Here's what people are saying about

Picky Parent Guide:
Choose Your Child's School With Confidence
The Elementary Years (K-6)

"As the son of a public school teacher, the father of four children educated in public schools, and someone who has spent over 30 years working to improve public education, I can say this book will be an invaluable guide for parents who are seeking what's best for their children."
—JAMES B. HUNT, JR., Former Governor of North Carolina

"Picky Parent Guide is phenomenal – just what parents need to stay calm and productive during the admissions process. I would consider the child of any family that has read and used this book an attractive candidate."
—JEFF ESCABAR, Director of Admission, Marin Country Day School

"There's not a parent in America who wouldn't benefit from the ideas and tools in Picky Parent Guide. If you have choices, this book will help you choose with confidence. If you don't, use this guide to press for the changes our nation needs — more options and higher school quality for every child."
—HOWARD L. FULLER, Ph.D., Distinguished Professor of Education, Marquette University and Chair, Black Alliance for Educational Options

"This wonderful new book will help parents understand the many excellent options they have within the public education system."
—BART PETERSON, Mayor of Indianapolis

"Picky Parent Guide addresses a neglected part of the educational choice movement: parent education. Parents need a guide to the spectrum of options that confronts them, and this is it! I would like to give this to all our families."
—EMILY LAWSON, Founder and Executive Director, D.C. Preparatory Academy

"This excellent book will guide parents of academically gifted children in selecting appropriate educational options. The advice is on target and very appropriate."
—JAMES T. WEBB, Ph.D., Co-author of the award-winning Guiding the Gifted Child: A Practical Source for Parents and Teachers

"Picky Parent Guide is an outstanding guide for parents. It provides them with an invaluable resource that will only strengthen the choices they make regarding their children's schools. In this day and time, it is a must read for parents contemplating this important decision."
—MICHAEL J. FEDEWA, Superintendent of Schools, Catholic Diocese of Raleigh, NC

"This is a first rate, practical guide for helping families match their children's needs with the right school. You'll learn everything from the secret ingredients of great schools to how to crack the mystery of securing a slot in the school of your choice."
—BRUNO V. MANNO, Ph.D., Senior Associate for Education, The Annie E. Casey Foundation

"A terrific and useful book that does not obsess over distinctions and labels about public and private but instead shows parents how to really get inside of all kinds of schools and make the right decisions for their children."
—ANDREW J. ROTHERHAM, Director, 21st Century Schools Project, Progressive Policy Institute

"Picky Parent Guide is a great tool for parents of preschool children. It can help transform what is often an overwhelming and anxiety-provoking process into a manageable and empowering experience that serves both parents and children throughout the elementary years."
—JACQUE GRILLO, Executive Director, Lone Mountain Children's Center, San Francisco

"I have a feeling that the Hassels will be keeping parents and schools on their toes for some time to come."
—TOM LOVELESS, Ph.D., Director, Brown Center on Education Policy, The Brookings Institution

"Choosing a school is hard, but when it works, it unlocks worlds and possibilities for families. The Hassels have created an indispensable guide to help parents undertake this most challenging responsibility: matching their kids with schools. The tools provided are the right ones to make the smart call. The lively and accessible format, the checklists and the charts are all informed by the reality of today's schools. Armed with this knowledge, families will find choice truly satisfying, and great learning will take place."
—JOHN AYERS, Executive Director, Leadership for Quality Education, Chicago

"Picky Parent Guide is a tremendous resource for parents and school leaders alike. All parents should have this book by the time their kids are 3 years old, if not sooner. It provides thoughtful guidance so that parents have tools to match their children's strengths, needs and interests to the schools that will serve them best. It also helps school leaders better answer the questions posed by informed parents."
—JOHNATHAN WILLIAMS, Co-Founder and Co-Director, The Accelerated School, Los Angeles, The Time Magazine Elementary School of the Year 2001

"I love this book! Choosing a school is a very personal decision, and Picky Parent Guide *will enable parents to make the best decisions possible for their children. In writing this book, Bryan and Emily Hassel have provided a real service for parents, children and schools."*
—GAYNOR MCCOWN, Executive Director, The Teaching Commission

"Picking a school for a child is the single most important decision a parent can make. Picky Parent Guide *provides well-written, common-sense advice that will help parents make better, more informed decisions. Your child deserves to have you read this book."*
—THOMAS W. CARROLL, President, Foundation for Education Reform and Accountability, Founder, Brighter Choice Charter School in Albany, New York

"These tools eased our worries and helped us choose just the right school for our child and family. When our needs changed, we switched schools with confidence that we were making the right move."
—GRAY DUNAWAY, Mortgage Broker and Mother of Two

THE ELEMENTARY YEARS (K-6)

Choose your child's school
with CONFIDENCE

Bryan C. Hassel, Ph.D. & Emily Ayscue Hassel

Armchair Press
Ross, CA
www.armchairpress.com

Picky Parent Guide
Choose Your Child's School With Confidence
The Elementary Years (K-6)
By Bryan C. Hassel and Emily Ayscue Hassel

Published by:
Armchair Press, LLC
P.O. Box 215
Ross, CA 94957 U.S.A.
orders@armchairpress.com
www.armchairpress.com
(415) 460-9750 phone
(415) 460-0850 fax

Picky Parent, Picky Parent Guide, Fit Factors, Great School Quality Factors, Confident Choice, Confident Choice Tools, Light'ning List, Smart à la Carte, Snap To It and the phrase *"with Confidence"* are registered and unregistered trademarks of Armchair Press, LLC.

The *Picky Parent Pal* and *Great School Superhero* characters, *Great Fit Triangle, Fit Factor Funnels,* Armchair Press logo and all other illustrations are registered and unregistered copyrights of Armchair Press, LLC.

Copyright © 2004 by Armchair Press, LLC.
First edition: May 2004
ISBN 0-9744627-7-2
LCCN 2003099067
Parenting/Education

Printed in the United States of America
First Printing, this edition, May 2004
10 9 8 7 6 5 4 3 2 1

Logo, Cover Design, Interior Design and Illustrations by BGDI, Inc.
Typesetting by Karen Quigg

Dedicated to our own first teachers,
Sedley, Chris, Emily and Ozzie,
who parented us well, jumped through hoops
to choose the right schools for us along the way,
and encouraged us to participate in those choices.

And to our own children, Margaret and Christopher,
who put up with us.

Contents

Step One
Get Started

Step Two
Solve the Great Fit Puzzle – Child, Family and School

Discover Your Child's Needs

Step Four
Get the Scoop on Schools

Step Five
Make Your Choice, Make It Happen

Step Six
Make the Most of It

The List of CONFIDENT CHOICE Tools

(In order of first appearance.)

Acknowledgements

Great thanks to the many parents who shared their stories, past and present. These tales brought life and personal meaning to our ideas. We cheer those parents who have overcome social pressure and practical barriers and put their children's needs first in making education choices. We thank each and every parent who uses our work to choose the right school for a child and to help shape excellent schools for the future.

We admire immensely those teachers who, without the benefit of an excellent school to support them, manage the heroic task of providing an excellent education for their students. They have boosted their students' minds and spirits for a lifetime and presented the possibility of educational excellence for all.

We laud the school leaders who have overcome organizational and practical barriers to build schools in which all students achieve and all are challenged, despite overwhelming pressure to settle for something less.

Thanks to the brilliant thinkers, researchers and authors of works on children and education on whose shoulders we stand to help parents choose and shape Great Schools.

We are thankful to all of the Public Impact staff, former teachers and education nonprofit professionals, who have contributed so much to our thinking about education over the years. We are especially grateful to Lucy McClellan Steiner for her enthusiasm about this topic and her excellent reviews of relevant research, much of which undergirds our thinking and writing here.

We thank the dozens of people who reviewed part or all of the manuscript before it was published. Their thoughtful reactions have improved the book immeasurably. We especially thank Malcolm Campbell for insightfully reviewing our early material, tutoring us on the world of book publishing, and encouraging us ceaselessly.

Many thanks to our colleagues in the education field who share our commitment to every child's success. We have learned from every one of you, and we would not have been able to complete this project without your support and insights.

Thanks to Ozzie Ayscue and the staff and contractors of Armchair Press for excellent editing, design, and fast-track sailing through the sea of publishing red tape to bring this book to parents quickly and in good form. Kudos to California design firm BGDI for doing a terrific job of giving the book just the right look. Thanks to Karen Quigg for speedily assembling hundreds of pieces into one book. Most especially thanks to Ozzie for adopting this project and applying his considerable talents to it, truly treating it like his own baby.

A special thanks to family and friends – you know who you are – who shared both ideas and personal support during the arduous process of researching, writing and publishing this book. We are obligated to inform you that our parents are not responsible for any grammatical errors in this book.

Preface

As professionals, we have been working for years to improve quality and variety in K-12 education. We're not alone. Well-meaning educators, academics and politicians are working diligently to improve quality and parental access to choice among schools. In our work, it occurred to us over and over that parents have largely been left out of the discussion. Very little has been done to help parents choose and work with their children's schools. What is available tends to be academic, narrowly focused, or largely based on authors' personal and political opinions. You should have more than that to rely on when making decisions that will affect your children for the rest of their lives!

By coincidence, after we'd launched this project, the public schools in the city where we lived at the time adopted a new city-wide choice program under which parents could choose from among schools throughout the district. Add to that a healthy set of private, charter and magnet schools, and parents around us were swimming in a sea of excitement and confusion. We were amazed at how frequently the topic of choosing a school or dealing with the one they had chosen came up in conversations among parents, whether they were choosing schools for the first time or questioning the wisdom of prior choices. The level of commitment among parents from all walks of life to doing right by their children fueled our fire. The most striking aspect of these conversations was that many parents seemed to be very much adrift, either completely lacking confidence or locked onto easy-to-see "window dressing" and popular school offerings. Parents were on a journey about which they cared intensely, but for which they had no roadmap or sense of direction.

As we conducted our research for this book – including formal and informal interviews with parents – we were awed. We were awed by the amount of time, effort and emotional involvement many parents commit to choosing and working with their children's schools. We were awed by the level of savvy that parents develop about the specific issues that arise concerning their own children, often after years of seeking desperately to understand their children's needs and how to meet them. Parents can and do learn about very "specialized" areas of education when their own children's learning and joy are at stake. We found parent after parent who had rebounded after near-misses, full-blown disastrous decisions, and good-decisions-gone-bad to find the right schools for their children. We recount for you some of their stories here. More importantly, we translate the wisdom they earned with great angst into a series of litmus tests for you to use in seeking a school that fits your child's and family's top needs.

We, too, are parents. And we ourselves are not too persnickety about most things. Living life with children – plus work, a household to run, relationships to nurture, and other activities – can make for a bumpy ride. It's a rare day that doesn't hold one surprise or another – a last minute schedule change, a child in tears, a mountain of unexpected work, a plumbing leak – you name it. When life is full to the brim, even we, who know a thing or two about schools, have felt both fretful and meek about our children's educations when things weren't quite right. We know it's hard to asked pointed questions when you don't feel you have enough expertise to back you up. We know it is easy to defer to teachers and principals, even when you know in your heart that your child isn't getting what he needs. As our personal and professional worlds have merged, we've become convinced of this: some matters are more important than others, entirely and unquestionably worth being picky about, and your child's education is high among them.

As we completed our research and began writing this Picky Parent Guide, we became committed to helping parents be not just careful, but also confident. You can be both with no hesitation, because this book will:

➤ Raise your standards by using the best available research about school quality

➤ Help you consider your personal needs and values, for both child and family

➤ Organize the process so that you can relax and seek a school without wasting precious time, knowing that you are doing all you can for your child

➤ Expand your understanding of the school options available to your child, and

➤ Motivate you to choose wisely and to stay engaged in your child's education.

Expert ideas, your values. That's a whole lot better than relying on pushy pals, nosy neighbors, forceful family members or anyone else who'd like to shoe-horn you into their view of the school world, regardless of real quality or fit with your particular needs. This book is about putting parents in their place – at the front and center of their children's educations. We are your partners in the process. We want what's best for your child and family. Enjoy!

Bryan C. Hassel
Emily Ayscue Hassel
Chapel Hill, North Carolina

Photo: Can't Hide Talent Images

About the Authors

BRYAN C. HASSEL is Co-Director of Public Impact. A Rhodes Scholar, he is a nationally recognized expert on school choice and school reform who speaks frequently on these topics. He has advised leaders across the political spectrum, from city halls to the White House, on educational issues. He has organized and led national conferences. He has authored and edited dozens of books, articles, toolkits and other publications for schools, policymakers, and parents. President Bush appointed him as one of 19 members of the President's Commision on Excellence in Special Education. Bryan received his undergraduate degree from the University of North Carolina at Chapel Hill, which he attended as a Morehead Scholar. He earned his doctorate from Harvard University, where he concentrated his studies on education policy, and his masters from Oxford University.

EMILY AYSCUE HASSEL is Co-Director of Public Impact. Emily previously worked as a consultant and manager for an international human resources consulting firm, helping for-profit, non-profit and educational organizations to maximize the effectiveness of their employees. In addition to assisting parents with their school choices, she has authored publications on school leadership, professional development and selecting school designs. President Clinton's Secretary of Education chose to distribute her professional development toolkit, *Learning From the Best*, to all 15,000 U.S. school districts. Emily received her undergraduate degree in psychology and graduate degrees in law and business administration, all from the University of North Carolina at Chapel Hill.

BRYAN AND EMILY each attended both public and private schools. Between them, they personally experienced assigned public, magnet, neighborhood, traditional, open, single-sex, private day, and co-educational boarding schools, as well as at-home tutoring.

BRYAN AND EMILY are also parents of two school-age children, one girl and one boy. Their children have attended both public and private schools. They have personal experience with the challenging process of selecting schools for their children in this era of burgeoning parental choice.

Visit us at PickyParent.com

Check us out online. You will find more tips related to this book, links to other resources and opportunities to give us feedback and share ideas and stories about your search for the right school and the ups and downs of educating, developing and nurturing your child. So come and visit. Tell us your stories. Let us know what you like and don't like about this book. And read what others have said.

STEP ONE

Get Started

■ ■ ■ ■ ■ ■ ■

CHAPTE

Chapter 1

A Pep Talk for Parents, Picky or Not

The Olsons have three very different children. Rising kindergartener Heidi seems very advanced in her learning, while her twin brother Elan seems more in-the-middle but has exceptional social skills for his age. Their older son Colter is emerging from the confidence paralysis of dyslexia. Is there any hope of sending all three children to one school next year – with confidence?

■ ■ ■

Sam is an "on target" first grade student who is struggling to read. After politely asking for changes at school, with no results, his parents hire a tutor. Sam's reading improves immediately. "Is something wrong with this picture? What should I do next?" his mother wonders.

■ ■ ■

Lucy is a very academically gifted child who is bored in school. Her parents feel embarrassed to ask for "special favors" from her school to keep her challenged. And they fear that she'll begin to feel socially isolated. Is there any hope that Lucy's needs can be met in elementary school?

■ ■ ■

Karen has a mild learning disability that her current school is ill-equipped to handle. But her parents are hesitant to consume her time outside of school with tutoring or switch her to a school away from her two siblings. What should they do?

■ ■ ■

Annie spends most of her school time standing around and watching other students do their work. She has become disengaged from school work and socially detached, as well. Her parents know something's wrong, but just can't put a finger on the problem.

■ ■ ■

Ming and Li Zhang, native Chinese speakers who moved to the U.S. as children, want their rising kindergartener Margaret to learn about her heritage. Their lives bring them into contact with few other Chinese speakers, especially now that Ming's parents have moved back to China. Both busy professionals, Ming and Li have little time to create these connections for their child. They wonder how school, where their daughter will spend so many hours, might help.

■ ■ ■

Mary and Erasmus grew up poor and bright, and they worked hard to build a successful business together. They want their only child Nikki to have the college opportunity they both missed. Not rich, they will need to curtail their spending to afford college. What should they do? Can they save money for college and meet Nikki's school needs now?

■ ■ ■

Your life is brimming with activity. You have children. Need we say more? You do not have time to fret about things of little consequence. You might not worry when the laundry piles up once in a while. Your children probably shouldn't eat off your pristine-only-when-you-moved-in kitchen floor. But you, and parents like you, care how your child spends time. You make an effort to craft experiences that allow your child to become the terrific person he or she is meant to be.

It's O.K. to be picky when making important choices for your child.

Whether you choose a school proactively or not, the effect on your child will be considerable. During the long school year, your elementary age child will spend more time in school and related activities than in any other task besides sleep. School matters. The school you choose for your child and how you interact with that school matter, too.

How frustrating, then, that parents have had so little guidance to make this critical decision. We're here to help! Based on the best available research and personalized with the experiences of real children and families, this is the definitive guide to finding a *Great School* that *fits* your child and family.

Now, you might have read or heard other advice about choosing a school. This book is different. Why? What we share about school quality is based *only* on the very best available research, not our personal opinions or our own parenting style. When we offer our opinion, we tell you.

We used both research and interviews with parents making school choices to cover a very broad range of child and family needs. And we've built this book to help you put your finger on what kind of school will be best for *your own* child and family.

How do we do that? We offer you:

➤ *A step-by-step process* for seeking a high quality school that fits your child and family. This logical method ensures that you turn over all the right rocks on the path to finding the right school. For example, we don't just help you identify your child's school-related needs. We also tell you what to look for in a school to meet those needs, and we help you decide what questions to ask in your school hunt. Our *Confident Choice Tools* help you focus on the right information at the right time, quickly and decisively.

➤ *A little mantra* to help you remember two features that count most when looking at schools: academic quality and how well each school *fits* your child's and family's needs. The mantra? **Great School, Great Fit**. With this in mind, you'll come to expect that your child's school will strive for the seven Great School Quality Factors and meet the four Fit Factor needs important to you. You'll find the memorable mantra and Factors useful even if you don't follow all the steps we recommend here.

You will feel confident for these reasons and more. Most importantly, you will understand your child's school better and become more engaged in your child's education, both in and out of school.

This Book is For You

Every year, at least twenty million parents make choices about their children's schools (some proactively, some not). Each family has its own circumstances, its own values, its own reasons for choosing. But whoever you are, this book is built to help. You will find the material here useful if you are:

➤ Making your first school choice for a rising kindergartener
➤ Moving to a new city or school district
➤ Moving to a different part of town
➤ Facing new options because of new choice policies in your public school district
➤ Facing new choices because of changes in your family's circumstances

➤ Concerned about your child's current schooling situation
➤ Content but curious about whether your child's school is really meeting all of your child's and family's important needs
➤ A parent with a child graduating to the next level and to a new school within the elementary years
➤ A parent of a newborn or toddler who wants to learn about what's ahead
➤ Hoping to understand your child's needs better
➤ An educator who wants to know what savvy parents seek in schools.

More Choices Than Ever

When most of us were growing up, our parents didn't have much choice about where to send us to school. Almost all of us went to our assigned public schools. The remaining few attended a narrow spectrum of private schools. There was little sense of picking a school to fit our needs as children. And to many of our parents, "quality" meant having a star teacher or two, a firm principal, and a nice facility. Some of us thrived as students, some of us got utterly lost in the shuffle, and many of us just bumped along for the ride.

Today, things are different. Most parents have far more options for their children, created by the birth of magnet schools, charter schools, choice within and between public districts, and growth in numbers of home schooling families. Private schools continue to educate large numbers of children, as well.

Consider these facts for a moment:

➤ The percentage of children attending a school *other than* the assigned public school has increased steadily over the past decade.
➤ By 1999, one of every four children in grades 1 – 12 attended a school other than the assigned public school – about 12 million children.
➤ Half of American families – including roughly 23 million children – say schools influenced their decision about where to live.
➤ 43 states and the District of Columbia now allow some choice across or within school districts.
➤ In 1975, only 14 school districts had magnet schools. By 1995, 230 did.
➤ In 1991, there were no charter schools. Today there are about 2,700 charter schools educating 700,000 children.
➤ By 1999, about 850,000 children were homeschooled, a number that has grown so quickly the government only recently began to track it.
➤ A growing number of districts allow parents to choose from among all their schools.
➤ A new federal law *requires* school districts to offer choices to families if their schools fail to improve adequately.

Because they have so many options, many parents who choose their children's assigned public schools are scrutinizing them as never before. These parents too are making proactive choices.

Smart à la Carte

Get Smart About School Types

Many parents make broad, sweeping assumptions about whether one *type* of school will offer better quality for their children. In fact, when parental education and income are factored out, research has not consistently shown that any one type of school educates children better than other types. (You might also be interested in school designs, such as Montessori, Core Knowledge and the like. See Chapter 10 for more about that.)

Still, it's good to know about the different types of school that may be in your community:

➤ *District public schools* typically are funded mainly through a combination of local, state and federal funding, "owned" by the public, and controlled by the local board of education.

➤ *Magnet schools* are also public schools, but typically have a special curriculum or teaching method. They draw from a cross-section of a city or town rather than specific neighborhoods.

➤ *Special programs within schools.* More and more schools run special programs for a subset of students, such as foreign language and International Baccalaureate programs.

➤ *Charter schools* are also public and in most states are funded with a combination of local, state and federal money, but they are "owned" and controlled by independent groups of citizens. They can lose their public funding if they do not meet performance goals.

➤ *Private independent schools* are funded mainly through a combination of tuition and fees charged to parents and fundraising campaigns, owned by non-profit organizations (although not always), and controlled by boards of alumni, parents, staff and interested citizens.

➤ *Private religious schools* typically are funded through a combination of tuition and fees, fundraising campaigns and money from a larger religious body. They are owned by nonprofit entities and controlled by boards mostly made up of people whose religious affiliations match the schools'.

➤ *Home schooling* means teaching your child at home, either alone or in conjunction with other home-schooling parents. You own, you control, and – in most areas – you pay for materials and equipment.

For your child, the opportunities for better school quality and a better school fit have never been greater. Indeed, some families have treasure troves of schools from which to choose. Jewels can be found in some very surprising places. But there's lead amongst the treasure. Low quality – more often *mediocre* – schools that really *won't* fit your child and family abound. Schools that for decades have touted themselves as "superior" and "elite" have become mediocre as the world has moved past them. And in some communities, families still don't have as many compelling choices as they should.

But a new era in education is dawning for parents. Choice is taking root and spreading nationwide. If trends continue, it won't be long before every family has a range of compelling possibilities from which to choose.

Why Making a Proactive Choice Helps Your Child

Even if you can choose, why bother? After all, life is hectic enough. How much precious time do you really need to spend on this? Regardless of which school you ultimately choose, and even if you decide to stay put with your older child, choosing a school thoughtfully is worth the effort for your child and your family.

Parents who proactively choose schools are more satisfied with their children's schools and more involved in their children's education. Their children perform better in school, too.

Recent studies show that when parents proactively choose schools:

➤ They are more satisfied with their children's schools.
➤ They are more involved in their children's education.
➤ Their children perform better in school.

Why? The research doesn't tell us for sure, but we'd bet it has to with all of the following:

➤ Students whose families take time to choose end up in *better schools*, on average.
➤ Those students' needs – including their capabilities, interests, and ways of learning – and their families' needs and resources *better fit* the schools they have chosen.
➤ Parents who take time to understand their child's and family's needs are *better able to work with* teachers and principals.
➤ Parents who have made a proactive choice better *understand the shortcomings* of their chosen schools, and they fill these gaps for their children at home and with non-school activities.
➤ Parents who have invested time to choose certain schools push for positive changes within those schools.

Even if you end up sticking with your child's current school, or choosing the one you thought you'd pick, or not having as many choices as you'd like, you will still reap the benefits of a proactive choice. You will have ideas about how you can make up for the school's shortcomings. Many of you also will gain the confidence to encourage change within your children's schools, both to meet the particular needs of your children and to better meet the needs of all students and their families. In the last chapter of the book, we'll tell you how.

Guess what: I.Q. is not fixed for a lifetime. Your child's I.Q. may rise 20 points or more during the elementary years with proper challenge and instruction.

How to Find a Great School that Fits *Your* Child and *Your* Family

When your child's success and happiness are involved, you can make a great choice with just a little guidance. Parents may not always know the solutions, but they often are laser accurate about the problems. A driver doesn't need to be an engineer to know the car engine's not working well. But she may need a shot of smarts and confidence when the mechanic says "can't find a problem here, Ma'am!" You, too, can get both smart and confident about whether a school is working well for your child and family. But how?

This book gives you a step-by-step approach you can use to find the best school that meets your needs. More on that soon. Even more important, this book helps you identify *what to look for in a school* – what we call **quality** and **fit**.

Let's take a moment to define "quality" and "fit," since those two ideas will run through every page of this book.

Quality. Put simply, some schools are just better than others. Quality is what sets a Great School apart from a mediocre or bad school.

What makes a school great? Is it great teachers? Well, yes, but not just that. Teachers are human like the rest of us, and there are only going to be a limited number who can be great every day, year in and year out. Great schools have figured that out. Spiffy grounds and buildings? Well, they might make parents feel better, but flashy facilities won't help your child excel academically. So what is important?

Let's start with this question: what does a Great School accomplish with students that average or bad schools don't? ***Great schools are ones in which students of all abilities and types achieve dramatically better academic results than similar students in other schools.*** Having a lot of college professors' children does not make a school great, any more than having children of less-educated parents makes a school bad. But the tests scores of two such schools might differ quite a bit. We really have to know how much those children learn compared to similar children who attend school elsewhere to know whether the school is making the difference.

Luckily, decades of research have uncovered what makes a school great. In study after study, the same characteristics keep coming up. Researchers know what they are. Teachers and school leaders know what they are.

Now it's time for parents to know what they are, and to use that information to find Great Schools for their children. In Chapters 11 – 14, you'll learn about the seven Great School Quality Factors that set top schools apart. You'll follow the story of one family, the Olsons, as they seek one school for their three very different children. You'll read how Great School Elementary comes to the rescue while schools Good Try and Yesteryear fall short. By the end, you'll know how to tell whether a school is Great or not. For now, the box "Great School Quality Factors" gives you a preview.

Smart à la Carte

Great School Quality Factors

1. Clear Mission Guiding School Activities
2. High Expectations for All Students
3. Monitoring Progress and Adjusting Teaching
4. Focus on Effective Learning Tasks
5. Home-School Connection
6. Safe and Orderly Environment
7. Strong Instructional Leadership

Fit. Parents know that there are no peas-in-a-pod when it comes to children. One child jumps right in and joins the group without fail. Another child stands back and surveys the scene every time. One child seems to know answers before you've asked questions. Another child has to learn the same facts over and over before remembering. One child learns best working alone, while another must chat with a friend or teacher while she works. One child bursts at the seams in a regimented classroom, while another breaks down crying in the confusion of a cluttered setting. One child is whip smart, but doesn't perform well in school. Another child tests "average" in ability, but is a hardworking academic dynamo.

Parents tend to be keen observers of their own children. As we talk to parents about their kids and school, we hear:

➤ My child's enthusiasm just disappears at school (or in similar settings).
➤ My child goes into a shell in a group.
➤ My child isn't moving along as fast as she could in basic subjects.
➤ My child is quiet at school, but talks my ear off when we're alone.
➤ Few adults seem to appreciate my child's special qualities and gifts.
➤ My child is struggling academically, and nothing seems to help.
➤ I'm worried (or already know) my child will get in trouble for not sitting still.
➤ My child's performance is uneven, and nobody seems to know why.

Families also come in lots of shapes and sizes. Yours has its own values, its own priorities. You also have constraints when it comes to money, time, and other practical matters. So it's not a surprise that when we talk to parents about their *families'* needs, we hear a whole range of concerns:

➤ Our family has strong values. Will our child's school reflect them?
➤ We want our child to attend a top college.
➤ We don't like what we hear about how children behave in school these days.
➤ We hope school will expose our children to a wide variety of people.
➤ It would be nice to find a school that all of our children could attend.
➤ We're not sure we can afford private school.
➤ We need a school that's convenient to our home and workplace.

Quality is like "good nutrition": all the fruits, vegetables, whole grains and protein everyone needs. Fit is like choosing personal favorites from each healthy food group and picking your dessert.

Since children and families are so varied, your needs and the importance of your needs *for school* can differ dramatically even among the closest of friends, neighbors and family members. "Fit" is about how closely a school meets your needs, particularly the most important ones that you cannot meet outside of school.

Just as chocolate cake excites most of us more than oatmeal (health nuts excepted), it is most often fit that inspires our *passion* for a school, even though it is quality that most determines the academic success of our children. If quality is your "good nutrition," all the fruits, vegetables, whole grains and protein *everyone* needs, then fit is about choosing your personal favorites from each healthy food group *and* picking your dessert.

You can think about the match between child needs, family needs and school offerings as a triangle. The completeness of your child's education will be determined by how well your child, family and school fit together. We call this the "Great Fit Triangle":

Great Fit Triangle

How Well Does Your School Fit
Your Child & Family?

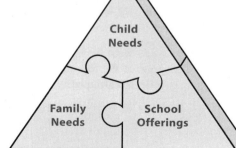

But your child and family have so many needs and values. How can you possibly decide which ones matter most for school?

This book helps you identify your *highest priority needs and values* by sorting them into four Fit Factors. You'll think about:

➤ *what* your child should be learning in school (like what content and at what level);
➤ *how* your child learns best (like what kind of teaching style really connects);
➤ what *social issues* matter (like your and your child's friends); and
➤ what *practical issues* (like location and cost) make a difference.

Using the four Fit Factors, you'll go from a confusing flurry of considerations to a concise list of what matters most – and what to look for in a school to get that.

Smart
à la
Carte

When to Start?

It's OK to think generally about school choices at any time, but begin your serious planning in late summer or early autumn the year before your child will start school or switch schools – August is ideal in most locations. Start much earlier and there is a decent chance that your child, your family or one of your Target Schools will change enough to alter your plans. Start later, and you may miss out on schools with early application or registration deadlines. We hear that in some instances you must schedule interviews the spring in advance of the fall you will apply for your child, but this is rare. Individual schools vary, and so you must find out the schedule and steps for each school you seriously consider!

The Step-by-Step Process to Make the Right Choice

Quality and fit will be your compass. But even with a compass, most of us still need a map. So we've developed a step-by-step guide to help you organize your school choice process.

1 Let's walk through this map, which appears on page 14. From your starting point at the top, the map forks off in two directions, one toward fit and the other toward quality.

2 Take fit first. On the map, Solve the Great Fit Puzzle has two branches. Going down the left branch, you'll start with Discover Your Child's Needs. Of all your child's characteristics, what matters most when choosing a school? In Chapters 2-5, we'll help you figure that out.

The right branch of Solve the Great Fit Puzzle leads you to Uncover Your Family's Needs. Your family has values, preferences and constraints you'll want to take into account when picking a school. Chapters 6-9 will help you zero in on the ones that really matter for your school choice.

After considering your child's and family's needs, you'll come to Know What You Need from a School. We'll show you in Chapter 10 exactly *what a school should do* to match the needs you've identified. We'll help you summarize your decisions in a handy one-page *Personalized Great Fit Checklist* to take along on your school hunt.

(3) That's fit. What about quality? The next step, back up toward the top of the map, is to Learn About Truly Great Schools. Chapters 11-14 let you in on the research that tells us what makes Great Schools great. You'll also learn specifically how to gauge the quality of the schools you consider. We will provide you with a *Great School Quality Checklist* you can carry around as you visit schools.

(4) The next step is what we call Get the Scoop on Schools. In Chapter 15, you'll come up with a list of top schools available to your child. We'll help you ask the right questions to get the information you need. Using your fit and quality checklists, you'll investigate your options, learning as much as you can about whether each one meets your priorities.

(5) Then, it's time to Make Your Choice and Make It Happen. Chapter 16 brings you to the moment of truth, using all the information you've gathered. You weigh the pros and cons of the schools you're considering and figure out which one is the best school that fits.

From there, you're on to Chapter 17, where we help you up the odds of getting your child into your top pick school.

(6) And in the final chapter, you Make the Most of It. Here we offer a mini-guide to working effectively with your child's principal and teachers, developing your child outside of school and changing your child's school for the better.

At the end of the book, we also offer you:
➤ A glossary of the "education speak" terms you might encounter in your school hunt.
➤ A list of other resources you may find helpful in your school search and in helping your children get the education they deserve.
➤ An appendix containing the critical *Confident Choice Tools* you will use to identify your needs, choose the best fit and quality school, and round out your child's education outside of school.
➤ A list of our sources.
➤ A thorough index so you can use this book as a ready reference guide anytime an education issue arises for your child.

Even if you do not have time to take every step here, seeking your child's top fit need and real quality in a school will improve your child's life and school performance.

How to Find a Great School That Fits:
a Step-by-Step Approach

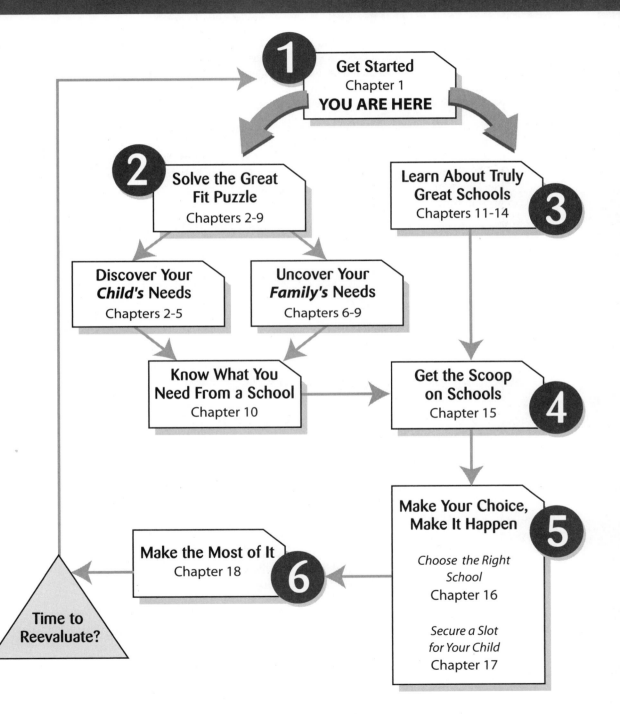

1 Get Started
Chapter 1
YOU ARE HERE

2 Solve the Great
Fit Puzzle
Chapters 2-9

3 Learn About Truly
Great Schools
Chapters 11-14

Discover Your
Child's Needs
Chapters 2-5

Uncover Your
Family's Needs
Chapters 6-9

Know What You
Need From a School
Chapter 10

4 Get the Scoop
on Schools
Chapter 15

5 Make Your Choice,
Make It Happen

*Choose the Right
School*
Chapter 16

*Secure a Slot
for Your Child*
Chapter 17

6 Make the Most of It
Chapter 18

Time to
Reevaluate?

Recurring Picky Parent Guide Features

Throughout the book, you will find the following recurring features:

➤ *Light'ning List* – at the start of each chapter, we lighten the load and enlighten you in a flash with a chapter summary for the busiest of parents.

➤ *Snap To It* – suggested action steps at the end of each chapter to help you make progress on your school decision – when you are ready.

➤ *Smart à la Carte* – We think you really are so smart. And you'll be even smarter after reading these boxes we've cooked up for you on hot topics of special concern to many parents. Read those that interest you most.

➤ *Definitions* – simple, clear meanings of terms you'll encounter in your school hunt, throughout the book where you need them and in the book-end glossary.

➤ *Viewpoint* – a series of boxes providing brief overviews of prominent, modern child development theories affecting school choice, in Chapters 2 through 5.

➤ *Stories and examples* – tales about parents who've made both uplifting and unfortunate school choices – and the big consequences for their children and families. We've included a mix of real-life stories and examples we crafted to illustrate important points. Among these, you'll find conclusions to the stories begun in this chapter.

➤ *Confident Choice Tools* – tools supporting the Snap To It activities walk you through a step-by-step approach to choosing a school. You will use these worksheets and tables to zero in on your priorities, record your ideas and stay on top of the process.

How to Use this Book

Strategy A: In-Depth

Some of you will devote much time to reading and thinking about your child's school options. If this is you, do this:

➤ *Read* this book from start to finish. Enjoy yourself. Chat with your spouse or friends about it.

➤ *Start observing and thinking* about your own child and family right away. Take mental notes, or use our "Quick Thinks" on pages 37 and 109 to record your ideas.

➤ *Complete the Snap To It activity sections* (look for the handy symbol as you flip through). Use the *Confident Choice Tools* provided here to stay organized.

Strategy B: Complete but Focused

Others of you may want the "big ideas," but need a faster route through. If this is you, do this:

➤ *Read* Chapters 2 (your child), 6 (your family), 10 (matching a school to your needs), 11 (school quality), and 16 (making the choice).

➤ *Read the Light'ning List* at the beginning of each chapter you skip.

➤ *Complete the Snap To It activity sections* (look for the handy symbol as you flip through). Use the *Confident Choice Tools* provided here to stay organized.

➤ *Delve deeper* only into other chapters that apply most to your child and family. Use the Light'ning Lists at the beginning of each chapter to guide you.

Strategy C: Quick Action

Still others of you would rather skip the "big ideas" and get right to the steps. If this is you, do this:

➤ *Read Light'ning List* at the beginning of each chapter to get the main ideas.

➤ *Complete the Snap To It activity sections* at the end of each chapter (look for the handy symbol as you flip through). Use the *Confident Choice Tools* provided here to stay organized.

➤ *Read the other book sections and use the reference tables* in the Appendix as needed to help with activities where you want the big picture (book sections) or where you need more detail (tables).

We also encourage you to visit the book's companion website, *PickyParent.com*, where you'll find more information, up-to-date links to great resources and the opportunity to share ideas and experiences with other parents.

A Clear View: We Are a Team

This book is your steady platform: we will help you stand firm on the shoulders of great educators, great thinkers about children and schools, and great parents to provide the very best for *your* child. We will lift your head above the clouds of a busy life and other obstacles to make clear, confident decisions about how your child will be educated – in school and out.

So, go ahead. Be picky, and show it. Do it with confidence. We'll help you turn your pickiness in to positive parent power – not just pointless whining – to improve your child's school performance and life. At some point, all parents fear the slow drip of time that passes until the bucket is full and your chance to influence your child's development has passed. You don't have to go there. This book is about helping you reach your highest hopes for your child. We say: every child, including yours, is born with great gifts. Help your child discover, build and enjoy those gifts.

You will need to do mind-work, soul-searching and legwork. But you'll know that your efforts are high-impact, that you are achieving all a parent can, and that your child will feel your love and concern. You will *feel great* about being picky when it counts most. Ready? Let's go.

Solve the Great Fit Puzzle– Child, Family and School

■ ■ ■ ■ ■ ■ ■

Discover Your Child's Needs

LIGHT'NING LIST

What To Know from Chapter 2

➤ **A Great Fit school will meet your individual child's most important needs.**

➤ **The child characteristics most helpful for picking a school** are sorted into the **four Fit Factors:**

 ✔ What *Your Child Learns* – these are things about your child that indicate *what subjects and at what level of difficulty* your child should be taught.

 ✔ How *Your Child Learns* – these are things about your child that indicate *how a school should teach and interact with your child.*

 ✔ *Social Issues* – this is your child's own desire and need to attend school with *friends.*

 ✔ *Practical Matters* – this includes scheduling your child's essential *non-school activities* (as well as any practical concerns arising from other child needs).

➤ **You can identify the parts of each Fit Factor most important for** your **child** in four ways:

 ✔ *Observe* your child directly, alone and in groups of other children.

 ✔ *Compare* your child to other similar-age children.

 ✔ *Test* your child formally through a professional educational tester or psychologist.

 ✔ *Get Smart* about the characteristics that may be most important for your child.

➤ **Every aspect of every Fit Factor is not important for every child.** You must prioritize to find a school that meets your child's few top needs.

➤ **Even if you identify only one critical need of your child's**, and seek to meet it through school or at home, **your child will be far better off** than without your effort.

➤ **The less certain you feel about identifying your child's top needs, the more important Great School Quality Factors #2 and 3 become** in your school hunt.

Chapter 2

Ladies and Gentlemen, Introducing...Your Child

Amy soars academically, as long as she can discuss her ideas. Make her sit quietly and do worksheets all day and her mind wanders away from the task at hand. Margaret excels in art. She also writes complicated, detailed stories – as long as she can start with a picture. Sonya loves math, and she can see the symbols and do problems in her head. Sure, she can read and write well enough, but it's math that makes her feel supercharged about school. Arthur does well enough in school, as long as he has one or two close friends to pal around with during recess and lunch. Take that away and he shuts down. A solid student, Mark's behavior unravels without very clear rules and consequences. Give him clear rules, and he actually turns into a class leader. Alexander thinks of complicated science projects and experiments he wants to pursue every week. He bemoans going to school, since it takes his time away from his "real work."

Sorting Out Your Child's Unique Needs

Children vary in so many ways! Your child is like no other, yet possesses so many qualities in common with others. Like a star that twinkles a little differently with each view, your child may seem to be many different people combined into one. Through the still unknown recipe of genes and upbringing, your child is a unique concoction of capabilities, wants, needs and motives.

Indeed, children's bodies, minds, emotions and spirits combine to make unique individuals. This mix affects the kind of environment in which each child learns best. As a parent, you probably have some sense of this. But many of us feel at a loss to understand and respond to our own children's capabilities, needs and personalities, even in our daily parenting, much less for school.

What Matters for Matching My Child to a School?

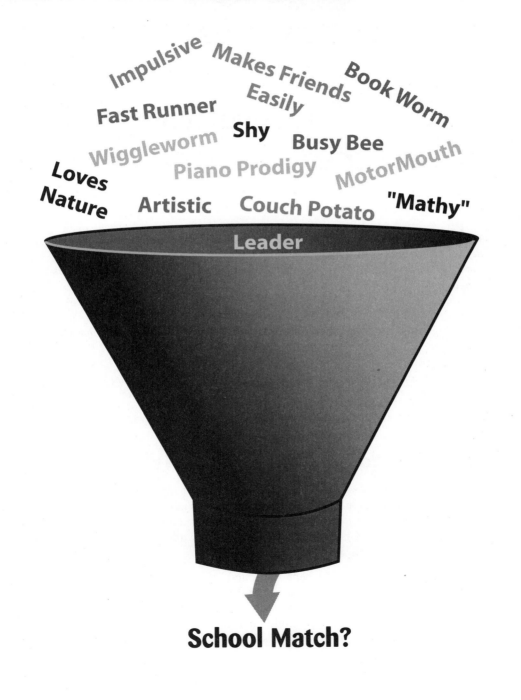

Impulsive Makes Friends Book Worm
Fast Runner Easily
Shy Busy Bee
Wiggleworm Piano Prodigy MotorMouth
Loves Nature Artistic Couch Potato "Mathy"
Leader

School Match?

Parents aren't the only ones to wonder what really matters. For decades, educators and child development experts have considered children from many angles, and they have sliced this apple many different ways. Every leading expert's ideas are useful for understanding some children better. Every leading expert's ideas are useful for teaching some children better. (See the box *One Child, Many Viewpoints* on page 29 if you'd like to know more.) But for the most part, parents have been left in the lurch when trying to discern what their individual children need at school.

At one time or another, most of you will feel stuck on one of these challenges:

➤ You need help understanding what your child is really like.
➤ You understand your child quite well but aren't sure which characteristics are important for school.
➤ You know what aspects of your child will affect his school success but are uncertain of exactly what he needs at school as a result.
➤ You feel uncomfortable asking for "special favors" from a school to meet your child's particular needs.

Regardless of how prepared you feel right now, we say this: *you the parent are in the best position to know your child's needs and ensure that they are met, at school and elsewhere.* Most parents know far more about their own children than they will admit even to themselves. If you feel cloudy – or even clueless – about any of these matters, read on. This book will:

➤ Focus you on *your* child
➤ Help you figure out what is important for choosing a school for your child
➤ Prepare you to hunt for a school that meets more of your child's needs from the start
➤ Help you find a school where you'll have fewer "favors" to request because the school already does the things your child needs
➤ Equip you to help teachers meet your child's needs
➤ Equip you to help your child outside of school

The Great Fit Triangle

The burning question for you now is this: which qualities, in their unique combination within your child, really matter for choosing a school? Which of your child's features will help her learn and feel better in some schools – with certain teachers, peers, materials, and expected ways of learning – and worse in others? Which of your child's strengths and weaknesses can be addressed at school, and which can be developed at home?

Great Fit Triangle

Matching Child and Family Needs with School Offerings

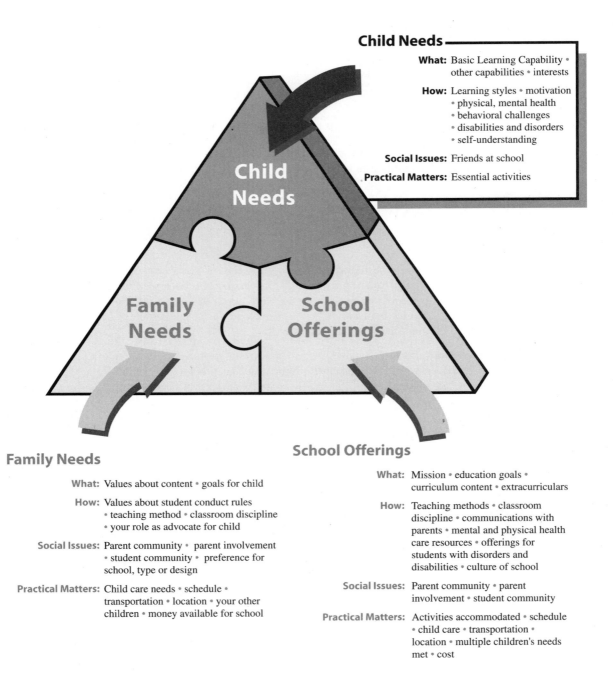

Child Needs

What: Basic Learning Capability • other capabilities • interests

How: Learning styles • motivation • physical, mental health • behavioral challenges • disabilities and disorders • self-understanding

Social Issues: Friends at school

Practical Matters: Essential activities

Family Needs

What: Values about content • goals for child

How: Values about student conduct rules • teaching method • classroom discipline • your role as advocate for child

Social Issues: Parent community • parent involvement • student community • preference for school, type or design

Practical Matters: Child care needs • schedule • transportation • location • your other children • money available for school

School Offerings

What: Mission • education goals • curriculum content • extracurriculars

How: Teaching methods • classroom discipline • communications with parents • mental and physical health care resources • offerings for students with disorders and disabilities • culture of school

Social Issues: Parent community • parent involvement • student community

Practical Matters: Activities accommodated • schedule • child care • transportation • location • multiple children's needs met • cost

When your child's and family's needs fit well with what your child's school offers, we call it a "Great Fit." We use the Great Fit Triangle to illustrate how these "pieces" work together.

Focus on the Four Fit Factors

Fortunately, we can focus on a limited number of characteristics that affect how well children fare in different kinds of school environments. We developed this targeted list by scanning the research about child development and by talking with parents of many different kinds of children about their children's needs. From all of that information, we organized the many characteristics of children into four easy-to-grasp categories: the four Fit Factors. These Fit Factors are simply a way of sorting out your child's (and later, your family's) many features in a way useful for identifying your school needs. The four Fit Factors for children include:

➤ **What *Your Child Learns:*** these are aspects of your child that affect *what subjects and at what level of difficulty* your child should be taught at school. These include your child's Basic Learning Capability, other capabilities, and interests.

➤ **How *Your Child Learns:*** these are aspects of your child that affect *how a school should teach and interact with your child* both in and outside of the classroom. These include your child's learning styles, motivation, physical and mental health challenges, behavior challenges, learning disabilities and disorders, and self-understanding.

➤ *Social Issues:* this includes the need for social contact with particular friends from the *child's* perspective.

➤ *Practical Matters:* this includes essential extracurricular activities that may be compelling choice factors for some children.

The burning question for you now is this: which qualities, in their unique combination within your child, really matter for choosing a school?

The four Fit Factors help you by taking the jumble of characteristics that define your child and funneling them down into a manageable set. And this book will help you narrow even that organized list down into your own personalized high-priority list of your child's needs.

In the following three chapters, we'll describe the child characteristics within each of the four Fit Factors in detail. If you find that your child has additional needs that must be met at school, fear not. Chapter 10 will help you think for yourself to find the right school. For now, take a peek at the *Child Needs Summary* on page 38.

What Matters for Matching My Child to a School?

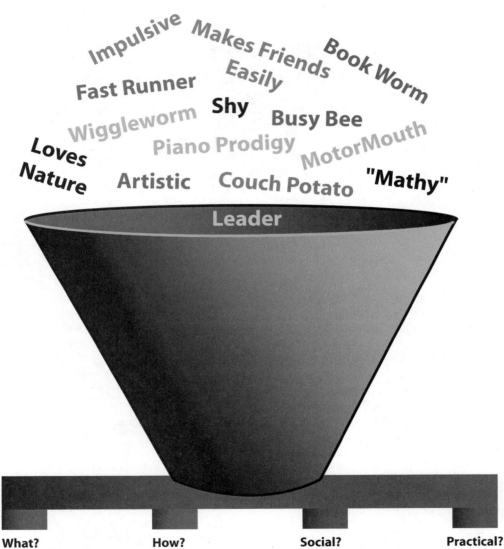

Impulsive

Makes Friends Easily

Book Worm

Fast Runner

Shy

Busy Bee

Wiggleworm

Loves Nature

Piano Prodigy

MotorMouth

Artistic

Couch Potato

"Mathy"

Leader

What?
- Basic Learning Capability
- Other capabilities
- Interests

How?
- Learning styles
- Motivation
- Physical and mental health
- Behavior challenges
- Learning disabilities and disorders
- Self-understanding

Social?
- Friends at school

Practical?
- Essential activities

How to Learn More about Your Child

Not every Fit Factor characteristic is important for matching every child to the right school. You'll need to decide which ones are really important for your child. To do that, you'll need to take a fresh look at your child now.

Know that many parents find it challenging to see their children in the truest light. Naturally, we want to think our children will be standouts in anything they undertake, especially in the first societal litmus test of success: education. In fact, your child has a much greater chance of success in school and life if you approach this process with an honest and open mind about your child's strengths and challenges. By finding a good fit for your child, you'll place him in a school environment that makes the most of his strongest abilities, while also recognizing and developing his weaknesses.

Viewpoint   One Child, Many Viewpoints

People are complex, no doubt. A visitor from outer space would be hard pressed to describe humans along any one dimension. Our bodies alone include multiple physical and chemical systems working together. Our minds alone are complex and, to some extent, still unfathomable. Even when we understand, we do not always know the importance of each aspect of our incredible brains and how they interact with the world around us.

The very best thinkers and experts have tried repeatedly to explain humans in straightforward terms, using lists and scales simple enough for the rest of us to understand. Great thinkers and educators have in recent decades come to see children as a unified collection of critical characteristics, though they may disagree about what those critical characteristics are. Notable experts and viewpoints include Howard Gardner's multiple intelligences, Mel Levine's eight learning abilities, learning styles, whole child thinking, and a rainbow of others focusing on narrower aspects of child development.

Viewpoint boxes appearing throughout the Child chapters include sketch summaries of some popularly accepted ideas about what is most important for children's growth, development, and learning. We've highlighted some of the most influential and complete models of children's minds and ones you are most likely to run across in parenting life. Use them to improve your thinking and understanding of your child, but know that we have included them all in some way in our four Fit Factors to help you determine what your child needs from school. If something jumps out at you as "just the thing" that describes your child, make a note of it.

If all children were formally assessed at preschool age and reassessed throughout the school years, you would have a "moving profile" of your child. This kind of tool would be invaluable for school placement, teacher assignment, teaching and parenting. Many Great Schools do this with their current students. But when you are choosing a school, it's up to you to lead the process of gathering the information you need to understand your child.

You will best understand your child if you have had time to observe, compare with other children and discover more about the child characteristics important for choosing a school.

You should *start with those things about your child that really stand out:* obvious strengths and challenges, likes and dislikes. Our *Child "Quick Think"* activity on page 37 will help get you going.

Focus on those one, two or few things that matter most for your child. Meeting just those needs, at school or home, can significantly improve your child's life and school performance.

Then, in the following chapters, we'll give you specific ideas for clarifying and organizing your child's needs using the four Fit Factors. The suggested activities will include a combination of these:

1. *Observe*
2. *Compare*
3. *Test*
4. *Get Smart*

There's no need to dive into these activities right now. As you consider each of the four Fit Factors, we'll prompt you with specific ideas about what to observe, how to compare, what tests to consider, and how to "get smart" by reading more about specific topics. For now, though, here's an overview of each way of getting to know your child better:

➤ *Observe* – if you have spent a fair amount of time alone with your child and have observed her in a group setting, you may have a good grasp of her needs already. If not, and you have some time before you'll need to choose a school, make the most of the opportunities you have to observe your child directly.
  ✔ Think about how well your child's current school or child care setting fits. The box Signs of a Great and Not-So-Great Fit can help
  ✔ Schedule one or more appointments to observe your child at school or day care (it is best if you can observe without your child seeing you, but this is not always possible)
  ✔ Pay attention when your child has friends over to play
  ✔ Watch your child at the park
  ✔ Use other chances to observe how your child works and plays, both alone and with others, at home and elsewhere
  ✔ Follow our specific advice in the following chapters for characteristics that really jump out at you

Smart à la Carte

Signs of a Great and Not-So-Great Fit Between Child and School

If your child is in school, even preschool or day care, you may have gotten an intuitive feeling already that the situation is a Great Fit for your child – or not. If your child has not participated in any group learning yet, you may have no idea. But if yours has – as most young children in the U.S. have – you may recognize some signs of a great or poor fit.

Signs that a school or other group setting *fits your child* include these:
➤ Your child is eager to go to school (or preschool or day care)
➤ Your child acts energized and happy at the end of the school day
➤ The pace of learning in core subjects is, overall, about right for your child: challenging but achievable
➤ You see tremendous progress in your child's overall development – academic, physical, social and emotional – throughout each school year
➤ Your child feels that her abilities and interests are appreciated at school
➤ Your child is achieving and performing academically ("cognitively" in younger years) at the level of which he is capable
➤ Your child has friends and acquaintances who like and accept him at school
➤ School work and friends are important, but not all-consuming, parts of your child's life

If school or another group setting is a *poor fit for your child,* you might see some of these signs:
➤ Well into the school year, your child is hesitant, or even adamantly opposed to going to school (and other stressful events in your child's life, like a new baby, can't explain these feelings)
➤ Your child is not just tired, but worn down and unhappy at the end of most school days
➤ Your child has made little progress in the past year, either academically, socially, emotionally or physically
➤ Your child often says "school is boring"
➤ Your child is not performing as well academically as you think he can
➤ Your child expresses little interest in what she's learning at school
➤ Your child often says that teachers or other kids do not understand her or do not like her
➤ Your child doesn't seem to have any close friends or friendly acquaintances at school
➤ Your child shows symptoms of stress only when school's in session (e.g., sleeplessness, fatigue, excessive clinginess and whining, new nervous habits, regressing to younger behaviors)

You can learn a lot just by interacting directly with your child and by noticing what your child is like when playing alone and with other children.

➤ *Compare* – for choosing a school, it is helpful if you understand how your child is similar to or different from other children of the same age. Your child's teachers and other caregivers often are in a terrific position to give you valuable details about how your child acts in a group and how your child compares to others of the same age. Ask questions, listen and learn. Some parenting books include "typical" child development schedules, and those can be helpful for comparing your child's current capabilities to others of the same age. If you've got more time and energy, use opportunities to observe and get to know other similar-age children, either with your child present or not, such as:

✔ Volunteer in your child's classroom (or another of same-age children)
✔ Teach a class of similar-age children at your religious institution
✔ Invite children over to play with your child, one-on-one or in a playgroup
✔ Observe other children (and compare your child to others) in informal play at the park, birthday parties and so forth
✔ Observe other children (and compare your child to others) in structured, non-school, group activities – while your child participates in athletics, for example
✔ Follow our specific advice in the following chapters for characteristics that really jump out at you

➤ *Test* – seek limited or complete testing through a combination of public schools, private psychologists and education counselors. You may be able to obtain basic test results only, or you might choose comprehensive parenting and school choice counseling. Many of you will find that testing is not necessary, as your child's most outstanding characteristics are relatively easy to pinpoint.

But if:
✔ Your child has an extreme characteristic that you want to understand better, or
✔ You've had little time to observe your child, or
✔ You do not feel confident making judgments about your child after reading this book, or
✔ You want a thorough assessment of your child's capabilities and needs, or
✔ You feel more comfortable taking action with the backing of an objective, expert assessment,

then consider seeking professional testing and counseling. See our box, *Getting Help*, to get started on finding and working with a professional tester. And visit *PickyParent.com* for information about common child assessments.

➤ *Get Smart* – use books and other tools for understanding more about children who you think may be *similar to your child.* Your time is limited, so focus your research carefully. Easy-to-obtain resources include:

    ✔ Other books about specific characteristics of some children (such as gifted or learning disabled). See our Resources for Parents section starting on page 354.

      ✔ Websites for helping parents and children with specific needs, also listed in our Resources section.

        ✔ *PickyParent.com*, for up-to-date links and resources.

Smart à la Carte

Getting Help: Professional Testing and Counseling

If you decide to get help from a professional counselor to identify or clarify your child's needs, your first task will be to find one. Ask your child's teacher, principal or school counselor, or even your friends (or look in your local phone book) for names of child psychologists and education counseling specialists who do school-related assessments. A private tester will cost at least a few hundred dollars for a basic I.Q. test, perhaps one other short test, and simple feedback for you.

You may find free or less expensive alternatives in your community. If your child has indication of certain learning disabilities, public school systems provide free testing (call your local school district central office). Many private schools offer assessments as part of the admission process, though feedback may be too late to help you target the right schools. Some preschools offer inexpensive developmental assessments for current students and, if they have a kindergarten or "junior" kindergarten program, prospective students.

Your counselor need not have a Ph.D., although the more thorough the testing, the more important training in use of assessments will be. Whatever your counselor's background, testing should include use of "standardized" scales that compare your child to many other similar-age children, not merely the counselor's personal opinion.

Before you get help from professionals, ask what kind of tests they do, whether testing is done individually or in groups, how long testing takes, what kind of feedback you will get and when, and the total cost. The younger the child, the more important it is to have individual testing. You may find the range of tests fairly limited. At the least, most such counselors can assess your child's I.Q., academic development (yes, even for preschoolers), learning style preferences, and major learning disabilities. The feedback that you get from such testing may be limited, but you most certainly will find it helpful to learn about or confirm characteristics of your child important for choosing a school.

Prioritizing Your Child's Needs: Must Haves and Nice to Haves

You're on your way to knowing your child. In the following chapters, we will walk you through each of the four Fit Factor characteristics for children and help you identify which are most important for your individual child. You will quickly see that many issues are not critical for your child, and you can avoid bogging down your school hunt by setting these aside.

Most children will have only a *small number of characteristics that are top priorities* for selecting and working with a school. These we call "Must Haves," simply because your child really must have these needs met, ideally at school. If you see other non-essential needs – ones that just aren't a top priority or that you can easily address at home – consider them "Nice to Haves." We call them this simply because it would be *nice to have* these needs met at school, but not really essential. Later, you can use your Nice to Haves as tiebreakers between equally appealing schools. Do your work well, and this will be your prize: you can focus on finding a truly Great Fit school for your child's top needs.

Viewpoint   Whole Child

One field of thinkers and experts focuses on the "whole child." Several such authors have called for education, parenting and child care to focus on the various aspects of children's development, rather than on "subjects" we want to teach children (e.g., math, reading). Elements of the "Whole Child" that experts have addressed include these:

1. *Cognitive* – how children think and learn in traditional academic areas. This includes memory, problem solving, connecting old ideas and creating new ones in language, math and other subjects.
2. *Social* – how children get along with others, both one-on-one and in a group (as leader, follower, team member).
3. *Emotional* – how children feel, understand their feelings and control their behavior in response to feelings.
4. *Physical* – how well children perform using small motor skills (e.g., handwriting, building with small objects), large motor skills (e.g. running, dance) and coordination of the body in general.

In addition, some have included a fifth element:

5. *Spiritual* – How connected does your child feel to a higher power beyond human beings or to a sense of oneness with humanity as a whole?

For many parents, what rises to the top of the Must Have list for school will depend on what you, as a parent, can offer your child outside of school. If your budding musician's needs can be met with private lessons in non-school hours and you can foot the bill, then this interest/capability may be just a Nice to Have at school. If you, upon realizing that your child's lack of social skills is holding him back, feel very capable of helping your child close the gap (e.g., with lots of play dates and positive coaching), then choosing a school with the perfect-fit social group becomes less important.

But you must be honest with yourself. Accept the fact that there may be things you cannot or do not want to do for your child outside of school. If one of these barriers realistically will keep you from meeting your child's important need elsewhere, then make the need a Must Have and seek to meet it through school:

➤ You face practical or logistical barriers (time constraints, multiple children's schedules, lack of money, conflict with your work and so on)
➤ You do not want to push your own child academically or otherwise and would feel more comfortable having other adults play this role
➤ The basics of parenting – keeping your child fed, warm and safe, let alone teaching discipline, manners, morals and values – are daunting enough, and you don't want to add to an already overfull parenting basket

Viewpoint   A Rainbow

Some experts and authors have focused on characteristics that seem to make certain children stand out, but are not described with just one dimension or scale. Some popular examples include the "Spirited Child," the "High Need Child," the "Difficult Child" and books describing common differences between boys and girls. If your child fits one of these models, then these categories can be helpful for guiding much of your parenting life. But for choosing a school, you will need to peel apart the layers of these categories, as they typically include a combination of child characteristics that may demand different school settings. You can use our Fit Factors as a guide to untangle this web both for choosing a school and parenting outside of school. For example, if your "High Need" child is gifted academically – as a good portion of these children seem to be – then she really needs a school that meets her academic needs (or you will need to accommodate elsewhere in her life). Similarly, your "spirited child" may be a very strong visual learner and thus have a very high need for visual order in the classroom (e.g., few class changes, a neat classroom, a space of her own) regardless of other characteristics that make her "spirited." Your boy may need extra emotional skill development – or not. Your girl may need help balancing her social concerns with setting high goals for herself – or not.

Conclusion

The one sure bet is that there are no "generic" children. Your first job as a parent is to *know your child* so that you can make great choices about his school and life. Sound daunting? After you've read Chapters 3 – 5 about your child, you will find your confidence rising: you can not only understand your child but find the right school to fit his needs. (And if you do the *Snap To It* Activities you'll feel all the more confident, and rightly so.)

What To Do

➤ *Use Child "Quick Think"* on the next page to "brainstorm" the things about your child that you think really stand out compared to other children. Estimated Time: 10 minutes

➤ *Skim the Child Needs Summary* on page 38 to get a complete preview of the specific child characteristics included in each of the four Fit Factors. You do not need to follow the instructions at this time – we will walk you through each item in Chapters 3-5. Estimated Time: 5 minutes

Need more? Want more? Got more to share? Visit PickyParent.com.

Child "Quick Think"

Stop and think for a few minutes about your child. Write your responses here or on a separate page. Compare and discuss your answers with anyone else involved in school decision-making (e.g., your spouse or child). Keep your notes handy to use later in your school hunt.

What strengths, challenges and other characteristics stand out about your child?

➤ What your child likes or is able to do well

➤ What your child doesn't like or has difficulty doing

➤ How your child works and interacts best with adults and other children

Child Needs Summary

How to Use This Summary:

➤ Use this checklist to help identify your child's most important characteristics for choosing a school. Use Chapters 2-5 and the *Know Your Child's Needs* table on page 368 for further clarification.

➤ Write an "M" in the square box beside needs that are Must Haves: truly essential for your child's school to address. Most children will have a small number of Must Haves.

➤ Write an "N" in the square box beside needs that are Nice to Haves: not essential, but helpful for school to address.

➤ Leave empty boxes beside items not important for choosing a school for your child, because either (1) an item is not important for your child or (2) you do not need school to address an item.

➤ Record Must Haves and top Nice to Haves on your *Personalized Great Fit Checklist* on page 59.

WHAT YOUR CHILD LEARNS

☐ **BASIC LEARNING CAPABILITY:** A child's readiness for learning in core academic subjects. A Must Have for all. Check highest category that fits.

○ **Extremely Challenged:** very delayed math, language; or I.Q. below 70; social difficulty as peer of Typical children

○ **Challenged:** consistently delayed in math and language; or I.Q. between 70 and 85

○ **Typical:** close to expected math, language, but may be somewhat behind or ahead; or I.Q. between 85 and 120

○ **Bright/Gifted:** advanced or learns quickly; 90th-97th percentile on achievement tests; or I.Q. between 120 and 130

○ **Highly Gifted:** very advanced math and/or language; 97th percentile and up on achievement tests; or I.Q. over 130; may have social difficulty as peer of Typical children

OTHER CAPABILITIES: look for strengths (early or very strong capabilities) and weaknesses (late or very weak capabilities) compared to other children of same age. A Must Have only for extreme strengths and weaknesses. Mark Must Haves ("M") and Nice to Haves ("N"), if needed.

☐ *Musical:* senses, appreciates, composes, and/or performs music, including rhythm, pitch, and tone

☐ *Artistic:* understands and appreciates others' art; creates original works of art pleasing or interesting to others

☐ *Physical & Hands-on:* displays strength, agility, speed, balance and/or flexibility; or uses all or part of the body to create ideas or objects and to solve problems

☐ *Social & Leadership:* understands & interacts well with many kinds of people; or organizes/leads other children

☐ *Creativity:* thinks of new ideas and ways to do things, rather than imitating others; may apply to varying activities

☐ *English as Second Language:* understands, speaks, reads, and writes English at age-appropriate level

☐ **INTERESTS:** something your child loves to do or think about often, regardless of skill; interest must be long-held and something your child wants to continue pursuing frequently at school to make it a Must Have. Write interest here, if any:_____

Continues...

Child Needs Summary *...continued*

HOW YOUR CHILD LEARNS

☐ *LEARNING STYLES:* a Must Have if child is very strong in one style only or very weak in one style. Check extreme strengths or weaknesses below.

◯ *Visual:* learns best seeing things written or in pictures; stimulated by how things look; bothered by disorder, clutter. Strength or weakness?: _____

◯ *Auditory:* learns best listening, talking, discussing; stimulated by sounds; bothered by loud, disorganized noises. Strength or weakness?: _____

◯ *Kinesthetic:* learns best moving body; and/or using hands ("tactile"); stimulated by activity; bothered sitting still. Strength or weakness?: _____

☐ *MOTIVATION:* how self-motivated is child to achieve academically? A Must Have if this is a strength or weakness. May be a Must Have if child is Typical and parent cannot provide general supervision of child's work and progress. Check category that best fits.

◯ *Strength:* child sets challenging goals for self, tries hard things on own, works to overcome barriers and problems

◯ *Typical:* child works to meet goals set by teachers, parents; or sets achievable goals for self; stops if problems arise

◯ *Weakness:* child not bothered when does not perform well; or is bothered but takes no action

☐ *PHYSICAL OR MENTAL HEALTH CHALLENGES:* any physical restrictions or handicaps; ongoing illnesses requiring daily treatment or special facilities; or ongoing or recurring emotional upset (severe depression, anxiety, other mental health challenges). Write here, if any: _____

☐ *BEHAVIOR CHALLENGES:* significant, unresolved behavior or discipline problems in group settings that prevent your own child or others in class from effectively learning.

☐ *LEARNING DISORDERS AND DISABILITIES:* a Must Have for any recognized learning disability; or learning disorder severe enough to require special services at school to meet academic, social, emotional or physical needs. Write disability here, if any: _____

☐ *SELF-UNDERSTANDING:* child's demonstrated ability to understand self, including own strengths, weaknesses and interests and to use that understanding to make decisions. A Must Have only if child is very weak in this area.

SOCIAL ISSUES

☐ *FRIENDS:* a Must Have if your child has well-established friendships with children attending a certain school, and your child does not have social skills to make new friends, and you are unable to help your child continue current friendships outside of school or establish new friendships. List specific friends here, if any: _____

PRACTICAL MATTERS

☐ *ESSENTIAL ACTIVITIES:* Must Have if child has non-school activities that must continue and can't be done at school. Write activity here, if any:_____

LIGHT'NING LIST

What To Know from Chapter 3

➤ **Fit Factor #1 is** *What Your Child Learns:* these are things about your child that indicate *what subjects and at what level of difficulty* your child should be taught.

➤ **The three** child **characteristics for Fit Factor #1:**
  ✔ *Basic Learning Capability* = your child's readiness for learning in core academic subjects. Is your child gifted? Challenged? Or more in the middle?
  ✔ *Other Capabilities* = your child's extreme strengths and weaknesses in other endeavors like Music, Art, Social & Leadership, Physical & Hands-on, Creativity, English as a Second Language, and others.
  ✔ *Interests* = your child's strong interests that need to be addressed in school.

➤ **You can identify the Fit Factor # 1 characteristics most important for** your **child** by (1) Observing (2) Comparing (3) Testing and (4) Getting Smart. Start with the tools listed in Snap To It at the end of the chapter.

➤ **Remember, you must identify the** few most important **characteristics of your child** to match with schools for a Great Fit.
  ✔ Basic Learning Capability will be a Must Have for all children.
  ✔ Other Capabilities and Interests will be a Must Have for a limited number of children if they are *extreme* relative to other kids.

Chapter 3

Child Fit Factor #1:
What Does *Your* Child Need to Learn?

Jane was bored in school for years until in third grade her parents switched her to a school that raised the bar as fast as she could scramble in math, reading and writing. She bounds out of the house every morning now, revved to go to school!

■ ■ ■

Ben tuned out in the basics until his parents moved him to a performing arts magnet where his unusual talents and interest in music and dance were revered. His schedule booked to the gills with motivating arts activities, he now shines in the basics as well.

■ ■ ■

Roger, exceptionally creative in his free time and astonishing in his ability to organize and lead other young children, was deflated by the structured, just-the-facts approach of his traditional school. His parents switched him to a school where much of the learning is project-based and students are invited to design and produce works outside the traditional worksheet format. In his first month, Roger organized several kids to write a class creative writing newspaper for the weekly writing assignment. The writing of all the students involved soared as they spent large amounts of free time pursuing the activity. Roger's creativity and social leadership, already strengths, have soared as well.

Identifying Your Child's Content Learning Needs

What schools teach differs in three big ways: the level of challenge offered to individual students, the range of subjects taught, and the thinking skills emphasized.

As a parent, it's not always easy to know exactly *what* your child should be learning in school. Most parents know that their children need the basic subjects, but how challenging should the work be? And what subjects, topics and non-academic skills does your particular child need to learn about at school? In short, what subjects and level of difficulty will engage your child's mind and make the most of his talents?

These questions all fall under Fit Factor #1: What Your Child Learns. In this chapter, you will explore the characteristics of your child that affect what subjects and at what level of difficulty your child should be taught at school. If you explore your child's needs in this area, you will be better able to choose a school that fits your child. You will also be more likely to offer the right kind of opportunities outside of school.

There are three big differences from school to school in *what* students learn. One is the level of difficulty and pacing. In some classrooms, the whole class is working on high level work. In others, everyone's tackling simpler tasks. In still others, teachers try to get each student working at his or her own level. Different classrooms move individual kids forward at different rates as well ("pacing").

The second big difference is the range of subjects taught. All elementary schools cover the three R's of reading, writing, and arithmetic. Beyond that, schools differ in how much time they spend on everything from science and social studies to art, music, character-building, and social-emotional skills ("breadth").

The third big difference is the degree to which schools stress basic skills versus critical and creative thinking. Basic skills are things like memorized facts and dates, letter sounds and vocabulary words, repetitive math problems, and how to write a sentence with a capital letter at the beginning and period at the end. Critical thinking includes problem solving, comparing and contrasting, and other ways of *using* basic skills and knowledge. Creative thinking is coming up with new ideas and doing things in new ways, rather than the standard way.

What kind of school is right for your child when it comes to *what students learn*? Well, it depends on your child's specific needs. Fortunately, you can zero in on these needs quickly by thinking about the three characteristics of your child that make up Fit Factor #1:

➤ Basic Learning Capability
➤ Other Capabilities
➤ Interests

Basic Learning Capability

Lucy just began second grade. For two years, she has learned little in school. When she began kindergarten she was already reading at a second grade level and by the end of the year was reading at a fifth grade level, though the teachers focused on teaching letter sounds to the entire class for the year. Lucy's parents had engaged in repeated discussions with her teachers about how to challenge Lucy at school, to no avail. The teachers assured them that Lucy was "doing just fine" at school – making grade level and not misbehaving – and that the one-hour weekly pull-outs for gifted students would start later in second grade. Her parents started to feel embarrassed requesting special favors for their child. They began looking at other schools. They sought – and found – a school that monitored children's learning and adjusted the lessons upward every week for children who were ready. Lucy would be grouped with other children at her current learning level – from her own class or others – for at least half of each school day. All children at this school were organized into small learning groups with ever-changing membership, so she would not be labeled a "brain."

■ ■ ■

Sam, a personable and athletic first grader, was an "on target" student, his teacher said. Yet he was still struggling with reading, and his parents did not believe that this was very "on target" at all. His school had a large population of gifted students and also many who were challenged. His parents' dismay grew as they realized how little attention the kids in the middle, like their son, were getting. After no response despite several polite meetings with his teacher, his concerned parents hired a private tutor once each week (for Sam and a classmate to share). Sam's reading skills developed quickly. "Am I crazy, or is something wrong with this picture? What should I do next?" his mother asked in frustration. Assured that indeed there was something wrong, she and several other parents scheduled a meeting with the new principal. The principal, eager to improve results for all students, formed a committee to plan significant changes in the school's reading program. The resulting changes, including targeted strategies for readers at differing levels, raised reading scores for children across the board in only one year's time. Sam's parents were thrilled and stopped feeling guilty for being "pushy."

■ ■ ■

> *Approach this process with an open mind about your child. A Great Fit school will make the most of your child's strengths and develop his or her weaknesses.*

Basic Learning Capability: What It Is, Why It's Important

Basic Learning Capability (BLC) is a child's current readiness for learning in core academic subjects, before intervention by a school. It is one very important factor in determining what a child will be ready to learn at each age – and therefore *what* he should be taught.

Definition

Capability: A person's readiness for performance or accomplishment in a pursuit.

Basic Learning Capability: A child's readiness for learning in core academic subjects.

"Core" academic subjects: Subjects that all students must master in preparation for independent adult life and further education in our society, including at least reading, writing and math.

BLC includes traditional measures of "intelligence," which assess mental processing speed and agility in areas such as logical problem solving, comparing, and contrasting ("analytical" and "conceptual" thinking). But not that alone. An individual child may take a bump up or down in BLC based on previous *exposure to core academic* material. A "typical" child who has been offered a very rich and stimulating environment – at home or school – that encourages language and mathematical/logical development may be ready for more challenging school work in core subjects than a child who has not had much stimulation.

It is important to identify the state of readiness for academic work that your child brings to school, because you will want to *find a school that provides children like yours the twin joys of facing challenges and being successful in facing them.* Core academic work – reading, writing, math and the like – consumes much of school time and focus.

➤ *If academic work is far too hard* without the intensive support and unrelenting expectation for success that an academically *challenged* child needs, he will learn neither the ultimate joy of success nor how to overcome challenge (nor the basic knowledge he needs for adult life).

➤ *If academic work is far too easy* for an academically *gifted* child, he will not learn the tenacity to face and overcome challenge, since he will not encounter it until much later.

Both over-challenged, under-supported children and the never-challenged ones lose an opportunity to strengthen their intellectual gifts and reinforce good work habits.

Definition

Analytical thinking: Solving problems by breaking them down into logical, orderly steps. One of the two major capabilities assessed by traditional "I.Q." tests.

Conceptual thinking: Making comparisons between things not obviously related, seeing similarities and large patterns in a collection of smaller events. The second major capability assessed by traditional "I.Q." tests.

If your child is properly challenged at school, he can make enormous progress in classic "intelligence," increasing his thinking abilities by leaps and bounds. A child's I.Q. may increase by 20 points or more during childhood – a *huge* change – with proper stimulation and challenge. A child can progress from one BLC category to another entirely with combined, consistent high expectations, effective teaching approaches and commitment by the child to work hard. The discipline and confidence a child gains from such an experience can last a lifetime.

Indeed, a Great School that expects much of every child – no matter where each starts – can make all the difference. This is one reason why school *quality* hinges significantly on challenging individual students of all capabilities to make constant *progress*. But we'll get to that big point later. Meanwhile, you need to know where your child is *now* to choose a school that will offer your child the opportunity to move forward.

Most schools are designed to target children in the middle. The impact on children of low BLC – who just don't grasp the basic facts they need – can be devastating. Not only will they not learn what is expected, they may feel bad about it and show it with angry behavior, acting up or tuning out in class. And the very high BLC child – who grasps the basics immediately and is ready to move on – will suffer, as well. He will begin to "feel different" from his engaged peers, may demonstrate bored behavior like not paying attention and not sitting still, and will not learn the tenacity that comes with being challenged to learn something new and hard. A high-quality school will overcome these challenges, but you must make sure that a school is strong in the specific ways that will fit your child right now.

Do not worry that you are limiting or pressuring your child by "pegging" her early. Think of this as a starting point, neither a cap on your child's academic potential nor a guarantee of performance in school. We all know that motivation and hard work accompany any long-term success, and your child can bring these to the table regardless of other capabilities.

All students can influence their own success by working hard and overcoming barriers. The right kind of challenge and support can teach your child to do just that.

Some students just have a harder time initially learning new things, solving problems, seeing how ideas are similar and different and coming up with new ideas. Others seem to breathe in knowledge and solve problems before the rest of us even know there's problem at all. Most are somewhere in between. All students can influence their own success by learning to work hard and overcome barriers along the way. Indeed, the right kind of academic challenge and support in school can influence how well and how early children learn these lessons.

Categories

The five categories of Basic Learning Capability are these:

1. *Extremely Challenged:* very delayed math and language; difficulty relating as peer of Typical children; I.Q. below 70. About 2–3% of children fall here. These children are included under the umbrella term "special needs" because of their learning challenges.

2. *Challenged:* consistently somewhat delayed in math and language; I.Q. between 70 and 85. About 13–14% of children fall here.

3. *Typical:* close to expected in math and language, but may be somewhat behind or ahead in some areas; I.Q. between 85 and 120. Most children, nearly 7 out of 10, will fall here.

4. *Bright/Gifted:* advanced or learns quickly in math and language; or 90th–97th percentile on achievement tests; or I.Q. between 120 and 130. About 13–14% of children fall here.

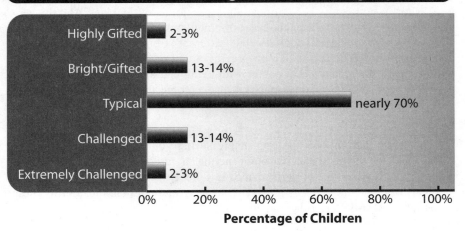

Where Children Fall on the Range of Basic Learning Capability

5. *Highly Gifted:* very advanced math and/or language; or 97th percentile and up on achievement tests; some may have difficulty relating as peer of Typical children; I.Q. over 130. About 2–3% of children fall here.

We'd like to have narrowed these to three big buckets – On Target, Below and Above. But parents, educators and researchers who know about Extremely Challenged and Highly Gifted children will tell you that these two groups tend to be much more different from their peers academically than children even a bit closer to the norm. Those mental differences often create social challenges, too, so it's especially important to get a handle on things if your child is near either extreme.

Viewpoint   Multiple Intelligences

Howard Gardner, the highly regarded developmental psychologist who pioneered thinking about "multiple intelligences" in *Frames of Mind,* originally divided intelligence into seven categories. He sees the intelligences not as goals to be met, but as strengths to appreciate in their own right and to be drawn upon for teaching different children traditional academic subject matter (e.g., using music to teach math). His basic intelligences include these:

1. Linguistic – the ability to learn and use language (words), both spoken and written.
2. Logical-mathematical – the ability to analyze problems (i.e., to break problems down into parts and weigh the value of different parts), to do math, and to investigate "logically" (working through the different elements of problems in order).
3. Musical – the ability to appreciate, compose (write rhythm and pitch), and perform music.
4. Bodily-kinesthetic – the ability to use all or part of the body to create new things, accomplish goals and solve problems.
5. Spatial – the ability to understand and *use space and the objects in it* to create new ideas and solve problems.
6. Interpersonal – the ability to understand and act on the feelings, thoughts, abilities and motives of *others*.
7. Intrapersonal – the ability to understand and act on *one's own* feelings, thoughts, abilities and motives.

You might be wondering, "How does Basic Learning Capability compare to these seven?" BLC includes a combination of the first two of Gardner's intelligences: Linguistic and Logical-mathematical. Many of the other intelligences are part of child characteristics presented later in this chapter and the next.

When is This a Priority for Your School Hunt?

In most cases, we encourage you to discard any Fit Factor element that isn't a clear, top priority so you may focus on those that are. But Basic Learning Capability is the one exception. You – and all parents – will best be able to choose the right school if you know where your child's Basic Learning Capability falls.

You may be tempted not to bother if your child is right in the middle, particularly since so many schools are designed to fit children of "typical" academic capability. But too many right-in-the-middle children miss out because their schools either have set low learning standards or, having set challenging standards, fail to reinforce basic subjects adequately and interestingly. We have heard too many parents of these children lament in retrospect that schools did not ask enough of their children or failed to drive home the basic building blocks of knowledge in reading, writing and math. Consider finding a school that fits your child's BLC a Must Have even if your child is quite the norm.

Smart à la Carte

Take Care When Having Your Child Tested

We'll say it here as you identify your child's needs, and we'll say it again later regarding testing for school admissions: take precious care of your child before and during testing times. All children are susceptible to stress from testing situations – the younger the more so. If you yourself are stressed about your child's testing, your child may absorb that stress and take it on as his or her own. Your child will not "over test," but she may "under test" if she's too preoccupied, tired, sick, hungry or otherwise "not herself" to show what she knows. So:

➤ Try a slightly earlier than usual bedtime for your child for at least a few days before tests.
➤ Pay special attention to your child's diet during the week prior – good nutrition, plenty of water, not too many sweets (the usual suspects).
➤ Make sure your child gets regular exercise.
➤ Schedule only one testing event in a week if possible, and never two days in a row (but it's fine to have multiple tests in one multi-hour session – discuss your child's stamina with the tester if you are concerned).
➤ Limit new and unusual activities to essentials in the days prior.
➤ On test day, ensure that your child has a healthy breakfast, plenty to drink, and healthy snacks to maintain energy.
➤ A hug goes much further than a lecture just prior to testing time.

Identifying Your Child's Need

If you're not sure about your child, a simple I.Q. test is a good place to start. But if we'd meant I.Q. alone, we'd have said it. Your child's previous exposure to academic material matters, too. Your child may be ready for *more* challenging work more quickly than others in his I.Q. range if he's had a lot of academic exposure and challenge previously. Likewise, your child may need more catch-up than others in his I.Q. range if he hasn't had the same level of academic exposure and challenge.

If you'd prefer not to test – or at least not right away – you may be able to make an approximate guess of your child's BLC. Your best strategy is a process of elimination. Start with the most extreme categories and move to the center until you find one that seems best to describe your child. Children who are either Extremely Challenged or Highly Gifted will often show clear behaviors that are markedly different from others of similar age – Challenged and Bright children somewhat less so. Typical children are, well, typical in mental processing and have a better chance of just seeming to "fit in" academically and sometimes even socially.

> *Remember: I.Q. is not set in stone. Your child can learn analytical and conceptual thinking skills and increase I.Q. by 20% or more during the elementary years.*

Smart à la Carte

When Your Child's I.Q. and Academic Skills Don't Match

If you believe, or a tester confirms, that there is a great difference between your child's I.Q. and academic know-how, you'll need to find a school prepared to nurture your child appropriately across the gap. Going for a high quality school, not just one that fits today, will be critical. If your child has had less academic exposure than most children with his mental processing capability (I.Q.), your child's school will need to guide your child *rapidly* up the ramp of academic basics rather than holding him back or skipping steps. If your child works in overdrive and seems to perform "beyond herself," then the school will need to allow your child to continue challenging herself while watching for academic gaps and over-achiever stress.

If a very large gap shows between I.Q. and actual learning – either in an expert assessment or later school performance – you'll want to have your child checked for learning disabilities and disorders, too. This is especially true if you know that your child has had great exposure to academic learning materials and activities, either at home or in school or day care.

To get a read on all of this, check out the Basic Learning Capability section of our *Know Your Child's Needs* table, which starts on page 368.

If you're not sure after thinking it through and you feel motivated to get testing, you're in luck. I.Q. tests and those of verbal and mathematical/ logical development are some of the most refined tests available. That said, know that children are susceptible to stress from the usual burdens of growing up and even the testing situation itself – the younger the more so. Your child probably will not "over test," but she may "under test" if she's too preoccupied, tired, sick, hungry or otherwise "not herself" on the day of the test. If test results do not seem correct to you, consider a retest. But it will be easier on you and your child if you simply take special care of your child's health and well being before the first test so your child is relaxed, undistracted, and mentally alert. For more on this, see the box *Take Care When Having Your Child Tested* on page 48.

Smart à la Carte

When Your Child's Reading, Writing, and Math Skills Don't Match

Your child may apply his or her Basic Learning Capability unevenly to academic subjects. The fact is that any specific academic work – reading, writing, math, or particular aspects of each – uses several parts of your child's brain. Your child may have particular strengths (what he *can* do) and preferences (what he *likes* to do) unrelated to the "thinking skills" assessed on an I.Q. test. Your child may apply thinking skills to any of the three core academic areas, and other pursuits, too – or not.

If your child has an exceptional *capability* in one core academic area, such as writing or math, treat your child as Highly Gifted in that subject. Seek in a school the individualized goal-setting and instruction *in that subject* that your child needs. Use the sections of the Child tables addressing Highly Gifted children to help with your hunt. Ideally, you'll find a school that challenges and nurtures the strength, while also meeting your child where he is in other academic areas. Similarly, treat a very strong *interest* in one academic area over the others as just that – a strong interest to be addressed through school or elsewhere (use the Interests section on page 55 to help).

That said, vast differences in skill and learning across core subjects may indicate a learning disability. For example, if your brilliant mathematician or chatty 7 year old child can't read, consider testing for dyslexia and other disabilities.

Identification strategies include:

➤ Have a straightforward I.Q. test conducted by a professional tester. The tests will differ for young and older children, and the expected results vary by age, but a qualified tester will be able to explain the specifics to you.

➤ Have a developmental test of language and math conducted by a professional tester, which will capture not just I.Q. but previous exposure to academic material compared to children of similar age.

➤ Ask your child's school, preschool or day care teachers how your child compares to other children of same age whom they have observed.

➤ Observe and compare your child's language to similar age children – the clarity of speech, difficulty of words used, complexity of ideas expressed, and length of paragraphs.

➤ Watch for behavioral indicators, especially compared to other children. Use to identify or eliminate Highly Gifted and Extremely Challenged categories, and possibly to identify or eliminate Bright and Challenged:

  ✔ *Extremely Challenged:* is very delayed developmentally overall. Clearly seems "slow" to master daily life challenges, not just academic ones. Does not connect as true peer of children who seem more typical.

  ✔ *Challenged:* seems slow, is behind developmental lists you've seen. But is able to get along and learns in daily life and learns ideas and skills that are repeated often in your home, at school or in child care.

  ✔ *Typical:* seems close to expected.

  ✔ *Bright/Gifted:* seems quick in language and math, but not so different that social interactions with more typical children the same age are challenging.

  ✔ *Highly Gifted:* seems very advanced or quick in math and/or language; very mentally energetic. Always "on" compared to other children, asking many questions, concocting many new ideas, endlessly pursuing current interests. May get bored easily in big group.

➤ See our Resources for Parents section starting on page 354 or visit *PickyParent.com* for more assessment resources.

➤ *If you get overwhelmed, aren't sure where your child falls and aren't able to get professional testing, do this:* focus on school quality, in particular Great School Quality Factors #2 and 3 detailed in Chapter 12, to help ensure that your child's needs are met.

Other Capabilities

What They Are, Why They're Important

Because basic academic subjects are the fundamental building blocks of so much of school and adult work, it is easy for parents and educators alike to forget how much joy and success can come from other aspects of life. Music, art, athletic activities, making crafts and other work by hand, interpersonal and group relationships, creative thinking of all kinds and just being able to converse in a common language are all endeavors that bring both pleasure and function to life. Most children will gain both joy and success from having at least a threshold level of *appreciation and ability* in these areas. At the other end of the scale, children who truly excel in one or more of these areas can enjoy great success in life and work as a result.

Categories

You will want to consider helping your child make the most of extreme strengths and ensure that your child has at least minimal capabilities in each of the areas listed below:

➤ Musical
➤ Artistic
➤ Physical & Hands-On
➤ Social & Leadership
➤ Creativity
➤ English as a Second Language (ESL)

Whether or not you want school to play a role in developing your child's capabilities in these areas is a personal decision (with the exception of English as a Second Language, which you really should deal with at school). But if your child has an

✔ extreme strength or
✔ extreme weakness

in one of the areas listed above, then consider making use of the long school day to address the matter.

When is This a Priority for Your School Hunt?

If your child has an *extreme strength* in one of these areas (or similar one), consider how you can best help your child make the most of it. Seek a school where your child can use and develop her strength often. Like a muscle, even great talent needs to be exercised to grow in strength. But do consider your child's interest in the matter before committing too much of your child's time to one

Capability	May be a Strength if your child...	May be a Weakness if your child...
Musical	Senses, appreciates, composes, and/or performs music, including accurate rhythm, pitch, and tone.	Rarely enjoys pleasing music created by others. Rarely attempts musical or rhythmic activities.
Artistic	Understands and appreciates others' art; creates original works of art genuinely pleasing or interesting to others.	Rarely seems to notice pleasing works of art created by others. Rarely chooses to create art of own.
Physical & Hands-On	Displays strength, agility, speed, balance and/or flexibility; or creates ideas or objects and solves problems very well using whole body or small muscles of the hand.	Lacks coordination and strength of either the whole body or small muscles of the hand. Unable to perform or create using body.
Social & Leadership	Understands and interacts well with many kinds of people; or organizes and leads other children.	Shows little understanding of others' feelings or consistently communicates poorly – and unable to make friends.
Creativity	Thinks of new ideas and ways to do things, rather than imitating others or using "standard" methods; may apply to varying activities.	Rigidly and consistently insists on thinking and doing things the way others do them or the way they have been done before.
ESL (English as a Second Language)	When English is the child's second language, understands, speaks, reads and writes English at level expected of same age children for whom English is first language ("age-appropriate").	When English is the child's second language, does not understand, speak, read or write English at age-appropriate level.

endeavor. Your amazing musician may be better off letting her interest catch up to advanced abilities than spending a great deal of time exercising an ability that she doesn't enjoy using. Your stellar athlete may be as interested in academics as sports, and you'll want to take that into account. Make an extreme capability a school Must Have only if your child *actually* spends a great deal of time on it and *wants to continue* doing so.

If your child is very late or **weak** in one of the listed capabilities compared to other same-age children, then finding a school to help your child develop *at least basic skills* may be your best route. You need not enroll your tone-deaf child in a school for the performing arts (indeed, that would be torture), but you may want to find a school with a basic music program. If you've just now focused on a particular weakness and feel that after-school activities or other aspects of family life can serve to develop your child, then this may be a mere Nice to Have in your school hunt.

But if your child's weakness in one of these areas may affect not only his enjoyment of that particular skill but his ability to use his strengths, make it a Must Have. Seek a school that will make the most of the long school day to improve your child's competence. For example, if your child is already weak socially, don't starve his social skill development by home schooling (unless you take care to include group activities with a stable set of peers in the plan). Your child will thank you when he finds out as a teenager and adult how important getting along with others can be, not just for social life but also for work. If English is your child's second language, seek a school with an intensive English as a Second Language skill development program. No matter how capable she is in other areas, your child needs to be able to communicate in the dominant language of the land to make the most of her other skills.

Identifying Your Child's Need

Identification strategies include:

➤ Ask your child's school, preschool or day care teachers how your child compares to others they have observed. Lead teachers may have an especially good grasp of physical and social skills, creativity and ESL mastery. Consider asking more specialized teachers who have contact with your child about Music and Art, if your child's school, preschool or care center uses them.

➤ Behavior indicators, especially compared to other children. See the box on page 53, and go to the Other Capabilities section of our *Know Your Child's Needs* table beginning on page 368 for more.

➤ A straightforward test of capability by a tester qualified to test in that subject matter (Music, Art, Physical & Hands-On, Social & Leadership, Creativity,

English as a Second Language, or other area you value). In most cases, you need not take this step unless you suspect a weakness in one of these three areas: Physical & Hands-On, Social & Leadership, or English as a Second Language.

Interests

What They Are, Why They're Important

Your child's interests are a strong indicator of the kind of thinking and topics that excite his mind. This is true particularly when an interest is long-term and deeply held. For a child who has a very strong interest in a particular subject, attending a school that does not address the area thoroughly may be boring and perhaps a waste of your child's potential. Your avid young botanist, bird watcher, poet, dancer, or foreign language aficionado would be well-served in a school that addresses the interest well. The same is true for any very strong and consistent interest your child may have, whether in a traditional academic field or another – the arts, athletics, or a particular way of thinking such as creativity or logical problem solving.

Such strong interests will often coincide with unusually strong capabilities, but not always. Allow your child to be passionate about an interest without being the "best" at it. She'll learn much from pursuing an area of personal interest, even if it turns out not to be a lifelong calling. But you will have to make the reality check and judgment call about whether your child must pursue the interest *at school* – or whether you are able to provide materials and opportunity for your child to pursue the interest outside of school.

So, should you sign up your five-year-old boy who likes trucks and fire engines for truck-driving school or firefighting classes? Probably not. But *do* take delight in your child's interests, and use them to help your child prepare for school.

Categories

Interests will be Must Haves for very few elementary age children. You should consider choosing a school focused on your child's interest only if the interest is both

- ✔ strong and
- ✔ unusual relative to other children.

Common types of interests include:
- ➤ Subjects and topics
- ➤ Ways of thinking (analytical, conceptual, creative)
- ➤ Other interests, regardless of talent or current skill (e.g., interpersonal, musical, artistic)

When Is This a Priority for Your School Hunt?

If indeed your child's interest is strong and unusual, then it may be a school Must Have. If you find that your child's passion is also his *talent*, then it may rise right to the top of your gotta-have-it list. But "interests" are one school selection item that will fall away for many. If this turns out to be you, remember that there are typically many other avenues besides school to help your child enjoy and pursue special interests.

Identifying Your Child's Need

➤ Ask your child's current school, preschool or day care teacher (or any teacher of similar-age children) what interests are typical for children your child's age.

➤ Ask your child's current school, preschool or day care teacher whether your child's interest is displayed in school.

Smart à la Carte

Your Five Year Old Truck Nut: What To Do?!

Do you really need to send your truck-crazy preschooler to "trucks & transportation" school? Certainly not. But it is easy enough for parents to get caught up in the typical passions of young children, be they "all things pink and purple" for your girl or "all things on wheels and with 'saur' at the end" for boys. In the case of the five-year-old boy who loves trucks, you need not choose a school that covers this topic. Even if the interest is long-held, it is not unusual. Many boys this age like trucks, and truck-related items certainly are used in many schools to teach reading and other basic skills. Inexpensive opportunities to use trucks for learning at home abound, as well: small truck models, ABC truck puzzles, books and other truck learning toys are widely available. Many fire stations allow visits from neighborhood children to check out the real thing, too. You can do much to support your child's current interests and use those interests to build your child's "worldly" and academic knowledge.

If you aren't sure what's typical, just ask your child's current teacher, preschool teacher, day care operator or even one who doesn't know your child at all: "what's typical of a child this age?" As a parent, you will have to make an assessment that balances all of the issues above to determine if your child's particular interests are truly important for your school selection.

➤ Observe and compare your child's behavior. Consider the factors below to determine whether your child's interest is strong and unusual enough to seek a school that will fit, and see the Interests section of our *Know Your Child's Needs* table, which starts on page 368:

✔ **Time spent:** your child chooses to spend large quantities of time on the interest, and

✔ **Long term:** the interest has been held for a long time (a year or more for young children, several years for older children), and

✔ **Will continue:** your child wants to continue pursuing the area of interest, and

✔ **Unusual:** your child's interest is one not shared by many children his own age (so that most schools would not address it in the regular curriculum). Ask your child's current school, preschool or day care teachers for guidance on "typical" same-age child interests. Assume that a very extreme level of interest, even in a traditional academic subject, is unusual, period. And . . .

✔ **Difficult to accommodate outside of school:** your child's interest is one that would be difficult for you to address at home or in extracurricular activities.

SNAP TO IT

What To Do

➤ **Refer back to your Child "Quick Think"** on page 37 to refresh your memory regarding things that really stand out about your child. Estimated Time: 2 minutes

➤ **Use the Child Needs Summary** on page 38 to get a quick fix on the Fit Factor # 1 What Your Child Learns characteristics. Estimated Time: 5 minutes

➤ **Use the Know Your Child's Needs table** on page 368 to further clarify your child's Fit Factor # 1 characteristics and the importance of each for choosing a school. You need not read the whole table: focus only on items you suspect are important for your child. Estimated Time: 15 minutes

➤ **Record your Must Haves and Nice to Haves** on your *Child Needs Summary* (page 38). Estimated Time: 10 minutes

continues...

SNAP TO IT *continued...*

Optional Activities

➤ *Discuss your child's needs* with your spouse or other parenting partner. Estimated Time: As needed.

➤ *Plan now to schedule professional testing for your child* if you are not at all certain of which Basic Learning Capability category your child fits into. If you have narrowed to two BLC categories, you may want to consider testing. Consider professional testing also if you suspect your child may have an extreme weakness in Social, Physical & Hands-On, or English as Second Language skills. Estimated Time: 30 minutes to find a tester and schedule an appointment.

➤ *Mark your calendar to ask current school, preschool or day care teachers* about your child compared to other children. Estimated Time: 2 minutes to mark your calendar, 5 minutes to schedule time to talk with teachers, 45 minutes to talk with teachers.

➤ *Make a plan to observe your child and read other resources*, as needed. For some readings on topics covered in these chapters, see the Resources for Parents section starting on page 354. Estimated Time: 10 minutes to plan; you decide how much for observing and reading other resources.

Need more? Want more? Got more to share? Visit PickyParent.com.

A CONFIDENT CHOICE Tool

Personalized Great Fit Checklist

School Name: _____

▶ In the first blank column, list in pencil the precise names of your top child & family needs based on your *Child and Family Needs Summaries* (pages 38 and 110) and on your reading of Chapters 2–9 and related tables. For example, write: "Basic Learning Capability, Typical." See a complete example on page 176.

▶ Check whether each of your needs is a Must Have or Nice to Have.

▶ In next big column, make note of the characteristics a school must have to meet your need based on your reading of Chapter 10 and related tables.

▶ Include specific questions to ask school principal, teachers, parents, and others (or use our *Interview Forms* on page 273).

▶ Make an extra copy and fill in notes for each school you consider.

▶ After you gather the information you need, grade each school on how well it fits each Must Have and Nice to Have item:

    A perfect fit   *C* halfway fit

    B very good fit   *D* poor fit   *F* very poor or no fit

FIT FACTOR	CHILD & FAMILY NEEDS: Must Haves & top Nice to Haves	MUST HAVE	NICE TO HAVE	WHAT TO LOOK FOR *and* QUESTIONS TO ASK	NOTES ABOUT THIS SCHOOL	GRADE
What Your Child Learns						
How Your Child Learns						
Social Issues						
Practical Matters						

LIGHT'NING LIST

What To Know from Chapter 4

➤ **Fit Factor #2 is** *How Your Child Learns:* these are things about your child that indicate how a school should teach and interact with your child.

➤ **The six** child **characteristics for Fit Factor #2 are:**
  ✔ *Learning Styles* = strengths and preferences your child has for using the senses – particularly sight, hearing/talking, and touch/movement – to absorb new information and act in a learning environment.
  ✔ *Motivation* = your child's internal drive to learn and perform academically.
  ✔ *Physical or Mental Health Challenges* = special challenges your child may face because of physical barriers or serious or recurrent mental illness.
  ✔ *Behavior Challenges* = behavior control problems that affect your own child's or other children's learning.
  ✔ *Learning Disabilities and Disorders* = problems your child may have with important parts of physical or mental functioning. These often reveal themselves through great imbalances: between your child's potential and actual achievement or between seemingly related capabilities (e.g., spoken and written language).
  ✔ *Self-Understanding* = your child's *understanding* of his own strengths, weaknesses, interests, needs and wants and the *self-control* to make decisions accordingly.

➤ **You can identify Fit Factor # 2 characteristics most important for** your **child** by (1) Observing (2) Comparing (3) Testing and (4) Getting Smart. Start with the tools listed in Snap To It at the end of the chapter.

➤ **Remember, your goal is to identify the** few most important **characteristics of your child** to match with schools for a Great Fit.
  ✔ Learning Styles; Motivation; Physical or Mental Health Challenges; Behavior Challenges; and Learning Disabilities and Disorders will be Must Haves for some children.
  ✔ Self-Understanding will be a Must Have for a limited number of children.

R 4

Child Fit Factor #2:

How Does *Your* Child Learn Best?

Jeff, a chatterbox from an early age, tuned out for academics and was constantly in trouble for disturbing others in his school, which focused almost exclusively on individual work. A switch to a school where much work is done in pairs and small groups, both with and without teachers, turned him into an academic and social star.

■ ■ ■

Maddy is bright but not interested in things academic unless a caring adult spends quiet time with her each day. Her perceptive parents noticed this about her and jumped through financial hoops to send her to a small school with very small classes and daily one-on-one teacher interaction. Highly motivated by these personal relationships with her teachers, she now writes short stories with astonishing insights about feelings and relationships.

■ ■ ■

Phillip suffered a spinal injury in a car wreck as a second grader, losing the use of both legs. Working in careful coordination with his school principal and teachers, his parents have ensured that Phillip participates in every aspect of school life, including physical education. His teachers keep a close eye on his mental health, as well, and help Phillip focus on his areas of talent and interest. Through their parent support group, his parents know of several similarly disabled children who have become isolated and depressed at school. Not Phillip!

■ ■ ■

Early in first grade, Karen's teachers became concerned about her slow reading progress, since she seemed to be fine in other subjects. Testing revealed a form of dyslexia. Her current school had few resources to address the problem, and Karen's parents did not want to take large quantities of Karen's time outside of school. But they were torn about switching schools, since Karen's older and younger siblings attended the same one. They sought and found a school with an intensive program for helping young learners understand, address and in some cases overcome dyslexia. Karen reentered her former school in third grade and now reads slightly above grade level, in line with her performance in other subjects. Karen is proud of her progress and sees herself as an I-can-do-anything kid.

Kids Learn in Different Ways

Your child's distinct combination of qualities also will factor into *how* she learns. Think of the children who lock onto learning only when they can busily work with their hands: how easily they get into trouble for not paying attention in more traditional "look and listen" schools, and how they flourish in hands-on "touch and do" schools. Think of the bright child who is just not motivated in school – unless he has some one-on-one time with the teacher. Think of the child who is the "model student" – *unless* the classroom is too noisy or disorderly. Think of the child who couldn't read until his dyslexia was diagnosed and his teachers deployed appropriate teaching techniques. Or the many other sometimes "fuzzy" characteristics that make a child learn and perform better and with more enjoyment in some settings than others.

If you have a gut feeling that a school does not fit your child, listen to your intuition and try to figure out why.

Many parents with whom we have worked initially referred to these "how" learning factors as their "gut" concerns or "intuition" about their children. They knew there was something a little different, extreme, or special about their children, but couldn't always put it into words. Sometimes it only hit them when they went to visit the school they'd assumed their child would attend – a family or neighborhood favorite. They'd come away with their "gut" screaming and head spinning: something about the school didn't fit, but it was "just a feeling."

Quite often this unsettled feeling is born of a parent's mind trying unsuccessfully to see how her child would fit into a school. These things about our children that are hardest to put into words often fall into the How Your Child Learns category. The ones that we specifically address here from your *child's* perspective include:

➤ *Learning Styles*
➤ *Motivation (to learn and perform in school)*
➤ *Physical or Mental Health Challenges*

➤ *Behavior Challenges*
➤ *Learning Disabilities and Disorders*
➤ *Self-Understanding*

These things affect *how a school ought to teach and interact with your child,* both in and out of the classroom. If your child has a strong need in one of these areas, you will be well-served to hunt for a school that fits from the start.

Learning Styles

Annie attended a school where children were encouraged to follow their own interests to engage in hands-on learning activities. A bright child who had been developmentally advanced most of her preschool years, Annie would surely benefit from the self-pacing of this elementary school, her parents thought. But Annie was a very strong "visual" learner, an average "auditory" learner and a very weak "hands-on" learner. She spent most of her school time standing around and watching other students do their work. She was disengaged from school work and became socially detached, as well. Her irritated teachers began to wonder, "What's wrong with Annie?" The answer: a very poor school fit. Annie's parents switched her to a traditional "look and listen" school where the average student was bright – so that the group learning pace was just right for her – and where learning activities were geared to watching and listening. Annie happily engaged in school activities, and her teachers think she's "just great."

■ ■ ■

Carl's mother still frets that her son attended a fairly traditional elementary school for far too long. Her son was constantly engrossed in planning and building complex structures of various kinds – with blocks, paper clips or whatever materials were available to him. His designs and buildings were feats of wonder. But because he was so exceptionally engaged in his own work, he was constantly in trouble for not listening and following directions. This mother finally realized that her child required a more open setting in which he could learn through individual projects of his own choosing. Fortunately, there was a public magnet school in the city with a self-paced teaching method and plenty of hands-on learning. It was a perfect fit, and her son flourished. Today, she believes that the years of being the one "in trouble" hurt his self-image. His talents and temperament are highly valued in many jobs, including the engineering path he has chosen. But it took a change of schools for him to feel valued at school and to have time at school to learn the way he learned best.

Learning Styles: What They Are, Why They're Important

Children, and adults, learn in many ways. We use different parts of the brain – and the body it controls – to absorb, make sense of and act in the world. We all learn by observing others and the things around us, by listening and discussing, by jumping in and doing something with our hands or bodies. Most of our brains are not equally developed throughout. Some parts of our brains are stronger and more active than others, leading us to find learning and acting in certain ways more engaging and enjoyable than doing so in other ways. Learning styles are simply our preferred ways of learning new things, depending on which of our senses – particularly sight, hearing/speech and touch/movement – we find most natural and engaging to use.

How many of you:
➤ Can't remember something you've heard unless you write it down?
➤ Can't remember something you've read unless you talk about it?
➤ Can't connect with an idea unless you have a model that you can make or touch with your hands, or unless you can dramatize it with your body?
➤ Learn and perform your work well – unless it is too noisy?
➤ Get bored unless you are in a room with lots of color and things on the walls?
➤ Never could memorize poems, but learned all the words to your favorite songs?

Life is not just about the destination, but also the joy of the journey. A learning style match can greatly influence whether your child loves school or not.

If any of these fit you, then you most likely have one or more very strong learning styles (and perhaps weaker other ones). You can imagine, then, how powerful a good school match can be for a child with extreme learning style strengths and weaknesses. While there is little evidence yet that a learning style match will improve your child's long-term academic achievement, we all know that life is not just about the destination, but also the joy of the journey. Your child will love the learning more when teaching matches your child's learning style strengths. Those of you who faced extreme mismatches – or perfect fits – as children know exactly what we are talking about.

So we ask all of you to step into your children's shoes for a moment and see school through their eyes. If your child has big strengths or weaknesses in learning styles, a good match with your child's styles is a powerful tool for creating a love affair between your child and school.

Categories

The three long-recognized learning styles include these:

1. *Visual:* Child learns best by seeing things written or in pictures and may use written or drawn "props" to reinforce own learning. Child is stimulated and engaged when surroundings are visually interesting. Child may be easily bothered by disorder, clutter, lack of neatness, and changes in location.

2. *Auditory:* Child learns best by listening, talking, and discussing. Child is stimulated by sounds, including voices, and will usually talk or make noise to fill a silence. Child may be easily bothered by loud or disorganized noises.

3. *Kinesthetic/Tactile:* Child learns best by moving body ("large motor skills" or "kinesthetic" learning) and/or working with hands ("fine motor skills" or "tactile" learning). Child is stimulated by physical activity, moving while working (kinesthetic) and hands-on projects (tactile). Child likes, and is able, to do detailed work with hands (tactile), such as handwriting, drawing and building with small parts. Child may be bothered by sitting still for long periods without using body or hands.

Your tasks are first to identify your child's preferred learning styles and then to note if your child has either:

✔ extreme strengths or
✔ extreme weaknesses.

When is This a Priority for Your School Hunt?

Your child's learning style(s) may be a Must Have – you really must meet your child's need at school or elsewhere – if:

1. Your child is very strong in one style only (and weak in other two) or
Your child is very weak in one style

   And

2. Your child has trouble learning, is not interested in school, or is easily upset when the teaching method and classroom environment do not match her style strengths.

Take note: most children won't meet this fairly stringent test. For one or more learning styles to be a Must Have, your child must have *extreme* strengths or weaknesses *and* face big learning challenges as a result. If your child falls in the more typical range of learning styles, you can set this aside in your school hunt.

Many great quality schools (and great quality teachers in other schools) will recognize each child's learning style strengths and weaknesses and will encourage three paths: building the strengths, developing the weaknesses, and learning to use the strengths to help the weaknesses. Some schools even make it part of their mission and curriculum to do just this (an effort that may be unnecessary for a child who already has balanced learning styles).

But more often, individual schools are geared toward one or two styles. If this is the case, then you'll want to make sure your child's extreme strengths (if any) are valued in your child's school. Building on your child's strength can help your child feel more confident and successful in school. Moreover, you will want to avoid a school that uses a teaching method geared solely toward your child's extreme weakness (if any). Your child *may* learn as much content, but probably won't enjoy the learning.

You may want a school both to build on your child's style strengths and improve his weaker learning styles. If so, look for one that uses a variety of approaches to teaching and learning – looking, listening, hands-on activity and body movement. You'll want to take into account what materials and activities you can offer your child outside of school, both for building and enjoying strengths and developing weaknesses. The more you offer outside of school, the less important a perfect learning style match becomes.

Identifying Your Child's Need

Many parents will be able to pinpoint extreme strengths and weaknesses just from their children's behavior. But if you are not sure, or you're about to bank your entire school pick on this matter, consider having your child tested.

Identification strategies include:
➤ Have a straightforward learning style assessment conducted by a professional tester. The expected results vary by age, but a qualified tester will be able to explain the specifics of your child's test to you.
➤ Ask your child's school, preschool or day care teachers how your child compares to other children of same age whom they have observed. You may want to ask specific questions about your child's behavior from the lists below.
➤ Observe and compare your child's activity to that of similar-age children. In what kinds of activities does your child choose to engage, and what does your child resist doing? How does your child's skill level appear compared to same age children?
➤ Use the behavior indicators below. These describe learning style strengths. Weaknesses are opposites of these. For more, see the Learning Style section of our *Know Your Child's Needs* table, which starts on page 368.

Visual Learners:

➤ Like to see things written down or in a picture:
  ✔ Remember what they see well
  ✔ Want to see and show others timelines, illustrations, charts, diagrams
  ✔ Learning aided by copying and organizing notes for own visual reinforcement

➤ Very attuned to physical environment – desk or table arrangement, things on walls, how things look:
  ✔ Bored by lack of things on walls
  ✔ Excited by stimulating, but neatly organized, physical environment
  ✔ Overstimulated and bothered (may become upset) if materials and equipment are disorganized
  ✔ Have trouble focusing without own workspace that child can organize neatly – own desk or assigned place at table
  ✔ May have difficulty with changes involving new physical surroundings

Auditory Learners:

➤ Like to talk:
  ✔ Remember what they say well
  ✔ Want to discuss and talk through what they have heard, what they are thinking
  ✔ Thrive on discussion
  ✔ Like to read out loud
  ✔ Will repeat ideas and words aloud when they are trying to remember
  ✔ Will assume you remember what they've told you (because they will)
  ✔ Silence rare – they are bored by silence and will interrupt it with talk
  ✔ Difficulty working quietly at desk for a long time – need to talk to selves or others

➤ Stimulated by sound:
  ✔ Remember what they hear without visual or physical cues, without writing it down
  ✔ Like teachers to explain things orally
  ✔ Like and ask for storytelling without books
  ✔ Overstimulated and bothered by extreme or poorly organized noises – crowds, loud music, very noisy classrooms

Viewpoint   Learning Styles

Learning styles are a widely accepted way to categorize children. Different children will have different learning style strengths and weaknesses. Some children may be strong in only one or two, some will have great weaknesses in one or two, others will be balanced in their learning approach. Recently, the idea of learning styles has been expanded and made more complex in an effort to weave in more child characteristics. The commonly accepted learning styles understood and used by educators are Visual, Auditory and Kinesthetic/Tactile – the ones we use here to help you choose a school.

Kinesthetic/Tactile Learners (your child may *be one and not the other)*

➤ Like to move their bodies ("kinesthetic"):
   ✔ Like to act out a situation or do simulations
   ✔ Like to be busily moving while working
   ✔ Like to do hands-on projects to represent their ideas
   ✔ Express enthusiasm with large physical movements (jumping, running in circles)
   ✔ May wiggle body constantly; may be labeled hyperactive
   ✔ Difficulty sitting still for long periods

➤ And/or like to touch ("tactile"):
   ✔ Like to build, do detailed work by hand, and handle materials constantly
   ✔ Handwriting and other detailed handwork a strength
   ✔ Understand ideas best when they can touch a physical object
   ✔ Take notes or doodle to keep hands busy, even though may not look at notes later
   ✔ Like to make a physical product by hand
   ✔ May fidget constantly; may be labeled hyperactive
   ✔ May have trouble focusing and completing tasks unless holding something in hands

Motivation (to learn and perform in school)

John was a typical kindergartener in many ways – right on target in his development when he started school. But what he cared about most was hanging out with his friends. Recess and lunchtime were the highlights of his school days, hands down. He wasn't really bothered when he didn't master letter sounds or counting. He didn't feel loved by his lead teacher, and that bothered him much more than not telling letter "b" from "d." In January, his frustrated teacher, with the help of the assistant teacher, reorganized her time to ensure that the she spent 20 minutes each in math and reading one-on-one with John each week. She tutored him, gave him specific weekly goals: a simple set of exercises for his parents to complete with him at home, and a very simple set of activities he could do on his own (next week when we meet I want you to name all the things you can think of that start with the "m" sound for me). John, very motivated by these personal, one-on-one interactions, leapt forward in his learning and was at grade level by the year's end. His parents were grateful to John's teacher, but knew that what she did was not the norm. They did not want to "fight" for the same special attention every year at this school. The next year, John's parents switched him to a small school with small classes where every teacher spends one-on-one time with each student in reading, writing and math every week. John consistently performs at grade level or higher, and he feels great about that. He's also learned how to set goals for himself.

■ ■ ■

Jane was a supercharged toddler, a supercharged preschooler and a supercharged elementary school student – constantly trying to do the next harder thing. Having had her tested, her parents knew that she was just a little above average in basic "intelligence." Yet her never-stop approach to life led her to work hard constantly on whatever task was put before her, and she excelled academically as a result. In second grade, she was not chosen for the Gifted and Talented program at her school; admissions were based solely on I.Q. testing, and she didn't pass muster. Her riled parents asked for a special exception and were denied. They quickly began to seek an alternative school for the following year. They chose for Jane a school where children could work at their own pace using a "contract" they made with the lead teacher each week. Jane excelled, regularly performing 15 percentile points higher on end of grade tests than her I.Q. would predict.

Motivation: What It Is, Why It's Important

Your child's abilities (what she can do) and motives (what she likes and wants to do) may not always be the same. Even the brightest intellects vary tremendously in motivation to learn and perform academically, which is simply how self-motivated they feel to:

➤ Set challenging goals for themselves in school work,
➤ Plan in advance to do what needs to be done to meet the goals, and
➤ Overcome barriers along the way to completing the work.

The motivation to learn and perform academically can be a crucial fit need for children at either extreme – highly motivated or not much at all. Different motivation levels are one major reason why children's (and adults') performance in the real world often differs from "raw" capability. Mediocre students can excel in the work world, largely fueled by extremely high motivation to learn and perform (and the work habits to back it up). Bright stars sometimes fizzle when the going gets tough. We won't speculate about what magic formula sparks that drive and determination some seem to have and others lack. But what we do know is this: when a school fails to fit a child at either extreme, the child's learning in school will almost certainly fall short of what it would be in a better-fit school.

Categories

Your child's motivation will fall into one of these three categories:
➤ *A strength* – *high* levels of self-driven motivation to learn and perform academically
➤ *Typical* – solid self-driven motivation
➤ *A weakness* – low levels of self-driven motivation to learn and perform academically

When is This a Priority for Your School Hunt?

If your child's motivation is either:
✔ a strength or
✔ a weakness
then this most likely is a Must Have, and your child will benefit from a school with a teaching approach that fits her motivation level.

But even a child who is typical may need a more-than-common motivational boost from school in some circumstances. If your child is:
✔ *typical* in motivation and
✔ either your *time* with your child or your *confidence* overseeing your child's academic progress is limited,
then you may want to seek the same qualities in a school that a child with weaker motivation would need. If you are raising your child as a single parent, if both parents are working full time, or if you do not feel confident with school work yourself, consider seeking a school with the kind of structured oversight of your child's progress that a child with lower motivation would need. You'll also want to let your child's teachers know that you *want* them to hold your child to high standards even when you can't.

You will almost certainly want to make motivation fit a top-priority Must Have if your child is both:
✔ low in motivation *and*
✔ either *challenged* or *gifted* in Basic Learning Capability.

Low in motivation, challenged in BLC. A child with this combination will need significant academic and personal support, both at home and at school, to develop into a successfully independent adult. School work will be hard for this child from the start, and the low-motivation tendency to give up easily will be reinforced if the child faces failure after failure. In most cases, this child will need not only academic tutoring, but also intensive help learning to set step-by-step goals, persevere through disappointment, and feel good about other positive qualities (e.g., social skills, non-academic strengths).

You will want to find a school offering either a highly structured curriculum and a "no excuses" policy for meeting grade level *or* high levels of teacher/child contact (in very small groups or one-on-one). Ideally, you would seek both of these qualities in a school. Your child almost certainly will need some one-on-one time with a supportive adult, not just for academics but for personal support and to learn life skills such as goal-setting and tenacity.

Low in motivation, academically gifted. A child with this mix is probably the most at risk for underperforming compared to her potential (even more so for the highly gifted child). This child may meet even high academic standards without actually learning new material. She will not complain or demand more challenging work as will her more motivated academic peers. This child will need the school to set more challenging goals for her – and help her learn to face challenges and overcome barriers – if she is to reach the level of learning of which she is capable. If the school does not play this role, it falls to the parent. What an uncomfortable dynamic it is for a parent to push her child who is already making A's and B's to "do better"! And yet, the ability to face and master challenging work is one best learned young. If your child has this twin combination of academic gifts and low motivation, you may want to make finding a school that will *challenge* your child with individual learning goals and nurture her with individual attention a very top-priority Must Have.

As with many fit items, Great *quality* Schools will meet the needs of children with all motivation levels. In general, highly motivated students need to be allowed to set their own goals beyond other students and have their work *formally* recognized (through an activity log, work portfolio or other record-keeping, and possibly in report cards). A child with little motivation needs clear, challenging expectations imposed by others and regular monitoring of progress. A Great School will set high minimum standards for all (higher still for advanced students), assess students' "starting points" at the year's beginning, track individual progress and push and prod students to meet goals. But given that most schools have quality strengths and weaknesses, you'll want to ensure that your child's school has the right strengths for your own child if motivation is a Must Have need.

A significant motivation problem at school can indicate a severe misfit between child and school. Address the underlying cause, and you may solve the "motivation problem."

Identifying Your Child's Need

In many cases, your child's motivation level may not be as obvious as some other characteristics until your child grows older. But some children show signs of one extreme or the other early on, and most parents have the close-up view needed to see the signs. Consider your child's motivation about things schoolish and academic, for sure, but also her general tendency to set and overcome challenging barriers to accomplish what she wants to do. Of course, any child (or adult, for that matter) may choose to "turn it off" if an insurmountable, or even just unsavory, barrier gets in the way. (Don't think your teacher – or boss – likes you, respects you, or admires your work? Convinced there's no way you'll succeed on that test or work project? Turn down that motivation dial!) Consider your child's general tendencies, and if you aren't certain, then assume your child is *Typical* in motivation for the purpose of choosing a school.

Identification strategies include:

➤ Ask your child's school, preschool or day care teachers how "self-directed" and "willing to overcome challenges" your child is compared to other children of same age whom they have observed. Ask especially about academic tasks, but also other individual achievement activities.

➤ Look for behavioral indicators. The motivation section of our *Know Your Child's Needs* table (starting on page 368) provides some help. But here's a start. Your child's motivation is:

A *strength* if your child frequently
- ✔ *sets challenging* learning or achievement goals for self,
- ✔ *initiates* trying hard things on own,
- ✔ *plans ahead* to meet goals, and
- ✔ usually works to *overcome barriers* and problems without giving up.

Asking for adult help is not a sign of a less-motivated child if your child asks for help to complete a specific task in pursuit of her larger goal (e.g., your kindergartener asks, "Mommy, will you please show me how to make a sign that says 'Cold Drinks' for my lemonade stand?") In general, the goals these children pursue for themselves will exceed any reasonable expectations of grownups around them.

Typical if your child usually
- ✔ works to meet goals set by parents or teachers, or
- ✔ sets and meets clearly *achievable* learning goals for self, and
- ✔ *stops or lowers goals* when problems arise (as they almost always do!)

A typically motivated child will express frustration, anger or sadness when he fails to meet a reasonable goal set by someone else (teacher, parent), and will *feel* the need to do better next time without being told, "try harder." But when it comes to taking action, this child may need encouragement to overcome challenging barriers. In general, this is the child most teachers expect: one who will do the assigned work, but who might need a push or nudge when the going gets tough. Most children will fall into the "Typical" category.

A *weakness* if your child
- ✔ rarely sets goals for herself in work or play.

And one of these:

✔ is not bothered when she does not perform as well as she is able on self-initiated tasks or ones others (teachers, parents) ask child to complete, or

✔ is bothered when she does not do as well as she or others expect on tasks, but takes no steps at all on her own to improve.

Physical or Mental Health Challenges

Physical Health Challenges

What They Are, Why They're Important

A physical health challenge should be a factor in choosing a school if it is one that would make it difficult, if not impossible, for a child to participate fully in routine, daily school life without assistance or some accommodation. This includes not just physical handicaps, but also ongoing illnesses requiring physical restrictions or treatment during the school day.

It is important to find the right fit not only for your child's physical well-being, but also for his social, emotional, and academic benefit. If any of these areas may be affected in addition to physical health, then it is no doubt worth the effort to seek a Great Fit school. If your child has a long-term physical challenge – whether caused by birth, accident or illness – then you will certainly want to make sure that your child's school has the *facilities* needed for your child to participate fully in school life and the *staff* to administer needed medications or other care. Your child may be eligible for special education services in public schools.

Categorizing, Prioritizing, and Identifying Your Child's Need

Unlike some other How Your Child Learns items, this is one where most parents do not need help identifying the issue. You certainly know that your child has needs differing from most other students, though you may not be certain how much help you should expect from school.

Use this as a guideline: a physical health challenge is a Must Have if your child needs *special facilities or care* at school to *participate fully in academic classes* and any *other aspects of learning that you consider vital* for school (e.g., social, emotional, physical). If your child's physical health challenge is manageable without help from school, then you might use this as a tiebreaking Nice to Have to choose among schools – in case the condition worsens or you need occasional assistance and flexibility.

The more specific you are about your child's physical health challenge, the better you can understand what your child needs and communicate with schools about how to interact with your child.

➤ Start by summarizing your child's general condition, noting the cause, if known.

➤ Next, make a list of the specific activities for which your child may need accommodation in order to participate fully. Common possibilities include physical education and sports; drama, music, and visual arts; field trips; school projects that involve lots of physical activity; and class or school-wide social events.

➤ For each activity note any accommodations that you have found to be helpful for allowing your child to live and learn as fully as possible. Get ideas from your child's previous teachers or day care providers about what did and did not work.

➤ Add to the bottom of your list any specific care that your child needs during the day – medications, regular medical or therapy appointments – for which he'll require on-site care or need to be excused from school.

➤ Use this list as your guide for:
   ✔ Deciding which very *specific* needs your child must have met at school and which needs you may be able to meet elsewhere.
   ✔ Asking specific questions about what each school will and won't provide your child.
   ✔ Sharing helpful information about your child with the school you choose.

If your child needs medication during the school day, then certainly you will want an on-site school nurse to administer medications and to help you watch for problem side effects or loss of drug effectiveness. If your child needs frequent therapy, then certainly you will want to ensure that appointments may be coordinated with the school schedule. Nearly all schools allow children some time off for medical appointments. If your child has a certain routine, check that the schools you are considering have policies allowing you to continue necessary treatments. In higher elementary grades, some school schedules are packed full with academic and expected extracurricular activities; you will want to enquire about flexibility to meet your child's treatment needs.

Even if your child's condition does not require accommodation or assistance from school, if it is a noticeable physical handicap then you also will need to explore the social culture of the school. If it is one in which taunting and teasing are acceptable behaviors, your child will undoubtedly suffer a great deal. Look for a school with a character program emphasizing respect and tolerance – not just posters on the wall, but clear expectations and consequences for rude student behavior. We have been amazed at the real differences among schools in this regard. Talk with parents of other children with similar challenges to learn both how their children have fared and how other students have acted towards their children.

Mental Health Challenges

What They Are, Why They're Important

Mental health challenges include both *ongoing* (long-term) and *serious temporary* mental illnesses. Whether your child's condition is caused by a family event (e.g., divorce, death), stressful occurrence (e.g., car accident, injury), an inherited trait, or an unknown cause, you may want to find a school that can partner with you to help your child navigate the stormy seas of academic and social pressures associated with school. If your child suffers from a mental illness, her academic, social, emotional and physical development can be affected significantly. It is important to recognize and deal with your child's condition sooner rather than later, whether or not you engage your child's school in the effort.

Categorizing and Prioritizing

Examples of common mental illnesses include depression, anxiety or panic attacks, and bi-polar disorder (manic-depression). We will not attempt to help you make clinical diagnoses of the many complex and varied mental illnesses. We do say this: if you see significant negative changes in your child's academic, social, emotional or physical state that are not otherwise explainable (or even when they are explainable, do no just "go away" after a few days), you should seek diagnosis from a psychologist or psychiatrist. Many school counselors can help you take the first steps or recommend local professionals.

To decide whether this is an item you should consider in choosing a school, consider both of these:

➤ *How much is your child's condition likely to affect her life at school?*
Consider not just academic performance but also social, emotional and physical development.

➤ *To what extent do you need or want help from school?*
Examples include administering medications, providing counseling, allowing a flexible schedule or even just keeping a watchful eye for problems.

If your child's condition is very severe, this certainly will be a Must Have. You will need your child's school to actively, if discreetly, help you keep tabs on your child's condition and assist with treatment as needed (if only allowing some schedule flexibility for counseling or other therapy). Your child may be eligible for special education services in public schools.

But even if the illness is milder or recent in occurrence, you may want to seek a school that could be helpful, so that you have backup resources should the illness become prolonged. In other words, you may want this to be a Nice to Have and seek a school that will be socially and emotionally welcoming (or even helpful) to your child as a tiebreaker.

Identifying Your Child's Need

➤ If your child displays troubling symptoms, take your child for professional diagnosis by a psychologist or psychiatrist. Many school counselors can help you take the first steps or recommend local professionals.

➤ Look for these general signs of mental illness:
   ✔ Big changes, or ongoing problems, in your child's sleep – sleepy all the time, not able to sleep, or suddenly begins erratic schedule (e.g., sleepy all day, awake all night).
   ✔ Big changes in or ongoing problems with your child's eating – packing it away in gorging sessions or prolonged loss of appetite. Extreme or sudden weight gain or loss is also a sign of a problem.
   ✔ Loss of joy – your child always seems to be unhappy, laughs very little.
   ✔ Loss of excitement – your child loses interest in school or activities that used to get her excited.
   ✔ Loss of self-control – your child is lashing out in anger frequently, acting violent towards siblings or parents, or wildly excited for extended periods.
   ✔ Social changes – your child is suddenly not interested in former friends, without explanation. Your child suddenly stops talking with you and/or siblings.
   ✔ Changes in academic performance – your child's grades drop suddenly.

Behavior Challenges

What They Are, Why They're Important

What child doesn't have a few of these, you might ask? And true, all children are by definition still learning how to behave themselves. But some children have further to go in learning both *what is expected* and *how to control their own behavior* in a group setting.

Children who have significant discipline/behavior problems that:
➤ prevent themselves or other children in the classroom from learning effectively
   or
➤ have led to serious or multiple formal disciplinary actions
need schools that will work with parent and child to improve social and emotional skills. These children can disrupt not only their own learning but that of

other students around them until they learn how to identify and respond to their own strong emotional states.

The challenge for parents is to distinguish those times when poor behavior is a result of other easily changeable circumstances from those times when the child has a "behavior problem" resulting from underdeveloped social and emotional skills or a behavioral disability. Mild to moderate behavioral problems can result from a school (or preschool) that is a very poor fit in critical ways. For instance, shoehorning your child into a school with the wrong academic pace or teaching method can lead to mild behavior problems for all but the child with terrific self-control. A bright child who is bored or a struggling student who is lost often will wiggle excessively and fail to pay attention to school work. A strong learning style misfit between school and child also may lead to an excessively wiggly or upset child: a strong kinesthetic learner (who needs to move and touch) in a "look and listen" school may wiggle endlessly, and a strong visual or auditory learner in a too-chaotic school may be easily upset by the noise and disorder.

In the case of the school misfit, you will notice that your child behaves very well when she is in environments where she feels both engaged and successful. For these children, the burden should be on the school and teacher, not the child, to address the problem, or on you to seek a better-fit school. These behavioral problems should disappear with a better school fit or changes in how your child's teacher interacts with the child. If your child is very extreme in some way – very gifted or very challenged academically or very lopsided in learning styles, for example – then she will *need to learn better self-control than most other children,* because she may often find herself a "misfit." You'll give your child a great gift if you recognize the ways in which she is very different from peers and help her learn to recognize her feelings and manage her behavior when she feels out of place.

But these behavioral "problems" – though grave to parents when dealing with them – will pale in comparison to those of the child who is repeatedly violent towards teachers or peers or who consumes excessive teacher time by frequently violating basic behavior rules. The child who needs help with *behavior* specifically will have significant or repeated disciplinary problems *in most all group settings.*

The earlier parents and school jointly intervene to provide a stable, clear set of behavior expectations and consistent, appropriate rewards and consequences for actual behavior, the sooner the child will develop self-understanding and self-control in group settings. You are doing your child a disservice when you ignore or defend true behavior problems. Instead, it is a great gift to a child to learn these behaviors as soon as possible, since continued problems will prevent him from realizing his potential in other areas and enjoying life (not to mention driving teachers and parents batty).

Categorizing and Prioritizing

If your child has had
➤ significant, unresolved behavioral or discipline problems in group settings, or
➤ repeated behavior that prevents your own child or others in school, preschool or day care from learning effectively, or
➤ repeated behavior that puts your child at risk for formal disciplinary action,

then you should consider this a Must Have.

If this is a Must Have for your child, you will need to seek a school with a planful, consistent approach to discipline that is consistent with your parenting values so that your can work with the school to reinforce good behavior and reduce the inappropriate behavior. The method of discipline must also be effective with your child. If your own parenting style, limited time with your child, or an inconsistent approach among your child's caregivers may have led to repeated behavior and discipline problems, you may need to make changes at home, not just school. Think about what environments have worked best in past: when does your child behave well in a group – and why?

If you are still not sure what to seek, look for a school that proactively teaches about expected behaviors and self-control, not just one that punishes bad behavior. Think "clear expectations, consistent consequences (both rewards and punishments), frequent praise and discussions about good behavior, and firm but fair punishments when needed."

Regardless of the discipline approach, you will need a school with very frequent, personal communication between parents and teachers. This clearly is easier in a school with parent-teacher contact structured into the daily routine (e.g., classroom drop-off and pickup available and encouraged, rather than bus or impersonal carpool lines). In addition to this frequent informal communication, you should look for schools with a formal policy for working with students and parents to develop behavioral discipline.

Identifying Your Child's Need

Most likely, you are aware of the problem if your child has been in any kind of group setting thus far. You will have experienced:

➤ At school, preschool or day care: *Repeated* calls from teachers, principal or guidance counselor about your child's violent *or* disruptive words and actions.

➤ In group settings with you present (e.g., social or religious gatherings): *Repeated* moments when your child is mildly violent – using words or actions – *and your child fails to correct himself after your reprimands.* "Mildly violent" includes pushing, hitting, pinching (and the like) or spoken threats to harm other children or adults.

➤ In any setting: Any single very violent action, such as hitting or beating another person to the point of causing a serious injury, use of any weapon (knife, gun, or the like) against another person, or verbally threatening any of these actions.

If you are not sure and believe that your child's previous teachers (school, preschool or day care) may not have divulged important information about your child's behavior, just ask. Remember, all children are still learning to behave themselves, and it is important to consider whether your child's behavior is typical for one of similar age. Also consider whether a major misfit between child and a particular group setting might be stimulating poor behavior.

Learning Disorders and Disabilities

Todd was constantly "disturbed" about his schoolwork. He avoided homework in his traditional, Catholic school like the plague, finishing only after long and exhausting work sessions with threats of "no fun until it's done" by mom. He excelled marvelously in some classes (math and science) but seemed utterly defeated in others – namely the language arts, especially writing. His feelings about school and himself academically were dimmed by his frustration with any assignment that required writing of any kind – most difficult in a school that emphasized not only the content of writing, but also penmanship. The toll was not simply lower grades in some subjects, but Todd came to think of himself as less capable than his older brother. After years of growing frustration, his parents at last took him to a child psychologist for testing. In short order, they found that their son had a recognized writing disability making it extremely difficult for him to think and write at the same time. He soon began to record his homework answers and his "written" papers on a small tape recorder. Then, as a separate step, he transcribed what he had recorded into writing acceptable to his teachers. His parents – with his consent – switched him to a school with a Paedeia program, which emphasizes oral discussion and presentation. He was at home at school, at last, and his grades and academic self-confidence showed it.

■ ■ ■

Learning Disorders and Disabilities: What They Are, Why They're Important

All people possess learning strengths and weaknesses. All of us are simply better at some things and worse at others, thanks to the mysterious mix of genes, experience, hard work and luck. Children also develop at different rates, so slight delays in some areas may not be important in the long run. How weak must an area be to call it a "disability," and what areas of weakness count? The school hunt bottom line: what weaknesses rise to the level of "disabilities" or "disorders" that might affect your choice of schools?

In general, think of it this way: a *disability* is a problem with an important, basic part of your child's physical or mental functioning that is significantly different from your child's other capabilities or that significantly hampers your child's learning. A *disorder* is a *problem* with an *important, but not necessarily basic* part of your child's physical or mental functioning. Both disabilities and disorders may keep your child from fully utilizing her other capabilities.

In other words, disabilities and disorders are imbalances that have the potential to keep your child from learning and performing at the level of which she would be capable *if she did not have the disability or disorder.* This does not include just academic learning, but also social, emotional and physical development. If your child has a major weakness in one area, it will surely keep him from doing his best in the other areas, as well. If you are thinking that this sounds similar to "whole child" thinking, you're right. But for a weakness to rise to the level of "disability," it must be significantly different from your child's other capabilities or it must impair his learning or functioning in some significant way.

Categorizing and Prioritizing

Any disability or disorder should be a Must Have, though only you can decide where it falls in the school hunt pecking order, based on:
➤ the severity of the disability or disorder, and
➤ how well you can accommodate it outside of school.

Consider the extent to which your child's participation or success in school (academic, social and physical activity) may be hampered if the school does not address your child's specific needs. The more severe your child's disability or disorder, the more your child's overall development may be harmed by an inappropriate school setting. Also consider how well your child will function socially in a classroom of more typical children for some activities.

As with other weaknesses, you will need to make a decision about the approach you want your child's school to take. Ignoring or working around a disability or disorder entirely may leave your child unprepared for the "real" world in which accommodations are not always available. Use this opportunity to help your child understand himself better and learn to develop his own weaknesses (and to help his teachers do the same). Most experts now agree that the least restrictive environment in which a child can achieve academic and social success is best for a child with a disability.

Viewpoint   All Kinds of Minds

Physician and child-development expert Dr. Mel Levine focuses on eight critical abilities, controlled by various pathways in the brain, needed for children to function well in school and life. A shortfall in one pathway may prevent a child from using great strengths in another. Levine has developed training for educators to identify weaknesses in children and change how they teach to address the natural differences in children's "wiring." In *All Kinds of Minds*, he provides very child-friendly stories to help parents and children identify and address weaknesses in each area. In *A Mind at a Time* he clarifies his vision for how parents and educators should work to meet the needs of individual children with varying strengths and weaknesses.

When one set of functions is weak, it is a "disorder." His sets of disorders are different from disabilities, because they describe a broad set of functions and are found in many, many children. Levine has encouraged educators to assume that most children have learning strengths and weaknesses. His teacher training program helps educators learn to teach in ways that help every child reach at least a minimum level of functioning in each major area, while also appreciating and reinforcing each child's strengths.

Levine's eight categories of capability are these:
1. *Attention* – ability to concentrate and focus on one thing, finish tasks and control one's own behavior
2. *Temporal-Sequential Order* – ability to understand and use steps and things that fall into an orderly pattern (e.g., alphabet, step-by-step instructions)
3. *Spatial Ordering* – ability to see and understand how things are organized in space around us, including small areas like a piano keyboard and large areas like a room or space
4. *Memory* – ability to store and recall information at a later time
5. *Language* – ability to speak, write and understand language using sounds, symbols (letters) and combinations of words
6. *Neuromotor* – ability to use the brain to coordinate all of the muscles of the body
7. *Social Cognition* – ability to succeed in social relationships, one-on-one and in groups, with peers and authority figures
8. *Higher Order Cognition* – ability to understand and solve problems, learn new things and create

Levine's work has been a godsend for many adults and children who have been hampered by seemingly basic matters such as paying attention and staying organized, getting along with others socially, and remembering important facts. If you suspect that your child has a major weakness in one of these eight areas, investigate further to see if this is a Must Have for school or if you feel you can enhance your child's development outside of school. Nearly every parent (and child) can benefit from a basic understanding of these eight pathways. See the *Resources for Parents* section on page 354 or visit **PickyParent.com** for links to Dr. Levine's resources.

Children will learn to cope with their weakness better if they have the opportunity to learn and interact among children who do not share the disability.

This does not mean that you should ignore your child's disability, only that segregating your child into a group of similarly disabled children may rob him of important coping skills. That said, you may find such a setting preferable if the "regular" schools available are of low quality or ill-equipped to meet your child's needs.

Most importantly for our purposes here, seek a school that recognizes and develops a wide range of children *and* that attracts a supportive social group. Avoid using a disorder as an *excuse* for your child not enjoying or using his strengths. Indeed, make sure that your child's school *fits his strengths very well.* Allowing your child to enjoy success from his strengths may give him the confidence and energy to develop weaker areas.

Identifying Your Child's Need

Learning disabilities and disorders can be hard to diagnose. Indeed, many go undiagnosed for years.

Whether you know your child has a problem or only suspect it, you will need professional diagnosis of the specific disability. No parent should go it alone, because the effects of misunderstanding – or not recognizing – your child's needs can be devastating for your child and family. On the upside, many milder disabilities can be overcome or well accommodated if they are detected and addressed early in a child's life. Call your local public school district central office to inquire about free testing or seek private testing through a child psychologist or psychiatrist your area. The U.S. Department of Education publishes the current definitions of disabilities recognized as eligible for special needs services in public schools and information about your rights as a parent if your child has a disability (see *PickyParent.com* for details).

Some signs that your child may have a hard-to-detect disability include these (even one sign can indicate a possible disability):

➤ Your child does well in most or all *subjects*, except one.

➤ Your child does well with most *aspects* of his school work, except one that may cut across many subjects (e.g., reading, writing, speaking aloud).

➤ Your child speaks well, but *does not write* well compared to others of same age (e.g., takes a very long time, makes many errors, gets very frustrated).

➤ Your child writes well but *does not speak* so that others understand (compared to others of same age).

➤ Your child follows written instructions well, but *not spoken instructions*.

➤ Your child follows spoken instructions well, but *not written ones*.

➤ Your child *does not focus* on his school work for long enough periods of time to accomplish what is expected of children his age.

➤ Your child is unable to work and learn in a *group of children;* behavior problems or emotional outbursts regularly prevent him from doing his school work.

➤ Your child has extreme difficulty forming relationships with others his own age.

➤ Your child has trouble *moving or working his body*, so that typical, day-to-day activities are difficult.

Self-Understanding

Samantha was a "born follower." She tagged along with her older sister Laura for most activities, having no same-age friends or interests of her own. Laura, age nine, was an avid competitive swimmer. When at age six it seemed that Samantha's swimming talent outstripped her sister's, Laura began to feel jealous and stopped letting Sam play with her friends when they came over. Sam quickly lost interest in swimming. Laura also possessed great talent and interest in drawing and painting. Samantha had never displayed the same early talent as Laura in this area. But Sam insisted on taking art lessons, though she fretted continuously over her dim results. This pattern continued – Sam avoided competing with her sister when she might excel beyond Laura, and she pursued the same activities as Laura when Sam had little talent or interest. When this pattern began applying to academic work, Sam's parents took note. They sought and found a school for Samantha that paid close attention to students' personal development, focusing on the "whole child." At first, Sam continued the same pattern, befriending outgoing bully types who would tell her "what's what." But by the end of her first year, Sam had her own set of likable friends and had developed her own interests. She could tell her parents matter-of-factly what she liked to do and what she was good at – in academic and extracurricular activities. Her parents were thrilled that the "real Samantha" had been revealed.

■ ■ ■

Self-Understanding: What It Is, Why It's Important

If your child has a great understanding of her own strengths, weaknesses, interests, needs and wants and has the self-control to make decisions accordingly, you will have more flexibility in choosing a school. This child will certainly let you know if something is not going well in school and may have laser-accurate views of her teachers' strengths and weaknesses as well! Of course you still want to seek a Great Fit school for your child. Just because your child *understands* how a school is not the perfect fit, she will have little power until she is older and more independent to do anything about it.

On the other end of the scale, a child with very weak self-understanding will regularly make choices that are not appropriate for her abilities, interests, needs and wants – often just following the path of a sibling, friends or others. These children need help developing their self-understanding and learning to make life decisions. An appropriate school setting is one way to tackle the problem.

Self-understanding can help your child succeed not just in school, but in life. Give your child this gift by allowing your child to make choices (amenable to you) from an early age.

Categorizing and Prioritizing

If your child seems to have low self-understanding – little awareness of her strengths, weaknesses, interests, needs and wants – then this should be a Must Have in your school hunt. She will not understand and communicate when things aren't working well at school. She may have trouble making choices and prioritizing her activities to enjoy her strengths and develop her weaknesses.

Identifying Your Child's Need

➤ Ask your child's current school, preschool or day care teacher about behaviors listed below compared to other children of the same age.

➤ Observe and compare your child. Look for consistent choices that seem inappropriate to you, such as:
  ✔ Focusing little time on activities she enjoys and does well, or
  ✔ Spending too much time on activities that are of little consequence (no enjoyment to her, no help for schoolwork or other achievements, and no help to others), or
  ✔ Having few interests of her own (usually lets a sibling, parent or friend choose), or
  ✔ Choosing friends who are unkind to her or who do not bring out the best in her, or
  ✔ Expressing little recognition of her own strengths and weaknesses

If these describe your child, then you will need to find a school that closely fits her other needs, proactively teaches self-understanding, and communicates frequently with parents about children's individual progress. If you cannot find these things in a school, you certainly will want to take the initiative to guide your child and her teachers.

SNAP TO IT

What To Do

➤ *Refer back to your Child "Quick Think"* on page 37. Estimated Time: 2 minutes

➤ *Use the Child Needs Summary* on page 38 to get a quick fix on the Fit Factor # 2 characteristics. Estimated Time: 5 minutes

➤ *Use the Know Your Child's Needs table* on page 368 to further clarify your child's Fit Factor # 2 How Your Child Learns characteristics and the importance of each for choosing a school. You need not read the whole table: focus only on items you suspect are important for your child. Estimated Time: 20 minutes .

➤ *Record your Must Haves and Nice to Haves* on your *Child Needs Summary* (page 38). Estimated Time: 10 minutes

Optional Activities

➤ *Discuss your child's needs* with your spouse or other parenting partner. Estimated Time: As needed

➤ *Plan now to schedule professional testing for your child* if you want help identifying your child's learning styles, physical health, mental health or behavioral challenges, and learning disabilities and disorders. Estimated Time: 30 minutes to find a tester and schedule an appointment

➤ *Mark your calendar to ask current school, preschool or day care teachers* about your child compared to other children. Estimated Time: 5 minutes to schedule time to talk with teachers, 45 minutes to talk with teachers

➤ *Make a plan to observe your child and read other resources,* as needed. See the Resources for Parents section starting on page 354 for readings and websites related to how children learn. Estimated Time: 20 minutes to plan; you decide how much for observing and reading other resources

Need more? Want more? Got more to share? Visit PickyParent.com.

CHAPTE

What To Know from Chapter 5

➤ **Fit Factor #3 is Social Issues:** your child's own desire and need to attend school with friends.

➤ **Fit Factor #4 is Practical Matters:** scheduling your child's desired, essential *non-school activities*.

➤ **Remember, you must identify the** few most important **characteristics of your child** to match with schools for a Great Fit.
- ✔ Attending school with current friends will be a Must Have for some elementary age children.
- ✔ Scheduling essential non-school activities will be Must Have for a limited number of children.

Chapter 5

Child Fit Factors #3 and 4:
What are *Your* Child's Social and Practical Needs?

Social Issues: *Your Child's Friends*

Kelli is a shy, only child and one very slow to make new friends. In three years of preschool she developed very close friendships with two other girls, Sara and Lila. She plays with each of them weekly after school and has a good, positive relationship with both. Both friends have older siblings attending the same school. In September, when her parents mentioned that they were beginning to look at "big kid" schools for next year, Kelli panicked and said, "but I am going to go to Sara's and Lila's big brother's schools, right?" Kelli became obsessed and fretful over the possibility that she might not get to stay with her best – and only – friends. Her parents wanted her to stop worrying, but they also thought that kindergarten might be a good chance for Kelli to learn how to spread her social wings a bit. By February, Lila's parents had decided to send her to a different school. As it turned out, this school was a better fit for Kelli's top priority academic needs, as well, and so her parents opted for this school, too. They requested that Kelli and Lila be in the same classroom, a wish that the school principal granted. The three girls still get together at least twice a month for play and are taking ballet together after school. Kelli loves her new school and is learning how to make new friends while keeping the old.

■ ■ ■

Friends: What They Are, Why They're Important

Many parents form strong preferences about whom they want their children to befriend, and those feelings can grow stronger through the years. But from your child's perspective, it's not so much a matter of how she *ought* to feel but how she does *in fact* feel about friends – both current ones and the prospect of making new ones.

The more your child has developed bonds with particular peers, and the less apt she is to make new friends, the more you may need to consider her friends in your school choice. For some children, school friends are the rudder than keeps them headed in the right direction academically and emotionally, not just socially. If your child's school social group is critically important to *your child* – whether those friends are from your neighborhood, your child's current school, pre-school, day care or elsewhere – then you may need to make this a Must Have in your school selection.

You might also consider whether having friends of the same gender is important to your child. Single-sex schools at the elementary level are unusual, and most co-educational schools take great pains to balance the number of boys and girls in each classroom. But small programs, very small schools, and other options with few children may have imbalances in a given year. Even if this is not a Must Have at first glance, keep your eyes open for schools where your child may become isolated socially. If you are concerned, find out the school's policy on gender balancing.

Categorizing and Prioritizing

Choosing a school that your child's current friends will attend should be a Must Have for your school hunt only if your child:

➤ Has close friendship(s) with child(ren) who will be attending certain schools, *and*

➤ Does not have friends attending other schools you might choose, *and*

➤ Your child does not have the social skills needed to meet and make friends with new children, *and*

➤ You are unable to help your child continue current friendships outside of school or establish new friendships.

If the first three bullets describe your child, but you are able to help some in addressing the need, this can be a Nice to Have tie-breaker for schools meeting your other needs. Many, but by no means all, parents can help their children see old friends and make new ones with a little effort. One-on-one playtime outside of school is a simple and common way to accomplish both, but you will have to honestly say whether that's a role you can take on. Your child can wish for friends, but often needs you to make the playtime happen until an older age.

What are the reasons you might *not* consider your child's current friends in your school selection?

✔ Your child's school friends are secondary to non-school friends or to academics and other activities.

✔ Your child likes to meet and befriend new people.

✔ Your child is not particularly happy with or well-suited to his current set of friends.

✔ You think your child is ready to stretch his social wings, to learn how to get along with new children.

✔ You have time to help your child keep up with old friends and make new ones (with play dates, joint non-school activities and the like).

Identifying Your Child's Need

Identification strategies include:

➤ Ask your child's school, preschool or day care teachers how your child compares socially to other children of same age whom they have observed. Does your child play and work with other children? How well and how often? Does your child make new friends or just stick with the same ones every day?

➤ Observe and compare your child's social interactions to similar age children. Does your child seek out interaction with other children? Does your child approach new children successfully or stick to the same one(s) always? Does your child consider other children's needs in interactions? How do other children respond to your child?

➤ See the Social & Leadership sections of the *Child* tables at the end of the book for more help identifying and deciding whether you can deal with your child's friendship needs outside of school.

➤ Have a developmental test of social and related emotional skills conducted by a professional tester. This may include paper and pencil work, an interview and observation. Expected skills will vary according to the child's age, and a qualified tester should be able to explain how your child compares to the typical child of similar age.

➤ If you are on the fence, ask your child how she feels about the matter. Does your child express dread at the thought of making new friends? You may be surprised to find that she's ready for a fresh start!

Many parents can help their children see old friends and make new ones with a little effort. One-on-one playtime outside of school is a simple way to accomplish both.

Practical Matters:
Essential Activities (outside of school)

Evan was a second grader attending his assigned public school in a medium sized New England city. From an early age, it became clearer and clearer that he possessed unusual singing talent. The first week of second grade, Evan got the lead part in a locally staged version of the hit "Oliver." During the play's run, a Broadway producer happened to see his performance and approached his parents about Evan's participation in a revival of the same musical on Broadway. Evan's school principal was not impressed and said they would have to make home schooling arrangements if Evan took the part. Neither feeling qualified to home school him nor possessing the money to hire a full-time tutor, Evan's parents searched for another more accommodating school. Fortunately, a local performing arts magnet school had a special program for children like Evan, including shippable weekly packages of learning and instruction materials and internet and phone tutoring. With Evan's parents acting as facilitators but not instructors, Evan was able to excel in both academics and his theatrical life.

■ ■ ■

Extracurricular Activities: What They Are, Why They're Important

While the practical needs of most *families* loom large (and are the focus of Chapter 9), elementary age children have few that will affect the choice of a school. Most practical needs arise out of another child need, such as medical care for a health problem, and you can address them as such.

One need – uncommon but not unheard of – is for a child's participation in *essential* activities outside of school. Does your young soap opera star have daily shoots to attend? Does your violin virtuoso have concerts scheduled around the world? Does your Olympic hopeful have a rigorous workout routine? If your child's strong capability or interest has led to a demanding schedule of practice and performance, then fitting in these "extracurriculars" may not seem like an extra at all, but an essential factor in your choice among schools.

Categorizing, Prioritizing, and Identifying Your Child's Need

If your child has extracurricular interests or needs that:
➤ cannot be met at school,
➤ must continue, and
➤ often conflict with typical school scheduling,
then this should be a Must Have in your school hunt.

If your child fits this category, you surely know it. Whether your child is a nationally renowned pianist, has started an early career on stage, or has another combined passion and talent, you will want to find a school with the flexibility to meet your child's non-school demands. If you're not sure, we say this: do not pressure your child to pursue a demanding and time-consuming activity outside of school unless your child's own interests, capabilities and motivation have led the way.

Schools may meet your child's need in various ways: by offering on-site practice facilities, flexible scheduling, or cooperation with outside tutors. What's most important is that your child is allowed to continue the outside activity without sacrificing the long-term academic, social, physical and emotional benefits of school. Check periodically to ensure that your child's passion for the special activity is enduring. If his academic, social or emotional needs get short shrift, he may begin to crave a more typical school life for a while. Listen and be willing to help your child make changes when needed.

SNAP TO IT

What To Do

➤ *Refer back to your Child "Quick Think"* on page 37 to refresh your memory regarding things that really stand out about your child. Estimated Time: 2 minutes

➤ *Use the Child Needs Summary* on page 38 to get a quick fix on whether Fit Factors #3 and 4 may be Must Haves for your child. Estimated Time: 5 minutes

➤ *Use the Know Your Child's Needs table* starting on page 368 to further clarify your child's Fit Factor #3 Social Issues and #4 Practical Matters characteristics and the importance of each for choosing a school. Do this only if you suspect these items are important for your child. Estimated Time: 10 minutes

➤ *Record your Must Haves and Nice to Haves, if any,* on your *Child Needs Summary* (page 38). Estimated Time: 10 minutes

Optional Activities

➤ *Discuss your child's needs* with your spouse or other parenting partner. Estimated Time: As needed

➤ *Plan now to schedule professional testing for your child* if you are concerned about your child's social development and ability to make new friends. Estimated Time: 30 minutes to find a tester and schedule an appointment

➤ *Mark your calendar to ask current school, preschool or day care teachers* about your child's ability to make new friends compared to other children. Estimated Time: 2 minutes to mark your calendar, 5 minutes to schedule time to talk with teachers, 15 minutes to talk with teachers

➤ *Make a plan to observe your child,* as needed. Estimated Time: 5 minutes to plan; you decide how much for observing

Need more? Want more? Got more to share? Visit PickyParent.com.

Uncover Your
Family's Needs

LIGHT'NING LIST

What To Know from Chapter 6

➤ **The family characteristics most helpful for picking a school** are organized into the **four Fit Factors:**

✔ What *Your Child Learns* – your family's values and needs that influence what subjects and at what level of difficulty your child should be taught.

✔ How *Your Child Learns* – your family's values and capabilities that influence how a school should teach and interact with your child.

✔ *Social Issues* – your desire for your child to attend school with particular students and parents, or to attend a particular school or school type.

✔ *Practical Matters* – your family's logistical and financial needs.

➤ **You can identify the elements of each Fit Factor most important for your family** by taking time to think about and discuss your family's needs, wants, values, and capabilities.

➤ **Every aspect of every Fit Factor is not important for every family.** You must prioritize to find a school that meets your family's top needs.

Chapter 6

Psst! Yeah You – Your Family Has Needs, Too

Alison and Patrick Smithson wanted a traditional focus on the academic basics for their three children. They had recently moved from another city to a country club community. The Smithsons began to feel that this life, however relaxing for them, was isolating for their children. They wanted their children to be exposed to others from differing backgrounds and were concerned about how similar all of the children at their assigned neighborhood school appeared to be. They were a little worried about what their neighbors would think if they didn't support this school, as the neighborhood association had pushed hard to get a new school built nearby. They could afford private school if they scaled back on travel, but wanted to consider other public schools, too. Because they lived on the outskirts of their city, transportation was an issue if no busing was available. Their search revealed a traditional, back-to-basics public magnet school with much more diversity than their neighborhood school. While it was a 30 minute ride, the school bus would pick up in front of their house. Sara was accepted late in the summer before her kindergarten year. The Smithsons were thrilled.

■ ■ ■

Anthony Rockman, a widowed father of two who worked full time as a dock supervisor, wanted nothing more than for his girls to attend college. His late wife Cassandra had died of brain cancer just one semester away from finishing her accounting degree in night school. Both girls were quick learners, but he couldn't keep up with all of their school work. To him, a school that stayed on top of his girls' academic performance was a top priority. But he was just as worried about keeping them from falling in with the wrong crowd, especially without Cassie to guide them. He wanted a school with a strict code of conduct and strong moral values. In addition, a good, affordable after-school program was a must. He was busy and tired and couldn't get much time off from work to meet with teachers, so he needed a school he could count on. He felt biased towards the Catholic school many neighborhood children attended, but wanted to consider other affordable options, too. As he looked, he was surprised at how engaged, interested and helpful the staff members at this school were. He really couldn't believe how everything that he and his girls needed seemed to fit the school, and so that is the school he chose. Almost every week, one or both girls got to go home with another family with a stay-at-home parent for an afternoon. He felt they'd joined a big family, not just a school.

What Makes Your Family Tick?

Your family life is a unique expression of who you are as "team family." The things that make your family different from others are the things that make you a unique group of humans, bonded together by love and values. Whether you know it or not now, you most likely have very real family needs and preferences. When you get down to the business of choosing a school, you most likely will have several "ah ha" moments when your family's needs, wants and values crystallize into a reassuring, clear picture before you. After you have considered your family's needs for school, we think you will feel excited about being able to better put into words who you are and what you're about as a family!

But without guidance, many parents find it difficult to express and prioritize among wants and needs, much more so to stick with their goals during the school hunt. Values. Schedules. Child care. Money. Goals for your child. Passionate feelings about what your child learns. Social concerns for your child. Concerns about your own social life. What really matters? *Which family needs should lead?*

For example, you may find yourself thinking more than one thought like these:
➤ "If my child comes out of school with good grades in the basics, I'll be happy."
➤ "Children are exposed to too much, too soon. I want school to reinforce our own family's values."
➤ "I am worried about how peer pressure will influence my child."
➤ "I feel nervous around other parents at my child's school. I don't want to feel this way."
➤ "I plan for my children to attend college, and I'll do what it takes to see that it happens."
➤ "My child has a lot to live up to in our high-achieving family, and I want to support his efforts to 'be his own person.'"
➤ "Private school would be a financial stretch, but we'll manage if that's what it takes."

➤ "With our crazy work schedules, we're nervous about the transition from full-time child care to school plus afternoon care."

➤ "I've given a lot of time and money to my alma mater – how could I not choose it for my own children!"

Sorting and prioritizing your family's wants and needs can be confusing, just as with your child's needs.

Questions like these – in varying combinations – are all real and important to many families. If you feel concerned about finding what your family desires in a school, your fears are not unfounded. At some point in the school hunt, most parents will stumble across at least one of these barriers to a great family–school fit:

➤ Uncertainty about what values you want to pass on to your child through school

➤ Uncertainty about what kind of education you want for your child at school

➤ Not knowing what a school should offer to fit your family's needs and values

➤ Lack of confidence about asserting your values and needs in your school hunt

➤ Pressure to attend a particular school – an alma mater or local favorite

➤ Pressure to pony up piles of money for private school, just to show you care enough

➤ Uncertain finances

➤ Pressure from family, neighbors, friends to make a decision based on their needs and values, not yours

Smart à la Carte

Signs of a Great Family-School Fit

If your child's school *fits your family,* you might see some of these signs:

➤ You feel confident that your child is learning about important things at school

➤ You feel confident that your child is getting every opportunity to perform at the level of which she is capable in school

➤ You feel confident that your child is developing sound social, moral and ethical values

➤ You feel good about the teaching and learning methods used at school

➤ You feel good about how your child is behaving in school

➤ Both teachers and principal listen and respond to your satisfaction when you have a question or request

➤ You feel comfortable visiting and contributing time to your child's school and being with other parents

➤ You feel good about what your child learns from other students and their parents

➤ School fits into your daily routine and yearly calendar without causing great family stress

➤ Your child care needs outside of school hours are met

➤ School fits into your budget without causing undue family stress or significantly shortening the time you spend with your child

Family needs are different from child needs. A huge barrier to meeting your child's needs is simply understanding what those needs are. Once you understand your child's needs, it is an accepted parental privilege that you may make choices – including a school selection – to meet those needs. In most cases, family needs are much easier than child needs to identify. But the path to choosing a school that truly meets your family's needs and reflects your values is one filled with peril. The realities of a busy life, uncertain finances, and — most of all — peer and family pressure can be treacherous and great barriers to choosing the right school.

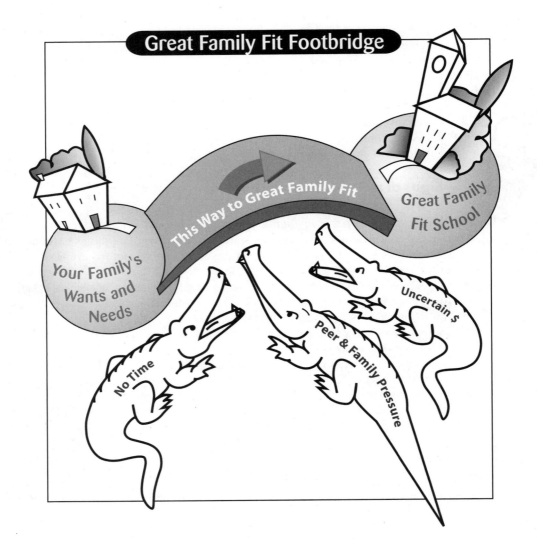

All parents need a safe bridge to cross from knowing their own needs to choosing a Great Fit school. Even the most pragmatic of parents can face moments of confusion and feelings of defeat. The following pages and chapters will help you not only clarify your family's wants and needs, but also find confidence and courage to seek a school that fits.

Regardless of how prepared you feel right now, we say this: you are in the best position to know your family's needs and ensure that they are met, at school or elsewhere. This and the following chapters will:

➤ Focus you on *your* family
➤ Help you decide what is important for choosing a school that fits your family
➤ Prepare you to hunt for a school that meets more of your family's needs from the start
➤ Help you find a school where you'll have fewer favors to ask and fewer moments of that sinking feeling that the school just doesn't fit you and your family
  ➤ Equip you to work with your child's school to better understand and meet your family's needs
    ➤ Equip you to meet your family's needs outside of school

Your family life is a unique expression of who you are as "team family." Find courage to be the family you want to be, and make your child's education part of the package.

Smart à la Carte

Signs of a Poor Fit Between Family and School

If your child's school is a *poor fit for your family,* you might see some of these signs:
➤ You worry about whether your child is learning about important things at school
➤ You worry that your child's school is not providing her opportunities to perform as well as she could academically
➤ You are worried about the social, moral or ethical values your child is developing
➤ You do not agree with the teaching and learning methods used at your child's school
➤ You are worried about how your child is behaving or the effect of other students' behavior on your child in school
➤ The teachers or principal do not listen well or respond to your satisfaction when you ask questions or make requests
➤ You feel uncomfortable or unwelcome at your child's school or with other parents there
➤ You are worried about what your child is learning from other students or parents
➤ You feel embarrassed about your child's school or very uncertain about it overall
➤ You often wish your child attended another school
➤ Your multiple children's conflicting school schedules or inadequate transportation leave you frazzled
➤ The extra work you must do to pay for a private school means you have little time to spend with your child during waking hours

The Great Fit Triangle

The big question for you now is this: which of your family's wants and needs matter most for choosing a school? Which will affect your family's life and goals greatly, and which are really low-priority afterthoughts? Which needs must be met at school, and which are better met at home and elsewhere? What will the impact be on your child and family when school is not a perfect fit with your family?

The Great Fit Triangle (page 103) shows how your family's characteristics combine with your child's and chosen school's to make a Great or not-so-Great Fit.

Focus on the Four Fit Factors

Fortunately, we can focus on a limited number of factors that determine how well a school fits a family. As we've talked to parents about their school choices, these are the issues that come up again and again, the ones that truly make a difference when it comes to finding a school that fits. We have taken all of these considerations and sorted them into four Fit Factors that parallel the issues you considered when thinking about your child. These Fit Factors are simply a way of organizing your family's many needs in a way useful for finding a school that meets them. The four Fit Factors for families are:

➤ **What** *Your Child Learns:* these are aspects of your family that affect *what subjects and at what level of difficulty* your child should be taught at school. These include your family's values about what *content* should be taught and particular *goals* you may have for your child.

➤ **How** *Your Child Learns:* these are aspects of your family that affect *how a school should teach and interact* with your child both in and outside of the classroom. These include your family's values about how children should *behave* at school, values about how children should *learn and be taught* at school (teaching method and classroom management), and your ability to *act as an advocate* for your child at school.

➤ *Social Issues:* these include your parental preferences about the student and parent community of a school, preferences about your own or other parents' involvement in the school, and your biases about particular schools and school types regardless of quality and other aspects of fit.

➤ *Practical Matters:* these include your family's needs for child care during non-school hours, daily and yearly schedule, transportation, school location, coordination of your multiple children's educations, and your financial constraints.

In the following chapters, we'll describe each of the four Fit Factors in detail. If you find that your personal fit hot buttons aren't included here, fear not. Chapter 10 will help you think for yourself to find the right school. For now, have a look at the *Family Needs Summary* on page 110.

How To Identify and Articulate Your Family's Needs

With your child, you've spent time observing and comparing, perhaps doing a bit more reading and some formal testing. Defining your family's needs is a bit different, relying less on research and testing. In large part, you'll need to do some good, clear thinking, discussing and prioritizing.

You'll start by brainstorming those things that really stand out about your family: obvious wants and needs, strengths and challenges. Use our *Family "Quick Think"* on page 109 to get you started.

Next, the following chapters will provide you with specific ideas for clarifying and organizing your family's needs using the four Fit Factors. You will need to set aside time to think, discuss, plan and put into words your family's wants and needs in more detail. Involve your spouse or parenting partner in the process, as you will need to decide jointly which needs and wants reign supreme. If you are part of a two-parent family (or both parents are involved in child-rearing decisions), then you'll need time together.

You may want to think and tinker with separate copies of the *Confident Choice Tools* for a while before comparing notes and deciding where you stand. Or you may want to sit down and hash it through together the first time. Whether planning alone or in tandem, you most certainly will need time away from your children for this. Know that you may need to have two "meetings," one to nail down the obvious things and another after you've had a chance to think a bit more and assess your financial situation. If you are raising your children alone, you will want to set aside similar quiet time for yourself to think and plan.

Prioritizing: Must Haves and Nice to Haves

In the following chapters, we will walk you through each of the four Fit Factor elements for families and help you identify which are most important for your own family. You will quickly see that many issues are not critical for your family, and you can avoid bogging down your school hunt by setting these aside.

Most families will have only a small number of needs and wants that are top priorities for selecting and working with a school. These we call "Must Haves"

Great Fit Triangle

Matching Child and Family Needs with School Offerings

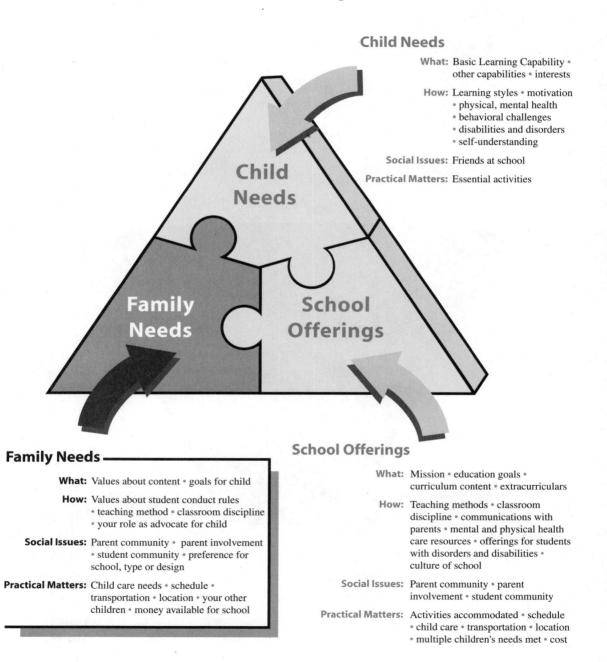

Child Needs

What: Basic Learning Capability • other capabilities • interests

How: Learning styles • motivation • physical, mental health • behavioral challenges • disabilities and disorders • self-understanding

Social Issues: Friends at school

Practical Matters: Essential activities

Family Needs

What: Values about content • goals for child

How: Values about student conduct rules • teaching method • classroom discipline • your role as advocate for child

Social Issues: Parent community • parent involvement • student community • preference for school, type or design

Practical Matters: Child care needs • schedule • transportation • location • your other children • money available for school

School Offerings

What: Mission • education goals • curriculum content • extracurriculars

How: Teaching methods • classroom discipline • communications with parents • mental and physical health care resources • offerings for students with disorders and disabilities • culture of school

Social Issues: Parent community • parent involvement • student community

Practical Matters: Activities accommodated • schedule • child care • transportation • location • multiple children's needs met • cost

What Matters for Matching My Family to a School?

Social Preferences

Our Family Values

College

Our Other Children

Schedules

Parent's

Money

Work

Social Needs

Child Care

Transportation

What?	How?	Social?	Practical?
• Values about content	• Behavior values	• Parent community	• Child care
• Goals for your child	• Teaching method	• Parent involvement	• Schedule
	• Classroom management	• Student community	• Transportation
	• Your role as advocate	• School biases	• Location
			• Other children
			• Money

because your family *must have* these needs met, ideally at school. If you identify other non-essential needs – ones that aren't a top priority or that you can accommodate easily at home – consider them "Nice to Haves." We call them this because it would be *nice to have* these needs met at school, but not really essential. Later, you can use your Nice to Haves as tiebreakers to choose between equally appealing schools. Do your work well, and this will be your prize: you can focus on finding a truly Great Fit school for your family's top needs.

Smart à la Carte

Values, Morals, Ethics and Religion: When Does School Matter *More*?

Religion, morals, ethics, and other values: when does school matter? For some families, finding a school that reinforces religion, morals or ethics – both in what your child learns and in the behavior that is reinforced – will be a clear Must Have. Not sure? Here's some help. If your family or child has one of the following characteristics, then you might find religious, moral or ethical education rising on your list of Must Haves:

➤ *Your time with your child after school is limited,* so that you have little chance to reinforce your family's values. If you are a single working parent or both parents are working full-time, then incorporating moral, ethical or religious teaching into weekday school may be more important. You certainly will have less opportunity to reflect on the day with your children, to guide them and to help them learn from interactions at school. If a parent is at home with children in the after-school hours, then there simply is more opportunity to share stories from the day, help children learn from their own behaviors and that of others (e.g., your child comes home with questions like "Toby used *X?!* word. Is it nice to say that?"). By dinner or bed time, the conflicts and lessons of the day will be harder for many tired children, particularly younger ones, to remember and share.

➤ *You have difficulty teaching the religious, moral or ethical lessons you want your children to learn.* You may feel ill-equipped to convey the information and behaviors you want your children to learn. You may feel uncomfortable discussing religion. Or, you may feel comfortable discussing religion, perhaps because you have a concrete Bible, Talmud, Koran or other document to back you up, but when it comes to morals, ethics and other values you feel fuzzy and not sure what to say.

➤ *Your child is particularly susceptible to peer influence.* You know your child. If she is one who quickly adopts undesirable behaviors of children around her and who rarely thinks of religious or ethical concerns on her own, then reinforcement at school may become more important.

Some families will find that their multiple needs pose conflicts. You value social connections you can get only in an expensive private school, but cannot afford one. You strongly prefer a teaching method that leaves lots of room for exploration, but logistically cannot swing that way-across-town magnet school that fits the bill. And so on. If this turns out to be you, then you will need to prioritize among your family's needs even before you get to the challenge of reconciling them with your child's needs.

Smart à la Carte

Values, Morals, Ethics and Religion: When Does School Matter *Less*?

Some parents may feel little need for weekday school to teach or reinforce religious, moral or ethical beliefs. Many children, in fact, will learn in positive ways from observing the differing behavior and standards of other children (and teachers). Your child need not lose her moral compass from observing the behavior of others. If you've ever seen another person blow up at something you yourself were angry about, and found your anger diminished by the experience, you know that sometimes observing others' poor behavior teaches us to control our own. You may have less need for religious, moral and ethical teaching *at school* if:

➤ *Your religious beliefs, morals and ethics are wound carefully into your afternoon, evening and weekend life.* For many families, religious practices and discussion of values fit comfortably into a daily routine without taking school time. You may have a stay-at-home parent in your family, or a work schedule that leaves you the time to teach the knowledge and behaviors you want to impart to your children. If you have been a working parent who stopped working outside the home, then you know how much more influential you are able to be in this after-school time than in the nightly bedtime scramble.

➤ *You feel comfortable reinforcing religious, moral or ethical teachings at home.* You are just one of those people who feels comfortable talking with your children, or you have learned to do it despite your discomfort. Even if your time with them is quite limited, you may feel very confident about your ability to influence your children.

➤ *Your child is an independent thinker who is able to withstand peer influence.* You know your child. If he is the one calling his peers to task for their rude playground behavior or bad language (or if he notices and reflects on those behaviors with you later), you can be more confident that he will withstand peer influences that may be negative. While this is a child characteristic, it is one that should influence how important it is for your family's values to be reinforced at school.

For many parents, those things that rise to the top of the Must Have list will come down to those things that you can least well accommodate at home. You can sign your child up for ballet and soccer with the elite social set, but you cannot feasibly increase your family income to fund private school. You can keep your child's afternoon calendar clear for plenty of unstructured "imagination" time at home even if you cannot change your work schedule to cart your child ten miles to and from that magnet school. Every family brings different capabilities and constraints to the table. Be honest with yourself about your family's aspirations and requirements.

You must start with a true and clear picture of your family needs, and trust yourself to balance these with your child's needs and with your search for a good quality school. Giving short shrift to your own needs as parents, or to the impact on your other children, will only cause problems down the road. Facing up to your real needs now will help you appropriately prioritize your school-hunt efforts and ultimately find a better-fit school. Your hunt may lead you down paths you never imagined! But focusing on what's most important now – in the planning phase – will lead you where you need to go. Trust yourself as a parent, both to be honest about your own needs and to bend later if your child's needs pull you in a different direction.

Focusing on one, two or the few family needs that matter most can significantly improve your family life and your partnership with school to educate your child.

Smart à la Carte

How Does a School Reinforce Values?

A school can reinforce – or call into question – your values in several ways:

➤ *What your child is taught,* including explicit teaching of religion, morals and ethics
➤ *How the school interacts with children* including general school policies (dress, honor code, disciplinary policies and expected manners), teaching methods and classroom discipline
➤ *The social environment,* including values and behaviors of teachers, other students and their parents

The fact that a school teaches your religion in its curriculum does not necessarily mean that your values and ethics are reflected in other school policies, the teaching method or social environment. You'll need to consider the broader school culture, not just what's taught in the classroom. Confused about what to seek? Fear not. The following family and school matching chapters will unscramble the puzzle for you. If values are an important element of schooling for your family, let your school hunt priorities reflect this. Whatever your needs, biases or preferences, it's best to recognize them now and decide how important they are to you before you start sorting through your school options.

Smart à la Carte

The Challenge of "Being Your Own Family"

Have courage to express your own family's values and meet your own needs. Be both who you are and who you want to become as parents – even when the picture you paint of your own family is different from what your friends, neighbors, colleagues, siblings, parents or others might want it to be. Choosing a school is just one more parenting decision like the other important ones you have made already, though perhaps a bit more public one than most. You may find that even good friends are very different from you when it comes to school needs. And you may find values, needs and interests remarkably similar to people with whom you have felt very little in common previously. Many parents find that early childrearing changes adult friendships: values are put into action with discipline, manners, material goods and other choices about how to mold and shape your children. Your heightened understanding of your own and others' values can unexpectedly bring you closer to, or drive small wedges between, you and other parents.

Don't be deterred by fear that your family will be "different." Let your school choice – and how you make it – be as much an individual family expression of ideals and values as all of your other crucial childrearing actions. Don't be hoodwinked by your well-meaning acquaintances and friends when they make definitive statements of what you ought to seek in a school for your child or which schools are "the best." They may be wrong, or they may be right for their family and very wrong for yours! Take time to articulate what you want and need as a family so that you can listen to friends and neighbors with the courage and know-how to separate your needs from theirs. Enjoy the journey of self- and family-discovery that choosing a school for your child can bring.

SNAP TO IT

What To Do

➤ **Use Family "Quick Think"** on the next page to brainstorm the things about your family that you think really stand out. Estimated Time: 10 minutes

➤ **Skim the Family Needs Summary** on page 110 to get a complete preview of the specific family wants and needs included in each of the four Fit Factors. You do not need to follow the instructions at this time. Chapters 7-9 will walk you through identifying your Must Haves and Nice to Haves. Estimated Time: 5 minutes

Need more? Want more? Got more to share? Visit PickyParent.com.

Family "Quick Think"

Stop and think for a few minutes about your family. Write your responses here or on a separate page. Compare and discuss your answers with anyone else involved in school decision-making (e.g., your spouse or other parenting partner). Keep your notes handy to use later in your school hunt.

What values, needs, strengths and challenges *stand out about your family?*

➤ Values about *what* your child should learn and achieve through school

➤ Values about *how* children should behave and learn at school

➤ How you and your child interact with the school community, socially and otherwise

➤ Your family's practical constraints (scheduling, transportation, finances, child care, your other children's schools)

Family Needs Summary

How to Use This Summary:

➤ Use this checklist to help identify your family's most important characteristics for choosing a school. Use Chapters 6–9 and the *Know Your Family's Needs* table on page 375 for further clarification.

➤ Write an "M" in the square box beside needs that are Must Haves: truly essential for your child's school to address. Most families will have a small number of Must Haves.

➤ Write an "N" in the square box beside other needs that are Nice to Haves: not essential, but helpful for school to address.

➤ Leave empty boxes beside items not important for choosing a school for your child, because either (1) an item is not important for your family or (2) you do not need *school* to address an item.

➤ Record Must Haves and top Nice to Haves on your *Personalized Great Fit Checklist* on page 59.

WHAT YOUR CHILD LEARNS

VALUES ABOUT WHAT CONTENT IS IMPORTANT: a Must Have if you strongly value a subject and need for school to cover it. Mark Must Haves ("M") and Nice to Haves ("N") below:

☐ Core academic subjects (reading, writing, math)

☐ Other academic subjects (foreign language, etc. – make your own list of subjects you value)

☐ Morals, ethics, character, religion

☐ Other non-academic: social, emotional and physical development

☐ Other topics important to you

GOALS FOR YOUR CHILD: a Must Have if one of these is your goal for your child, and your child is at risk of not meeting the goal (if goal is learning a particular subject, use *Values about content* above). Mark Must Haves ("M") and Nice to Haves ("N") below:

☐ Grade progression: child at risk of failing required subject or not meeting standard for grade progression

☐ Academic performance: child is capable of performing above grade level but at risk of not achieving potential

☐ College opportunity: you want child to attend college and child is capable, but child at risk of not achieving goal

HOW YOUR CHILD LEARNS

☐ ***VALUES ABOUT SCHOOL-WIDE EXPECTATIONS AND RULES ON STUDENT CONDUCT:*** a Must Have if you have strong opinions about school rules on children's social behavior, especially if

1. your time with your child is very limited or
2. you have difficulty teaching the religious, moral or ethical lessons you want your child to learn or
3. child is very susceptible to peer influence or
4. you are very concerned about values and behaviors your child is adopting at current school

Check expectations and rules important to you below:

○ Manners with other children and adults   ○ Honor code

○ Dress   ○ Discipline

○ Other behaviors _____

Continues…

Family Needs Summary ...*continued*

HOW YOUR CHILD LEARNS...*continued*

VALUES ABOUT HOW CHILDREN SHOULD LEARN: a Must Have if you have a strong opinion about how children should be taught and behavior managed in school

☐ *Teaching method* (check preferred method below)

○ Teacher directed: teachers transmit their knowledge directly to students and guide student activities in detail

○ Student discovery: teachers help students figure out new knowledge for themselves and choose own activities

○ Mixed approach: some of both teacher directed and student discovery learning

☐ *Classroom behavior management* (check preferred method below)

○ Controlling/Strict: teachers maintain order through clear rules, rewards and consequences

○ Developmental: maintain order by coaching and developing students' self-control; use peer and parental pressure

○ Mixed approach: some of both controlling/strict and developmental approaches

☐ **YOUR ROLE AS ADVOCATE FOR YOUR CHILD:** a Must Have if you have difficulty understanding and communicating your child's needs to teachers and principal (because of time constraints, lack of confidence, language barriers, cultural differences, or other reasons)

SOCIAL ISSUES

☐ **PARENT COMMUNITY:** a Must Have if you want your child's school to have parents with particular characteristics (make a list and check preferred items below)

○ Friends: Parents you already know?

○ Neighbors: Neighborhood parents?

○ Location: Parents from a particular neighborhood other than your own?

○ Values: Same values as you? Which values?

○ Social behavior and manners: Ways you want, or don't want, other parents to act?

○ Social and economic status: Do you have preferences about the diversity or makeup of the parent community?

○ Race and ethnicity: Do you have preferences about the diversity or makeup of the parent community?

☐ **PARENT INVOLVEMENT:** a Must Have if you have a strong preference about the level and type of parent involvement in your child's school, including (check preferences, if any)

○ Helping: helping with school's daily life (e.g., volunteering for classroom activities, media center, field trips)

○ Decision making (e.g., volunteering as member of school advisory or governing board)

○ Fundraising activities (see last item below, Money, about your own donation dollar amounts)

Continues...

Family Needs Summary *...continued*

SOCIAL ISSUES...*continued*

☐ ***STUDENT COMMUNITY:*** a Must Have if you want your child's school to have students with particular characteristics (make a list and check preferred items below)

○ Friends: Want to keep your child with current friends? Seeking new friends for your child?

○ Neighbors: Your child's neighbors?

○ Location: Students from a particular neighborhood other than your own?

○ Values: Same values as you? Which values?

○ Social behavior and manners: Ways you want, or don't want, other students to act?

○ Student achievement: Higher, lower or same-performing students compared to your child?

○ Social and economic status: Preferences about the diversity or makeup of the student body?

○ Race and ethnicity: Preferences about the diversity or makeup of the student body?

○ Gender diversity: Do you want an all-boys or all-girls program for your child?

○ Other student characteristics you do or do not want?

☐ ***I WANT MY CHILD TO ATTEND A CERTAIN SCHOOL, SCHOOL TYPE, OR SCHOOL DESIGN:*** a Must Have only if you would choose a certain school type (e.g., public, private, religious) or design over a different school of better quality and fit

PRACTICAL MATTERS

☐ ***CHILD CARE:*** a Must Have if you do not have other affordable child care options for hours needed
  ○ Before and after school   ○ Holidays and Summer

☐ ***SCHEDULE:*** a Must Have if you have unchangeable commitments (e.g., work, other children's schedules) and can not use transportation or child care to accommodate a different schedule
  ○ Daily hours   ○ Yearly (start/finish and holidays)

☐ ***TRANSPORTATION:*** a Must Have if you have unchangeable commitments preventing you from providing transportation and you cannot use non-school transport (e.g., carpool, city bus)
  ○ To school and home from school   ○ After school activities

☐ ***LOCATION:*** a Must Have if you need to have your child's school near work or home (e.g., you have time or transportation constraints, or you plan to visit your child's school very frequently)

☐ ***YOUR OTHER CHILDREN:*** a Must Have if you definitely do or do not want child to go to same school as siblings. Same or different schools? _____

☐ ***MONEY AVAILABLE TO PAY FOR SCHOOL:*** a Must Have if money available to pay, including possible scholarships or vouchers, is less than most expensive school option

Current $:[1]_____   Target $:[2]_____   Maximum $:[3]_____

1 Current: Amount you actually spend on education now (tuition, fees, child care, supplies, gifts, donations)
2 Target: Amount you could spend without major changes in work, lifestyle or debt (may be same as Curr. or Max.)
3 Maximum: Most you are willing to spend, with acceptable changes in work, lifestyle and debt.

Conventional wisdom works
only if you are conventional.

LIGHT'NING LIST

What To Know from Chapter 7

➤ **Fit Factor #1 is** *What Your Child Learns:* these are your family's values and goals that influence what *subjects and at what level of difficulty* your child should be taught.

➤ **The two family characteristics for Fit Factor #1 are these:**
   ✔ *Values about Content* = you the parent strongly value a subject or subjects and need for school to cover the subject(s), such as:
   - Core academic subjects (reading, writing, math)
   - Other academic subjects (foreign language, etc. – make your own list)
   - Morals, ethics, character, religion
   - Other non-academic: e.g., social, emotional and physical development
   - Other topics important to you
   ✔ *Goals for Your Child* = you the parent have particular goals for your child *and* your child is at risk of not meeting the goals, including:
   - Grade progression: child at risk of failing required subject or not meeting standard for grade progression
   - Academic performance: child is capable of performing above grade level but at risk of not achieving potential
   - College opportunity: you want child to attend college and child is capable, but child at risk of not achieving goal

➤ **You can identify the Fit Factor # 1 characteristics most important for** *your family* by thinking about and discussing whether there are particular subjects/topics you consider essential and whether you have goals for your child that your child may be at risk of not meeting.

➤ **Remember, you must identify the** *few most important characteristics* **of your family** to match with schools for a Great Fit.
   ✔ *Values about Content* will be a Must Have for some families.
   ✔ *Goals for Your Child* will be a Must Have for some families.

Chapter 7

Family Fit Factor #1:
What Do *You* Want Your Child To Learn?

Paul and Andrea are both computer systems analysts. They definitely want their only child Lisa to use computers at school, especially since time at home is limited.

■ ■ ■

Richard and Kitty value well-roundedness. Kitty, now a lawyer, went to college on full scholarship (as did her twin brother) because of her combined academic, athletic, and leadership prowess. They want their children to attend a school that teaches and promotes the same values.

■ ■ ■

Sandra is a single mother and works as a fundraiser for nonprofits serving the homeless. She wants her only child Anders' school to reinforce the importance of community service and social welfare. After failing to pass kindergarten, Anders was recently diagnosed with dyslexia, and so Sandra is very concerned about having a school that will not only address his disability now, but stay on top of things to ensure that he makes grade level. She's wondering if one school can meet all of her needs and wants.

Identifying Your Family's Learning Content Values and Goals

You may have strong opinions about two aspects of *what* your child learns in school:
➤ *Values about content:* what subjects or topics are covered in school
➤ *Goals for your child:* whether the topics taught will help your child meet *goals you have* for your child (e.g., grade progression, academic performance and college attendance).

Some parents may have strong, clear preferences, while others may merely have assumptions lurking beneath the surface. When you take time to think about it, most of you will have some idea of what you expect your children to learn and how that content will help them in life. Your thoughts on the content of your child's learning may be driven by many things: your own childhood experiences, your ethnic and cultural background, your religious beliefs, your reading of parenting books and articles, your work experiences or your "gut" feelings.

If you do not have strong preferences about what your child learns, don't sweat it! You may be open to new ideas and willing to follow the curriculum of the school that fits best in other ways. Many of you will be content to follow the needs of your *child* in selecting learning content. If so, you can move on to the next chapter. But *if* you have strong opinions about what should or shouldn't be taught – confess now and include your wants in your school hunt.

If you do not have strong preferences about what your child learns, that's O.K. A high quality school will meet your child's needs in the core academic subjects.

Values about Content

Roger and Sophia both grew up traveling the world in military families. Roger is fluent in two languages and Sophia in three. These capabilities have brought them not only career success (in the Foreign Service) but also much pleasure and convenience during leisure travel. They very much want their twins Anna and Zan to experience the same benefits of fluency in multiple languages. But the parents settled into jobs in the U.S., making "on the street" learning for their children unlikely. Fortunately, two foreign language immersion magnet programs opened at a high quality public school in their city, one in Chinese and another in Spanish. Anna wanted to learn Spanish and Zan Chinese. Anna was admitted for kindergarten through the lottery process, but Zan was not. Roger and Sophia did not give up. They kept Zan in the private preschool/kindergarten program the children had attended previously and kept him on the magnet waiting list. When a student's family moved and opened up a space in the Chinese program, Zan was admitted mid-year, much to his parents' delight.

■ ■ ■

Tamara and Greg are not picky about many things at all. They pride themselves on "letting our children grow up to be who they are meant to be, not who we want them to be." To this end, they care very much about their children having early opportunities to become well-rounded. They want their children to be socially capable, emotionally self-aware and physically active, not just academically high-achieving. After settling on a popular, nearby private school for their first child's kindergarten, they were feeling more committed and energetic two years later when child #2 was ready for school, too. A careful search revealed that another school – requiring a 45 minute bus or car ride – was committed to the kind of "whole child" approach they valued. With a wide variety of school clubs and physical fitness opportunities, explicit teaching of "emotional intelligence and social awareness," and a school-wide mission to "help children discover and be who they want to be," the school was a perfect fit for this family's strong values about content.

Values About Content: What They Are, Why They're Important

The content of your child's school education includes the subjects and topics covered at school, both through the main curriculum and other school activities. You may be a "just the facts, Ma'am" type of person, and therefore want a school that focuses mostly on the basic subjects (reading, writing, math). Or you may crave breadth and want a school that presents the basics in the *context* of science, social studies, foreign language, music, art and other "interesting" subjects. You may have strong moral, religious or ethical concerns and want to have those taught formally in the school curriculum. You may highly value the growing importance of computerized technology and want your child's school to reinforce this with more exposure than you can offer at home. Or you may want your child's school to promote well-roundedness – an understanding and appreciation of *many* academic subjects and topics, as well as social, emotional and physical well-being, too. Whatever your preferences, you need to decide now if they are ones that will influence your school choice.

If you are nodding to yourself that, yes, indeed you do have strong notions about what topics your child should study in school, think about the origin of your feelings. Your preferences may have something to do with your *own childhood* experiences. If you found math drills mind-numbing, you may be seeking something a bit more inspiring for your child. If you feel that the basics got short shrift in your early schooling, and this neglect affected your ability to perform in school or work, you may want to ensure your child gets a more solid start.

Then again, what you want your child to learn in school may have more to do with your *adult* view of the world. Many of you will find that you have a world view – your personal perspective on what is important for people to do, to know, to think, to feel and to be – that dictates your own sense of what's important for your child to learn at school. Your world view may come from your religion, your work, your background, or other aspects of your adult life. Your religion may dictate that your children absorb particular knowledge, and nights and weekends may not leave enough time. Your own work may require specific skills, knowledge or capabilities that you would like your child to begin learning in

Your child is part of your family, but your child is not you.

school. You may want your child to be exposed to, or even immersed in, a culture and language that's part of your family's heritage. You may enjoy foreign travel or live in an ethnically diverse area and want the study of foreign languages and culture to be an important element of your child's education.

Schools differ in their focus on learning content, or what subjects they teach and how much time is spent on each. Some schools focus primarily on the basics. Others balance the basics with other subjects. Some schools teach only alternative subjects, covering the basics entirely *through* these others. We want to jog your memory to help you discern any preferences *you* might have as parents, independent of your individual child's needs.

The Basics. All schools cover the basics – reading, math and writing – in some fashion. The relative investment that schools make in these three subjects – including staff time, materials, facilities and your child's time – varies according to each school's priorities.

Schools vary not only in their focus on the basics versus other subjects, but also in the relative emphasis among the three basics. Some schools focus largely on reading and math, and only somewhat on writing. While you might think reading and writing are connected – and they most certainly are – reading is often emphasized over writing in grade-level testing. Hence, some schools that seem to focus on "the basics" give writing short shrift. Others give writing, and communication in general, great emphasis, perhaps adding oral presentations, debate and speechmaking to the standard fare. In some schools, either math or language arts (reading and writing) are emphasized.

In later chapters we'll help you figure out what subjects are covered in schools you consider. For now, though, you need to decide whether you have a strong opinion about the extent to which the three basics are emphasized over other subjects, and what strong views you have, if any, about the comparative emphasis on these three.

Additional Subjects. Subjects such as foreign language, science, geography, computer technology, art, music and physical education can serve three purposes. First, they can *motivate an otherwise uninspired student* to learn the basics. A child who thinks writing letters and learning letter sounds is as inspiring as cleaning up toys may come to life when learning about the planet Mars while studying the letter M. A child who finds math tedious and unimportant may feel the spark when using fractional measuring cups and spoons to make a green, gooey slime in science. A student who doesn't see the point of writing stories may change his tune when he gets to write a short autobiography as part of a social studies lesson. In each case, and many more examples like them, children who do not feel interested in school can feel differently when the subject matter is interesting. Thus, some schools will use non-basic subjects to inspire an interest in basic reading, writing and math skills.

Second, additional subjects can *stimulate multiple areas in the brain* and provide context for better memory. For example, there is some evidence that learning a foreign language helps children understand and use the English language better. Some research also shows that early exposure to music improves mathematical ability, perhaps because music provides a context for counting and numerical relationships. For a struggling student, tapping into multiple areas of the brain and providing context for memory – through interesting sights, sounds, ideas or hands-on experiences – may mean the difference between making the grade or not.

Third, schools can teach non-basic subjects for their *intrinsic value* – the knowledge and skills gained in each subject. You may want your child to study foreign languages not to benefit her study of English reading and writing, but to learn the foreign languages themselves. You may want your child exposed to a great variety of subjects and topics not just to help with the basics but to get a taste of the richness of our world. For many parents who have a strong preference about what topics their children learn, this will be the driving factor.

When is This a Priority for Your School Hunt?

You will need to decide how important your preferences about the content of your child's schooling are. Whatever your needs and desires, be honest about them up front so you may focus your school search accordingly. Make this a Must Have only if you have a strong opinion.

Goals for Your Child

Mary and Erasmus both grew up poor and bright. They worked hard, often juggling 20 or more hours of work each week while attending high school. They met waiting tables at a local family diner. After school, they got married, borrowed money from Mary's uncle, and started a restaurant together, building it into a successful business over 10 years' time. Neither had the time to attend college, but both regret their lost opportunity. They want their first son Nikki to have the opportunity they did not. Nikki is a seven year old attending a local religious school, a financial sacrifice his parents are happy to make. But they are not happy that Nikki is not being challenged in school. Reading before age four, Nikki is well ahead of the structured curriculum in his school. The teachers love him, but have little to offer him academically. While they treasure the values the school teaches, Mary and Erasmus know that they cannot be satisfied until their son attends a school where he is challenged and on a clear path toward the college of his choice. A short hunt revealed, to their surprise, that Nikki's assigned public school provides extensive services, both in and out of the classroom, for very gifted children. This fact has attracted many families with children like Nikki into neighborhoods assigned to the school. Nikki would spend at least half of his school time working with similar children on challenging work in core subjects. Mary and Erasmus, with their son's consent, switched him for second grade and donated a portion of their former tuition money to their church and a portion to Nikki's college fund.

Goals for Your Child: What They Are, Why They're Important

Many parents live with the dream that their children will achieve things in school that they, the parents, did not. In our society where hard work and tenacity carry you far, many parents can provide opportunities for their children that they themselves didn't have. Many parents are satisfied with the content of any curriculum, *as long as* it will help their children achieve the goals they have set for them. We have listed a few very common goals parents have for their school-age children. If you have goals for your child not listed here, by all means include them in your school hunt.

Three common goals parents have for their children and fear their children won't attain are these:
➤ Grade Progression (moving from one grade to the next without being held back)
➤ Academic Performance (at a specific level acceptable to *you*)
➤ College Opportunity (getting admitted to a college acceptable to you)

Your goals may arise from your own childhood experiences or your adult view of the world. If you yourself were held back a grade – or just missed a chance to attend the college of your choice – you may have very strong feelings about grade progression or college attendance. If you come from a family of high academic achievers, you may have similarly high goals for your child. If your life has been enhanced or diminished by your own education achievements, you may have goals for your child that would help her avoid or obtain the same experiences you have had.

Some family situations make it more challenging for children to achieve their academic potential. They include at least these: being the child of a single parent, of immigrants who are not fluent in English or savvy about the American educational system, of parents who did not themselves achieve highly in school, and of parents living in poverty. If your child is challenged in Basic Learning Capability or faces other learning barriers described in the Child section of this book, he also may struggle to meet common parent goals.

Whatever your goals, you will want to consider these questions:

➤ *What is the goal, specifically?*
Is it that you want your child to go to Harvard only, or is it that you want your child to be able to go to the college of her choice?

➤ *How likely is it that your child will not meet the goal?*
If your child is challenged in Basic Learning Capability, then you might be most concerned about simply ensuring progress from grade to grade each year. If your child is ahead academically, then your child most certainly will make progress and achieve at satisfactory levels; you might be more concerned about your child being prepared to attend a high school offering advanced courses and good college placement.

➤ *Is the goal consistent with your child's interests and abilities?*
Are you really ready to decide that little Charlie will go to an Ivy League college? Is your artistic child likely to pursue the engineering career you wanted to pursue and didn't? If not, consider carefully whether or not to make this goal a factor in your school choice.

When is This a Priority for Your School Hunt?

If, upon reflection, you:

✔ do indeed have a specific goal for your child and
✔ are concerned about your child's ability to meet the goal,

then make this a Must Have, and find a school to help.

SNAP TO IT

What To Do

➤ **Refer back to your Family "Quick Think"** on page 109 to refresh your memory regarding things that really stand out about your family. Estimated Time: 2 minutes

➤ **Use the Family Needs Summary** on page 110 to get a quick fix on the Fit Factor #1 *What Your Child Learns* characteristics. Estimated Time: 5 minutes

➤ **Use the Know Your Family's Needs table** on page 375 to further clarify your family's Fit Factor # 1 characteristics and the importance of each for choosing a school. You need not read the whole table: focus only on items you believe may be important for your family. Estimated Time: 15 minutes

➤ **Discuss your family's needs** with your spouse or other parenting partner. Estimated Time: As needed

➤ **Record your Must Haves and Nice to Haves** on your *Family Needs Summary* (page 110). Estimated Time: 10 minutes

Need more? Want more? Got more to share? Visit PickyParent.com.

LIGHT'NING LIST

What To Know from Chapter 8

➤ *Fit Factor #2 is How Your Child Learns:* these are your family's values and capabilities that influence how a school should teach and interact with your child, both in and out of the classroom.

➤ *The three family characteristics for Fit Factor #2 are these:*
   ✔ *Values about school-wide expectations and rules on student conduct* = you have strong preferences about school rules and expectations regarding students' social behavior, including both school policies and the actual behavior that results. You may have specific preferences about manners with other children and adults, dress, discipline, honor codes, and other behaviors.
   ✔ *Values about how children should learn* = you have strong preferences about how children should be taught and behavior managed in the classroom at school.
      • Teaching method: how teachers teach
      • Classroom behavior management: how teachers manage classroom behavior
   ✔ *Your role as advocate for child* = your ability to understand and communicate your child's needs to teachers and principal. The lower your ability and comfort in these matters, the more important to find a school that will help.

➤ *You can identify the Fit Factor # 2 characteristics most important for your family* by thinking about and discussing your values, preferences and abilities in the listed areas.

➤ *Remember, you must identify the few most important characteristics* of your family to match with schools for a Great Fit.
   ✔ *Values about student conduct rules, how children should learn* and *your role as advocate for your child* will be Must Haves for some families.

Chapter 8

Family Fit Factor #2:

How Do *You* Want a School to Interact with Your Child?

Lissa and Sean have one child, McKinsey. With his father in the Foreign Service, Sean grew up living in several countries, and he attended Montessori schools through fifth grade. Lissa attended very strict traditional schools through high school, and always felt trapped. Both Lissa and Sean want a school where McKinsey can discover herself and follow her own passions.

■ ■ ■

Les and Anita are less concerned about teaching method than with behavior. Anita, a former teacher turned corporate trainer, strongly believes that behavior problems are the major issue in schools today. So they are looking for a school with strict behavior rules both in and out of the classroom, a strong honor code, and a high-standards dress code (uniforms would be ideal).

■ ■ ■

Christine is a widow who works part time (good life insurance spared her from full time work) while raising four children. Though she's gotten more assertive by necessity, she feels uncomfortable asking for much from her children's schools. "I use up all of my toughness just keeping a roof with no leaks over our heads." She already feels as though she's constantly asking for favors just to make her schedule workable. She needs schools that will work hard to meet her children's differing needs (and differ they do!). She needs schools that will stay in touch with her and let her know when something seems amiss with one of her children.

How Your Child Learns:
The Family Perspective

Families can have strong views, and a tremendous influence, on how children learn at school. In fact, many parents are more concerned about the environment in which their children learn than the subjects their children study. Regardless of what subjects your child learns, you may have expectations regarding how students are taught and treated at school. And you most certainly can affect how well teachers understand and respond to your child's needs. So, you should consider whether any of these is an important factor in choosing your child's school:

➤ *Values* about *school-wide expectations and rules on student conduct,* not just in the classroom but in less formal interactions, too (including expected manners, dress, discipline and honor code)

➤ *Values about how children should* **learn,** including:
   ✔ *Teaching method* and
   ✔ *Classroom behavior management*

➤ *Your role as advocate* for your child at school

Values about School-Wide Expectations and Rules on Student Conduct

Jan and Andy Smith were full-time lawyers and parents of three. They chose a school with a "character program" that included weekly class time devoted to topics like making friends, the effects of teasing and taunting, and so on. These were good, solid values lessons that these busy parents were worried they wouldn't have time to reinforce. When Jan decided to make the switch from full-time professional to full-time parent and volunteer, she began spending far more time at the school. She was shocked by the values that the school's culture informally promoted. The student body of the school was highly homogeneous. Scholarships were limited in number, and the high tuition bill ensured that only children of high earners could attend. The school had developed a "keep up with the Joneses" culture of conformity and focus on money. While formal manners were emphasized with adults, students were rude to each other and intolerant of others who looked or acted "different." There seemed to be no emphasis at school on monitoring this informal behavior outside of the classroom. The school friends that her child brought home to play largely reflected the values of the school. These values were not at all aligned with hers and her husband's. She began to realize that the informal social environment of the school was far more influential than the formal character program. They sought and found a school where both the formal rules and informal expectations better fit their values about student conduct.

■ ■ ■

Janet, a divorced mother of one son, enrolled her child Mark in a school where students were expected to set their own group norms for behavior and work through conflicts on their own. Janet liked this approach, as it reflected her belief that children must learn to set their own personal boundaries. But in November, Janet was called to the principal's office to discuss her son's behavior. The principal liked Mark, and thought he just needed a little coaching to improve his behavior. The principal was confident that Mark could work things out, all kids could really, and he just wanted her to be aware of the issue. One month later, Janet was horrified to overhear another mother telling a friend about how her son had been bullied repeatedly by "this awful pack of boys, especially a boy named Mark – do you know him?" To which the other mother replied, "No, but I have heard about that group. I guess they're just still learning. They are boys, after all." The next day, Janet began to hunt for another school for her son. She found one for the following year that had a very clear focus on values that were like hers, but where the discipline policy was very clear, with specified, increasingly unsavory punishments for "bullying." Within a year, her son seemed happier and more affectionate towards her, but just as important his behavior had changed significantly, and he was, as his teacher told her, "one of my easy kids."

Values about School-Wide Expectations and Rules on Student Conduct: What They Are, Why They're Important

You probably have expectations about how your child should behave at home and elsewhere, and you have values that underlie those expectations. Kindness. Respect for others. Honesty. These are all social values that communicate how we expect our children to relate to others. The particular social behaviors parents value most differ from family to family.

You may want your family's values and expectations for behavior to be reinforced actively by your child's school. A school reinforces values not just with what's taught in the classroom, but also through its rules, behavioral expectations and other aspects of "culture." If you have strong preferences, and feel that your values must be reinforced at school, then you'll want to ensure that your child's school culture fits. A school's culture is defined by both formal policies that set *expectations* for student behavior and *actual* student and teacher behavior allowed, both in and out of the classroom. Common cues parents can observe include these:

➤ Manners expected with other students and adults
➤ Dress (expected and actual)
➤ General discipline policies and practices
➤ Honor code (concerning both academic honesty and other student responsibilities)
➤ Other behaviors expected in the school community

While there are many cultural aspects of a school that most adults would agree are more desirable than others (e.g., kindness among children is reinforced, rudeness is discouraged), some values are more subject to opinion.

If you give your children a strong moral compass, they can be adventurous in the world knowing they won't get lost.

For example, consider three schools with differing dress codes. School A requires navy and white uniforms to establish equity in appearance among students in an economically diverse population. School B's dress code requires collared shirts for boys, no jeans, and prescribed dress lengths for girls, to establish a sense that all students are meeting a certain standard of social refinement. School C's dress code simply requires that students be fully clothed (shoes, shirts and pants or dresses) and otherwise allows individuality of attire.

The other cultural aspects of those three schools would, most likely, reflect the underlying values expressed through their differing dress codes. School A most likely has a clearly expressed behavioral code, for students and staff, that includes values like "respect for others" regardless of economic background, interpersonal kindness, and a focus on common community goals. School B most likely has a strict code of discipline and reinforces formal manners in student-teacher interactions. School C would be more likely to encourage individuality and tolerance for diversity in social and academic interactions.

All three approaches have costs and benefits, but each creates a distinct social environment which may or may not align with your family's values. Dress codes are not always so well aligned with the rest of school culture, but they are one important cue.

When is This a Priority for Your School Hunt?

This is a Must Have if you have strong opinions about school rules and expectations regarding children's social behavior and general conduct. Consider the following factors that make this a more likely Must Have:

1. Your time with your child is very limited, or
2. You have difficulty teaching the religious, moral, or ethical lessons you want your child to learn, or

3. Your child is very susceptible to peer influence, or
4. You are very concerned about the values and behaviors your child is adopting at his or her current school, or how your child is treated by others at school.

If this is a Must Have for you, you should make your own list of the behaviors you want your child's school to reinforce and the cultural cues (manners, dress code, etc.) that are most important to you.

As you begin to take a closer look at schools, you will notice that some are more adept at reinforcing their intended values than others. Ones with explicit character programs – in which students and teachers actually spend time discussing values and behavior each week – are more likely to reinforce stated values and expected behaviors than schools with just a written policy. But even a school with a concrete character program may allow and even reinforce unintended behaviors in other ways. Look for warning signs such as students who are polite and respectful with adults but rude and mean-spirited with other students. If you have particular concerns related to your child or family (e.g., a child with an obvious physical disability, a child of a race different from most other students in a school), ask to speak with parents in similar situations to get the real scoop.

Values about How Children Should Learn

Jane and Carter were dissatisfied with the strict, structured environment of their second grader Sandy's classroom. They envisioned school as a place where their child should "learn how to learn." In Sandy's school, assignments were very much directed by the teachers, with explicit instructions and little room for students to pursue their own interests. The classroom reflected this, with desks all lined up in neat rows facing the front of the class. Jane and Carter hadn't really formed their opinions until they'd seen Sandy's classrooms in action over the years through their monthly classroom volunteering. They felt like Sandy was a robot, just following detailed instructions all the time. With their resolve building, Jane and Carter sought a school where their daughter could do more learning and discovery on her own and where teachers would earn her respect, not fear. They considered several schools and finally chose one with a "balanced" approach to learning. Sandy would spend about half of her learning time on self-directed activities and half on teacher-directed ones.

■ ■ ■

Jack attended kindergarten at a small private elementary school where children were encouraged to choose learning activities from work centers scattered throughout the classrooms. His parents had chosen the school for its small, friendly environment. Teachers were "facilitators" to guide children when needed. Over the summer, Jack and his parents attended a family reunion including many cousins, two of whom were about Jack's age. Jack's parents were astonished to find that one of the cousins had begun reading in October and the other was just starting. Jack didn't even know the letter sounds yet, as he rarely chose to do the "letter" work center at school. Concerned, they called the school director when they returned home. The director politely told them that the school did not "push" reading onto children until 3rd grade when end of grade testing began, but that children who were ready could certainly read at school if they wished. This reflected the philosophy of the school, which parents of students were expected to accept when they enrolled their children. Jack's parents immediately sought and found another school with more structure. They found one where all students were expected to know letter sounds and begin reading by end of kindergarten, and the curriculum and teaching method supported this goal. Students still had a one hour block of time every day for activities of their own choice, but the rest of the day was teacher-directed (though often in small groups). By December of first grade, Jack was reading on a second grade level. He was very proud and called himself a "bookworm."

Values about How Children Should Learn: What They Are, Why They're Important

Many parents have either explicit or assumed values about how children should learn, and be taught, at school. These values often stem from a larger world view about the balance between following authority and the freedom of individuals. In the case of schools, the balance is between the authority of teachers to direct children and the freedom of children to explore and follow their interests. Even if you do not know of a specific teaching method you like best, you probably have an opinion about the authority vs. freedom issue.

This issue comes to the fore in two main ways: the *teaching method* used to instruct students, and the techniques employed for *classroom behavior management*.

Teaching Method. Teachers can help students learn in two major ways. They can use "teacher-directed" methods: telling children what they need to know through lectures, readings, chalkboard displays or other methods. Or they can use a "student discovery" approach: providing appropriate materials, perhaps with guiding questions and goals, that allow students to figure out new knowledge for themselves, often in activities of their own choosing. The first teaching style is that of "expert": let me teach you what I know. The second is one more akin to "coach": let me use what I know to stimulate and motivate you to learn for yourself. Both styles can be effective when used well. The question for you, as parents, is whether you have a strong personal preference about how your child should learn. You may even have a strong desire for a *mixed* approach that uses both teacher-directed and student-discovery methods.

Classroom Behavior Management. A teacher's authority over children's behavior in the classroom can take different forms, "controlling" (strict) and "developmental." A controlling approach will include establishing clear rules and consequences for breaking them (as well as occasional rewards for adhering). A developmental approach includes more subtle tactics for influencing students' behavior: coaching students to improve their self-control; frequent recognition and reward for positive behaviors and progress; and effective use of peers, parents and the principal to reinforce good behavior. Again, the question for you as parents is whether you have an inclination towards a particular classroom disciplinary style, and whether that is a Must Have for your child's school. You also may have a strong preference for a mixed approach, teachers who employ both controlling and developmental tactics as each situation requires.

When Are These Priorities for Your School Hunt?

Teaching method is a Must Have only if you have a strong opinion about how your child should learn and be taught at school. Classroom behavior management is a Must Have only if you have a strong opinion about how behavior should be managed in your child's classroom.

What if you philosophically favor a certain approach, but your child needs something different? For now, make note of your preferences. Better to be honest with yourself about your biases so you can take them into account. Later, you'll have the chance to weigh them against your own child's needs.

Your Role as Advocate for Your Child

Your Role as Advocate: What it Is, Why It's Important

The last family characteristic that will affect *how* your child learns at school is your ability as a parent to help your school understand your child's needs. We hope this book will go a long way towards helping you *understand* your child, but you also have the sometimes intimidating task of *communicating* with your child's school. In some cases, you may need to induce changes in your child's school or even "go to the mat" to get what your child needs.

How well you are able to accomplish those tasks – understanding your child, communicating with and influencing a school – to meet your child's needs will greatly affect the importance of finding a perfect fit school for your child. *The more comfortable and capable you are acting as your child's advocate, the less important it is for you to find a school that perfectly fits your child.*

Some common barriers to acting as your child's advocate include time constraints, lack of confidence, language barriers, and cultural differences. You may have other barriers, either temporary or permanent.

Assess your abilities as a family team. In some families, one parent will be more comfortable than the other talking with teachers and principals. In others, a tag team effort will produce the best outcome. If you are a single parent, you may find help from friends or extended family members who know your child. We don't recommend showing up at the principal's office with all 25 members of your family clan! But it is perfectly acceptable for an aunt, uncle, grandparent or close friend who can be helpful in understanding and communicating about your child to get involved.

When is This a Priority for Your School Hunt?

Consider this a Must Have if you think that lack of time, confidence or other barriers will prevent you (or your family helpers) from acting as your child's advocate at school. In this case, it will be more important to seek a school that fits all your child's needs very closely, or one that offers a program highly individualized to each child. You will also want to look for a school that communicates well with parents, in both directions: sending out information about what's happening at school and how individual children are doing, and welcoming parents as partners in crafting each child's education.

What To Do

➤ *Refer back to your Family "Quick Think"* on page 109 to refresh your memory regarding things that really stand out about your family. Estimated Time: 2 minutes

➤ *Use the Family Needs Summary* on page 110 to get a quick fix on the Fit Factor #2 *How Your Child Learns* characteristics. Estimated Time: 5 minutes

➤ *Use the Know Your Family's Needs table* on page 375 to further clarify your family's Fit Factor #2 characteristics and the importance of each for choosing a school. You need not read the whole table: focus only on items you believe are important for your family. Estimated Time: 15 minutes

➤ *Discuss your family's needs* with your spouse or other parenting partner. Estimated Time: As needed

➤ *Record your Must Haves and Nice to Haves* on your *Family Needs Summary* (page 110). Estimated Time: 10 minutes

Need more? Want more? Got more to share? Visit PickyParent.com.

LIGHT'NING LIST

What To Know from Chapter 9

➤ **Fit Factor #3 is** *Social Issues:* these are your family's preferences about characteristics of other students, and their parents, at your child's school. The four family preferences for Fit Factor # 3 are these:

- ✔ *Parent Community:* Your preferences about the parents of students attending your child's school.
- ✔ *Parent Involvement:* Your preferences about the level and type of parent involvement in your child's school.
- ✔ *Student Community:* Your preferences about the students attending your child's school.
- ✔ *School or School Type:* Your preference for your child to attend a certain school, school type, or school using a certain design.

➤ **Fit Factor #4 is** *Practical Matters:* these are your family's logistical needs and financial constraints affecting your choice of schools. The six family items for Fit Factor #4 are these:

- ✔ *Child Care:* your needs for care during non-school hours.
- ✔ *Schedule:* your daily and yearly scheduling needs.
- ✔ *Transportation:* your need for your child's transportation to and from school.
- ✔ *Location:* your need for your child's school to be located in a particular place.
- ✔ *Your Other Children:* coordination of your multiple children's educations.
- ✔ *Money:* money available in your family to pay for school and related expenses.

➤ **You can identify the Fit Factor #3 and #4 characteristics most important for your family** by thinking about and discussing your values, preferences and needs in the listed areas and by assessing your financial resources.

➤ **Remember, you must identify the few most important characteristics of your family** to match with schools for a Great Fit. Each of the Fit Factor #3 and #4 items will be a Must Have for some families.

Chapter 9

Family Fit Factors #3 and 4

What are *Your* Family's Social and Practical Needs?

Regina, single mother of a boy, age 5, and a girl, age 7, works cleaning houses while her children are in school. At night, she waits tables at a nearby pub. Her mother keeps the children until she gets home at midnight. She needs a school that ends as early in the day as possible. With her cleaning done by 2:00 p.m., she wants to spend the rest of the afternoon with her children. But she also is concerned about the social group in her children's school. She has seen the depressing downfall of so many boys in her neighborhood and wants her own son to be exposed to many boys (and their parents) with high expectations for a bright future. The neighborhood school won't do. Private school is out for financial reasons (and she doesn't see scholarships as likely for her children right now). She is happy to discover – and fortunately able to get both children into – a public charter school with the right schedule and a diverse group of students from all over the city.

■ ■ ■

Ming and Li Zhang's first child Margaret was a chatty preschooler. Ming and Li had both moved to the United States as children with their parents. When Margaret was born, they were determined to help her fit into the dominant culture. But as she grew, they realized how little she knew of her heritage (Ming's parents had moved back to China and Li's parents were deceased). They live in urban San Francisco, in the Marina district, where Ming is a radiologist and Li a patent attorney. While the city as a whole has a strong Chinese culture, their neighborhood and preschool have few children of Margaret's ethnic heritage. They read in the newspaper about an experimental Chinese language and culture immersion program in which half the children are native English speakers and half native Chinese speakers. Investigating further, they were convinced of the program's academic rigor. They applied, and Margaret was waitlisted. Late in the kindergarten year, she was admitted off the waiting list. They jumped at the opportunity for Margaret to spend time in a community with the perfect mix of students.

■ ■ ■

Donna, an investment banker, and her developer husband Ran, were in conflict between two private schools. One is a large, old-line traditional favorite of their social set, and is just five blocks from their home. The other is a new school, located 25 minutes away in good traffic, which has drawn many families away from the traditional schools with its focus on diversity (many scholarships are offered to achieve this goal), community service, and individualized instruction. The social connections among parents at the old-line school are strong and would be beneficial to both Donna's and Ran's businesses. Yet, Donna became concerned about the "bubble world" in which many of the children attending this school seemed to live. She was just not impressed by the lack of worldliness of these children, and frankly, many of their parents. The new school seemed to have drawn away just the sort of people she wants to influence her child and family. Satisfied with the quality of the new school, Donna and Ran ultimately chose it for its parent and student community, so in line with what they want to foster in their own family. They formed a carpool with neighbors to limit their driving.

■ ■ ■

SOCIAL ISSUES

Some parents begin the search for schools with social issues at the top of the list. With so little information available about the core job of schools – educating children – parents turn instead to easier-to-observe social matters. But even if you are concerned primarily with academic affairs, you should pause a moment to consider your social needs and preferences.

There are four broad social issues that you will want to consider:
➤ The parent community
➤ Parent involvement in school life
➤ The student community
➤ Your biases or preferences for a particular school, school type or school design

The Parent Community

What It Is, Why It's Important

Some parents very much want to take advantage of the parent community brought together by their children's schools. Others will not spend much time with other parents (but remember that your child may) because of work or lack of interest. You must set your own priorities and decide both how important the parent community is to you and what characteristics you seek.

Some characteristics of other parents you might want to consider include these:

➤ *Friends:* Is it important for your child's school to have parents you already know, or even particular parents?

➤ *Neighbors:* Is it important for you to have neighbors at your child's school?

➤ *Location:* Is it important for you to have other parents from a particular location (other than your neighborhood)?

➤ *Values:* Is it important for other parents to have the same values as you? Which values?

➤ *Social behavior and manners:* Are there particular ways you want, or don't want, other children's parents to act?

➤ *Social and economic status:* Do you have preferences about the diversity or makeup of the parent community?

➤ *Race and ethnicity:* Do you have preferences about the diversity or makeup of the parent community?

➤ *Other characteristics:* What else do you want, or not want, in the parent community at your child's school?

When Is This a Priority for Your School Hunt?

Be honest with yourself. If rubbing shoulders with those in a certain social set is important to you, confess to yourself right now. If your children are living an exclusive life of privilege and financial wealth, and you want your entire family to be exposed to more economic diversity, then make that a priority. If you want to be part of a community that includes many others from your ethnic or cultural background, say so. And so on. Think about it, talk about it, and decide what's important to you. Make this a Must Have if you have strong preferences about any of the items listed above.

Parent Involvement

What It Is, Why It's Important

Some parents, but by no means all, want to become actively involved in their children's schools. Let us tell you what the research says about this. *Scads* of articles, in both the popular press and academic journals, have appeared calling for more parent participation in schools. This goes beyond helping your own child. It is about expressing your commitment and contributing your talents to improve and operate your child's school for the betterment of all students, not just your own.

There is good research linking parent involvement *at home in your own child's education* to student achievement. In fact, the research is detailed enough that we pretty well know how parents should – and shouldn't – help their children outside of school hours (see Chapter 18).

Even avid parent volunteers will average only a few hours per week at their children's schools. Your child will spend at least 30 hours per week there.

But despite all the time and effort put into recruiting and organizing parents to become involved in schools generally, there is little evidence that parent volunteerism at this level helps children's academic learning overall. The kind of parent effort we are talking about includes volunteering in the classroom or media center, attending school meetings, etc. Some studies have found a small correlation between the level of parent involvement and test scores. However, the schools with higher test scores also are those in which students start school *already* achieving at higher levels – and the parents of these fast-start kids are also more likely to volunteer at school. So, it is more likely that what the parents have done *at home* to prepare their kids for a good start in school, rather than the less focused volunteer time at school, brings up the tests scores.

That said, should you care about volunteering at your child's school? Oh yes! Here's why:

➤ If your volunteer activities are appropriately focused, you can *simulate the proven, beneficial* at-home interactions for children who do not have parents able to play this role.

➤ If your volunteer activities enhance one or more Great School Quality Factors (e.g., allowing teachers to work with smaller groups of children), then you may directly improve school quality.

➤ Your targeted activities may improve the school's fit with your needs or your child's.

➤ You may have special skills to do necessary work that your school would otherwise have to fund from the school budget, freeing up money for quality-focused expenses.

➤ You will feel good about it and enjoy getting to know teachers and other parents.

➤ You will understand your child's school environment better and thus be able to help your own child better with both academic and social challenges.

➤ Your child's teacher will feel appreciated and may return the favor with attention for your child.

➤ If fundraising proceeds are used directly to support one or more Great School Quality Factors or a Fit Factor important to you, then your fundraising activities can directly improve the school's offerings.

You must decide whether you would like to be active in your child's school, what role you would like to play, and how important this is to you for choosing a school. Many parents who very much want to volunteer at school have a preference for the type of volunteer work:

➤ *Helping with school's daily life.* This includes volunteering for classroom activities, helping in the media center, chaperoning field trips and the like. These activities, if properly focused to meet school goals, can contribute to the quality of a school.

➤ *Decision-making.* This includes volunteering as a member of a school advisory or governing board and similarly empowered roles. Parents who understand school quality can have a powerful impact in these roles, influencing and helping the school to improve in significant ways. But parents sometimes pressure schools to focus on misleading quality "red herrings." If you're reading this book thoroughly, consider yourself a good candidate for a decision-making role in your child's school.

➤ *Fundraising.* This includes organizing or participating in fundraising activities, such as school carnivals, book fairs, dances, candy and wrapping paper sales, and so forth. Some parents want to contribute time to such activities only if the fundraisers also serve an educational purpose (e.g., book fairs), while others prefer those that promote social interaction among parents (e.g., dances, dinners, auctions and the like).

Parent volunteers focusing time directly on Great School Quality Factors can make all the difference for the children they affect.

When is This a Priority for Your School Hunt?

If you have a strong preference about the type and level of time contribution parents ought to make, then this is a Must Have.

➤ If you strongly prefer a very active parent community and are able to commit this time yourself, you will want to look for a school that expects and gets the parent involvement you want.

➤ If your time or interest is limited, you will want to ensure that parent volunteer expectations or requirements are not too burdensome for your situation.

Make this a Must Have if you have strong needs or preferences one way or the other.

The Student Community

What It Is, Why It's Important

With abundant news stories about scary incidents in schools, and some about inspiring activities initiated by students, most parents are at least somewhat concerned about the student community at a school. Many of you have great hopes and great fears about the values and behaviors of your child's peers, and how they will influence your child. Indeed, your child's peers, both in her classroom and elsewhere in a school, will most certainly influence her view of the world and her behaviors. That influence may be to reinforce your own family's values, or to take your child in a very different direction from what you as a parent anticipated. This issue often takes a great leap in importance as children move from elementary to middle school, but many parents are concerned about their children's school peers from the start.

You will need to identify the student body profile you want and decide how important it is to you that your chosen school fits this profile. You may find that what you want in a student community mirrors what you want in a parent community, reflecting your overall values.

Characteristics you may want to consider for the student community include these:

➤ *Friends:* Do you want your child to have school friends he or she already knows, or do you want your child to forge new friendships?

➤ *Neighbors:* Do you want your child to go to school with children from your neighborhood?

➤ *Location:* Do you want your child to go to school with children who live in a certain place (other than your neighborhood)?

➤ *Values:* Is it important for other children to have the same values as your family? Which values?

➤ *Manners and social behavior:* Are there particular ways you want, or don't want, other children to act?

➤ *Student achievement:* Do you want your child to go to school with students who generally perform at higher, similar, or lower levels than your child?

➤ *Social and economic status:* Do you have preferences about the diversity or makeup of the student body?

➤ *Race and ethnicity:* Do you have preferences about the diversity or makeup of the student body?

➤ *Gender diversity:* Do you want an all-boys or all-girls program for your child?

➤ *Other characteristics:* What else do you want, or not want, in the student community at your child's school?

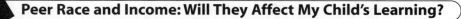

Smart à la Carte

Peer Race and Income: Will They Affect My Child's Learning?

One question that many parents have is whether the makeup of the student body at a school will affect *their children's academic achievement*. Should you avoid schools with certain kinds of student populations, or seek out schools with some other profile? The short answer is "no." The main determinants of whether your child will succeed in a particular school are the school's quality and fit with your child and family needs (particularly those needs affecting academic learning). As you look at schools, these should be your focus.

Why? Interestingly, many parent assumptions about peer effects do not hold water under high quality research scrutiny about student results. Those that do are almost entirely explained by school quality shortfalls, not characteristics of the students. Does that mean the makeup of the student body is irrelevant? Not necessarily. Mediocre and low quality schools often fall into two traps in response to their student populations. The traps are created not by the peers in the school, but by the sub-par response of the school to its students.

The first trap is this: seemingly homogeneous student populations (e.g., all white, all African American, all middle class, all poor) can tempt school leaders and staff to assume that all of the students are the same, when in fact (as you know from our Child Chapters 2 - 5) individual students' needs vary considerably. These schools mistakenly adopt a one-size-fits-all approach, which often lowers expectations for many students who could progress further academically, both to grade level and well beyond. So not surprisingly, high quality research shows that students attending very homogeneous schools, with children all of one race (all white, all black) or all poor, achieve inferior academic results *compared to their peers in somewhat more diverse schools*.

The second trap is this: extremely diverse schools that do not have a strong quality backbone to support an individualized approach to education can fail for many children, too. More and more, these schools are catching and riding the wave towards differentiated learning, which as you'll see in our chapters about school quality, is critical to individual children's academic success.

In summary, the academic effect of peers is not always what parents have imagined. It's often not the peers that are the challenge, but the response of the school to its student population. Use our Great School and Great Fit tools if you want to ensure that a school does the most for your child academically, regardless of who else attends the school. (An important note: high quality research about peer effects has been conducted almost exclusively in student populations of white and African-American students. We look forward to sharing more information about other growing populations in the United States when high quality research is available.)

When is This a Priority for Your School Hunt?

You will need to decide what aspects of the student community are Must Haves for you. Research has consistently indicated that the seven Great School Quality Factors we explain in later chapters have a far more positive and potent impact on student achievement than a student's peers. You simply can't judge a school's quality based on what kinds of students make up the school community.

But you may have strong social preferences unrelated to your child's academic learning. These may be a stronger factor in your school choice if your ability to influence your child is limited or your child is very susceptible to peer influence.

I Want My Child to Attend a Certain School, School Type or School Design

What It Is, Why It's Important

Some of you may be embarrassed to admit it, but you would never send your child to a private school even though you can afford one. Others of you feel certain that no public school could offer the quality of education, or social contacts, you want for your child. Still others have it nailed down even further: the school you attended, your alma mater, produced the very best years of your life and you want your child to have the same experience. Or conversely, some feel you would never send your child to the school you attended; it was an awful place for you, and you'd never subject your child to that! Or you might have a bias towards a particular *design*, such as traditional, Montessori, or International Baccalaureate. Carefully consider whether you have strong feelings about a particular school, school type or design, including:

- ✔ Bias *toward* a *certain school*
- ✔ Bias *against* a *certain school*

- ✔ Bias *toward* a certain school *type*
- ✔ Bias *against* certain school *types*

- ✔ Bias *toward* a certain school *design*
- ✔ Bias *against* certain school *designs*

Whatever your bias, it's healthy for you to be candid with yourself about it. Remember that there are several school *types*:

➤ District public schools
➤ Public magnet schools

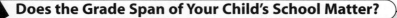

Smart à la Carte

Does the Grade Span of Your Child's School Matter?

Among the schools available to you, you may find varying grade spans. Some stick to a three-part model: elementary only (grades K–5 or 6 typically), middle only (grades 6 or 7–8), and high only (grades 9–12) or something quite similar. But some schools serve students in grades K–12, others K–8, K–3 or other configurations. And more and more schools include a pre-kindergarten year. Does it matter which grade span you choose?

Here's the scoop. The traditional grade breaks are largely based on social maturity and behavior changes typical among children. Indeed, even K–12 and K–8 schools often divide students into different campuses to avoid mixing of children in very different social phases. In a high quality school, grade breaks will matter little for academics, as Chapters 11 and 12 explain. But *you* may have preferences about whether your delightfully naïve 7-year-old should be exposed to overly-confident, worldly 13-year-olds. If so, make a note of it when considering Social Issues.

Perhaps more important to many a parent considering selective or limited-admissions schools, both public and private, is concern about getting your child admitted in later grades if you do not enroll in the earliest years. See the box *Up Your Odds: Understanding the Admissions Game* in Chapter 17 for more about that.

➤ Public charter schools
➤ Private religious schools
➤ Private independent schools
➤ Home schooling

And there are many school *designs*, which *may be used in any type* of school, including:

➤ Traditional
➤ Montessori
➤ International Baccalaureate
➤ Core Knowledge
➤ Many, many others! See pages 172-73 for more.

You may feel a bias because of family pressures, particularly if you live in the town or city where you grew up. For example, it might simply be easier for you to opt for the school your siblings have chosen for their children or that your parents have supported with financial gifts.

If choosing a certain school is indeed a Must Have, make it so. But you will need to make sure that your anointed school does not fall far short on any of your child's Must Haves and do a thorough quality exam, too. You will need to ensure that you accommodate for the school's shortcomings. You will feel only regret down the road if you realize that family or personal loyalty led you to put your child in a school where he was destined to be a fish out of water. On the other hand, if you ensure that your very creative child focuses her non-school activities (and some out-of-school friendships) on creative interests, then sending her to your traditional alma mater might be just fine. And so on.

If your child's best fit school is a type or design you had not considered, being *aware* of your bias might actually help you overcome it in the best interest of your child. Research has *not* consistently shown one *type or design* of school to be superior in quality – consistently producing students who achieve more than other students whose parents have similar incomes and education levels. The seven Great School Quality Factors have a much greater effect on student learning than the type or design of school.

Nonetheless, you may hold biases from your personal experience. Your feelings may be entangled with your values about teaching method, classroom behavior management, social peers for yourself and child or other aspects of school culture. You may, in fact, be able to find several schools that fit your needs and wants without adhering to the precise school, school type or design you had in mind. If you feel a bias about a certain school, school type or design, take time to jot down in words, or to discuss with your spouse or a trusted friend, *why* you feel that bias. As you become savvier about assessing school quality and fit issues, you will better be able to put this "gut" feeling into words and analyze it to see whether your bias still holds true.

When Is This a Priority for Your School Hunt?

We say: clarify your biases and include them in your decision process. If you would choose a certain school (or type or design) over a different one of better quality and fit, make this a Must Have. Or, note it as a Nice to Have in the event of a tie. Rest assured that it is better to be honest about what you want and need as a parent and family. Trust yourself to reconcile your bias with your child's needs and quality issues later.

PRACTICAL MATTERS

If logistics and finances are not big factors for you, then you might wonder how any parent could, in good conscience, pick a school based solely on these factors.

But many of you will find one or more of the following circumstances strongly influencing your school choice:

➤ Dual careers – limited time with child
➤ Multiple jobs – limited time with child
➤ Long work hours for the working parent (even when the other stays at home)
➤ Single parenting
➤ Multiple children
➤ Long distances (rural areas)
➤ Long commutes (crowded urban areas)
➤ A budget already stretched too thin

Most families have some restrictions on time, not to mention money, which will place constraints on school options. Certainly there are exceptions. Some families drive long distances and perform budgeting feats to place their children in the perfect school. But this should be necessary only if your child has unusual needs or if your area has very limited school options (of poor quality or poor fit).

Take stock of the practical constraints on your family and include them in your school hunt. For most families, practical matters will be Nice to Haves that you will be willing to bend if a school of superb quality and fit comes along. But if there are logistical elements that are truly Must Haves, by all means include them in your school search! Most of the practical matters are straightforward. Money is the one exception, and we will help you think about this one in some detail. But first, let's tick through the others so that your school hunt list will be complete.

The practical matters you will want to consider include these:

➤ *Child Care:* Do you need child care before or after school, during holidays and vacations, or during the summer?

➤ *Schedule:* Do you have constraints on your schedule, because of your work, your other children's schedules or other activities? Consider both daily schedule and yearly calendar.

➤ *Transportation:* What are your transportation needs, before and after school?

➤ *Location:* How important is school location? Is proximity to your home or work important?

➤ *Your Other Children:* What other conflicts with (or impact on) your other children are you concerned about (logistical or otherwise)?

➤ *Money:* How much money is available for your family to pay for school and related expenses?

Child Care

For this you need to ask yourself what your current and future child care needs are likely to be: what kind of care does your child need, when, and how much you can afford to pay? Then you must consider all the *sources* of child care available to you. Finally, you will want to compare your best non-school option to school care, in terms of quality, convenience, time covered and cost.

Child Care Needs:

➤ Consider what coverage you need in the hours before and after school, as well as holidays, vacations and summer.

➤ Consider all of your children's needs if you have more than one child.

➤ Consider any changes you are planning to make in your work or other activities that will affect child care needs.

➤ What services will you need from your child care provider? This may depend on the ages of your children and the amount of time they spend in care. Do you just need a safe environment for an hour or so of free play each afternoon? Or are educational environment and developmental appropriateness issues? Help with homework and time to do it? Structured activities or free play?

➤ Will your child need transportation to and from care?

➤ How much can you pay for the child care that you need?

Child Care Sources:

➤ Your current care: what type of child care are you using now? Can you keep using this same source after your child begins (or changes) school?

➤ Day care center

➤ Family home day care (small group of children at someone else's home)

➤ Nanny, your own or shared with another family

➤ Relatives, neighbors or friends

➤ Church, temple or other religious institutions

➤ School

➤ What are other sources of care in your city or town? Seek out your local child care resource and referral agency. Many cities have them now, and they can be a terrific source of information about what's available to you.

➤ How much would each of your options cost? How much does your favorite option, aside from school care, cost? This will give you a clear number to compare as you look at schools and the care they provide.

To the extent that you will have child care needs not met elsewhere, you must decide whether it is desirable (Nice to Have) or essential (Must Have) for school to provide your child with care. Include this in your *Personalized Great Fit Checklist.*

Schedule

You will need to consider both your daily and yearly schedule needs. If your other children are in schools with an early or late schedule, then having your third child in one with a similar schedule might be ideal (particularly if you work or have many other activities to fit into your day). On the other hand, some stay-at-home parents are *happy* to have their children in different schools with different daily and yearly schedules, because this gives them precious time alone with each child. You will need to decide what factors prevail and how important each is in choosing a school. Things to consider include these:

➤ Timing of morning and afternoon transportation for child(ren), especially with regard to multiple school schedules and conflicts with parents' work
➤ Impact of schedule on children's extracurricular activities (e.g., late schedule leaves less time for most activities)
➤ Desirability of having time alone with each child, on daily basis and during holidays and vacations
➤ Desirability of having time for your children to be together (for your benefit or theirs), daily and during vacations
➤ Impact of schools with differing vacation schedules on your family's vacations (especially if you like to travel *during* typical school year)
➤ Other schedule issues you may have.

Transportation

Think about what you can provide in the way of transportation for your child. Then you can determine what assistance you need from your child's school.

➤ Can your child walk to school (with or without you)?
➤ Can you drive your child to school?
➤ Would a neighborhood carpool meet your transportation needs?
➤ For older children, are there alternative transportation means available, such as city bus or subway?
➤ Are your morning and afternoon transportation needs different?
➤ Do you have time constraints, such as a certain time by which you need your child to be picked up in the morning or dropped off in the afternoon?
➤ Does your transportation need to be coordinated with your child care?

Having considered the above questions, do you need school busing or other school-provided transportation? If so, what are your Must Haves and Nice to Haves in terms of timing, cost, pick up and drop off location?

Some of you may have strong feelings about one mode or another of transportation. Put your feelings into perspective when you consider your child. While some of you may have found carpooling a great way to ruin neighborhood friendships (how many of us make our best buddies when we're sleepy or worn out?), it saves gas and parent time. Carpooling also lets your children develop relationships with other adults. Children also have a chance to get to know other children who live nearby, even when they are not exactly the same age or best pals.

Busing has negative connotations for many parents, too. You may be concerned about the amount of time your child may spend on the bus. But riding on a school bus, even without a seat belt, is significantly safer than riding in a car (*and* environment-friendly). Many (but certainly not all) children enjoy the unstructured social time with a variety of other children that a school bus ride provides. Others find the lack of structure unnerving. A child who is the target of teasing may find the limited adult supervision typical on school buses excruciating. A socially outgoing child, or even a quiet but self-confident one, will be fine on a safe school bus in most instances.

Location

Location can be a significant factor if you begin to consider very far away or very close alternatives or if you have severe time constraints. A less-than-perfect school one block away might be preferable to an almost perfect school an hour's commute from home. Of course this depends on *just how different* the two schools are in quality, fit, and distance, and on how crunched *you* are for time. Your child's time is an issue, as well, since time on the bus or sitting in carpool is time that could be spent on favorite extracurricular activities, homework, exercise or good old fashioned down time. The extra time you have in the afternoon *may*, in some cases, allow you to accommodate for a nearby school's weaknesses.

You may prefer a school close to work rather than home. If you work outside the home, you will have extra time at work – and no less with your child – if you can pick her up from a school near your work.

Location also will also affect other Fit Factors, such as having neighbors and friends in school, your involvement in activities at school, transportation and child care. Only you can decide if closeness is a Must Have or merely a minor convenience. Consider these questions:

➤ Does location matter to you, and why?
➤ Do you prefer a location close to home, work, or your other children's schools?
➤ Does your child's school location impact your transportation or child care needs?

Your Other Children

If you have more than one child, you most likely will have touched upon the most obvious multi-child issues in the social and other logistical sections. The practicality of dealing with multiple schools as a parent, of ensuring transportation, of differing daily and perhaps yearly schedules may drive some of your school decision-making.

If you have children who are far apart in age, you may be dealing with multiple schools anyway. Unless you opt for a K–12 school with a single campus, or luck into appropriate schools with similar schedules located near each other, you're going to feel like a professional juggler before it's over! Of course, if you've juggled baby plus toddler plus older child already, you're no amateur. Your life is already full of twists and turns. You will have to decide whether having each child in a better quality, better fit school to meet their individual needs is worth a bit more complexity.

Living in a Sibling's Shadow

For any of you who followed a well-known older sibling to school, you know that an older sibling can cast a large and looming shadow in the mind of the younger. Most children yearn to find and express their individuality, and this pursuit most certainly is valued and encouraged in our society. But it can be hard for a child to find his own path when one has already been cut by a sibling; it means working harder to be himself than to follow along.

On the upside, siblings can offer personal, social and academic support to each other when they attend the same school at the same time. They are a ready-made chat in the hallway or at lunch time that puts both at ease. They can be on-the-scene trouble-shooters when problems arise. They are the people one can tell about the A+ right away without feeling like a bragger, or cry to about the unexpected F with no fear of rejection. If your children support each other, having them in the same school can be a treat.

However, if one sibling – no matter how smart or successful – makes the other feel small, constrained, less capable and empowered than the other would feel elsewhere, then having them in different schools where they can blaze their own trails may be the better decision. Sometimes, an extremely successful child can induce those feelings in a sibling unintentionally. Similarly, if you have a child who has had severe behavioral or academic problems, you might consider other schools for younger siblings. Siblings cast shadows both positive and negative. You won't want your younger child to feel hesitant about shining more brightly than the older one. Avoiding the good kid, bad kid comparison is easier when children are in different schools altogether.

We are not denying the many practical benefits to you as parents of having your children in the same school. If your children show many of the same interests, needs and talents, or they are quite self-confident about their different interests and talents, by all means consider the same school. But if you have a child, older *or* younger, who casts a very strong shadow, then consider the impact on your other children of having them in the same school.

Money

If you want to consider private schools for your child, you will need to spend some time determining just how much you can afford to pay. Will it be worth the expense? In some cases yes and others no. (See box *Does Paying More Get More for Your Child?*)

Your job for *now* is to determine how much money you can contribute towards your child's education, *if* needed. You'll benefit from this exercise even if you think you cannot afford private school. It will free you to consider more appropriate options, and at the end of the day you will be better for knowing exactly why you made the school decision you did. And even if you decide not to go private, you will know what funds you can make available for outside-of-school programs that meet your child's needs.

Don't let the money tail wag the quality and fit dog. Choose a school for quality and fit first, not the price tag.

Most private schools have some scholarship students and students whose parents work extra to afford private school, so don't assume you will be alone if you stretch to afford one. (Of course, if you are dripping with money from the sale of your soaring start-up or the family till, you may not need to bother with this exercise, unless you want to get some perspective on your child's classmates!)

Many of you are already spending money on your child's education and school-hour care. Any funds you currently spend on the following items can be rolled into one lump and reallocated for your child's education:

➤ Child care during school hours
➤ Child care immediately before and after school
➤ Preschool tuition, fees, donations and gifts
➤ School tuition, fees, donations and gifts
➤ School supplies for home
➤ Educational toys for home
➤ Extracurricular activities
➤ Educational outings and travel
➤ Clothing for your child
➤ Breakfast and lunch for your child

Smart à la Carte

Does Paying More Get More for Your Child?

Will paying more money get your child a better education? Maybe. Maybe not. High quality, unbiased research says there's little relationship between school cost and quality. There's little evidence that tuition-charging private schools, on average, teach children more than free public schools do. And public schools with more money to spend don't necessarily outpace schools with less (for similar students).

That said, money well spent – for example, to clarify high educational standards, to monitor individual student progress, to ensure that every student actually learns in school – improves quality. In fact, a wealthy school, private or public, that focuses its money on real quality and Fit Factors important to the stated mission can achieve phenomenal results for its students and their families. But the fact is that some wealthy schools, public and private, fritter away funds on flashy, parent-enticing gimmicks that do not improve student learning. Many well-established private schools, with their easy flow of student siblings, alumni children and new families looking for a sure thing, fall victim to the same complacency that haunts many public schools with captive audiences. No doubt, many private schools use their financial resources to provide exceptional quality for every child admitted. But some well-established schools begin to believe the myth that selective admissions make a student body homogeneous, allowing a cookie-cutter approach to instruction.

Sadly, we have heard parents tell tales of their children – *highly* gifted in academics, creativity, or the arts – whose gifts were left to rot on the vine despite a high tuition bill. Similarly, students who struggle, perhaps admitted by virtue of alumni or sibling status or with an undiagnosed mild disability, are asked to seek tutoring from outside sources instead of having their needs met at school. And so on. It simply takes too much effort to meet these children's needs consistently at school when that school has become complacent about individual children's learning.

No matter what you pay, many of you will want to know that your child is getting the best you can afford. How can you tell whether it's worth the money for private school? In some cases, it will be the best money you ever spend and the greatest gift you ever give your child. In others, it's a waste of your money and a loss for your child. Fortunately, you will have resources parents before you have not had. The seven Great School Quality Factors and your *Personalized Great Fit Checklist* will help you make an excellent assessment of your Target Schools' strengths and weaknesses. You will be able to compare schools directly on the factors most important for your child and family, and you can make a clear-headed decision about whether and when the extra money for private tuition will in fact buy a superior education for *your* child.

An Example

Let's assume that Ann, a widow, is paying $4,000 per year for her son Roger's full time child care, $600 for his clothes, $400 for his lunches on school days, plus an additional $1,000 for school supplies, educational toys and educational outings. So, she is paying a total of $6,000 for these items altogether.

A great quality private school offering the traditional approach that Roger needs is on Ann's way to work. The private school tuition is $8,000, seemingly out of reach on her wages. However, books are included in tuition. Uniforms are required, dropping Roger's annual clothing needs to $350. And Roger qualifies for a partial need-based scholarship that will cover $3,500 of tuition and a school lunch pass. Ann's mother, who felt uncomfortable keeping Roger by herself all day when he was younger, is happy to keep him from 3:30 when the bus drops him off until his Mom gets home at 5:30. If Ann's spending on school supplies, educational toys and outings stays steady, then her spending will actually decline by $150.

	Ann's Preschool Spending	Ann's Private School Cost
Tuition/Fees	$0	$8000-$3500 = $4500
Child Care	$4000	$0
Clothes	$600	$350
Lunches	$400	$0
School Books	$0	$0
Supplies/Toys	$1000	$1000
Total	$6000	$5850

If Ann had assumed that the private school was out of reach, then Roger – and Ann – would have lost out!

Steps to Determine How Much Money You Have for School

Your goal is to determine three facts about your family:

1. *Current* School Spending: How much are you paying for school-related child expenses *now*?
2. *Target* School Spending: How much could you *comfortably* pay, without unwanted changes in work or debt, once your child starts school?
3. *Maximum* School Spending: What is the *most* you could pay, with acceptable changes in work and debt, should your best quality, best fit school require it?

In some families, these three numbers will be the same: you are paying all you can now, and there is no tolerable way to increase your income. Or numbers 1 and 2 may be the same: you could obtain more money, but only by taking on debt or having a second job (or a stay-at-home parent going back to work unexpectedly). Only you can decide how far you are willing to push yourself and your financial security.

Take these steps to assess your finances (or use our *Heads or Tails Money Worksheet* on page 154):

1. Tally the ***amount you are spending now*** on your child's clothing, school-hour food, child care, school donations, teacher gifts and other education and care-related expenses. This is your "Current" spending.

2. Determine how much ***"extra" income,*** above your current yearly income, you are likely to make each year between now and when your child graduates from high school. (You may extend this timeline out to cover multiple children and college years, if you like). "Extra" income is anything more than you are making now, but not including an average 3.5% annual increase in pay. Possible sources include:
   ➤ Raises you expect that will exceed the 3.5% cost-of-living level.
   ➤ Increases in the amount of work you or your spouse does. For example, if Mom or Dad is staying at home and earning no income now, but will resume work when your youngest starts kindergarten in two years, then that expected income will be "extra" for each year of work.
   ➤ Other bumps up in income. If a parent is in a job in which pay goes up significantly after a certain number of years (e.g., by making supervisor, by making partner in a law firm), note the year that extra income will begin.
   You will need to make sure taxes have been subtracted from any income you add. The tax amount depends on your tax bracket, state income tax, and current tax laws. Subtracting 35% is a guideline for middle income earners. (For example: $10,000 of "extra" income is worth $6,500 after taxes are subtracted.)

3. Determine any ***"extra" expenses,*** above your current annual budget, you are likely to have each year between now and when your child finishes high school (or whatever time line you have chosen).
   ➤ "Extra" expenses are ones you do not pay for out of your current annual income, and that are beyond what would be covered by a typical 3.5% pay increase.
   ➤ Example extra expenses are college savings, retirement savings, new house down payment, roof or other major home repairs, having more children, allowance for medical and other emergencies, car or other major expenses not currently coming out of your regular annual income.

4. Determine what *expenses you are willing to cut from your regular spending.* Do not limit your thinking to education and child-related expenses only. Consider all of your spending. If packing your lunch for work four days each week would save $1,000 each year, is that worth it? Do you really need two cell phones in your family? Do you watch TV enough to justify the full cable package? And so on. Only you can decide what lifestyle changes, if any, you are willing to make in your family.

The total you get after all that is your "Target" spending, though many of you will choose to spend far less in the end, of course.

To get your "Maximum," consider alternative sources of money, depending on which are both available and amenable to you. Examples:

➤ An extra job for one or both parents
➤ Seeking overtime when available in wage-earning jobs
➤ Employment at your school of choice in exchange for reduced tuition
➤ Selling assets you own (e.g., your extra car, stock)
➤ Scholarships, both need-based (depending on your family income and assets) and merit-based (for your child's achievement or potential)
➤ Debt (e.g., a second mortgage, home equity line of credit, or credit card debt)
➤ Grandparents or other relatives
➤ School vouchers (in limited locations only)

Sometimes the question about money is "when?" rather than "how much?" For example, if a parent is in a job where pay starts relatively low but increases substantially later, your family might have enough money to pay for any school you want, but not soon enough to pay for elementary school. Or if a parent plans to return to work when children are in school, family income might increase substantially, but not *soon* enough for your oldest child's early schooling. In these cases, you will need to decide whether it is feasible and desirable to pursue a short-term source of money in the early years, remembering that you will pay both for school and interest if you take on debt.

Making Sense of it All

This chapter has covered a lot of ground, from social issues to practical matters. Add that to the other Fit Factors for your family, and to the child needs you've identified, and you're probably accumulating quite a list. But don't panic! In Chapter 10, you get the payoff – a clear sense of what you need to look for to find a school that fits your child and family.

No matter what, or whether, you pay for your child's school directly, be sure the school spends money where it counts – on quality and your top fit needs.

What To Do

➤ *Refer back to your Family "Quick Think"* on page 109 to refresh your memory regarding things that really stand out about your family. Estimated Time: 2 minutes

➤ *Use the Family Needs Summary* on page 110 to get a quick fix on the Fit Factor #3 Social Issues and #4 Practical Matters needs and preferences. Estimated Time: 10 minutes

➤ *Use the Know Your Family's Needs table* on page 375 to further clarify your family's Fit Factor #3 and 4 needs and preferences and the importance of each for choosing a school. You need not read the whole table: focus only on items you believe are important for your family. Estimated Time: 20 minutes

➤ *Discuss your family's needs* with your spouse or other parenting partner. Estimated Time: As needed

➤ *Assess your family's financial situation* and money available to pay for school and other education-related items. Use the *Heads or Tails Money Worksheet* on page 154. Estimated Time: 1 – 2 hours, or more depending on how good a grasp you have on your income and expenses

➤ *Record your Must Haves and Nice to Haves* on your *Family Needs Summary* (page 110). Estimated Time: 15 minutes

Need more? Want more? Got more to share? Visit PickyParent.com.

Heads or Tails Money Worksheet

STEP 1: Determine your current spending on education related items for your child. If you have multiple children, you will need to do STEP 1 for each child and add it up for each year.

Current Education Spending:	*$ Amount*
School or Preschool Tuition, Fees.....................	_____
Child Care During School Hours.....................	_____
Before and After School Child Care..................	_____
School Donations	_____
School Supplies for Home	_____
Educational Toys for Home	_____
Extracurricular Activities..........................	_____
Educational Outings and Travel	_____
Clothing for Child	_____
Breakfast, Lunch for Child.........................	_____

TOTAL $ _____ = *Current Spending*

STEP 2: Determine "extra" income above your current that you are likely to make each year between now and when your child graduates from high school. "Extra" is anything more than you are making now, not including an average 3.5% pay increase each year. Start with the year extra income will begin. Work in today's dollars; do not consider inflation. *Before you add income year by year, make sure taxes have been subtracted (-35% is a guideline).*

Sources:
"Extra" income you earn now but do not spend
Raises you expect above 3.5%
Increase in amount of work you or spouse plan to do (new or more jobs)
Other bumps up in income expected (e.g., promotions, making partner)

STEP 3: Determine "extra" expenses likely above your annual budget between now and the year your child will graduate from high school. "Extra" expenses are ones you do not currently pay for out of your annual income and that are beyond what would be covered by a typical 3.5% pay increase. Work in today's dollars; do not consider inflation.

Possible extra expenses include at least these:
Savings for college and retirement
New house down payment, new roof or other major house repairs
Having additional children
Allowance for medical or other emergencies
Car or other major purchases beyond current spending

STEP 4: Determine what expenses you are willing to cut from your regular spending every year. Do not limit your thinking to education and child-related expenses.

Examples:
Pack children's and your work lunches 4 days per week
Limit yourself to one cell phone per family, at most
Limit your cable TV package to the basics
And so on — think about expenses that are not meaningful to your family.
Amount we are willing to cut yearly: $ _____

Continues...

Heads or Tails Money Worksheet ...continued

STEP 5: Do the math, year by year, to find your "Target" spending: Determine how much money you will have each year for education expenses listed in STEP 1. This is your yearly "Target" (though you may choose to spend less).

Use this handy formula:

$$\text{Current Educational Expense} + \text{Extra Income} - \text{Extra Expenses} + \text{Expenses Cut} = \text{Yearly Available Amount ("Target")}$$

STEP 6: To find your "Maximum," consider extra sources of money to pay for school, including:

An extra job for one or both parents
Seeking overtime when available in wage-earning jobs
Employment at your private school of choice in exchange for reduced tuition
Scholarships, both need based and merit based
Debt: second mortgage, home equity line, credit card. Add debt interest to extra expenses.
Grandparents or other relatives
School vouchers (limited locations only)
Assets you could sell (e.g., extra car, stock)

Math Station

Year	Your Child's Grade	STEP 1: Current Spending ("Current")	STEP 2: + Extra Income	STEP 3: – Extra Expenses	STEP 4: + Expenses Cut	STEP 5: =Yearly Amount Available ("Target")	STEP 6: + Extra $ Sources? ("Maximum")
1	K						
2	1st						
3	2nd						
4	3rd						
5	4th						
6	5th						
7	6th						
8	7th						
9	8th						
10	9th						
11	10th						
12	11th						
13	12th						

NOTES:

1. This worksheet provides an estimate only and is in current dollars. We assume that increases in regular income will cover yearly increases in expenses, including education-related expenses.

2. Private school tuition may increase at a rate different from overall inflation or your pay increases.

3. If your income will cover private school in later years but not early years, borrowing money for earlier years may be an option. Include estimated debt interest in your Extra Expenses. Alternatively, consider private school an option for middle or high school but not elementary.

Know What You Need
from a School

LIGHT'NING LIST

What To Know from Chapter 10

➤ **Deciding what a school should offer to fit** your child and family needs is the next step. The *Great Fit Triangle* (page 162) and *Fit Factors Unfolded* table (page 177) show school differences that affect fit.

➤ **You can use our short-cut tables to identify the specific ways schools can meet your needs** – *Child Needs: What to Look for in a School* (page 380) and *Family Needs: What to Look for in a School* (page 400).

➤ **Think for yourself about how a school can meet your needs.** You should consider:
  ✔ *How exclusively focused on children and families like yours is the school? Or, how effectively does the school individualize learning for children?* If you choose a school focused on children or families like yours, make sure the school is a very good fit. A school adept at meeting many needs may have fewer children and families just like yours, but is more likely to fit your changing needs and multiple children.
  ✔ *How much will a school tap and build your child's strengths?* A school should appreciate and support children who have strengths like your child's.
  ✔ *How much will a school develop your child's weaknesses?* You shouldn't choose a school entirely focused on your child's weaknesses, nor one that will ignore them. Look for a school that will develop your child's weaknesses so that they do not keep your child from using and enjoying strengths.

➤ **School type** (for example, private or public) and **school design** (like Montessori) can matter for fit. But you'll want to look beyond a school's "label" and **find out what the school is really like** before making a choice.

➤ **Prioritize among your many child and family needs.** When you get down to the business of choosing a school, know that you may need to prioritize among even your Must Haves.

Chapter 10

The Puzzle Solved: A Personalized Profile of Your Great Fit School

What Kind of School Will Meet Your Needs?

You know your child's and family's needs, or at least you're headed in that direction. Now what? Even when you know your needs, it is not always easy to know the many ways that a school can meet them.

When you start looking at schools (or if you've already been around the block with your older child), you'll see that they vary in many, sometimes confusing, ways. One school says it has high standards because teachers cover a lot of subjects. Another also says it has high standards, but focuses mainly on the basics. One uses a tried and true teaching method, another seems to be trying several different approaches in the classroom all at once. One is beautiful – lovely, neat classrooms with stimulating displays – while another school is chock full of materials but not so neat looking. One school's classrooms are so quiet you can hear a pin drop, another school's classrooms seem to have constant buzz. One school's students are all dressed similarly, another's students wear uniforms, while still another's students are very different from each other in dress and other ways, as well. It can be overwhelming to experience so many different environments during your concentrated school hunt. Which school differences really matter for *your* child and family?

In this chapter, we'll help you determine what a school should offer to meet your child and family needs. With some needs, there is a clear best fit way to meet the need: other approaches are a distant second best. With other needs, there are a lot of ways to "skin the cat" (or the apple, for animal lovers). We'll help you explore all of the options and think for yourself on these matters, *with confidence* of course.

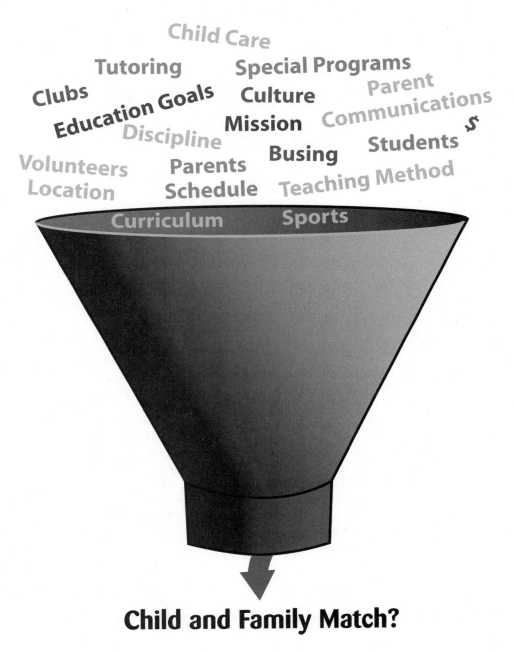

Specifically, Chapter 10 will prepare you to find a Great Fit school. It will help you:

1. *Identify what you should seek in a school* to fit your specific, common child and family needs using our tables

2. *Think for yourself* about what you want in a school to fit your child and family needs

3. *Understand how school type, school design and school culture* can affect multiple fit needs, and

4. *Prioritize* among your many child and family needs.

You'll likely find this chapter a satisfying confidence-builder, whether or not you are working through the *Confident Choice Tools* while you read. You'll start to get a picture of the school elements that may work best for your child and family. These elements will become so familiar to you that you'll soon be able to spot schools that fit (and those that don't) quickly and accurately. There's no better confidence-builder than being very well informed and ready to take action.

When you are ready, this book will help you complete your own *Personalized Great Fit Checklist* – summarizing on one page your child and family Must Haves and what *you* want in a school to meet those needs. This little tool will be your constant companion later as you explore schools available to your child.

The Great Fit Triangle: The Third Piece of the Puzzle

You won't be surprised to find that the Great Fit Triangle is our first stop on the way to matching your needs to school offerings. The third part of the Triangle shows the offerings of schools that differ to address the varying needs of children and their families.

It's no coincidence that the Great Fit Triangle has three interlocked puzzle pieces. School and family should work together as a team for you and your child. When they do, your child will benefit and you can share the education load with your child's school. When they don't, you or your child will suffer.

If family life develops your child in the ways that school doesn't, your child has the chance to grow and develop into a well-rounded adult without one area (e.g., social skills) inhibiting his ability to use the others (e.g., academic skills). Similarly, if school fills voids in your family life (e.g., time for physical exercise), especially when family time is very limited, your child will be all the better. And if you are

Great Fit Triangle

Matching Child and Family Needs with School Offerings

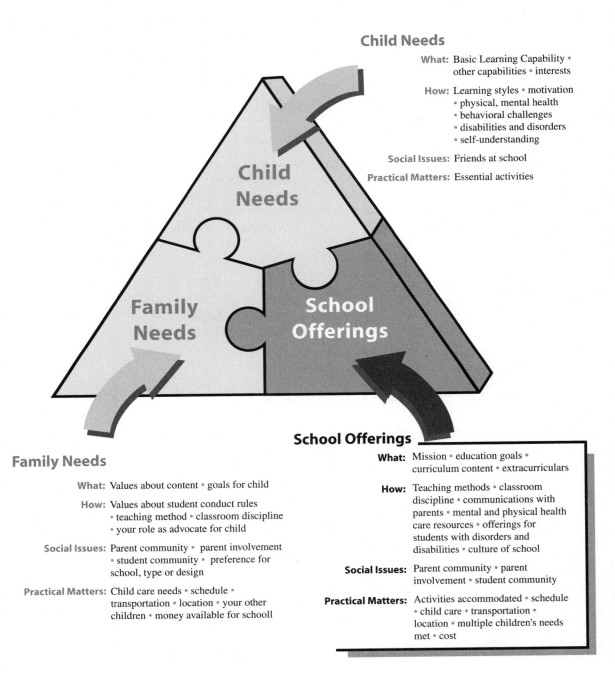

Child Needs

What: Basic Learning Capability • other capabilities • interests

How: Learning styles • motivation • physical, mental health • behavioral challenges • disabilities and disorders • self-understanding

Social Issues: Friends at school

Practical Matters: Essential activities

Family Needs

What: Values about content • goals for child

How: Values about student conduct rules • teaching method • classroom discipline • your role as advocate for child

Social Issues: Parent community • parent involvement • student community • preference for school, type or design

Practical Matters: Child care needs • schedule • transportation • location • your other children • money available for schooll

School Offerings

What: Mission • education goals • curriculum content • extracurriculars

How: Teaching methods • classroom discipline • communications with parents • mental and physical health care resources • offerings for students with disorders and disabilities • culture of school

Social Issues: Parent community • parent involvement • student community

Practical Matters: Activities accommodated • schedule • child care • transportation • location • multiple children's needs met • cost

fortunate enough for school and family to reinforce each other – promoting and teaching the same values along with a broad set of life skills – the more likely your child is to develop a *strong and well-rounded* set of knowledge, skills, values and habits consistent with your parental desires.

Focus on the Four Fit Factors

Some school differences affect school quality, some affect fit with child and family needs, and some affect both. Here, we are focusing on school differences that affect fit. (Chapters 11 – 14 will address quality.)

So how can you, the parent, make sense of the jumble of characteristics you see when you begin to investigate schools? As with your child and family *needs*, you can use our four Fit Factors to understand how one school's *offerings* differ from another's:

➤ *What Your Child Learns:* Schools differ greatly in their overall educational "mission," which is a statement of what a school aims to accomplish and why. Schools also vary in the range of subjects taught, how challenging the educational goals are for each child, and extracurricular offerings.

➤ *How Your Child Learns:* Schools differ in how teachers instruct students, both in their main approaches used for all students and alternative approaches used for students with particular needs and challenges. Schools vary in their disciplinary policies and practices (in and out of the classroom) and the overall culture of interaction between the school, students, and parents.

➤ *Social Issues:* When you choose a school, you're choosing a unique group of kids and adults with whom you and your child will spend time. Social Issues include the school's social norms and values as well as the characteristics of its students and parents. The types and levels of parent participation in the school community are part of this Factor, too.

➤ *Practical Matters:* Each school has its own daily and annual schedule, transportation system, and location. Some offer before and after school care, some don't. Some are free of charge, others charge anywhere from a lot to a little in tuition.

If you've given some thought to your child's and family's needs within the four Fit Factors, you're ready to start thinking about what school offerings will meet those needs. To see how school offerings line up with child and family needs, skim down the columns of our *Fit Factors Unfolded* table on page 177.

What Matters for Matching A **School** to My Child and Family?

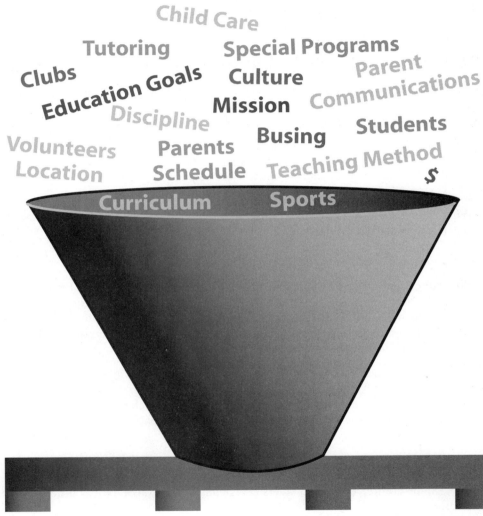

Child Care
Tutoring
Special Programs
Clubs
Culture
Parent
Education Goals
Communications
Mission
Discipline
Students
Busing
Volunteers
Parents
Teaching Method
Location
Schedule
$
Curriculum
Sports

What?
- Mission
- Goals for students
- Curriculum content
- Extracurricular offerings

How?
- Teaching method
- Discipline
- Communication with parents
- Health care
- Disability/disorder offerings
- Culture

Social?
- Parent community
- Parent involvement
- Student community

Practical?
- Activities
- Child care
- Schedule
- Transportation
- Location
- Meets needs of many children
- Cost

Short-Cut Tables for Common Child and Family Needs

We know you're picky about these matters (and we like that). But you're also busy. It takes work to think through all of these issues on your own. Fortunately, most children and families have needs shared by many others. We have taken some of the most common needs – those included in the *Child* and *Family Needs Summaries* – and identified the characteristics of schools that best meet those needs.

While we twisted your arm in Chapters 2 – 9 to get you to at least *consider* all of the many needs and wants your child and family might have, in this section we let you focus on those items most important to you. The specific school pre-scriptions for common child and family needs appear in tables rather than text, so you may focus only on the material that's relevant to you. "More tables?" you say. "Oh no!" Don't worry: you need read *only* those sections pertaining to your own child and family. We won't subject parents of typical kids to reading the really annoying prescriptions for "highly gifted" kids, and we won't rattle the rest of us mere working folk with ideas for parents who find themselves with extra cash on hand to support their children's educations!

If you begin to feel uncertain about what to seek, focus on one top child Must Have and Great School Quality Factors #2 and 3.

The tables *Child Needs: What to Look for in a School* (page 380) and *Family Needs: What to Look for in a School* (page 400) translate your common needs into matching school offerings. In reading the tables, focus just on the items that you have identified as Must Haves first, then circle back to your top Nice to Haves. In many instances, a school may meet your needs in one of several ways, leaving you more flexibility. As you go, note "What to Look For" on your *Personalized Great Fit Checklist* (page 59).

Thinking for Yourself: Matching School Offerings to Your Needs

Our *What to Look for in a School* tables will help you with specific issues, but you really can and should *think for yourself* about what to look for in a school. You may have needs different from the common ones listed in the *Child* and *Family Needs Summaries,* you may prefer to think things through for yourself, or you may just want a better understanding of how to find a Great Fit school. In many instances, you will find that there are multiple ways to address a need, which leaves you more flexible to seek quality and a better overall child and fam-ily fit, too. This section will give a sense of the *range* of school options and the tradeoffs you make with different kinds of schools.

Some fit needs, particularly family needs, are easier to translate than others. For example, if you need a certain location, schedule, child care or transportation, you can look for schools that directly fit the bill. If religious education is a school Must Have for your family's children – and you have no other conflicting Must Haves – you can narrow the list quickly to schools that address your religious group. If the kind of families and students attending a school is a major concern – e.g., you want school friends who live nearby or you want your child exposed to international students – you can ask pointed questions about each school's population. If you want a school addressing certain content, you can ask if and how each school covers that material.

Thinking for yourself never goes out of style.

In other cases, it is harder to translate your needs into school offerings. What *should* a school do to conform to your family's values? To meet the needs of academically challenged children? Gifted children? Learning disabled children? Go-get-'em, super-motivated children? Bright but unmotivated children? And so on. The answers are not always apparent, particularly when it comes to your *child's* characteristics.

Fortunately, many needs – even when they are compelling Must Haves - may be met in multiple ways. For example, most academically gifted students may be educated effectively in special schools for gifted children, in special programs within larger schools, in more diverse schools that break children into small (ever-changing) groups by current achievement level, in schools where learning is self-paced, or in schools that carve out one-on-one time for teacher and student (including home school). A similarly broad range of schools – from those that admit only children and families meeting certain criteria to those adept at individualized learning for many types of children – will address many of your needs.

So how do you distinguish among these options? Consider these three questions:
➤ How *exclusively focused on children and families like yours* is the school? (Or: how effectively does the school individualize learning for children?)
➤ How much will a school *tap and build* your child's strengths?
➤ How much will a school *develop your child's weaknesses*?

How exclusively focused on children and families like yours is the school?

Some schools target a particular kind of child or family – e.g., families of a certain religious or ethnic background, children who learn well sitting and listening in a big group, academically challenged children, bright children who need motivation – and set out to meet the needs of that limited population only. Other schools are adept at meeting the needs of a broad range of children and families. The more of the school day spent in activities tailored to your values and your child's capabilities, interests, learning styles and other characteristics, the more enjoyable and fruitful your child's schooling will be. But, the more specialized or focused a school is, the more important it is that you have made *just* the right match.

Many families choose schools, both public and private, with a one-size-fits-all approach only to find that the curriculum targets the wrong level of learning (too advanced without support for their struggling children or too slow) or wrong learning style. You must be *sure* to make the right match with highly focused or selective schools, so that your child will not be an academic or social fish out of water. Research clearly shows that there is lost opportunity in any school that focuses the curriculum entirely on the "average" student, even the average in that particular school. Even highly selective schools will have students with a broad range of abilities and learning needs (especially if siblings or alumni are favored in admissions). *Watch carefully for signs that your child's needs are not being met if you choose a school offering a one-size-fits-all curriculum or teaching method.*

Fortunately, many schools find ways to accommodate a broader range of children and families:

> ➤ *Providing a special program housed within a larger school* so that all of a child's academic work is done with similar children, but informal contact may occur with other children. You must make sure such a program is a good fit and that your child is comfortable being perceived as "different" by children not in the special program. Special programs are *not* effective if they are used to lower expectations for struggling students.

> ➤ *Dividing all students up into small work groups* to address their varying needs for most school work. Children will spend a large portion of the school day working at their current level of capability, and teachers are more likely to lock onto your child's interests and learning style than in large group. Watch out for schools that provide only a weekly pullout for "gifted" or "remedial" education, as these will provide little long-term benefit to your child. Instead, small group learning should consume a *large portion* of each school day and week and should be used to engage and challenge your child, not to lower expectations. Small groups should *not* be set for an entire school year, but should change very frequently as needed (weekly). Children learn in fits and starts, and frequent changes in the groupings should reflect this fact. Note: If your child is very strong visual or auditory learner, she may have trouble with the noise and feeling of disorder at transition times unless this process is managed with skill and discipline.

> ➤ *Rotating children through one-on-one teacher-child activities,* in combination with large group or small group activities. A great arrangement for chil-

If your child will be different from the norm in a school, find out whether children like yours are treated kindly and with respect.

dren who need the extra motivation that a little undivided attention inspires. Although less time in the overall day may be focused on work at your child's current level of capability, most homework and some class work can be *highly* tailored to individual needs.

➤ *Rotating all children through a* variety *of learning activities* geared to meet the needs of each student for at least some portion of the day. All students have the opportunity for a few inspiring and engaging moments and the chance to develop weaknesses as well as strengths. Your child *may* have less time in day working at the appropriate level (ask how activities are selected for children). Note: If your child is a very strong visual or auditory learner, she may have trouble with the noise and feeling of disorder at transition times unless this process is managed with skill and discipline.

How much will a school tap and build your child's strengths?

It is unlikely that your child will ever feel great about a school if your child's greatest strengths are not valued or addressed by the school. At best, yours will be one of those children waiting for the better days of college or work. At worst, your child may feel unappreciated and socially isolated (if the school tends to attract children very different from yours). On the other hand, even children with tremendous strengths – be they academic, artistic, social or other – need additional skills and knowledge to function happily and successfully in our world. So an overdose on your child's strengths, particularly if other important developmental needs aren't addressed, may not be the best choice, either.

You need to choose a school that, at the very least, respects and encourages your child's strengths. Beyond that, you and your child will need to decide just how much the child's strengths need to be addressed and how important it is for your child to attend school with children who have similar strengths.

How much will a school develop your child's weaknesses?

Help your child strike a balance: find a school that offers your child the chance to improve academic, social, emotional and physical weaknesses without dwelling on them for a large part of the day. Is your child academically challenged? Don't start a mover-and-shaker letter campaign to gain admission to a school that typically admits only very bright students. Do find a school that provides high academic expectations and the focus on basics, repetition and tutoring he'll need. Does your child have motivation challenges, such as difficulty setting goals and dealing with challenges? Don't torture her with an unstructured school where children are expected to be highly self-directed. Do find a school with a structured goal-setting process to ensure children are challenged.

Remember: it's not just your child's current achievement at stake, but also the long-term discipline and confidence needed to achieve your child's own goals for herself. You'll want your child to feel that she can overcome weaknesses, learn to enjoy strengths despite the weaknesses, and develop the concrete skills for making it happen.

School Type, School Design, School Culture

The *What to Look for* tables are helpful because they are very specific: they tell you particular things to seek to match your child and family needs. Many parents ask us: what about the "big picture"? Shouldn't we decide, first, whether we want a private or a public school? Or: isn't there some well-known "school design," like Montessori or International Baccalaureate, that we should be looking for above all else? Or: can't I just get a feel for a school's "culture" and go on that?

School type, design, and culture certainly can matter for fit. But here's our message: you can't learn everything you need to know about a school by looking at the label on the outside. The fact that a school is private or public, or a magnet or charter school, doesn't tell you much about whether it will fit your needs. A school's design and culture tell you more. But even within a well-defined design, there's a lot of variation from one school to the next. And while some aspects of culture are readily observable when you walk into a school, others that you can't see without digging a bit more deeply may or may not fit your Must Have needs. You still need to look inside the particular school and see what it's *really* like.

That said, type, design, and culture can make a difference. Here are some thoughts on how and when.

School Type

The types of schooling available in your community may include:

➤ district public schools (regular or magnet),
➤ public charter schools,
➤ private independent schools,
➤ private religious schools,
➤ special programs within other schools of all types, and
➤ home schools.

Research has not shown a consistent difference in *quality* based on school type alone. Because school type does not determine quality, and because it affects so few *child* needs, we encourage you to consider schools other than your top-pick type. Many parents who *never* dreamed they would "go public" or "go private" have done so when they realized that a truly critical child (or family) need could best be met in a school that did not fit their pre-conceived notions.

Nonetheless, the school type (or the particular school) is something you should consider *if* one of the following is a Must Have or top Nice to Have:

Family

➤ *Social Issues: I want my child to attend a certain school or school type.*
   If you determine that you strongly prefer (or don't like) one type of school, or one school in particular, then the school or school type is a matter for you to consider in your school hunt. Note *why* this is important to you on your *Personalized Great Fit Checklist.*

➤ *Practical Matters: Money available for school.*
   Some types of school will cost you more "out of pocket" than others, and you may not want to waste time exploring schools that simply aren't feasible financially. But, scholarships or vouchers may be available to your child to cover or reduce the cost of a private or religious school, so do not dismiss a school for cost alone until you've explored these wallet-builders.

School Design

Schools may use an existing design already in use by other schools, or they may hammer out their own. Common examples of pre-existing designs are listed and described in the table on page 172. Visit *PickyParent.com* for more information and links to websites of school designs you are considering.

For schools that have one, an overall design often means that the school mission, curriculum, teaching method and other elements of school life adhere to a pre-scribed way of thinking about children and education. A school's design *may* cover all aspects of school life, from philosophy to practical matters like the schedule. But many existing school designs cover only *some* aspects of school life, such as the content of what's taught and the teaching method.

Knowing a school's design can help you make a quick judgment about fit – when the design affects issues important to you or your child. Beware, though, that even schools subscribing to particular designs can vary quite a bit. Before you settle on a school, you'll need to ask questions about your specific needs to know just how well the school will fit. If you are considering a special program within a larger school, it is important to find out just how much the program's daily practices follow the routines of the larger school.

Many schools do not use a pre-existing design. Instead they create their own or pick and choose from among the elements of others. If you can't get a handle on a school's overall design, fear not: you can look for the specific things you need in a school using our short-cut tables, *Child Needs: What to Look for in a School* and *Family Needs: What to Look for in a School.* In fact, you need to do that even if a school says it's using a certain design.

What About "School Culture"?

Sure, a school may have an explicit design that determines what is taught, and how. But what about the more subtle aspects of a school: the dress code, expected and actual student behavior, manners among students and staff, the values of the children and families attracted to the school? All of these policies, practices and aspects of the school community define how a school expects people to treat each other and which values – such as honesty, kindness, respect for different ideas and teamwork – are reinforced and which are not. Together they make up a school's "culture."

Shouldn't parents seek a school culture that fits? Definitely. If you have worked through the Snap To It exercises in our *Child* and *Family* chapters, then you already have a good handle on which aspects of school culture are most important to you and what values you want reinforced at school. You may be able to make a quick judgment about a school if many aspects of its culture are aligned – or misaligned – with your Must Have values.

Prioritizing Your Many Fit Needs

If your child and family have competing needs – ones that would lead you to very different kinds of schools – then you'll really want to make careful choices about what to seek in a school.

A Great Fit school is one that meets both the most *important* and *difficult-to-accommodate* needs of your child and family. Few schools will meet every one of them. But some needs are more essential than others: for your child or family, you must address them either in school or family life. The more vital a need is to your child's being, or your family's needs and values, the more important it is that you find a school to address it.

For example, if your child is a social and leadership superstar, few venues will make up for the extraordinary opportunities in a school with significant small group interaction, unstructured time and extracurricular activities. If your child is challenged academically, tutoring will help; but a school that makes the most

School Designs Defined

This table provides brief descriptions of some common school designs. If you're exploring school designs, you won't want to stop here. Visit *PickyParent.com* for references and links to more information about these and the many other school designs.

DESIGN	GRADES	MAJOR PHILOSOPHY	KEY COMPONENTS
Accelerated Schools	K - 8	Provide all students with enriched instruction based on entire school community's vision of learning.	• Gifted-and-talented instruction that engages and challenges students is offered to all students. • Governance structure empowers school community to make key decisions about change through participatory process.
The Coalition of Essential Schools	K - 12	Students and teachers should be active partners in creating meaningful learning.	• Does not offer a specific curriculum, but rather a set of guiding principles. • These include: small classes, in depth coverage of material, personalization, teacher-as-coach, democracy, and demonstration of mastery. • Students should be engaged in "authentic tasks," and assessments should improve teaching.
Core Knowledge	K - 8	Focus on teaching a common core of concepts, vocabulary, skills, and knowledge.	• Sequential program of specific topics for each grade in all subjects. This sequence makes up 50 percent of a school's curriculum. • Instructional strategies are modeled for teachers, but the selection is left up to them.
Direct Instruction	K - 8	Aims to improve achievement significantly over current levels by using highly prescribed curriculum and instruction.	• Instruction is fast-paced and demands frequent scripted interaction between teachers and students. • Students are placed in small, flexible groups by performance level. • Student progress is assessed frequently.
Edison Schools, Inc.	K - 12	For profit educational management company that operates public schools nationwide using research-based school design.	• Grades are clustered together in academies, and students have the same teachers for several years. • Schools operate with longer school day and year. • Rich liberal arts curriculum with research-based instruction and ongoing student assessment.
International Baccalaureate	Pre K - 12	Develop whole child, including cultural capabilities, through study of prescribed international curriculum promoting thinking and transdisciplinary skills.	• Guidelines for what students should learn in six core content areas. • Prescribed teaching methodology that emphasizes: critical thinking, inquiry, risk-taking, global understanding, sensitivity and open-mindedness, moral principles, and reflective self-understanding. • Ongoing monitoring of individual student learning integrated with daily lessons. • Mastery of a second language.

 Continues…

School Designs Defined   ...continued

DESIGN	GRADES	MAJOR PHILOSOPHY	KEY COMPONENTS
Montessori	Pre K - 8	Develop culturally literate children by nurturing their intelligence, independence, curiosity and creativity.	• Classrooms are multi-age and students stay with one teacher for several years. • Method values and supports individual learning styles. • Curriculum is carefully structured to move individual children from one skill to the next. • Encourages independence and self-discipline.
Multiple Intelligences	Pre K - 12	Design instruction so that it supports student's natural abilities and talents in order to access a broad range of human potential.	• Maintains that traditional schooling supports some types of intelligence more than others. • Encourages teachers to be aware of and to value students' natural forms of intelligence. • Designed to support students' individual learning strengths so that they learn more effectively.
Paideia	K - 12	Foster more active learning and better use of teacher and student time.	• Focus is on active learning and developing critical thinking skills. • Individual schools have flexibility in how they implement basic principles.
School Development Program	K - 12	Meet the needs of urban students by improving educators' understanding of child development and fostering healthy relations with families.	• School-wide committee directs school improvement process and promotes parent involvement. • Schools receive some guidance with curriculum and instruction, but teacher and school-wide teams are expected to make most decisions.
Success for All	Pre K - 8	Structured research-based reading program designed to teach all children to read well in the early elementary years.	• 90 minutes a day of instruction for students in reading, writing, and language arts; one-on-one tutoring for young students struggling in reading; extensive family support services. • Students are grouped by reading level (reviewed by assessment every 8 weeks) and often work cooperatively.
Waldorf	Pre K - 12	Children learn best through experiences that awaken multiple senses and focus on capabilities.	• Students learn through experiences and personal exchange with teachers, rather than textbooks. • Focus on developing intellectual, emotional, spiritual capabilities, not just content learning. • Arts and physical activities used as learning tools. • Intense study of one subject over several weeks. • Students stay with same teachers in grades K–8.

of the long school day to *breathe life into and reinforce* the basics is hands down the best solution in most cases. If your family is cash-strapped, and your child does not have the particular strengths that might lead to a private school scholarship, finding the best public school truly is essential.

Few schools will offer everything you want and need for a perfect fit. You will need to decide for yourself which wants and needs you can handle elsewhere. Just because your child has an essential educational need does not necessarily mean that the need must be met at school. Many parents will be able to supplement the school experience with a broad range of extracurricular activities, tutoring, social experiences and so on.

Parents also can meet many of their own needs outside of their child's school experience. Had you counted on being part of the parent community at your neighborhood school or alma mater? You need not choose a second-rate or poor fit school just to satisfy these yearnings: get more involved in other neighborhood activities, and shore up your friendships with former classmates (or even continue to volunteer and improve your former school). You can find several ways to meet most needs, once you understand what they are and the range of ways to meet them.

You'll have another chance to think this through when it comes to decision time (Chapter 16). But it will be easier then if you've already narrowed down your Must Have list. You need not eliminate a need altogether from consideration – make it Nice to Have if you think you can meet the need outside of school. To get some help thinking about how you can meet needs outside of school see our helpful, you guessed it, tables: *Child Needs: Ways to Get What You Don't Get at School* (page 416) and *Family Needs: Ways to Get What You Don't Get at School* (page 428). You'll find the advice in these to be very basic, and we think you'll be able to add ideas to this list once you get started.

Chapter 16 will help you face the often wrenching choices about how to balance child and family fit needs – along with school quality. You can decide which kinds of school shortcomings would be easier for your child and family to accommodate outside of school, depending upon the schools available to your child. But before that, you need to learn more about the proven pillars of school quality that make a truly Great School.

SNAP TO IT

What To Do

➤ *Turn to your **Personalized Great Fit Checklist*** (page 59). You will use this checklist to investigate schools you are considering. If you haven't already, fill in the first column, "Child and Family Needs," with your child and family Must Have needs based on your *Child* and *Family Needs Summaries*. Include top Nice to Haves, if you have few Must Haves. Estimated Time: 15 minutes

➤ *Use our short-cut tables,* *Child Needs: What to Look for in a School* (page 380) and *Family Needs: What to Look for in a School* (page 400), to decide what you will seek in schools for a Great Fit. These tables also tell you what questions to ask principals, teachers and parents. Estimated Time: 10 - 20 minutes

➤ *Try to narrow your Must Have list as much as possible.* Consider carefully what needs you can meet outside of school. Use our tables to help: *Child Needs: Ways to Get What You Don't Get at School* (page 416) and *Family Needs: Ways to Get What You Don't Get at School* (page 428). Estimated Time: 30 minutes

➤ *Record top questions and things to look for in your school hunt* in the middle column of your *Personalized Great Fit Checklist*. You need not include every detail there. Include just as much as you'll need to feel confident investigating schools later.

  ✔ You may prepare separate interview sheets for principals, parents and teachers as needed. See our *Interview Forms* on pages 273-75

  ✔ You may want to mark or copy key sections of the tables to take with you to schools, if you find it helpful to have detail close at hand

  ✔ See the example completed *Checklist* on page 176
  Estimated Time: 30 minutes

➤ *Think for yourself as needed and as time allows.* Do you want a school focused just on children and families like yours or one adept at meeting varying needs? How much do you want a school to focus on developing your child's strengths? Weaknesses? Work these thoughts into your *Checklist*. Estimated Time: As needed

➤ *Note any school type, school design or school culture "big picture" thoughts to consider* as you cast your net in search of schools. Work these into your *Checklist*. Prepare a clean final *Checklist* that is now a truly personalized profile of your Great Fit school. Estimated Time: 0 - 10 minutes

Need more? Want more? Got more to share? Visit PickyParent.com.

Personalized Great Fit Checklist

School Name: _____

▶ In the first blank column, list in pencil the precise names of your top child & family needs based on your *Child and Family Needs Summaries* (pages 38 and 110) and on your reading of Chapters 2–9 and related tables. For example, write "Basic Learning Capability, Typical." See a complete example on page 176.

▶ Check whether each of your needs is a Must Have or Nice to Have.

▶ In next big column, make note of the characteristics a school must have to meet your need based on your reading of Chapter 10 and related tables.

▶ Include specific questions to ask school principal, teachers, parents, and others (or use our *Interview Forms* on page 273).

▶ Make an extra copy and fill in notes for each school you consider.

▶ After you gather the information you need, grade each school on how well it fits each Must Have and Nice to Have item:

A perfect fit **B** very good fit **C** halfway fit **D** poor fit **F** very poor or no fit

FIT FACTOR	CHILD & FAMILY NEEDS: Must Haves & top Nice to Haves	MUST HAVE	NICE TO HAVE	WHAT TO LOOK FOR *and* QUESTIONS TO ASK	NOTES ABOUT THIS SCHOOL	GRADE
What Your Child Learns	Child: Basic Learning Capability – Bright/Gifted	X		· Indiv. learning goals ahead of grade level or high overall goals · Frequent monitoring · Focus on critical thinking		
How Your Child Learns	Child: Motivation – Weak Family: Values about how – Classroom Behavior – controlling/strict	X	X	· Variety of teaching methods · Frequent feedback for parents · Individual work with teacher · Clear behavior expectations · Clear punishments & rewards		
Social Issues	Family: Student Community – critical mass of gifted children	X		· High % of children designated "gifted" or scoring at high levels on tests (not just % at grade level)		
Practical Matters	Family: · *Child-care* – need afterschool · *Transportation* – bus to & from · *Money* – afford up to $6,000 plus $1,000 for afterschool; prefer less	X		· Afterschool available · Bus to and from school available (for afterschool, too) · Tuition & fees minus aid is no more than $6,000, or total with afterschool no more than $7,000		

Fit Factors Unfolded

Each section of the Great Fit Triangle includes the four Fit Factors. Your child's, family's and school's most important characteristics must match to make a Great Fit.

	FIT FACTOR #1: What Your Child Learns	FIT FACTOR #2: How Your Child Learns	FIT FACTOR #3: Social Issues	FIT FACTOR #4: Practical Matters
Child Needs	• Basic Learning Capability • Other capabilities: musical, artistic, physical and hands-on, social and leadership, creativity, ESL • Interests	• Learning Styles • Motivation • Physical and mental health challenges • Behavior challenges • Learning disorders and disabilities • Self-understanding	• Friends at school	• Essential non-school activities
Family Needs	• Values about what content is important, e.g., academic basics, other subjects, religion, ethics • Goals for your child, e.g., grade progression, academic performance, college opportunity	• Values about school-wide expectations and rules on student conduct, e.g., manners, discipline, dress, honor code • Values about how children should learn: teaching method and classroom behavior management • Your role as advocate for child	• Characteristics you want in parents • Your preferred level and type of parent involvement • Characteristics you want in students • Preference for certain school, school type or design	• Child care: before/after school, summer, etc. • Schedule: daily and yearly • Transportation needs • Location • Your other children • Money available to pay for school
School Offerings	• Mission • Educational goals for students • Curriculum content (regular classes and special programs) • Extracurricular offerings	• Teaching method • Classroom discipline • Communication with parents • Mental, physical health care • Disability and disorder offerings • Culture of school (and special programs)	• Parent community characteristics • Parent involvement, expected and actual • Student community characteristics	• Activities accommodated • Child care provided • Schedule and schedule flexibility • Transportation provided • Location • Meet needs of all your children • Cost

STEP THREE

Learn About Truly Great Schools: The Secret Ingredients Revealed

■ ■ ■ ■ ■ ■ ■

LIGHT'NING LIST

What To Know from Chapter 11

➤ *You can learn to compare the quality of schools* with accuracy and confidence.

➤ *Great Schools* are ones in which children learn dramatically more in core academic subjects than similar students in other schools.

➤ *More than thirty years of repeated research* has revealed seven consistent characteristics of the highest quality schools. We call these seven school characteristics the *Great School Quality Factors*:

1. Clear Mission Guiding School Activities
2. High Expectations for All Students
3. Monitoring of Progress and Adjusting Teaching
4. Focus on Effective Learning Tasks
5. Home-School Connection
6. Safe and Orderly Environment
7. Strong Instructional Leadership

➤ *Seeking the Great School Quality Factors* is the most reliable way to choose the school where your child will learn the most in core subjects.

➤ *If you need a short cut, seek Great School Quality Factors #2 and 3*. A school pursuing these rigorously and vigorously will be forced to address other factors over the long haul. And it more likely will be a Great Fit for your child: quality supports fit.

➤ *Don't be fooled in your hunt for a Great School:*

✔ *Comparing overall test scores* of schools with very different kinds of students can be misleading and often reveals little about school quality.

✔ *Individual great teachers* working alone cannot make a whole school great. Even great teachers need support from a Great School to produce the best results with your child.

✔ *How happy your friends are with a school is not a* quality *indicator,* unless your friends know about school quality, have fit needs similar to your child's and family's and know about more than their own children's particular teachers.

➤ *We provide a Great School Quality Checklist* on page 200 for you to use when you are ready to investigate schools.

Chapter 11

What *Really* Separates the Best from the Rest?

Liza and Harrison Olson, after trying for four years to have a second child, had twins, a boy, Elan, and a girl, Heidi. The twins were moving from a private preschool to "big kid" kindergarten in the fall. Their older son Colter, now in second grade, would move to third grade. Colter had repeated first grade when he was unable to read near grade level. Finally, he was diagnosed with dyslexia at the end of the repeat year and allowed to advance to second grade only if his parents paid for outside "treatment" of his disability. Liza and Harrison were not pleased with Colter's school for failing to notice his special challenge for so long, but also mad at themselves for not getting a private assessment sooner. They were determined to make the right decision for their twins and even willing to switch Colter to a new school if a better one could be found. Elan, true to his name, brimmed with personal energy and could charm children and grownups alike with his engaging smile and friendly manner. In preschool, he was right on target in his learning so far. Heidi, more serious in her demeanor and more challenged making friends than her twin, was reading at a first grade level, full of ideas and questions and "very advanced," her teachers said. Liza and Harrison knew she'd make any school look good, but wanted one that would actively challenge her and not just leave her to work by herself all day. The Olsons' questions: Could they send all three children to the same school? What if Elan or Heidi grew to have a special need like Colter? How could they make this decision with confidence? With these uncertainties, the Olsons began their school hunt.

■ ■ ■

The Seven Great School Quality Factors

You know what makes a Great Fit, now. And if you've been working while you whittle away at this book, you have a sense of your own child's and family's unique needs. That's really important for choosing the right school. Aren't you glad you took time to think and learn about that? We hope you're feeling confident. "What more could I want?" you say.

Well, would you buy a house with a shaky foundation just because it had the right number of bedrooms? Would you purchase a car with the right headroom for your tall family if you knew it would break down a lot or wouldn't accelerate fast enough to get you onto the highway without a mild heart attack?

Fit matters, but quality counts, too. *We define high quality or "great" schools as ones in which **students of all kinds** learn dramatically more in core academic subjects **than similar students** in other schools.* That's what Great Schools accomplish. Great Schools meet the needs of more children and families more of the time. The results show both in "soft" measures, like parent satisfaction, and "hard" ones, like student test scores in the basics. This book will show you how to look for the signs of a Great School, one that you can count on to educate your child in core academics, year in and year out.

Definition

Great School: A high quality or "great" school is one in which children of all abilities and types learn dramatically more and perform better in core academic subjects than similar students in other schools.

Core Subjects: Core subjects are ones that all elementary students must master in preparation for independent adult life and further education in our society, including at least reading, writing and math.

But what are Great Schools made of? Sugar and spice and everything nice? Snips and snails and puppy dog tails? Wouldn't it be nice if you could rely on simple clichés – for raising your child and choosing a school? But parents of spunky girls and good-as-gold boys know that what seems true at a glance doesn't always hold true.

So how do you find these Great Schools? What's the magic ingredient to seek on the label so that you know you're getting real quality? Test scores, individual teacher quality and other parents' opinions are frequent *mis*leading indicators.

➤ *Test scores* alone reveal little unless you know whether you are comparing schools with similar kinds of students: ones of similar starting capabilities or from families with similar parent education levels and incomes.

➤ *Great teachers* are, well, great. But absent a Great School behind them, they are less likely to stay and spread their good work to other classrooms. Like all stars, they are likely to "burn out" over time without a fuel source for their challenging work. And you never know whether your child will be assigned to more than one or two star teachers over the years.

➤ *Your friends' glowing reports* of their own children's school experiences mean little unless your friends know about the real indicators of school quality, have fit needs similar to your child's and family's, and know about more than their own children's particular teachers.

Fortunately, decades of research by many different experts of differing perspectives have shown that a few consistent features of schools make them great. Not just for your one child – but for all of your children, and for the kids on the other side of the railroad tracks, too. Not just for today, but for tomorrow and the next year, too.

We call these consistent features the *Great School Quality Factors*. When compared to typical schools, Great Schools consistently demonstrate these seven pillars of school quality. You may recall them from Chapter 1. But we don't expect you to be an expert *yet* (though you're on your way), so here they are again:

1. *Clear Mission Guiding School Activities:* The school has a clear purpose and approach to education that *you* understand. The principal, teachers and parents understand this mission, and it guides all decisions and activities in the school. Precious resources like money and classroom time are focused to achieve the school's goals, not wasted on "window dressing" – things that may look good but don't further the school's mission.

2. *High Expectations for All Students:*

   ✔ The school has *high* minimum academic standards ("grade level") that prepare *all children* for independent adulthood in our society. Grade level standards may include both specific skills and knowledge a child should have in core subjects, as well as "thinking" skills. In a Great School, all students are expected to achieve at least grade level.

   ✔ The school also has higher, individualized standards for children who are ready to excel beyond grade level. No matter how bright the average child in a school and how high "grade level" goals are set, every school has students who are ready to learn beyond these goals. In Great Schools, these students are expected to meet increasingly difficult goals in core subjects.

3. *Monitoring of Progress and Adjusting Teaching.* Each child's individual progress is monitored frequently during the school year. Teachers change their teaching approaches as needed – adapting to individual student interests, learning styles and other differences – to ensure that students meet their

goals, both grade level and higher. When a child falls behind, the school takes immediate action, accepting no excuses for failure.

4. *Focus on Effective Learning Tasks.* Teachers use well-planned, well-tested approaches to instruction. Class time, material purchases and facilities are all allocated according to the school's mission; more important subjects are given more time and the best materials and facilities. Classroom interruptions are minimal. Materials and curriculum are frequently reviewed, and altered, to ensure they are working as planned.

5. *Home-School Connection.* Parents are told what their children will be learning, how to help at home, how their children are progressing during the year (frequently), and how to work with the school to solve any problems their children might face.

6. *Safe and Orderly Environment.* Students are kept safe from harm by other people, facilities and equipment. Students know how they are expected to behave in and out of the classroom, and they behave as expected because consequences are clear and consistent.

7. *Strong Instructional Leadership.* School leaders maintain clear, high expectations for teachers, recruit and keep great teachers, organize teachers to work together, monitor and improve teacher performance, and act on high and low teacher performance (ridding school of low performers, recognizing and rewarding high performers).

If you've already had a child in school, you may find yourself saying, "I knew it!" to several of the seven Great School Quality Factors. They each affect real, tangible activities in the classroom that you and your child cherish when they're present and sorely miss when a school is lacking.

Quality Supports Fit, Fit Supports Quality

Many parents feel guilty asking for elements of quality, because they think that school shortcomings affect only their own individual children. But Great Schools make it their business to fit many children, while keeping academic expectations high, because that's how they ensure that everyone achieves and makes progress in core subjects.

In fact, if you need a short cut to assess the quality of schools you consider, seek Great School Quality Factors #2 and 3. A school that pursues these rigorously and vigorously will be forced to address other Great School Quality Factors over the long haul. A school that doggedly sets and pursues challenging goals for every child, monitors individual progress and does back flips to ensure

learning for individual students will succeed for almost every child in core academics. Such a school will be forced to seek the most effective planning methods, teaching practices, learning environment, communication and management practices inherent in the other Great School Quality Factors. Indeed, we see "Rigor and Vigor" becoming the watchwords of schools that choose to be great.

In contrast, a school that focuses only on a clearer mission, the latest and greatest reading program, leadership training, better classroom behavior and the like is making a start. But without a clear expectation that all children will reach challenging goals, frequent measurement of how well individual students are learning and individualized responses to learning barriers, a school will leave many students, of all abilities, behind their academic potential. The school won't know that the latest, greatest reading program isn't working or is too easy for three out of every ten kids. And so on. What lost time and joy for those children left out!

With a one-size-fits-all approach, it's nearly impossible to fit even a carefully selected group of children all the time, year in and year out. Great Schools build many bridges to carry children from far-flung places to lofty destinations.

Meeting Individual Needs: Mission Impossible?

Thirty years ago, "great" schools offered a more challenging one-size-fits-all curriculum. Today, Great Schools challenge all children and respond to their individual needs.

When we tell parents to focus on Great School Quality Factors #2 and 3, they often ask: how on earth can a teacher respond to the *individual* needs of 20 or 30 students? So we thought we should take a moment here and explain what Great Schools *really* do.

Meeting individual needs is nearly impossible when students are taught cookie-cutter style in a big group all day. Thirty years ago, a school could be "great" (compared to others) if it simply offered a more challenging one-size-fits-all curriculum to all students. Now we know that this is only one half of one factor (#2). Today, Great Schools offer a challenging curriculum, and they help teachers understand and respond to individual children better.

They accomplish this in many ways, but always set aside a significant part of the school day for children to work at their current achievement levels with teachers in small groups or one-on-one. Small group and individualized attention do not guarantee success: staff must use that contact to assess what each child knows and push each child to the next level. But that's nearly impossible if all contact happens in a big group. Smaller class sizes might help, but they are no guarantee. You must know exactly how teachers keep up with individual children – as impossible when treating 16 children the same as when treating 28 the same.

Great Schools provide staff, materials and time to help teachers individualize teaching and learning. These supports help teachers more easily grasp and respond to each child's current learning level, interests, motivation, learning styles and other differences.

For example, some Great Schools…

Use additional staff wisely:
➤ Provide skilled staff to assess students' progress frequently, so teachers know exactly where each child stands and who needs a different approach to learn the material.
➤ Provide learning specialists (e.g., math, reading, writing) to conduct small-group or one-on-one instruction.
➤ Provide assistant teachers to supervise large group or individual work in the classroom while lead teachers conduct small-group or one-on-one instruction.
➤ Provide staff learning coordinators in core subjects to help teachers across classes and grades move students around into groups that fit their current learning levels.

Use teaching methods and tools that help teachers identify and respond to differing needs:
➤ Pull small groups out of the classroom, but many Great Schools accomplish individualized work in the classroom.
➤ Have self-paced materials children can use on their own.
➤ Have clear, ladder-like learning goals and teaching materials, so that it's always clear what a child should learn next, even above grade level.
➤ Individualize homework assignments, or offer layers of more difficult homework as an alternative available to any child willing to take the challenge.

Help teachers make the most of time and technology:
➤ Provide time during the school day for teachers to think, plan and make instructional changes to address the varying needs of students.
➤ Do school-wide scheduling to allow students to move from group to group in core subjects with ease.
➤ Provide time for teachers across grades and subjects to do joint scheduling and moving of students to the right current learning groups.
➤ Provide computer technology for tracking and reporting student progress, so teachers can see in a blink where kids stand.

Many Great Schools use a combination of these and other tactics to individualize instruction. This approach has more than one name, most commonly "differentiation," or "individualized learning." But some schools sling those terms around without actually making sure the rubber meets the road. In evaluating a given school, you need to know that teachers are clearly expected to take this approach

Great Schools help lead teachers determine what each child knows and how each child learns best.

and have school support to do it. Appropriate support will likely include many of the tactics listed above. Otherwise, your child will experience the teacher-by-teacher quality rollercoaster so common in mediocre and weak schools.

Great Schools do not just let children learn at their own paces. They also ensure that every child has challenging academic goals and actively monitor individual progress.

In a Great School, an individualized approach leads teachers to *raise* standards for children who are ahead, but *never to lower* what is expected of a child. Instead, teachers use close contact with students to figure out how to help each individual reach grade level and beyond. Some children need more repetition of the basics. Some need hands-on objects rather than words on a page. Others need to learn in the context of a topic that is personally interesting. Still others just need personal contact with a firm, caring grownup to get motivated. But nearly all children – even those who face learning challenges – can meet grade level standards. Great Schools believe that every child can achieve grade level, and teachers and support staff do back flips to make it happen.

Tracking versus Current Capability Grouping

When we were in school, many of our classes were divided, from the beginning of the year to the end, into two groups. Maybe you were a member of the Ponies, the kids across the aisle the Penguins. One group was ahead, the other behind – all year. When we talk about how Great Schools group for instruction, this kind of "tracking" is emphatically *not* what works best. Instead, Great Schools organize groups by *current* knowledge or skill levels. Children make learning leaps at different times throughout the school year, and so the grouping of children should change frequently, too – even weekly. We call this "Current Capability Grouping," but whatever you call it, it's what Great Schools do.

So, Can I Pick and Choose Great School Quality Factors?

To be great, not just good, a school must achieve or actively strive for *all* of the Great School Quality Factors. None alone will make a school great. Without any one Factor, a school and the learning your child does at school will suffer. True, a school that pursues both Great School Quality Factors #2 and 3 with rigor and vigor will be forced to improve the other factors *over time*. And if your time is short, or you must make tradeoffs, these are the two to pursue. But meanwhile, you'll not want your child to suffer from great, gaping holes in the other Great School Quality Factors.

Take these other thoughts into consideration when you're ready to examine schools available to your child: Some quality elements, such as basic safety and focusing class time on learning, are needed just to keep a school from being a

Smart à la Carte

How Small Should a Small Group Be?

Students in many Great Schools do a lot of learning in small groups. But how small is small enough to be effective? Research in reading instruction – one of the better researched curriculum areas – indicates that groups of up to four students are as effective as one-on-one (more may be fine if the students are very similar).

Smart à la Carte

What About This?

Many of you will not be surprised by the seven Great School Quality Factors. But some of you surely will be startled by what's not there. In this box and the *What About That?* and *But, But, But…* boxes are several items that interest many parents. Here's the general scoop: some of these are important, but only if used to support or detract from a Great School Quality Factor or if they address your fit needs.

➤ *Class size:* some research indicates that classes with 17 or fewer students are better than bigger ones. But teachers must use smaller classes to individualize instruction. Know this: in many classrooms across America, teachers with 17 or fewer students teach the same things to every child using the same approach with no changes for kids who need more help, higher goals, or a different approach. Similarly, many teachers achieve astonishing levels of learning among students in large classes – with the kind of school support detailed on page 187. True, it's easier with fewer children, but small class size is no guarantee and a potentially misleading indicator of quality. Look for Great School Quality Factor #3 instead to get the best results for your child.

➤ *School Size:* some research indicates that children learn more in small schools. Most likely, it is easier for those school leaders *who are striving for the Great School Quality Factors* to get everyone, staff and students, moving in the same direction in a smaller school. But a smaller school is neither required for academic excellence nor a guarantee of academic excellence. Instead of school size, look for Great School Quality Factors #3 and 7 as more accurate indicators of how "personal" a school will feel to your child and how well-managed it will be.

➤ *School Year Length:* up to a point, the more time your child spends learning, the more your child will learn. That goes to Great School Quality Factor #4, Focus on Effective Learning Tasks. But how is that time at school being spent? Your child is better off in a high-quality school with a traditional schedule than a mediocre one with a longer school year. That said, your child would likely learn more in a high quality extended year school than a similar quality one with a traditional schedule. Consider, though, whether *your* child might use that time for play with friends, physical activity and other valuable non-academic pursuits.

colossal failure. Others, like high expectations, monitoring student progress, and adjusting teaching approaches for different children, are essential for taking a school from good to great. But all seven Great School Quality Factors are ingredients that distinguish Great Schools from the rest.

As our Great School Superhero shows, each factor plays an important role in maintaining the strong body of the school. Clear Mission is the brains, High Expectations plus Monitoring Progress & Adjusting Teaching the ever-busy legs, Focus on Effective Learning Tasks the heart and body, Safety & Order along with Home-School Connection the supporting arms, and Strong Instructional Leadership the steady foundation.

As important as any of these Great School Quality Factors alone is that they are consistent with each other. "Healthy Body, Sound Mind" your child's school motto? Then facilities adequate for vigorous exercise – a playground, a big field, an indoor gym – are musts, along with time in the school day for exercise and some part of the curriculum addressing life balance. "Each Child Stretched to Individual Potential" the motto? Then a wide range of classroom materials and individual or small-group activities that allow children to push beyond "grade level" are musts, along with frequent monitoring of student progress and upward goal adjustment. Look for consistent, well-planned effort throughout the school to know if it is likely to achieve its stated mission and goals.

Also know that some Great School Quality Factors are somewhat more important for certain children and families. Few schools are perfect in quality, and almost none is perfect for everyone. You'll want to make sure your child's school is strong in the quality areas most important for your child and family. For example, academically gifted children *must have* schools that set higher, individualized goals for students who are ready. Academically challenged students and those with learning disabilities *must have* schools that frequently monitor student progress and make teaching changes to ensure that students grasp challenging material. Single parents, families in which both parents work and children with low motivation *must have* schools with strong home-school connections. Children with extreme behavioral challenges *must have* very orderly environments for learning the discipline to make their own decisions later.

But you need not translate quality into fit, because we've done it for you. Special quality considerations are already included in *Child Needs: What to Look for in a School* (page 380) and *Family Needs: What to Look for in a School* (page 400).

Don't be fooled into thinking, however, that some Great School Quality Factors aren't at all important for your child's learning. You and your child will sorely miss absent Great School Quality Factors, even the ones less essential for your fit needs today. But you, unlike parents who haven't read this book, will be aware

Smart à la Carte

What About That?

➤ *Multi-age Groups, Staying with Same Teachers:* a multi-age classroom lets your child play varying social roles over the years and often keep the same teacher, too. Having the same teacher for more than one year can help that teacher better keep up with your child's learning and get to know your child's needs better (especially in the absence of other school support to help her do this). But many a child has been stuck with a poor quality teacher or one whose one-size-fits-all approach was not a good fit with the child's needs – for two or more years! If you choose multi-age, ensure that your older student will be challenged and your younger one not left in the social and academic dust. Choose multi-age if you value the potential social benefit or if the school also is of high quality.

➤ *Academic Awards and Recognition:* yes these are a great way to express the value a school community places on academic striving and achievement, which can support Great School Quality Factor # 2, High Expectations. Look for progressively more prestigious honors within a school that reward kids who really go for it in each academic subject. Are mental fitness clubs (e.g., chess, Odyssey of the Mind) more prominent in the school, or are social and athletic ones more prominent? Do all kids who meet grade level make the "honor roll," or are there ever more prestigious honors that reward kids who really go for it in each academic subject? But public awards and recognition are not a substitute for expecting a lot from individual students day to day, throughout the year.

➤ *Grades vs. Portfolios vs. Class Rank:* grades are simply one way of expressing a teacher's monitoring of your child's learning and performance on a regular schedule. Portfolios the same. Grades are usually on a scale of what's expected for all students, so you can see how your child stacks up compared to the school's grade level standard (and sometimes compared to other students if teachers must limit how many students get As and Bs). Portfolios are collections of your child's work product, and they may be graded, simply "passed" or "failed," scaled in some other way, or just kept as archival proof of learning. Class rank tells you about pecking order, but little about how much anyone actually learned. As long as you are sure that a school will hold your child to high standards and monitor progress, the grading approach should be secondary, unless it is a school culture fit hot-button for you personally. More important than this for academic quality is the type and level of work that is rewarded and recognized in the school.

Smart à la Carte

But, But, But...

➤ *Homework Policy:* well targeted homework will likely help your child academically by allowing her to spend more time on core subjects (Great School Quality Factor #4). Homework can help keep you informed about what your child is studying in school and whether it is the right level of work for your child (Great School Quality Factor #5). But more homework that's too easy or too hard without a teacher is not helpful. If your child's school is using the long school day well, then homework time will not be hard for the school to limit. And limited it should be, in our opinion, in the elementary years. Your child is not just an academic robot. Homework should support academic learning, but allow time for other aspects of development, too. A homework policy helps you know how much time your child will have for other pursuits, but such a policy should be secondary to overall quality and your top fit needs.

➤ *Attendance Rates:* this should be an issue only if you are concerned about the social impact on your own child's attendance (family Fit Factor #3) or an accompanying extreme lack of order in a school (Great School Quality Factor #6). If so, eliminate a school with low attendance rates. Otherwise, don't let it outweigh other aspects of quality and fit.

➤ *Computer Technology:* this can be important in two ways. First, if you value your child learning computer skills and cannot provide tools at home, then make it a fit need to meet at school (family Fit Factor #1). Second, computers can be used to help monitor student progress and keep students challenged at just the right level (Great School Quality Factors #2 and 3). There are some terrific programs designed to do just this. But just as easily, computer time can be used to baby-sit or distract students from important content learning. What's important is how the computer time is used. If it's a fit concern for you, or if you notice that computer time is significant in the class schedule, be sure to ask how that time is used.

of what you're missing and better able to push for change or close the gaps outside of school.

In summary:
➤ All seven Great School Quality Factors are important
➤ If your time is very limited, seek Great School Quality Factors #2 and 3, while watching for great gaping holes in the others
➤ Look for a school with consistent *plans and actions* that cover all the factors
➤ Focus on Great School Quality Factors important for your fit needs today (these are already included in the tables about what to seek in a school for each fit need)

What About Test Scores? Don't They Tell Me All I Need to Know?

Standardized tests are just what they say – a standard or consistent way of comparing one child, classroom or whole school to another across a city, state or even nation. They are one measure of what students have learned in core academic subjects and are able to display by year's end.

They can be helpful to parents who are making a school choice. However, they also can be misleading. Why? First, test scores alone are poor indicators of quality if you are *comparing schools with different kinds of students*. A mediocre, one-size-fits-all school with lots of professors' kids may have better overall test scores than a very high-quality school with mostly kids of less educated parents. Yet your child – whether academically gifted or more typical – would probably learn more at the lower-scoring school.

When you've narrowed down the schools you are considering, you'll want to take the starting academic capability of students into consideration. One way you can do this is by examining the "growth" or "gains" of students over time – not just the level of performance at a school. *Growth scores tell you how much students have learned rather than how much they knew from the start.* If this kind of information is available, it tells you more than other test results about *how much learning* is going on in a school – which is what you really want to know.

Another way is to compare a school's performance with that of other schools with *similar student bodies*. If you can, find out the parent education and family income levels of students at the schools you're comparing, or look for information broken down this way. Then see how the students perform and improve compared to similar schools or similar groups of students. If you're comparing schools with very different students, you will choose a better quality school for your child if you give the Great School Quality Factors more weight than *overall* test scores.

Growth scores tell you how much students have learned rather than how much they knew from the start.

The second test score challenge is this: test results reported by your schools or the local newspaper may or may not be helpful for choosing a school for *your* child. You need to get both the right *types of scores*, and you need to get them for *children like yours*. Whatever your child's previous performance, background and personal characteristics, you'll want a school that has proven it expects and ensures high performance from kids *like yours*.

➤ *Types* of scores include at least these:
  ✔ *A number score* (sometimes called a "scale score"): the average number scored on a standardized test (e.g., 82 out of 100, or 155 out of 200)
  ✔ *Percent (%) at grade level:* the percent of students who scored the *target*

number score or higher for their *grade level* in each subject (or for all subjects averaged together)

✔ ***Growth or gain scores:*** a score that shows of the amount of progress students made over the school year

➤ *Kids like yours* might include at least these:

✔ ***Similar previous academic performance.*** If you have an inkling that your child may be among the top, middle or bottom scorers, you'll want to compare schools based on scores for kids like yours. If your child may struggle academically, how low is low: do they get *all* kids up to grade level? If your child is likely to be in the middle of the pack: do all kids meet grade level, and do more than just the "gifted" kids score near the top? If your child is gifted academically, how high is high: are top scorers scoring high numbers compared to the top students at other schools?

✔ ***Your child's race, gender and parent income*** might be important, too. Compare scores for children like yours across schools, especially if you think that some schools in your area do better with certain kinds of children.

Not sure which scores to consider for your child? Focus on the scores highlighted in the *Child Needs: What to Look for in a School* table on page 380 for children with current Basic Learning Capability like your child's.

You may feel frustrated if the scores reported by a school are not the ones you need or if a school does not publish its scores. You can try to obtain additional scores on your school district's website, from your state department of education, or simply by asking the schools you are considering. A school may be reluctant to share information with parents, fearing they'll misinterpret the information. If that's the case, tell the principal what you need to know and why.

Know this: multiple measures lead schools to focus on all kinds of kids. The best schools will use many measures. When a school uses only one measure – such as overall percentage of students at grade level – it probably isn't focusing on *all kinds of children* for *all core subjects*. If you just can't get all the test score information you need, fear not. Focus on the Great School Quality Factors, which, over time, will lead to higher test scores for all kinds of children.

Finally, last year's test scores don't tell you when a good school is about to head south (a "Falling Star") or a bad school is making all the right improvements (a "Rising Star"). Test scores alone show you a rear-view mirror. You also need to assess your Target Schools on the seven Great School Quality Factors for an accurate read on how a school is likely to perform in the future.

For all of these reasons, test scores should be a starting point only. You might be able to rule out some schools because of their abysmal test scores, or notice others that are consistent high flyers for kids like yours. But to get the real scoop on schools, you need to look for the seven Great School Quality Factors.

And What About Teachers?
If They're All Great, Is That Enough?

Never underestimate the power of a great teacher. The afterglow of a year when your child has had one is nearly incomparable. Indeed, many better schools of yesteryear relied on teacher recruiting alone. Not today. Great Schools have learned that even the best teachers need support and help to *be* their best and *stay* their best.

Great teachers, back then and now, use the seven Great School Quality Factors in their own classrooms: clarifying goals, expecting much of every student, monitoring progress and adjusting their approaches to reach every child, trying new tactics in a never-ending quest for the best, and so on. What tremendous respect we have for teachers who have accomplished these feats without support of the broader school! But teachers – or professionals of any kind, for that matter – who can maintain that level of performance year after year *without support* are rare indeed. And the fact of the matter is that most schools are populated largely with teachers who do not live up to the Great School characteristics, because they cannot or will not without help from the school. They *need* far more support, and you should expect more – for your child's benefit.

What About Teacher "Qualifications"?

Traditionally, when outsiders have tried to assess school quality teacher-by-teacher, they have looked at teacher "qualifications." Commonly accepted qualifications include teaching experience, certification, and specialized education. Unfortunately, studies conducted by unbiased, nonpolitical researchers who really just want to know what will work for children are few. And of the few good studies, the findings are inconclusive. In fact, the strongest, easy-to-measure-from-afar indicator of teacher quality is "verbal ability." You might be better off knowing your child's teacher's verbal SAT score than her experience level, certification or college major! But even knowing that would not give you the complete picture of how well a teacher would help your child learn.

Chances are that teacher characteristics not defined by *any* of the traditional measures matter most in the classroom. What leads a teacher to push, push and push for all students to achieve the most possible? What makes a teacher willing and able to detect many children's individual learning needs, empathize and connect with even the most challenging child through words and deeds that induce learning? Those are things researchers have begun to study but haven't nailed down yet. Meanwhile, we know that the seven Great School Quality Factors are what Great Schools – and the teachers within – pursue.

That said, here are tidbits to digest from the meager *good* research about traditional measures of teacher quality. "Experience" has been shown through consistent research to be important in this way: teachers with only one or two years of experience, all else being equal, will have lower performance than more experienced ones. Beyond that, the results a teacher achieves with students are due to factors other than time on the job. This is consistent with research about performance results in other professions, so it is not surprising. Avoid schools with large populations of teachers having almost no experience. If your child is assigned an inexperienced teacher, find out exactly how the principal and other staff will push that teacher up the learning curve fast (your child can't wait three years, after all). Great School Quality Factor #7, Strong Instructional Leadership, is critical always, but especially so in a school with many less-experienced teachers. As in many areas, the presence of a Great School to support teachers of *any* experience level matters most.

The importance of teacher certification is even less certain. It is a raging debate, with real results clouded by politics. Some research shows a benefit to certification, but most shows no impact at all. In the studies that do show benefit, the impact is small. And well-designed studies conducted by unbiased researchers are few, despite all the effort, money and political gab time spent on ensuring teacher certification. Go figure.

Finally, a teacher's subject matter expertise can make a difference, at least in math and science. But this is mostly true in higher-level courses, and so it's less relevant at the elementary level.

The impact of all these qualifications on your child's learning is dwarfed by the impact of the seven Great School Quality Factors. A highly experienced staff at a school where teachers are allowed to do the same old thing year after year, using a one-size-fits-all approach and comfortable but disproven techniques, won't do much for your child. In contrast, bright young teachers and professionals switching from other careers who teach in a school that implements only the best proven practices will do much for your child. A seasoned teaching staff willing to take a Great School approach is ideal.

What you as a parent care about is this: if you choose a particular school, what will a whole series of teachers *do for your child*? You can't tell by looking at experience or degrees of the teachers currently employed at the school. You and your child are better off knowing how well a school hires, expects, develops, supports and requires teachers to perform in the Great School mode.

Your Nagging Doubts: Can You Do This? Should You? Why Bother?

Can you, a parent who may have no expertise except having attended school yourself, judge the quality of schools? Definitely! Even if you focus only on Great School Quality Factors #2 and 3 and those aspects of quality most important for your child and family (after reading Chapters 2 - 10), you can ask and get answers to a few key questions that will let you compare schools and understand the strengths and weaknesses of the school you choose. Use the *Great School Quality Checklist* on page 200 and *Quality: What to Look for in a School* on page 409 to guide you. Don't be afraid to ask questions about issues you do not fully understand, as it is the job of Great Schools to explain their approaches to parents and make you a partner in the education process.

Is it possible that you will go through all of this and still find your child in an imperfect school? Yes. As with most things in this world, few schools are truly perfect. Most have areas that need improvement. But once you understand the strengths and weaknesses of the school you choose, you will be far better equipped to work with your child's individual teachers, push for school-wide changes, and organize your family life to fill school quality gaps. *Use Quality: Ways to Get What You Don't Get at School* on page 433 to help.

Will your search improve the quality of your child's school? Without a doubt! The questions you ask, the clear answers you seek, and the demands you make after choosing a school will improve not only your own child's school, but every school you have considered. You have the chance to impact every school where you ask questions about the *real* indicators of quality. By focusing on what counts in your school quest, you will send the signal over and over that these are the things schools need to improve. In this new era of parent choice, parents who take the time to seek real quality are quickly becoming key drivers of change within schools.

Keep Your Own Expectations High

In summary, you can and should expect a school and its staff to do these common sense things, year in and year out:
➤ Have a clear plan – that you understand – about what they'll do and how
➤ Expect a lot of your *child* and challenge *your child* to make progress in core subjects every day
➤ Have a handle on what *your child* knows in core subjects at all times and make sure *your child* learns what's needed, even if it takes back flips to do it

➤ Do what works best in the classroom, even when that means making changes
➤ Tell you what's what: what your child will learn, what to do at home, what your child has learned
➤ Keep your child safe and focused on learning
➤ Manage teachers and other staff so that the best stay, the worst leave, the rest learn from the best, and all staff members do their personal best work

Got it? Stay tuned, and you can learn more about each of the seven Great School Quality Factors and how to seek them in a school. If you are tired of filling out worksheets, or you're feeling guilty about not, get comfy in an armchair for a few quick chapters while you learn more about school quality. We've already created a *Great School Quality Checklist* for you (page 200), and you won't need it until you're ready to investigate specific schools. This checklist breaks each of the seven Great School Quality Factors into specific actions that you can look for and ask about in schools. The *Quality: What to Look for in a School* table on page 409 provides you with specific questions about quality to ask principals, teachers and parents.

Meanwhile, read on. The more you know, the more confident you'll feel. The more confident you feel, the more you can focus on choosing a school for what counts most. Later, if you're torn between two schools with differing quality strengths or are concerned about the quality of your child's current school, you'll be glad you invested some time in knowing what makes a Great School tick.

SNAP TO IT

What To Do

➤ *Skim the Great School Quality Checklist* on page 200. Estimated Time: 5 minutes

Optional Activities

➤ *Skim the Quality: What to Look for in a School table* on page 409 to help you phrase specific questions about quality to ask principals, teachers and parents. Estimated Time: 15 minutes

➤ *If your child is currently in elementary school,* take a few minutes to think about the quality strengths and weaknesses of the school. Use the *Great School Quality Checklist* as a guide. Discuss your thoughts with your spouse or other parenting partner. You can do a more complete assessment later, if you wish. Estimated Time: As needed.

Need more? Want more? Got more to share? Visit PickyParent.com.

Great School Quality Checklist — PAGE 1

School Name: _____

▲ Complete a separate *Great School Quality Checklist* for each school you consider.
▲ In Notes column, make notes about each school. Which factor elements are strengths? Weaknesses?
▲ After gathering available information, grade each school on each overall Great School Quality Factor:

✔ **A** school has all of the elements
✔ **B** school has most of the elements
✔ **C** school has about half of the elements
✔ **D** most of the elements are missing
✔ **F** school has none or almost none of the elements

GREAT SCHOOL QUALITY FACTORS	NOTES ABOUT THIS SCHOOL	GRADE
1. Clear Mission Guiding School Activities ● Written mission communicating focus and priorities ● Staff, parents & written materials state same mission ● School-wide goals support mission ● Student goals, curriculum & teaching support mission		
2. High Expectations for All Students: *High Minimum Expectations for All* ● Challenging but achievable student learning goals (standards) for each grade level ● School-wide plan and actions ensure that all students achieve at least grade level in basics, no excuses ● All or near all children achieve grade level ● Progress scores high for all, including lowest scorers *Higher Expectations for Students Who are Ready* ● Learning goals raised for ready students ● Clear, written progression of goals beyond grade level ● Plan and actions ensure students meet higher goals ● At least gifted students achieve very high test scores ● Progress scores are high for top students		

Continues…

Great School Quality Checklist   PAGE 2

School Name: _____

3. Monitoring of Progress and Adjusting Teaching
- School assesses individual student progress (weekly is ideal)
- Teachers change teaching approach to ensure that every child achieves his or her learning goals

4. Focus on Effective Learning Tasks
- Instruction approach proven to work
- Class time allocated according to subjects' importance
- Materials & facilities allocated in line with importance
- Principal and teachers limit class interruptions

5. Home-School Connection
- School tells parents what children will be learning
- School tells parents how to help own children learn
- School updates parents on own child performance
- School works with parents to resolve problems

6. Safe and Orderly Environment
- Students know how they are expected to behave
- Students focus on work in the classroom
- Consequences for behavior are clear and consistent
- School keeps students safe from harm

7. Strong Instructional Leadership
- Clear performance expectations for teachers
- Principal recruits, keeps great teachers
- Teachers work together within & across grades
- Principal monitors individual teacher performance
- Staff regularly identifies problems, improves school
- Professional development focused on school goals
- Principal acts on high and low teacher performance

LIGHT'NING LIST

What To Know from Chapter 12

➤ ***The Core Four Great School Quality Factors*** are essential to the teaching and learning that make a Great School great.

➤ ***Great School Quality Factor #1 is Clear Mission Guiding School Activities.***
The litmus test is this: the school has a clear purpose and approach to education that you understand. The principal, teachers and other parents understand this mission, and it guides all decisions and activities in the school. Precious resources like money and classroom time are focused to achieve the school's goals, and not wasted on "window dressing."

➤ ***Great School Quality Factor #2 is High Expectations for All Students.*** The litmus test is this: it is clear to you that the school will expect a lot of your child and challenge your child to learn in core subjects every day. Great Schools have:
  ✔ High minimum academic standards ("grade level") that prepare all children for independent adulthood in our society.
  ✔ Higher, individualized standards for children who are ready to excel beyond grade level.

➤ ***Great School Quality Factor #3 is Monitoring Progress and Adjusting Teaching.*** The litmus test: the school will have a handle on what your child knows in core subjects at all times and will make sure your child learns what's needed, even if it takes back flips to do it. Great Schools monitor each child's individual progress frequently during the school year, often weekly. Teachers change their teaching approaches as needed, to address individual children's needs. Barriers to learning, even non-academic ones, are addressed. When a child falls behind, the school takes immediate action, accepting no excuses for failure.

➤ ***Great School Quality Factor #4 is Focus on Effective Learning Tasks.*** The litmus test is this: the principal and teachers in the school can tell you how they know that they are doing what works best in the classroom, and they make frequent changes to improve. Teachers use well-planned, well-tested approaches to instruction. More important subjects receive more time and better materials and facilities. Classroom interruptions are minimal. Materials and curriculum are frequently reviewed, and altered, to ensure they are working as planned.

➤ ***The indicators of the Core Four*** in a school are included in the Great School Quality Checklist on page 200.

Chapter 12

Great School
Quality Factors #1 – 4:
The Core Four

Great School Quality Factor #1:
Clear Mission Guiding School Activities

The school has a clear purpose and approach to education that you understand. The principal, teachers and parents understand this mission, and it guides all decisions and activities in the school. Precious resources like money and classroom time are focused to achieve the school's goals, and not wasted on "window dressing" – things that may look good but that don't further the school's mission.

■ ■ ■

When Liza and Harrison Olson began their hunt, they identified three schools as possibilities for various reasons – one based on friends' recommendations, one a school Liza herself had attended, one their assigned district public school (we won't say which is which). They first investigated **Great School Elementary**, *whose motto was "Every Child Achieving, Every Child Challenged To Learn More." Every conversation they had – with the principal, three teachers and several parents of current students – made clear that this school met the learning needs of a wide variety of students, while also gunning hard for the highest levels of learning in academics. They talked with parents of gifted, typical and dyslexic children, and every parent claimed that the school was "just right for my child." When they investigated* **Good Try Elementary**, *which also had many different kinds of students, they were impressed by the nurturing posters and social charm of the staff they met. The school motto was "We Love Kids." But everyone Liza and Harry met at Good Try seemed to have* *a very different vision of the school, and they really never could get the principal to say what she saw as the school's mission. Teachers seemed to be using very different materials and teaching methods in the classes, mainly according to their personal preferences. One parent summed it up: "It hasn't been just right for our child academically, but we love the friendly atmosphere of the school." A popular third school they considered, **Yesteryear Elementary**, had a professionally-written mission statement that talked a lot about "nurturing all children" and "preparing them for the international world in which we live." The facilities, grounds and class equipment were impressive. But it was unclear to Liza and Harrison after an open house and tour how their children would benefit. The school used a one-size-fits-all curriculum and teaching method ("Perhaps O.K. for Elan?" they thought), plus a "guidance program" to help struggling students get appropriate tutoring elsewhere.*

■ ■ ■

"Clear" Means Clear to You

Great School Quality Factor #1 evokes that old saying that "if you don't know where you're going, you probably won't get there." A school must have a clear purpose and goals that *everyone* understands. That includes the school leadership, teachers, other staff and most certainly you as parents. If the people directly responsible for ensuring that a child learns lack a common understanding of *what the child should be learning and why*, it is ever so much harder for parent or teacher to bring a child along. But if everyone is aiming for the same target and reinforcing each other's efforts, more children will learn more of the targeted skills, knowledge and abilities.

When you start to consider schools available to your child, your litmus test for Great School Quality Factor #1 will be this: the school has a clear purpose and approach to education that *you* understand.

Clear, Consistent Communication

Having a school mission, goals or other guideposts written down in a desk drawer is not enough (but it is certainly an essential starting point). Instead, you should see and hear the mission throughout the school.

➤ If you are getting tired of hearing the same message spouting forth from the principal's, teachers' and parents' lips about the school's aim and approach to teaching, then that school is doing it right.

➤ If you hear what you need to hear when you interview the principal during your decision process – but then never again – then the school is only partway there.

➤ If you have to dig, dig, dig, to get even a hint of the school's goals and approach from the principal and teachers, then you can be sure that teachers in that school are all over the map when it comes to teaching and learning. Look for a very tired principal running around to fill the gaps caused by the lack of clarity. Listen for parents complaining about the inconsistent approach among teachers from year to year and within each grade.

Activities Support the Mission

Money, time and activities in a school must follow the mission or the mission will go unmet. Many schools start in the right place with a clear mission and plan for enacting it. But they veer off course – spending too much time and money on popular, easy or visible things. Great Schools constantly review to make sure that resources follow the mission, and they make tough decisions – about what to do and what *not* to do – to achieve the school's goals. They communicate their decisions to the whole school community, including parents, and explain how decisions will help meet the mission.

A school must live and breathe its mission for that mission to impact your child. If you read and hear that a school addresses children's various learning styles, but most teaching in a school is done with teacher standing and talking at the front of the class, something's wrong. If a school says no child will be left behind grade level, but does not monitor progress or quickly change the teaching approach for struggling students, something's wrong. If a school says it challenges every child, but then does not monitor student progress and raise goals for students who are ahead, something's wrong. If a school says its core values include exposing children to a diversity of people and perspectives, but the students and teachers are mostly quite similar, something's wrong. If a school's mission is to develop the "whole child," but all class time is spent on individual academic work, something's wrong.

If a school cannot tell you – the current or prospective parent – how and why it spends time and money the way it does, then it remains far from living its mission. Most frustrating for you, your child will not have the school experience you anticipated. In a Great School, the principal, teachers and most parents can tell you not only what the mission is, but how well the school is living up to its own standard and what changes are afoot to better meet the mission. In a Great School, you will get exactly what you expected – if you bothered to choose. And when you don't get what's expected, you will know that your comments and feedback are welcome by school leadership ever ready to make improvements.

By no means are we implying that schools should have any particular mission. All Great Schools commit to achieving strong academic results for all students. Beyond that, we have observed a wide variety of missions-in-action that work well for kids. Whether a school's mission focuses on "global awareness" or "engaging students in community service" is less important than whether the mission is clear, understood by all, and used as a daily guide to decision and action.

Great School Quality Factor #2: High Expectations for All Students

➤ High minimum academic standards ("grade level") that prepare all children for independent adulthood in our society. Grade level standards may include both specific skills and knowledge a child should have in core subjects, as well as "thinking" skills.

➤ Higher, individualized standards for children who are ready to excel beyond grade level.

■ ■ ■

*The Olsons learned more about the three schools they were considering. At **Great School Elementary**, the school used a set of continuous, step-by-step learning goals in core subjects and "critical thinking skills." Each subject and thinking area had a target minimum for each grade (which looked similar to grade level at Good Try, they noticed). Liza and Harrison were surprised to hear the principal and teachers call this level the "bare minimum" rather than "grade level." The staff told parents at the open house that most children would exceed the target in at least one subject each year. "This is what we tell our students, and we find that most children, even struggling ones, pick a favorite subject and really go for it," the principal stated with pride. The learning goals extended several grade levels above the sixth grade, even though this was the highest grade in the school. At **Good Try Elementary**, the teachers used a basic set of grade level standards used by many schools in the state. These standards stated end of grade goals only, but stated those quite clearly. After talking with several parents, it was clear that the school would provide extra help for struggling students and enrichment for advanced students if a child's parent requested it. "We do have a fair number of students with learning and family challenges, and we just know those kids won't meet grade level some years – but we love them anyway," the principal stated with pride. The Olsons wondered what that would mean for Colter. Or even Elan, if he too began to struggle. At **Yesteryear Elementary**, teachers stated with* *an air of pride that "our standards are higher than most schools in our area," and parents seemed to think the same thing. But the work the Olsons saw was well below Heidi's level. They asked a teacher, and she said, "Oh, don't worry. We always have a few kids like that, and they seem to take care of themselves! Plus, they always love our enriching mini-courses in January."*

■ ■ ■

How High is High?

We know from research that the more a teacher expects from a child, the more the child will expect of herself. And many parents considering multiple schools are seeking high expectations for their children. But even the brainiest child need not cram for calculus in kindergarten. So . . .

➤ How high should you expect a school to aim for "grade level"?

➤ How do you tell whether a school raises expectations for children who are ahead?

➤ And how do you tell whether teachers *really* expect students to reach the goals, whether grade level or higher?

If those seem like tough questions to answer, they are. While states, some national organizations, and many individual schools have clear, written learning standards, the rationale for them is not always clear. Most have been developed with the collective wisdom of teachers and other school staff who have a sense of what the typical student can master at each age. Yet we know that many children – fast or motivated learners, not just the supernova bright ones – go unchallenged in basic subjects for part of the school year. Furthermore, many children aren't making the grade even in schools with low-wattage standards. Standards are part of the solution, but clearly not the whole story.

Even if you don't know much about grade level standards, you know when your child isn't challenged or is academically lost at school.

You may not know much about grade level standards, but you know when your child isn't challenged or is academically lost at school. With a little effort, you can learn enough to make an accurate comparison among schools available to your child. The litmus test for you is this: it is clear to you that a school will expect a lot of *your child* and challenge *your child* to learn in core subjects every day.

Now let's dig deeper by making the term "high expectations" a little more real. Expectations are communicated in three ways:

1. *Grade Level Standards:* The minimum skills, knowledge and abilities required for all students to move from one grade to the next, often called "grade level standards" or "learning goals."

2. *Higher Goals When Students are Ready:* A clear, established process for setting higher goals to challenge individual children who are ahead of grade level in a subject.

3. *Words and Deeds:* The words and actions teachers use to communicate, formally and informally, that all children are *actually* expected to meet their goals, whether grade level or higher.

Grade Level Standards

Think of grade level standards and the next steps beyond for advanced students as a road map. If the school's mission is the ultimate destination, then the grade level learning goals should, all together, form a map to take your child through all of the school's grades (and beyond, for advanced students). The teaching methods and materials are the vehicles used to get from point to point on the map. Indeed, the very best of standards are constructed like a map, which allows teachers to focus on teaching and keeping students headed towards the destination.

If you compare schools' grade level standards (the minimum they expect all students to master) most likely you will find that the content varies in two ways:

➤ *How high? How difficult* are the skills and knowledge that all children are expected to master in each subject?

➤ *How broad? How many* academic subjects and topics are covered? How much of a child's overall development is addressed, not just academic, but also social, physical, emotional and spiritual?

Researchers have found that Great Schools have "high" standards in this way: students are expected to master more difficult material in the core subjects of reading, writing, math and, in later grades, science and social studies. In these basic subjects, teachers push students to learn more and think harder, not just memorizing more facts (although that has its place) but also solving problems, making logical arguments, comparing and contrasting ideas and creating new ones. (See box *To Think or Not To Think* on page 213 for more on the role of thinking skills.) Research, both in the U.S. and elsewhere, consistently shows that it is this push for higher levels of learning in core subjects, not breadth, that propels students to greater long-term academic performance.

Studies on breadth in education are few and inconsistent. Great Schools know this and do not confuse breadth with higher levels of learning in core subjects. They include breadth to reinforce core academic subjects, or because they value other subjects in their own right. However, they do not use greater breadth as an excuse for lowering expectations in basic academic subjects, nor as an alternative to raising expectations for children who are ahead in the basics. (See the box *Breadth: When Does More Do More for Your Child?*)

Smart à la Carte

Breadth: When Does More Do More for Your Child?

Breadth – more subjects, more topics, more of the "whole child" – has value, regardless of its impact on performance in core academic areas. Breadth communicates to students the richness of the world we inhabit – from the microscopic world of atoms to the outer reaches of space, from the English language to tongues that shaped the modern world but are no longer spoken, from the cultures we know and grew up enjoying to those with radically different values, religion, dress and behaviors. Breadth can engage the otherwise unengaged child, because it often captures what is lost when basic subjects are taught without imagination: the real experiences of people, the tangible and visible objects around us, the magic of things too far away or too small to see for ourselves. Breadth can help a child in the middle of the pack find special interests and talents that distinguish her from peers. Breadth in school can help children develop their social, emotional, physical and spiritual selves, especially important when family life is too busy to serve these traditional roles.

Breadth also can be used to reinforce and bring to life the basic subjects, when teachers collaborate to ensure that this happens. Indeed, breadth can become essential in a school that does not ensure children ahead of grade level are challenged in the basic subjects, preventing bored rebellion in an otherwise unengaged child.

In some circumstances, breadth may actually increase overall academic achievement, even in the basics. For example, there is some research evidence that language immersion programs – teaching the basic subjects in a foreign language – increase academic performance in the basics, particularly for non-native English speakers. For now, though, these studies are dwarfed by the seven Great School Quality Factors, which have appeared repeatedly over a long period of time as the major indicators of long-term achievement in students of all backgrounds. If you can find both quality and breadth in one school, go for it. If not, opt for quality and broaden your child's experiences outside of school.

You or your child may place special value on subjects or topics of particular personal interest, regardless of impact on overall academic achievement. The fit chapters (2-10) help you sort this out and include your personal favorites in your school hunt.

Many parents and their children value the content of broadening courses and will need to consider this in choosing a school (the fit chapters help you with this). However, breadth generally is not a substitute for ensuring that every child is challenged to greater heights of learning in the core subjects.

Higher Goals When Students are Ready

Children learn best when they are continually challenged to the next level of learning. Schools that focus entirely on making sure students reach grade level – even when grade level standards are set high – neglect any student who might be ready to progress further. Not only do "grade level only" schools fail bright and highly gifted learners, who may come into a grade already having mastered the material not expected until year end; they also fail the more typical "fast learners" and academically middling but highly motivated students, who may start in the middle of the pack but quickly learn the new material and are ready for more.

One mark of Great Schools is that all of their students, even the brightest and most academically capable, achieve more than similar students elsewhere. This is not by accident, but by design. These schools build in a consistent process for ensuring that "high" is as high as an individual child is ready to go. While the grade level standards form a firm floor, no individual child faces a ceiling beyond which the school stops offering academic challenge in the core subjects. Great Schools reflect this combined commitment to a firm floor and boundless ceiling in their written expectations, or "standards." They also reflect it in how they use the standards and in the actions of teachers.

Words and Deeds

Words: Comparing What's Written. Many parents will just accept a school's claim of "higher standards." But a school may mean higher in core subjects, broader, or just clearer. A school may have vague standards that the teachers don't understand, or ones crystal clear even to you. You won't know unless you take at least a little peek.

Almost all states have adopted a single system of standards for all of their *public* schools. Some public school districts have customized or raised these standards for all of *their* schools. Some individual public schools raise their standards beyond the district's, too. So if your search is limited to public schools within a single school district, the written state standards are a bare minimum.

You can obtain the basic standards for public schools in your area through your state department of education's website or your school district's website. You should also be able to look at an individual school's written standards in-person;

just ask at the school office. (If you aren't allowed to look, that's a sign that standards aren't used greatly in the school's daily life.)

If you're casting a wider net – considering private schools or a move to one of several districts or states – your job gets more complicated. You might want to get a free expert opinion about each state's or school's standards. Many state and national standards have been rated by teams of experts. You can assess a school's standards with help of the experts if the school uses recognized state or national standards as a base. If you are considering private schools, start by asking each school what standards it expects its students to meet. As with a public school, this can be useful in its own right: it will tell you whether each school uses its standards in everyday work. To find up-to-date websites that compile and evaluate state and national standards used by public and private schools, see our Resources for Parents section on page 354 or visit **PickyParent.com**.

If a school has detailed standards flowing continuously over many grades, then the expense may be too great for a school to share complete sets with prospective parents. Some schools break standards into grade-by-grade sections for sharing with parents, something they can easily share with the prospective parent as well. Ask for the samples you need, or offer to make copies at your own expense. If the grade level standards are available only in a 4-inch binder or not at all, you might ask how the school shares these learning goals with parents of students (chances are good that they don't).

Try looking at a limited sample to save time: two basic subjects in the grade your child would enter next year and in a grade two to four years above that. That's four sets to compare – all (or more than) most of you will have time to weigh! You might compare standards for math and reading (sometimes combined with writing into "language arts"), plus any subjects critical to you or your child after reading the fit chapters.

What Does a Grade Level Standard Look Like? Written standards will vary. The better they are, the more likely it is that a school *uses* them. Look for differences in Clarity, Continuity, Completeness, and Difficulty.

Continuous standards, with ever more difficult steps of learning, are more helpful in the classroom than end-of-year goals alone. For struggling and right-in-the-middle students, such a set of written standards makes tracking individual students' progress clear and consistent across classrooms. For advanced students, continuous standards make it far easier for teachers to challenge every child without regard to grade. Individual teachers do not have to reinvent the wheel when it comes to defining the next-step learning goals. Instead, they can focus on other Great School Quality Factors, like monitoring progress and adjusting teaching methods.

Shortcut: ask yourself, "Will this school's grade level goals challenge my child?" If so, go to Great School Quality Factor #3. If not, ask if goals are raised for advanced students.

Comparing Standards

	GOOD	BETTER	BEST
CLARITY	Standards are written for teachers to use, but are not simple or clear enough for most parents to understand	Standards are written for teachers, but are in simple form and clear language that most parents can understand	Standards are written with parents in mind, so that both teachers and nearly all parents can understand and use them
CONTINUITY	Written list of minimum skills, knowledge and abilities that children are required to master by end of school year ("grade level standards")	Written progression of ever more difficult skills, knowledge and abilities covering the typical range of students within each grade, with minimum year-end goals	Written progression of ever more difficult skills, knowledge and abilities that is continuous from grade to grade, with minimum year-end goals for each grade
COMPLETENESS	Written standards cover the basic subjects only: reading, writing, and math	Written standards cover more subjects that are taught in the school, not just the basics	Written standards cover all subjects included in the curriculum
DIFFICULTY	Skills, knowledge and abilities required for each grade level appear reasonable and achievable for typical children	Skills, knowledge and abilities required for each grade level are challenging for most typical children	Skills, knowledge and abilities required for each grade level are challenging for most typical children, and written goals extend well beyond even the highest grade level for ready children

Deeds: Comparing What's Done. Even when schools do not differ in their basic, *written* standards, they may differ enormously in their actual, day-to-day expectations. Studying Great Schools – that get great results with all kinds of students – has made two things clear. First, whatever the grade level standards may be, Great Schools pursue them relentlessly as a *bare minimum for all students*. What's more, Great Schools don't stop there; once a child masters a grade level target, he is asked to learn still more.

As with the school mission in Great School Quality Factor #1, a school must walk its talk. The school must truly *expect* all students to achieve challenging goals and must take *action* to ensure it. Within a given state, public schools will generally use the same written standards. Yet, if you ask, you will find that the principal and teachers in some schools make excuses for students not achieving this bar. At other schools, the state standards are treated as the absolute minimum, the bare bones bottom, the very least they expect. You can be sure that while the written standards are the same, more students will achieve more in the school with higher expectations.

Smart à la Carte

To Think or Not to Think? What Are "Thinking Skills"?

Great Schools stretch higher into the most essential subjects, which is one reason why even their students at "the bottom" perform better overall. Stretching higher does not mean just learning more facts, but also learning how to use facts to solve problems, make comparisons and think of new ideas. Many parents and educators worry that schools in the United States do not focus enough on teaching "critical" or "higher order" thinking skills. You might be thinking: "what does that mean?!" The most important "thinking skills" include these:

➤ *Analytical thinking* – solving problems that must be broken down into logical, orderly steps. A simple home example: how do you get five family members, luggage and the dog into your small station wagon for a trip? If you throw all the people and things in there, you run out of room and the dog sits on Mom's lap. If you make a plan about what goes where and when, taking all the different factors into account, that's analytical thinking: people need seats, dogs don't; the driver needs to see through the rearview mirror, so luggage can be stacked only so high; heavy suitcases on the bottom, food bags on top; bags we don't need on the road go in first; some of this luggage can stay home; etc. That's analytical thinking.

➤ *Conceptual thinking* – making comparisons between things not obviously related, seeing similarities and large patterns in a collection of smaller events. A home life example: you live in a beautiful neighborhood. But you never get as much exercise as you'd like. You rarely see your neighbors except through a car window. And even though you live within blocks of several great, reasonably priced restaurants, you always drive to them (and come to think of it, so do your neighbors). Though there are ways to address each problem individually and differently, it occurs to you that sidewalks would solve all three problems at once. That's conceptual thinking.

➤ *Creative thinking* – coming up with new ideas or new ways to use old ideas. A simple home example: your latest decorating project on a minimum budget means using grandma's knick knacks in ways you hadn't imagined before. That old butter churner becomes an umbrella stand, that potting table from her garage makes a charming entry way greeting table, her scarf collection sewn together makes snappy curtains for the den. That's creative thinking.

"Critical" thinking means making judgments. "Higher order" thinking is more and more complicated thinking of the types listed above. You don't need to be a rocket scientist to use thinking skills. Indeed, they are a big help just in navigating home life. More and more, they are not just helpful but essential for navigating a complex and ever-changing work world, too.

In all schools, you'll want to ask whether teachers *expect* all students to meet grade level and what *actions* the school takes to ensure that outcome. You'll want to ask and listen for specific examples of how teachers work with children to achieve grade level, especially if your child may struggle. You'll also want to ask what the school does with a child who masters the material before year end or who starts the year ahead of grade level, especially if your child is advanced or highly motivated. You should hear about a relentless, "no excuses," action-filled pursuit of the minimum grade level standards for every student, and a clear process to set higher goals for students who are ahead. Words of promise are not enough. Listen for a description of specific actions.

Do Clear Standards Hamper Great Teachers? Does so much clarity in standards inhibit the creativity of great teachers? Not really. Instead of devoting their time to clarifying *what* students need to learn, teachers guided by clear standards can focus on *how* the subject matter is taught and on ensuring that every student is challenged and making progress.

Great School Quality Factor #3: Monitoring of Progress and Adjusting Teaching

Each child's individual progress is monitored frequently during the school year, often weekly. Teachers change their teaching approaches as needed – adapting to individual student interests, nonacademic capabilities, learning styles and other differences – to ensure that students meet their goals, both grade level and higher. When a child falls behind, the school takes immediate action, accepting no excuses for failure.

■ ■ ■

*At **Great School Elementary**, the principal told the Olsons and other parents at the open house that each child has time either one-on-one or in a group of five or fewer children with the lead teacher in math, reading and writing most days of each school week. "Our lead teachers are trained to use this time to assess each child's mastery of material and to move the child to the next step. Teachers use a combination of interactive teacher-child materials and self-teaching materials appealing to different children's interests and learning styles. You will find this happening most of the day in every classroom. If a student is having persistent difficulty, we have school-wide learning resource teachers who help the lead teacher identify the root of the problem and address it right away." When the Olsons asked, the Great School principal told them that students not working with the lead teacher are shepherded through a variety of large group, individual, and small group activities by the assistant teacher –*

Smart à la Carte

Does My Child Need a Formal Assessment?

Is *formal* assessment of your child's abilities and learning characteristics, in writing or given orally, ever necessary? Well, yes. In some cases, an informal understanding of a child's work mastery is not enough. Two problems can arise. First, an academically gifted child who also has a mild learning disability, behavioral challenge or mental illness may be up to grade level, but actually capable of much more. This child will raise no red flags unless his academic work slips or his behavior becomes unmanageable in the classroom. For example, a very bright child with mild ADHD (attention deficit hyperactivity disorder), depression or dyslexia may perform "just fine" in the classroom but fall far short of his academic capability. Once the disability or impairment is addressed, his academic performance can rise to the full level of his capability.

Second, children who are typical in academic capability but who have mild learning disabilities, behavioral impairments or mental illness may be misdiagnosed as academically challenged. "Why isn't John paying attention? Because the material is over his head, so let's get him more repetition." Not the right solution for the depressed or clinically hyperactive child! If a child has certain disabilities or other challenges, even a star teacher working with a small group may not be able to diagnose the *cause* of the problem. And clearly, a child of any academic capability who has a severe learning disability or other impairment (physical or mental) may require formal assessment and significant treatment to learn as well as he is able.

What kind of formal testing might a school do? For starters, a formal test of each child's I.Q. (or similar) compared to performance will help identify that a gap exists between how we'd expect the child to perform academically and reality. Children whose performance lags need further assessment to pinpoint the exact problem – physical, mental or behavioral. In addition, brief formal tests of learning styles, interests and motivation are not essential but can help teachers anticipate individual students' needs.

As long as some children have learning disabilities and physical, mental and behavioral challenges, formal assessment at the beginning of each school year – or at times when academic performance changes suddenly – makes sense. This is a role that the Great School assumes but does not confuse with the three F's: frequent, focused and forward-looking monitoring of student progress (see page 217). If your school does not provide such formal testing, you may find it helpful to have your child tested by an education counselor or psychologist outside of school, to help with either your school choice or your communication with your child's teachers.

*with individual and small group work largely determined by each child's current mastery level. At **Good Try Elementary**, the Olsons learned that student progress is monitored every six weeks. If a child is struggling, and especially if a child's parents have expressed concern, learning resource teachers are available to work with small groups once each week in core subjects, especially reading. Starting in second grade, weekly pullouts for gifted students begin. At **Yesteryear Elementary**, the principal stated, and several teachers and parents confirmed, "Our standards are very challenging, so we really can just stick to our program." In response to the Olson's question about monitoring, one teacher said, "Oh, yes, we do end of grade standardized tests starting in second grade, so we know if there's a problem. And of course there are three report cards each year. And our guidance program funnels kids who aren't cutting the mustard to tutoring programs available in our city, if their parents choose."*

Smart à la Carte

Testing Feedback: Surviving the Jargon

If you are getting feedback from a testing professional about your child, know that testers may throw a bit of jargon at you. Some jargon you will already recognize, because you, having read this book, are an extra savvy parent. But there is one additional pair of terms you might want to know. There are two types of test scales that may have been used to assess or report on your child. One is called "norm" based testing and the other is called "criterion" based testing. If you feel your eyes glazing, don't sweat skipping this box. But if you are feeling a bit nerdy, read on.

Norm based testing compares your child to a large group of other children who've scored the full range of scores. On most characteristics, humans tend to fall on what's called a "normal" distribution: most of us are lumped pretty close together in the middle, a few of us struggle way below at the bottom, and a few of us score really high. Your child's score on such a test will probably be reported as a "percentile," indicating where she stands relative to other children. If your child scores at the "70th percentile," for example, she scored higher than 70% of children (7 out of every 10) her age.

Criterion based tests compare your child to a pre-set standard or criterion. For example, determining whether or not your kindergartener can count to three is a criterion-based test. But you'd also want to know, well, "Is that typical? How high can most kindergarteners count?" And "Can she count higher? How high? Are many other kids like that?" In the best of worlds, criterion tests are based on some real research about what is "typical," and they do not stop at the simple question "can you count to three" but go on to find out more about what your child knows and can do.

The Three F's That Keep Your Child Moving in Fast Forward

You might think that end-of-year testing is all it takes (and indeed many mediocre schools rely on this.) But the monitoring needed for Great School Quality Factor #3 need not be formal. Just *f*requent, *f*ocused on your child, and *f*orward-looking:

➤ *Frequent* enough that your child does not languish for long not "getting it" before the teacher tries another approach to make the material stick; and frequent enough that your child moves on to more challenging material when she's ready.

➤ *Focused* on your child's current level of learning and individual learning characteristics:
  ✔ Focused on your child's current learning level so that teachers can know how fully a child has mastered material he's currently pursuing, and
  ✔ Focused on understanding your child's characteristics – interests, learning styles, social and emotional development, and other needs and preferences – to help teachers ensure that your child learns.

➤ *Forward-looking* because monitoring is useless unless used to make changes – either to push a child to the next level of learning or to try a new approach for mastering the current material. Changes should happen as frequently as needed as a result of monitoring, in response to children struggling with new material and those mastering it earlier than expected.

The litmus test for Great School Quality Factor #3 is this: the school will have a handle on *what your child knows* in core subjects at all times and will *make sure your child learns* what's needed, even if it takes back flips to do it.

In a Great School, it is the teacher's job to know what level of learning each student has mastered and where each child struggles. Students start each school year at different levels of learning. Why? They will have learned at different rates during the previous school years. Some will remember what they learned, others will have forgotten and need review. Some will have been ahead from the start, others have always struggled.

It is the Great School's job to provide the resources – assistant teachers, learning specialists or other staff – that allow all lead teachers to have contact with students and keep track of individual progress. (Great *teachers* have organized volunteers to serve this role for years.) As long as she has small group or individual exposure to each child, even an average teacher should be able to determine the current level of mastery and appropriate next steps throughout the year. This is far easier, by the way, if the school also provides the kind of continuous learning goals or standards described in Great School Quality Factor #2. Great Schools also enhance teachers' ability to keep tabs on students by providing them with state-of-the-art data and data-tracking systems.

Great Schools do not leave teachers in the lurch. Instead, they provide teachers with consistent, well-planned support to identify and respond to each child's learning needs.

Teachers in Great Schools learn to do backflips to help all kinds of children learn challenging material. Even great teachers need school support to achieve this consistently.

It is also the teacher's job to identify and respond to individual learning characteristics in each child. Each student has his own academic and nonacademic capabilities, interests, preferred learning styles, and motivations. In a Great School, teachers are assisted in *understanding and using* these characteristics of individual children to foster learning. A Great School may weave this understanding of individual children's needs into daily learning. But at the very least, if your child is not making progress in an academic area despite repeated attempts using the school's standard tools and methods, you might see the teacher and school:

➤ Asking if there are any changes or recent stresses at home and helping you deal with the situation as it relates to your child

➤ Assessing your child's social, emotional and physical development; then working with you to design a strategy for addressing weaknesses that are impacting academic learning (see *Viewpoint: Whole Child* on page 34).

➤ Considering your child's overall brain development and trying new tactics to overcome weaknesses that are inhibiting your child's learning (see *Viewpoint: All Kinds of Minds* on page 81)

➤ Considering your child's "multiple intelligences" and trying a teaching approach that uses your child's strengths to promote academic learning (see *Viewpoint: Multiple Intelligences* on page 47)

➤ Assessing your child's learning styles and then using activities that play to your child's dominant style (see *Viewpoint: Learning Styles* on page 67)

➤ Suggesting and providing assessment for learning disabilities; if one is found, working with you to design a strategy for helping your child cope with or even overcome the disability

➤ Giving your child assignments that relate to a strong interest area (e.g., writing about interest, reading and researching about interest, doing math problems related to interest)

➤ Appealing to your child's motivations; for example, if your child needs to bond interpersonally with teachers, often sitting with your child at lunch or spending a few minutes of one-on-one teaching time with your child weekly

➤ Involving you in the process of understanding and helping your child learn

Each child's social, emotional and physical development can enhance or diminish academic learning. In addition, many children will at some point face a mental challenge of some kind, such as a disability, disorder or mental illness that diminishes learning. When teachers are expected and helped to identify and address all of these potential barriers to learning, children learn more.

Smart à la Carte

Do Schools Spend Too Much Time on Standardized Tests?

Many parents worry about overemphasis on standardized tests in schools today. Does the narrow focus of multiple choice tests on the basics lead teachers to neglect other subjects? Do these tests lead teachers to give short shrift to thinking skills in favor of rote memorization? Are schools spending too much time prepping kids to take the tests, instead of "really teaching them"? And what about kids who are already at or above "grade level"? What do they get out of constant drilling of material they already know?

Standardized tests – imperfect as they may be – are the best way found so far to compare the learning in *similar core* subjects of large groups of *differing* students attending *differing* schools. This is valuable for determining, for instance, how well students in a school are mastering core knowledge in basic subjects, and how subgroups within a school (by race, income or gender, for example) are faring. For these reasons, standardized testing is here to stay.

As a parent choosing a school, the key question for you is this: ***Is the school you're examining using standardized tests* the right way?** *Here's what to look for in a Great School:*

➤ *Standardized tests are only a small part of the school's assessment and monitoring system.* Annual fill-in-the-bubble exams are no substitute for the three F's. Teachers constantly monitor students' progress using other means.

➤ *The school uses standardized tests to track* **progress** of students over time, not just the percentage making grade level. Kids who are already at or above grade level don't waste time drilling for the exams; they do other work at their current level.

➤ *The school reports test results broken out by relevant categories* of students. It's common to see breakdowns by race and income. Less common but even more important: how much did kids with your child's starting performance level improve?

➤ *Tests reflect the school mission.* If a school says its mission is to develop strong critical thinkers, for example, the school should assess critical thinking, not just basic skills. Just as high schools assess critical thinking with Advanced Placement exams, elementary standardized exams can assess these skills, too.

➤ *The school tests what's important to you and your child.* Look back at your fit needs for what your child learns. Ideally, the school you choose "keeps score" when it comes to the content you think is most valuable. What's tested is what's valued, and that's where money and class time flow.

A Great School provides ongoing education to help teachers recognize and respond to students' individual strengths and weaknesses in all areas that affect learning. Teachers in Great Schools are expected to learn how to do new things they may think they can't do – to help your child learn things that your child may think she can't do. We call this doing "back flips." Whatever you call it, few teachers can do it consistently without training and intensive support from the school.

Great School Quality Factor #4: Focus on Effective Learning Tasks

Teachers use well-planned, well-tested approaches to instruction. Class time, material purchases and facilities are all allocated according to the school's mission; more important subjects are given more time and better materials and facilities. Classroom interruptions are minimal. Materials and curriculum are frequently reviewed, and altered, to ensure they are working as planned.

■ ■ ■

*At **Great School Elementary**, the Olsons heard one teacher say, "Standard educational programs are like fishing nets: a better one will let you catch more fish, but some students always slip through or we miss them entirely. We teachers work together in each grade and subject to make faster guesses about which programs work and what kind of kids need something different. And, well, we have a school-wide research team that reviews the latest curriculum research each summer to see if new materials or approaches have been proven to work." When asked, the principal pointed out that school rules limit mid-day announcements, visitors and other disruptions to keep the kids focused. She suggested that the Olsons take a look at the daily school schedules in kindergarten and third grade: "You'll notice that most of the day is spent on reading, writing and math, but we pack in foreign language, science, and critical thinking workshops for everyone, not just our gifted kids. We do more because the core subjects are so focused on individual kids' levels. There's not a lot of fluff time here where we're reaching only half the kids in the class like at a lot of schools." A mid-day tour (looking through two-way mirrors on classroom doors) showed the Olsons that indeed children seemed to be highly engaged in their work in the classrooms. At **Good Try Elementary**, different teachers seemed to be using different materials, "whatever we each feel most comfortable and familiar with, really," said one teacher. When the Olsons asked if the different approaches worked for all children, another teacher said, "Well, every classroom is different. I can't really speak for the other* *teachers." The Good Try principal confirmed that she trusted individual teachers to use their past experience and that keeping them happy was her biggest concern: "Good teachers aren't always easy to recruit, you know!" During their mid-day tour, the Olsons noticed that many children were focused, but several in each class seemed lost. At **Yesteryear Elementary**, several teachers told the Olsons that they'd been using the same reading and math programs for over a decade. "We were the first school in our area to adopt the reading program – the sales rep came here first, knowing that we are educational leaders in our community," the principal stated with pride. When asked if the program worked for all of their children, one teacher reminded the Olsons that some children "just can't cut it," and so ought to get outside tutoring. "But even they like school here, because so much of our school day is spent on enriching activities. We go on one field trip per week most weeks. And we have six playgrounds!"*

■ ■ ■

Focus, and Focus on What Works

If Great School Quality Factor #4 seems like a catch-all for good classroom instruction, it is. The core operations of a school occur in the classroom, and it is here that your child will experience the direct benefit of attending a Great School. Many schools that have relied only on finding great teachers or on adopting solid, but one-size-fits-all, teaching materials will be strong on this factor, even while being weak on others that require more ongoing support from the whole school. This factor alone is not enough to make a school great, but it is essential if your child is to experience strong learning in the classroom.

The litmus test for Great School Quality Factor #4 is this: the principal and teachers in the school can tell you *how they know that they are doing what works* best in the classroom, and they make frequent changes to improve.

Fortunately, there are simple signs that a school has a strong focus on effective learning tasks:
➤ Well planned, well-tested approaches are used.
➤ Class time, material purchases and facilities are allocated according to plan.
➤ Classroom interruptions are minimal.

Well planned, well-tested approaches are used. If a school is doing this, then teachers should be *able to tell you what approach and materials* they use in the core academic areas and why these were chosen. Listen with your common sense ears. You should hear about constant assessing, reworking and trying again of teaching methods and materials. If you hear that teachers are doing research to find the best current teaching methods and tools, discussing their methods and materials with each other in regular meetings, tossing out approaches that do not work with most children, tailoring proven methods to better fit the school's students, and other similar activities, then the school is doing it right. If you hear teachers complain that an approach is "required" by the school or school district, but that it doesn't seem to work with many students in the school, yet they are still using that approach, beware!

"Well-tested" need not mean "proven by academic researchers in a university." While that would be nice, the reality is that few instructional approaches have

Smart à la Carte

Learning to Read: My Way or the Highway?

Many parents of elementary age children are highly concerned about the method of reading instruction their children's schools use. Many of our strong feelings about the subject come from our own experiences as students. We may remember the dawning light when phonics was introduced in our own classrooms and we finally were able to figure out the words on a page. Or we may equate phonics with boring, repetitive class sessions.

In the raging debate about reading, you're likely to hear about two popular approaches, phonics and whole language. Phonics instruction includes teaching children not just letter sounds, but the sounds of common letter combinations that, all together, form words. Whole language means exposing children to reading materials so that they become familiar with common words, phrases and contexts of stories and are able to build off of those to read on their own. In reality, most schools don't go exclusively one way or the other. You'll want to get behind the labels and ask, "How, specifically, do teachers in this school help students learn to read?"

Fortunately, reading instruction is one of the best-researched areas of classroom instruction. From this research, we've learned that phonics advocates are right – the most effective reading programs do include explicit instruction in phonics for all students. But the research also tells us that the most effective teachers use a balanced approach. In addition to phonics, teachers should expose students to rich and interesting texts, lead discussions about the content of these texts, teach students to comprehend better by summarizing what they've read, and give students opportunities to read brief texts aloud in order to increase their "fluency." Importantly, Great Schools also give extra help, usually in small groups, to students who are slow to master phonics or read fluently.

been well-researched. That should not stop teachers from using "action research," or testing different materials and approaches in the classroom. Fortunately, there is a growing push to assess the impact of various instruction techniques and materials. Educators' understanding of what works for different kinds of children is a fast-moving target.

Meanwhile, it's clear that the particular materials used are less important than *how* they are used: to meet the school mission, to set high expectations for every child, to raise goals when children are ready and to approach children with differing needs in different ways. Great School Quality Factors #1 – 3 would lead a teacher to terrific teaching with a variety of instructional tools and techniques. **PickyParent.com** lets you delve deeper into the latest and greatest on curriculum and teaching approaches. We'll help you find out what research has said, if anything, about the particular approaches your prospective schools are using. (See box on *Learning to Read* for more about one raging debate.)

Class time, material purchases and facilities are allocated according to plan. When you visit a targeted school, you should see what you have *heard and read* about. Subjects and activities that are essential to the school's mission should be highly visible at the school – through top-notch facilities, materials and a large dose of class time. If you read in the school brochure that healthy mind, healthy body is the school mission, look for balanced academic and athletics facilities. If self-initiated, hands-on work is a core part of the school's agenda, but all you see is students sitting in desks with workbooks, ask how much time is spent doing this each day (it shouldn't be much). Beware the school that claims a science focus but has no science lab, no specialized science materials and only an hour a week of science. If you can't see how the school's priorities are met with the facilities and weekly class schedule, chances are that the school is not allocating resources in line with the mission.

Classroom interruptions are minimal. Just ask and then observe. First, the school should have a clear policy designed to limit classroom disruptions. For example, school wide announcements should be made during home room or the time early in the day before focused school work has begun. Children leaving class for doctor or other appointments should do so at the beginning of academic sessions, not in the middle. Students should be encouraged to use the toilet before and after focused class work (though younger children will certainly need more latitude on this to avoid accidents at school). Second, you should see behavior in classrooms that reflects the school policy. Teachers and students should be focused on class work. Blocks of academic time should go uninterrupted by distractions – visits from office administrators, loudspeaker announcements, toilet breaks, children leaving or reentering the class for reasons unrelated to their work, etc.

SNAP TO IT

What To Do

➤ *Skim Great School Quality Factors #1 – 4 on the Great School Quality Checklist* (page 200). Estimated Time: 5 minutes

➤ *Use the Quality: What to Look for in a School table* sections (page 409) for Great School Quality Factors #1 – 4 to help you think of specific questions about quality to ask principals, teachers and parents. Highlight or jot down the ones that are most informative for you, and record them as needed on your *Interview Forms* (page 273). Estimated Time: 10 minutes

➤ *Use the Quality: Ways to Get What You Don't Get at School table* (page 433) to help you decide what school weaknesses on Great School Quality Factors #1 – 4 you would find most difficult to make up for at home. Underline these in the left-hand column on your *Great School Quality Checklist.* Time: 10 minutes

Optional Activities

➤ *If your child is currently in elementary school,* take a few minutes to think about the Great School Quality Factor #1 - 4 strengths and weaknesses of the school. Use the Great School Quality Checklist as a guide. Discuss your thoughts with your spouse or other parenting partner. You can do a more complete assessment later, if you wish. Estimated Time: As needed.

Need more? Want more? Got more to share? Visit PickyParent.com.

Expecting a lot from people
does not mean you think less
of them, but more of them.
They're that important.
We're talking about teachers,
principals and schools, but
hey, it's true for children, too!

LIGHT'NING LIST

What To Know from Chapter 13

➤ **The Supporting Two Great School Quality Factors** enable children, teachers and parents to focus on the work of the school.

➤ **Great School Quality Factor #5 is Home-School Connection.** The litmus test is this: a school has a clear, consistent method for telling you what's what. In a Great School, parents are told what their children will be learning, what to do at home, what progress each child has made during the year (frequently) and how to work with the school to solve any problems their children might face.

➤ **Great School Quality Factor # 6 is Safe and Orderly Environment.** The litmus test is this: it is abundantly apparent that a school will keep your child and others safe and focused on learning. Students are kept safe from harm by other people, facilities and equipment. Students know how they are expected to behave in and out of the classroom, and they behave as expected because consequences are clear and consistent.

➤ **The indicators of the Supporting Two Great School Quality Factors** in a school are included in the *Great School Quality Checklist* (page 200).

Chapter 13

Great School
Quality Factors #5 and 6:
The Supporting Two

Great School Quality Factor #5:
Home-School Connection

Parents are told what their children will be learning, how to help at home, how their children are progressing during the year (frequently), and how to work with the school to solve any problems their children might face.

■ ■ ■

*Because of the delay detecting Colter's disability, and also because Liza was considering going back to work, the Olsons were concerned about communicating well with their children's teachers. At **Great School Elementary**, they didn't even have to ask about this, since the principal mentioned in the open house speech and the teachers they met all mentioned the school's required parent-teacher communication policy. Mini report cards were sent home every two weeks school wide. Not as comprehensive as the end of semester reports, they covered behavior, academics (broken down by subject), social development with peers and teachers, and physical development. Asked if this wasn't a huge burden, one teacher said, "This is O.K. for us, really, because we are keeping track of these things weekly, anyway. It's a bit of a scramble when they're due, but, frankly, we know you can help us more if you know where things stand. We often attach a sheet about the topics we'll be tackling with your child in the next few weeks. Standard instructions about how to help (and not* *help) children with homework were sent at the beginning of the year, with periodic reminders. At* **Good Try Elementary,** *when they asked, the Olsons found that the main communication occurred at the September class open house and the twice yearly parent conferences in November and April. "Some of our mothers, and occasionally fathers, volunteer to read stories in the classroom. Of course, we get to know those parents quite well," one teacher noted with a smile. Liza's stomach lurched as she worried whether that meant she shouldn't start working again – she wouldn't want to miss out on communicating with the teachers. At* **Yesteryear Elementary,** *when asked, the principal said with knowing certainty, "Oh, we have our first conferences in October, a whole month before most schools. And again in April, of course. And many of our parents help plan the January Chill, a fabulous party for parents and a great fundraiser for our school. We really get to know parents who participate that way." When Liza stuck her neck out and asked how teachers would let her know if Elan began to show the same disability as Colter, the principal said, "Don't worry, if your child is not going to make grade level, our guidance staff will help you find the right tutoring service for the next year."*

■ ■ ■

Your Child's First Teacher is You

Parent involvement has gotten a lot of press, political and popular attention in recent decades. As parents, you want your child to enjoy and succeed in school. As adults with other commitments – work, a household to run and other obligations – it is hard to help your child as much as you might like. The challenge is doubled if you don't know what your child is learning in school, much less have any idea how to help.

Great Schools recognize the pressures facing parents. These schools clarify what is expected of parents and shower them with helpful advice and materials throughout the year. They let parents know *what* their children are learning, before, during and after the learning occurs. They tell parents up front and during the year how to help their children at home.

So, when you are prospecting for your child's school, teachers should be able to tell you the specific process or steps that will occur for communicating with you and engaging you in your child's education. In addition, they should be able to give you an overview of the content most children will be learning in their grade (as well as a summary of next steps for children who are advanced, if you need this). If they can't tell you what your child would learn when they are "selling" the school to you, chances are slim that they will do it when your child is a student.

What you should hear about from principal, teachers and parents are clear and consistent:

➤ Steps and materials for telling parents what their children will be learning

➤ Process for frequently informing parents of each child's progress during the year (note that this is difficult if the school is weak on Great School Quality Factor #3: Monitoring)

➤ Expectations for how parents should help their children at home, and

➤ Process for dealing with problems, academic or behavioral, should they arise.

Many schools rely on a combination of quick parent-teacher chats at carpool pick-up and once-or-twice-per-year parent conferences. Schools in which most children ride buses may use one or two conferences per year only! But one-minute chat sessions and one or two meetings with the lead teacher are not enough to prepare you for helping your child at home and keep you informed of your child's progress. Great Schools are more planful and thorough about informing parents and getting them actively involved in their own children's education.

For example, in a Great School you might see a combination of these activities and materials:

Beginning of year:

➤ "Open house" gathering of all parents and teacher to give verbal overview of what children will be learning, teaching method and materials

➤ Short written descriptions of year-end goals (grade level), how struggling children will be helped, and how children who are advanced will be challenged. The teacher might show or give you a list of progressively more advanced learning goals for core subjects, not just year-end goals

➤ Meetings between parents and teacher to discuss each individual child's previous school experiences and important individual characteristics

➤ Clear invitation to communicate with teacher in a *variety* of ways accessible to parents (notes, phone calls, voice mail, email, special meetings, two or more regular conferences, drop off and pick up)

During year:

➤ Weekly written updates about what children learned last week and will learn next week, along with specific actions parents should take at home to support child

➤ Frequent homework overviews and descriptions of how parents should – and should not – help

You shouldn't have to beg to know what your child is learning. It's far harder to support your child's learning if you don't know what's being taught.

➤ Child's school work sent home in small, frequent batches, with explanations from teacher of assignment goals (if needed)

➤ At least two parent-teacher conferences to discuss child's progress (more is better and is essential if problems arise between conferences)

➤ Occasional parent-only classes to educate about key areas of children's learning, especially topics where parents may be less knowledgeable (e.g., computer skills, English as second language)

➤ Efforts to connect parents with social services they may need to build strong families and support their children's learning, when needed

End of Year:

➤ Written summary of child's progress and achievement in all major learning areas

➤ Discussion of suggested developmental goals for following year, assistance for parents considering school changes

The traditional celebratory family parties at the beginning and end of year are valuable, too, but they do not affect how much your child learns. They build a sense of community, help parents feel comfortable with the teachers and help parents meets each other. They can affect fit in many ways, but have little effect on quality. Since these do not help your child's academic progress and performance, they are not substitutes for the other steps that provide information about your child's learning in the classroom.

Great School Quality Factor #6: Safe and Orderly Environment

Students are kept safe from harm by other people, facilities and equipment. Students know how they are expected to behave in and out of the classroom, and they behave as expected because consequences are clear and consistent.

■ ■ ■

*At **Great School Elementary**, Harrison had heard the same things that Liza heard: the school kept in close touch with parents about their children's behavior. But Harrison was a "rule guy," and he wondered just how tough the behavior standards were. "They can report on it all they want, but if they don't expect much, who cares what they report," he grumbled. He was humbly surprised by the behavior he observed through the two-way mirrors on the classroom doors during his tour. "Wow, these kids are really focused. I look in there and I see all those different kinds of chil-*

dren thrown together, and, well, every kid focused on learning is just not what I'd expect. But that's what I see. I saw this one kid start to goof around – that teacher was all over it. It wasn't 30 seconds before they had him working on something." When he later looked at the school's "Behavior Policies" he liked the focus on "respect" and the worry-wart nature of the detailed safety procedures: all visitors had to sign in and wear a tag; a parent-staff committee conducted a once monthly walk-through to inspect the property and school equipment. "It would take a pretty crafty person – grownup or kid – to get past these safety rules," he thought. At **Good Try Elementary,** *the handbook had a safety and behavior policy, too. But the principal and teachers never brought it up except when they mentioned that the school had some kids from a "tough population." It seemed that they must deal with safety and behavior problems as they arose – or he just guessed that since they didn't really say much about it. When he asked about the visitor policy (having seen Great School's impressive one), the principal said, "Well, we want everyone to feel welcome here. In fact, on any given day, you'll see lots of adults who support our school visiting. Teachers are used to it." The principal was right. Harrison did see lots of strangers wandering around. In fact, he didn't have to wear a tag on his tour. "I could be anybody, a predator," he thought. At* **Yesteryear Elementary,** *he felt embarrassed after he asked about safety and class order. "Well, we have a great group of parents and kids, so it's not an issue," one teacher said. In fact, Harrison did think that the kids seemed pretty tame here. Even the ones who looked bored and tuned out in class seemed to be sitting still and not bothering other kids. "That's something," he thought.*

■ ■ ■

Many a parent in the past has been wooed by great landscaping and buildings, good manners in the classroom and a crystal clear honor or disciplinary code. And many parents have shied away from sending their children to schools where classrooms are noisy and chaotic, or buildings old and out of style. How can you tell what matters and what doesn't for the experience your child will have and how well she will learn in school?

The litmus test is this: it is abundantly apparent that a school will keep your child and others safe and focused on learning.

Great School Quality Factor #6 has shown up in many but not all studies of Great Schools. While it is a safe bet to say that most Great Schools adhere to Great School Quality Factor #6, it is a certainty that this factor does not guarantee greatness in the content of your child's learning. Safety and some degree of order are musts for a great educational environment, but they alone are not enough.

You certainly should eliminate schools with clear safety problems. But do not let prim and proper outweigh excellence in the educational basics. Instead, look for rock-solid safety basics and an environment where children can focus on learning. Then, use other elements of quality and fit to choose your child's school. Because safety is the more straightforward of the two matters, let's start there.

Safety

Your child needs both to be safe and feel safe to stay focused on learning. You should eliminate schools with serious safety problems, but do not choose a school solely for its safe environment. In reality, most schools are very safe for students – safer, often, than other places where children spend time. But as grim headlines have shockingly reminded us over the years, many schools also are lax about safety problems until a specific situation makes people aware of gaps.

You will need to consider not just the policies and practices of the schools you consider, but also the environment in which they operate. Schools located in suburban and rural areas may have less stringent safety policies for visitors because crime rates are generally low. Since the odds of a safety problem are low, these schools may choose to spend fewer resources to make the schools safer than they already are. In contrast, a school located in a higher crime area may need to be more stringent about certain safety procedures (e.g., visitors, screening for weapons) to meet the minimum bar for a safe school. You will have to make a judgment about how well the safety policies fit each school environment. Note that safety policies should cover all school-sponsored events and locations, including the school bus, athletic activities, etc.

How can you tell if a school meets the basic test for Safety? Look for these positive signs:

➤ The school has a clear policy for suspension, and ultimately expulsion, of any *student who threatens the safety of other students or staff with words or actions.* Even habitual pranksters who go too far are removed for the safety of others if they do not keep their behavior within safe boundaries.

➤ The school has a clear policy for suspension and ultimately expulsion of *students and staff caught using or selling illegal drugs* (or drugs with age requirements) at school or elsewhere.

➤ The school has a clear policy for suspension and ultimately expulsion of *students and staff caught in possession of weapons* on school grounds.

➤ The school has a clear policy of screening and identifying *all* visitors, not just those who *choose* to sign in. When you visit the school, you are subject to the policy and can observe that it is enforced. This is one policy that is infrequently followed in low-incident suburban schools until a problem occurs.

➤ Staff members are pre-screened for criminal records in all 50 states of the U.S. The school has and follows a policy about what previous crimes will exclude a staff member.

➤ Buildings, walkways, playgrounds, athletic fields, parking lot, buses and any other school facilities and grounds appear clean and in good repair.

➤ Equipment in the classrooms – from chairs and desks to science lab equipment – appears clean and in good repair.

➤ Cafeteria tables, chairs, kitchen and serving areas appear clean and in good repair.

Remember that flashy is not necessary. Do not choose a school because it has sparkling play sets or the best manicured lawn (unless it also shines in quality). But do eliminate schools that do not appear sanitary and safe.

Perhaps the most important contribution you can make to safety is teaching your own child to recognize, avoid and report unsafe situations. This is a developing field, and more and more advice is available to parents wanting to help their children get smart about personal safety.

Order

As with safety, you should eliminate schools with extreme disorder in the classrooms, but do not choose a school solely for its orderly environment. The most important aspect of "order" is not whether children are completely quiet and still, but whether they are engaged in learning.

Let us give a quick example. Many of the highest quality elementary schools – in which students of all kinds outperform similar peers elsewhere – use a combination of small group and individual work. If you step into a well-managed classroom like this, you will likely hear a low buzz of students and teachers interacting as they work. Nearly all students will be focused on their work, but you may at any moment observe a few staring into space or talking out of turn. You should see teachers redirecting those students towards their work.

To the casual observer, especially one who has a strong sense of order herself, the multiple groups doing different kinds of work, along with the buzz of activity, may look and sound chaotic. But to each child in the classroom, the work will feel great, because each child will be closely engaged in a task. Keep this school on your list!

Contrast this to a classroom in which young children are all in desks facing the teacher, potentially one of the most orderly arrangements (from the grownup perspective). But suppose that the teacher's words are clearly of little interest to many of the students. Many are looking off into space or doodling without looking at the teacher. This classroom also has a buzz, but it is caused by the rustling of the doodlers, the bumping of desks by bored (or lost), wiggly children, and the giggling of those in the back of the class! Few children are engaged in learning. The teacher does and says nothing about the situation, until a child makes a noise so loud that the teacher can't hear herself. Clearly, expectations for classroom behavior are low, and the students know this. The teacher, having but one set of material to teach in one way, has little in her arsenal to engage the children for whom the material is too easy, too hard or just plain boring. Yes, higher behavioral expectations, and consequences, might shape up the classroom, but the learning will not likely improve for many.

In another school, order is part and parcel of the school's approach, which includes lots of repetition and drilling in the basic subjects. In one of these classrooms, students are held fast by the teacher's gaze from the front of the classroom. The teacher holds up visual cue cards and drills the students on English sentence structure. The teacher asks a question, the students answer in unison. This classroom – indeed the whole school – is highly orderly. Don't eliminate it for lack of order. But is it the right place for your child? Maybe. You should not choose it for its order, but you should keep it on your list until you find out how it compares on other quality and fit items.

How can you tell if a school meets the basic test for Order? Look for these positive signs:

➤ The school has a clear, written policy about how students are expected to act toward each other, teachers and other school staff.

➤ When you visit the school, the behavior you see – in classrooms, hallways and elsewhere – matches the policy. In classrooms, all students appear focused on their work, whether working alone, in small groups or large groups. Teachers quickly, calmly redirect students who are not focused on work.

➤ School policy makes it clear that students who violate behavior rules face immediate, consistent consequences. Punishments are mild for minor offenses, but more severe for worse behavior and repeat offenders, including suspension and ultimately expulsion from the school (yes, even in public schools).

SNAP TO IT

What To Do

➤ *Skim Great School Quality Factors #5 and 6 on the Great School Quality Checklist* (page 200). Estimated Time: 5 minutes

➤ *Use the Quality: What to Look for in a School table* sections for Great School Quality Factors #5 and 6 (page 409) to help you think of specific questions about quality to ask principals, teachers and parents. Highlight or jot down the ones that are most informative for you, and record them as needed on your *Interview Forms* (page 273). Estimated Time: 10 minutes

➤ *Use the Quality: Ways to Get What You Don't Get at School table* on page 433 to help you decide what school weaknesses on Great School Quality Factors #5 and 6 would be most difficult to make up for at home. Underline these in the left-hand column on your *Great School Quality Checklist*. Time: 10 minutes

Optional Activities

➤ *If your child is currently in elementary school,* take a few minutes to think about the Great School Quality Factors #5 and 6 strengths and weaknesses of the school. Use the *Great School Quality Checklist* as a guide. Discuss your thoughts with your spouse or other parenting partner. You can do a more complete assessment later, if you wish. Estimated Time: As needed.

Need more? Want more? Got more to share? Visit PickyParent.com.

LIGHT'NING LIST

What To Know from Chapter 14

➤ **Great School Quality Factor #7 is Strong Instructional Leadership.** The litmus tests are these: the best teachers and other staff stay, the worst leave, and the efforts of all staff are consistently focused on the other six Great School Quality Factors. In a Great School, leaders maintain clear, high expectations for teachers, recruit and keep great teachers, organize teachers to work together, monitor and improve teacher performance, and act on high and low teacher performance (ridding the school of low performers, recognizing and rewarding high performers).

➤ **This is the Bedrock Great School Quality Factor.** Instructional leadership is the foundation upon which a Great School is built. Without leadership, fewer great teachers will stay, fewer teachers will perform their best, and the efforts of teachers will not consistently support the school mission, including both quality and fit.

➤ **If leadership changes, the school will change, too** – perhaps for better or worse – and often rapidly so.
  ✔ *Falling Stars are schools that have been great but fail to keep up* with the changing world or experience a decline in leadership. Great plans and practices put in place by former leadership can carry a school for a while, but not forever. Seek to avoid Falling Stars.
  ✔ *Rising Stars are schools making rapid quality improvements,* with new leadership committed to and capable of implementing the seven Great School Quality Factors. Seek Rising Stars to increase your range of options among potential Great Schools with a potential Great Fit.

➤ **The indicators of Strong Instructional Leadership** in a school are included in the *Great School Quality Checklis*t (p. 200).

Chapter 14

Great School Quality Factor #7:
The Bedrock

Great School Quality Factor #7:
Strong Instructional Leadership

School leaders maintain clear, high expectations for teachers, recruit and keep great teachers, organize teachers to work together, monitor and improve teacher performance, and act on high and low teacher performance (ridding school of low performers, recognizing and rewarding high performers).

■ ■ ■

Harrison and Liza were very interested in what the principals had to say. "After all, they ought to know what really goes on around there," Harrison noted. At **Great School Elementary,** *the principal was intense ("not the most relaxed woman I've ever met," laughed Liza), but she ticked right through the matters that most concerned the Olsons. After they heard her open house speech, they didn't just feel inspired, they felt that they really knew what to expect in that school. They were not disappointed when what they saw in the classrooms on their tour confirmed every claim the principal made. "I'm blown away," said Harrison. Despite his positive response to the principal's speech, Harrison still felt that he needed to grill her about her management. He, a manager himself, knew that a lot of blemishes could be masked by a motivating speech. The principal reminded him that the expectations for staff were included in the parent handbook. Later he looked and saw not just staff behaviors expected, but expectations about ensuring that 100% of kids met grade level, individualizing goals for kids who got ahead, weekly monitoring of each child's progress, as-soon-as-*

*possible identification of learning disabilities, and what this school called a "back flips" approach to understanding and motivating every child. The principal said, "Some teachers who think about working at our school think that we prescribe too much for our teachers, that we're tough on them, that we do not give them enough freedom. But let me tell you that our teachers are focused on your child and making the most of your child's potential. Yes, we expect a lot from our teachers, but our best performers love it. And they relish solving each other's problems in their weekly grade level planning meetings. Our turnover, which is low, is primarily teachers who need to leave for performance reasons. Our best teachers stay. Here, they can achieve and change the world one child at a time, and they know that I will do back flips to help them do just that." "Wow," thought Harrison, "I could take a few pointers from this woman for my own work at the bank." At **Good Try Elementary**, the principal was such a nice man that Harrison and Liza started to feel bad asking so many pushy questions. But they did, especially since they had a hard time grasping what the school was like from his open house speech. The principal said, "We have a lot of new teachers this year, so I am expecting things to look up for next year." When they asked whether it was an extra challenge having so many new teachers and why there were so many, he replied, "Well, the new ones do figure it out eventually. They can always meet with me if they're worried. Kids like them because they're young and friendly. And, you know schools just don't have enough money, so we lose quite a few of our star teachers to that bank of yours, Mr. Harrison." At **Yesteryear Elementary**, the principal's speech had focused mostly on the long history and traditions of the school. When asked, she said, "Oh, all of our teachers are great. They pretty much all stay unless somebody has to move out of town. Our teachers are very experienced." When asked about how teachers stay abreast of new ideas, the principal said, "If a teacher wants to study a new topic, we let them go to one conference per year of their choice."*

■ ■ ■

Great School Quality Factor #7 is the bedrock of school quality. Without it, an otherwise Great School will be uncertain as shifting sands. You will see, and your child will experience, inconsistent quality from classroom to classroom and year to year. The stronger a principal, director, leadership team or other leadership, the more consistent and stable you can expect a school's quality to be. This does not mean that the principal is necessarily an ace teacher herself, but rather that she helps others be great teachers. She sets clear expectations for other staff, helps them reach their goals for the school and rewards them accordingly.

This factor is really about how well the school leader *leads* the teachers. Some principals are good at setting a vision for the school, but poor at interpreting what that vision means for teachers. Some school leaders are great working with teachers to develop their teaching skills, but lack a vision of how those skills should support the school's mission and goals. The leadership skills required to set high standards for teachers, develop individual teachers' capabilities, lead group efforts to improve the school, and reward performance are rare to find all together in one person. The best of school leaders recognize their own strengths and weaknesses and form leadership teams to fill the gaps. Leadership teams may include teachers (e.g., grade level or subject matter leaders), parents (often in an advisory capacity) and others.

Some parents feel more comfortable asking about the quality of individual teachers than the performance of school leaders. But you cannot know the quality of a *school* by observing one or two teachers. Absent leadership, teaching quality and approaches in a school will be inconsistent and unpredictable. Even the very best teachers need to know what aspects of quality and fit are expected and supported by the school and how that translates into expectations for their work in the classroom.

Strong leadership is essential to the performance and staying power of even the best teachers. Great Schools do not rely merely on hiring great teachers. They support them with school-wide resources (materials, help in the classroom, and so on), reward them (with recognition, perks and money), and spread their good work to others. Nor do Great Schools focus professional improvement only on struggling and average teachers. Even the best teachers need to grow, improve and change with the times as student needs and research about "what works best" change. Great Schools get *all* of their teachers to do their personal best work by encouraging and rewarding improvement, achievement and teamwork. This approach sustains long-term performance of the best teachers and improves the performance of the rest.

You may wonder why *instructional* leadership is so important. After all, in any school, school leaders must take care of much business beyond managing instructional staff. Many leaders must spend time and energy on school finances, facilities and non-educational operations such as cafeteria and janitorial services. Indeed, these non-educational activities are essential for *sound* organization health. They distinguish schools that will survive from those that will fail to survive entirely. But rock solid finances, beautiful buildings and a great lunch menu tell you not one iota about whether your child will be challenged and nurtured to academic success. They tell you nothing about a school's quality in core academics.

Definition

 Instructional Leadership: Leadership of a school. Establishing a vision and/or goals and organizing and managing a group of people to implement the vision and goals in a school.

Great School leaders ensure that all school staff members are focused on implementing the first six Great School Quality Factors.

Even with a narrow focus on *instructional* leadership, many parents feel uncomfortable evaluating the leadership of a school from afar, and indeed it is easier once you've had more contact with a school as parent of a current student. But there's no reason not to take a stab at it as you investigate schools. Often a school's top leader will jump out at you as "just the thing" or "way off." But sometimes it is hard for parents to put into words and feel confident about their impressions of a principal or other school leader. Nonetheless, you will see the result of those leadership strengths and weaknesses as you look at other Great School Quality Factors.

Assessing School Leadership: Take the Leap

Fortunately for you, there are simple signs that a school's instructional leadership is strong or weak. If you have limited time or are just taking an initial look, probe your targeted schools on questions 1 and 6.

1. If you ask this...

Do you have clear expectations of teachers in your school?

You should hear this...

➤ We have clear, written goals and expectations for all staff

➤ All goals and expectations for staff were chosen to support our school's mission and quality

➤ We also expect certain behaviors from teachers when interacting with students, parents, and other staff, and they are...(fill in blank)

➤ We use these overall goals and behavior expectations to determine each teacher's development and improvement goals every year

Not this...

➤ Each teacher decides what's important in her class

➤ All of our teachers are great – they have a lot of experience

➤ Our teachers are professionals and can figure out what they need to do (true they are professionals, but all professionals in an organization need clear expectations)

2. *If you ask this...*

How do you get and keep great teachers?

You should hear this...

➤ We recruit for skills, competence and previous performance, not just years of teaching experience

➤ We recruit people who have already shown that they can meet the expectations we have of current teachers, in teaching or similar pursuits

➤ We would rather leave a position temporarily unfilled than bring in a teacher we're not sure about

➤ We don't let the district send us teachers who won't work well here

➤ Our best teachers stay because they are valued and rewarded

➤ Top teaching candidates want to teach here, because they know their work will be valued and rewarded

➤ We work hard to keep our current staff improving, and both our good and great teachers like this

Not this...

➤ We've tried but haven't had much luck

➤ We take who we can get and figure it out after they get here

➤ We recruit teachers with the most experience only

➤ The district assigns teachers to our school

3. *If you ask this...*

Do teachers work together in your school?

You should hear this...

➤ We have time set aside weekly for staff in the same grades and subjects to evaluate student progress, identify problems and plan changes together

➤ Everybody has strengths, and we expect staff to work together to make the most of their strengths

➤ Our best performers coach or model their work for our other teachers

Not this...

➤ When we have time

➤ We have a weekly all-school staff meeting for announcements

➤ Our teachers meet to chat and support each other personally, which they love (fine if they do, but not a school quality indicator!)

➤ Our teachers are professionals and can do what they want in their own classrooms

4. *If you ask this...*

What does your school do to help teachers improve their teaching?

You should hear this...

Most Important:

➤ We monitor individual teachers' strengths and challenges, and we start there to improve

➤ Teacher improvement is focused on better meeting our school's mission

➤ Teacher improvement is focused where student performance isn't meeting the school mission

➤ Teacher improvement is an everyday activity, not just for teacher workdays

➤ I observe teachers and give feedback about both strengths and challenges

And Also:

➤ I work with each teacher to develop both strengths and weaknesses

➤ Teachers observe each other and give feedback

➤ Teachers "coach" each other

➤ Development activities vary – workshops, training programs, independent study – but all focus on what teachers need to meet our mission

Not this...

➤ Teachers focus their development mainly on areas of personal interest

➤ Our teachers are professionals and they take care of their own development

➤ We hire only the best and so do not need to worry

➤ Teachers figure this out for themselves; they don't need help

➤ Our teachers attend conferences and workshops (fine, but only in combination with other efforts and only if workshops chosen to improve skills related to mission)

➤ Teaching is a natural talent; some people have it, and some don't

5. *If you ask this...*

Do you reward your high-performing teachers?

You should hear this...	*Not this...*
➤ We reward our high-performing teachers in many ways, such as: ✔ Recognizing their performance publicly ✔ Paying for them to attend conferences ✔ Providing extra funds for special projects ✔ Increased pay (e.g., annual bonus pay or higher salaries)	➤ We provide the same rewards to all teachers, regardless of performance and regardless of how that makes our best performers feel about the school ➤ We don't want to embarrass our solid performers by recognizing our best performers ➤ You can't really tell who the best performers are

6. *If you ask this...*

What do you do if a teacher is not performing up to expectations?

You should hear this...	*Not this...*
➤ We quickly focus on the areas that the teacher needs to improve and help her develop. If this does not work, the teacher is asked to leave our school (e.g., no more than 90 days from time problem is detected). ➤ We do not allow teachers who don't meet the school's performance expectations to stay ➤ While we respect our employees personally, the education they provide to students is our #1 concern	➤ We give teachers a few years to figure this out ➤ We are a public school, so we cannot get rid of low performing teachers ➤ We never have low performers ➤ It is too hard to find replacements, so we just don't let people go ➤ Employee job security is our #1 concern

Here to Stay? Rising and Falling Stars

Strong instructional leaders will not simply run from class to class telling everyone what to do each day (indeed, such leaders will irritate even mild-mannered teachers). Instead, they will work with staff to establish strong rudders that keep everyone moving in the same direction. Most of these rudders relate to another Great School Quality Factor. They will be *written for clarity* and they will be *practiced* day to day. They might include:

➤ A clear, written mission
➤ Clear grade level learning goals for students, and step-by-step progressive learning levels within each grade (ideally stitched together across grades)
➤ Clear methods and school-wide staff support for raising expectations above grade level when students are ready
➤ Clear expectations about teaching methods
➤ Clear direction about materials to use (and the flexibility teachers have to use others)
➤ Regular processes through which teaching is assessed and improved

Smart à la Carte

The Seven Great School Quality Factors: Make Them Part of You

The more familiar you are with the seven Great School Quality Factors, the more comfortable you may feel asking about them. Again, they are:

The Core Four
1. Clear Mission Guiding School Activities
2. High Expectations for All Students:
   ✔ High minimum academic standards ("grade level")
   ✔ Higher, individualized standards for children who are ready
3. Monitoring of Progress and Adjusting Teaching
4. Focus on Effective Learning Tasks

The Supporting Two
5. Home-School Connection
6. Safe and Orderly Environment

The Bedrock
7. Strong Instructional Leadership

These and other rudders will keep a school steady for some time, even through the stormy seas of a leadership change. But ultimately, if leadership changes, the school will change, too – perhaps for better or worse – and often rapidly so. Falling Stars are schools that have been great but fail to keep up with the changing world or experience a decline in leadership. Great plans and practices put in place by former leadership can carry a school for a while, but not forever. Seek to avoid Falling Stars. Rising Stars are schools making rapid quality improvements, with new leadership committed to and capable of implementing the seven Great School Quality Factors. Seek Rising Stars to increase your range of options among potential Great Schools with a potential Great Fit.

SNAP TO IT

What To Do

➤ *Skim Great School Quality Factor #7 on the Great School Quality Checklist* (page 200). Estimated Time: 3 minutes

➤ *Use the Quality: What to Look for in a School table* section for Great School Quality Factor #7 (page 409) to help you think of specific questions about quality to ask principals, teachers and parents. Highlight or jot down the ones that are most informative for you, and record them as needed on your *Interview Forms* (page 273). Estimated Time: 10 minutes

➤ *Use the Quality: Ways to Get What You Don't Get at School table* (page 433) to help you decide what school weaknesses on Great School Quality Factor #7 you would find most difficult to make up for at home. Underline these in the left-hand column on your *Great School Quality Checklist*. Time: 10 minutes

Optional Activities

➤ *If your child is currently in elementary school,* take a few minutes to think about the Great School Quality Factor #7 strengths and weaknesses of the school. Use the *Great School Quality Checklist* as a guide. Discuss your thoughts with your spouse or other parenting partner. You can do a more complete assessment later, if you wish. Estimated Time: As needed.

Need more? Want more? Got more to share? Visit PickyParent.com.

Get the Scoop on Schools

What To Know from Chapter 15

➤ *Your next step is to build a list of high potential Target Schools.*

➤ *Target Schools are ones you seriously consider; ideally you will narrow this list to no more than five schools* that appear to be of the best quality and fit for your child and family.

➤ *Investigating schools can be an emotional process.* At various times, you may feel excited, frustrated, impressed, disappointed, angry and elated, sometimes all about the very same school!

➤ *Your initial Target School list may include schools that you instinctively know you want to consider, including your "Default Destination" and others.* Your *Default Destination* is the school to which you would send your child if you did not bother to make a proactive choice.

➤ *Once your list is honed to the five highest potential Target Schools, you'll investigate those in detail.*

➤ *You will grade your top five schools on quality and fit,* identifying the quality and fit strengths and weaknesses of each using the *Great School Quality Checklist* (page 200) and your *Personalized Great Fit Checklist* (page 59).

➤ *At the end of this process, you will be prepared to choose one top choice school* based on your own fit needs and the best available research about school quality. You will be able to rank the remaining schools on your Target List.

➤ *You also will learn an enormous amount* about the schools you investigate and be prepared to work with the school your child attends and to parent your child outside of school.

Chapter 15

Sharpen Your Pencil: Grade Your School Options

The Active Hunt Begins: Surviving the Twists and Turns

You know what you want and need in a school. You're getting familiar with the true indicators of school quality. You are itching to look at schools available to your child – indeed we hope you are revved to go! But you also have a life busy with children, a household to run, work, volunteer activities and other commitments. You will need to focus your efforts so that your school hunt doesn't become a full-time job. Once you have taken time to identify your child's and family's fit Must Haves, learn about quality, and translate those into what you need in a school, you've come a long way.

Now it's time to:
➤ Build a list of high-potential Target Schools and
➤ Gather the information you'll need about each school to make a smart choice.

Many Starting Places on the Path to a Great School that Fits

Parents start in different places when it comes time to decide what schools to consider. You might:
➤ Know a few promising schools from which you'd really like to choose
➤ Have one strong Default Destination, a school you've always wanted your child to attend and want even more after learning about quality and fit

➤ Have a weak Default Destination, a school you could tolerate but that feels like "settling"; you need to explore this and other schools more rigorously

➤ Have a child already in elementary school, and want to make a change only if another school seems markedly better, or

➤ Have no clear path and want to consider a broad range of options.

Whoever you are, whatever your assumptions, we say this: you will be a better parent to your child and a better partner with your child's school if you seriously consider more than one school, one school type or very similar schools only.

Definition

Default Destination: The school your child would attend if you did not make a proactive school choice. This might be your child's current school, assigned public school, favorite private school, your alma mater, or favored school of your neighbors, friends or family.

This Way to a Smart Choice

So what path should you take to consider schools available to your child? All parents start with a "gut list" of schools they instinctively want to consider. This starting place often is defined by the potentially misleading indicators of quality and fit: overall test scores, knowledge of a great teacher here and there, other parents' personal opinions, and social pressure. But from there, the choice is yours. If you do it right, you will engage in an ongoing process of considering high potential schools of varying types and designs and deleting schools that really won't meet your quality and fit needs. You will screen schools using the highest priority questions and dig more deeply into those that make the initial cuts. You will seek to learn about promising schools you may not have considered previously.

At the end of this process, you will have three nuggets of parenting gold:

➤ A list of top Target Schools about which you know a lot

➤ Information you need to choose one favorite school (and rank order the rest), and

➤ Information you need to work well with the school your child attends and to parent your child outside of school.

Keep Your Eye on the Targets

Your Target Schools are the ones with the best chance of providing great quality and fit for your child and family. Your Target "short list" will change as you learn more about what schools are available and the quality and fit of each school you

The Path to Choosing Wisely

START

Default Destination
Based on Potentially
Misleading Information

Ongoing Investigation
Add High Potential Schools;
Delete Low Potential Schools

FINISH

Target School List
List of Best School Options
Based on Quality & Fit;
Understand Your Child's School

consider. Once you have pared down your list to a manageable number (ideally no more than five), you will investigate each school in detail to learn about its strengths and weaknesses. While this might seem a straightforward step, it can be fraught with emotional and practical challenges. The fearsome dragons of insecurity, uncertainty, embarrassment and scarce time rear their mighty heads. The rest of this chapter and the next will help you prepare and conquer each challenge with confidence, one by one.

Definition

Target Schools: Your short list of schools (up to five) with the best chance of providing great quality and fit for your child and family. Once you've pared your list down to a manageable number, these are the schools that you will investigate in detail.

You'll be a better parent to your child and a better partner with your child's school if you at least consider a variety of schools: different types, designs and features.

Riding the Emotional Rollercoaster

As you investigate individual schools, you may begin to feel a bond with the people you meet. This isn't like shopping for a car, when you typically won't see the salespeople you haggle with again, even the one who wins your purse. With at least one school – and you don't know *which* one yet – your initial exploration is the beginning of a long-term relationship. The principal and teachers you meet are the people who will one day soon take care of your child for six hours or more each day! If you are looking into a school that you yourself attended, you may already have relationships with school leaders and staff and feel especially squirmy about putting them in the hot seat. If you are trying to learn more about the school your child already attends, even more so.

You will feel a wide range of emotions during the active school hunting process and then again when you must make your final choice. At various times, you may feel excited, frustrated, impressed, disappointed and angry, sometimes all about the very same school! Proactively choosing a school is a bit like searching for a spouse. You want to keep your standards high and ask all of the right questions to make your choice. But meanwhile, some of the schools you consider will be assessing you, as well. You may feel like a cad when you reject some schools in the end, especially ones that invested time in you – responding to your tough questions, assessing your child and the like.

And you *will* be asking some tough questions, perhaps feeling embarrassed when there's no ready answer. You also may feel shy about how organized you are. As widespread choice is just coming of age, schools aren't yet used to seeing many parents who know just what they need and want in a school. Some school staff will be impatient or dismissive, brushing aside your questions. In the "Get the Real Scoop" section below, we offer some ideas about how to deal with these stresses.

But, trust us, most of you also will have moments of elation when you find that you've stumbled onto just the right place for your child and family, sometimes where you least expect. Many of you will find a school where you are impressed with the focus on real quality and find that the school fits your child's and family's needs quite well, to boot. You might even find a Great School with a Great Fit where you enjoy being part of the adult community from the moment you step in the door (all the more exciting if this is one of your Must Haves). You may feel even better when you realize that you have two or more good quality school options that fit your needs.

Of course, even your best option may not be perfect. Keep in mind that most families can make up for some school shortfalls outside of school and that a small, but vocal and committed, group of parents can help bring about tremendous changes in a school. Furthermore, you will learn a great deal about the school that you choose simply by having points of comparison with the schools you don't choose.

Know that if you find yourself on an emotional rollercoaster, you are not alone. Stay the course, continue your hunt, and find the right school for your child. You won't regret it for a moment when the hunt is done.

Build Your List of Target Schools

Your goal now is to craft a short list of Target Schools – those most likely to meet your quality and fit needs – that you can *really* get to know in detail. At first, you'll be looking into schools from afar: listing the schools you already think you'd like to consider, finding out what else is available in your community, and screening for basic quality and fit. Then you'll really start to dig in and focus on a limited number of higher-potential schools.

Start with Your "Gut" List of Schools

Start your Target School list with schools you know in your "gut" that you want to consider. First on your list is your Default Destination, if you have one – the school where you would send your child if you didn't bother to make a proactive choice or the school your child already attends. Then add others you know you want to consider, such as your assigned public school, friends' and neighbors' schools, the school you attended, and schools you've heard about that instinctively sound right. Don't feel obligated at this point to make a complete laundry list. Just include those schools that instinctively seem attractive for one reason or another. Use our *School List Tool* on page 272 to keep track of your Target Schools and important contact information (phone numbers, websites and the like).

Indulge yourself. Include that popular school that you now know won't work – you can eliminate it quickly after confirming that it just won't fit (or is of lack-luster quality). Some schools might surprise you, others won't. But this is your chance to give the nod to friends, family and neighbors when they ask if you *at least considered* their pet palace of pedagogy.

Definition

Pet Palace of Pedagogy: *The school that your friends, neighbors or family members think all children should attend – including yours – regardless of real quality or how well it will fit your child and family.*

Find Out What Else is Available in Your Community

Now it's time to broaden your horizons. Find out what other schools are available in your community, including ones that you wouldn't have considered before you became the education expert that you are now. This is your chance to peek outside your worka-day world into schools that might provide surprisingly good quality and fit. Use what you've learned so far to think more broadly than you might have otherwise.

Consider schools of different types and in different locations. If you've been thinking "only public," check out high potential private and religious schools. Their admissions policies and financial aid programs may make them a more realistic option than you thought. If you've always thought private is the only way to go, take a peek at high potential public schools. If you've been locked into thinking about neighborhood schools, look farther afield. Seek out information about special programs within larger schools that may fit your child's top needs. Even consider schools across district and state lines if you live near a border. Some public districts allow children from outside of the district to attend schools with open spaces for a fee. Private schools typically do not have residency requirements, so your child can even come across state lines to attend. The less potential you see in familiar or nearby schools, the more you'll want to look elsewhere to build your Target list.

There are several sources of information you might use. The *best* sources are different in every city and town. You will want to consider at least these to find out what schools are available to your child:

➤ Your local public school district's central office
➤ Friends and neighbors
➤ Parents you meet at your children's activities
➤ Your church, synagogue or other religious institution
➤ Your preschool or day care director
➤ The yellow pages of your local phone book
➤ Your local chamber of commerce or other "cheerleading" organization for your city or town
➤ Ads in local parenting newspapers and magazines (look at pediatrician's office, local library)
➤ The National Association of Independent Schools
➤ Articles or school guides in local newspapers or online
➤ Books about schools in your city (usually the very largest cities only)
➤ School choice advisors available to you (either private or through your public district)

Smart à la Carte

Special Programs within a Larger School

If you consider a special program within a larger school, you should assess quality and fit just as you would for a whole school. A special program may be significantly better or worse in quality and fit than the larger school. First, ask specific quality and fit questions about the program itself.

Then, ask about the effect that the larger school has on the special program. Do the larger school's policies and practices pervade the special program? If so, you'll want to learn more about the items that affect quality and your Must Have fit needs.

See our Resources for Parents section (page 354) or visit **PickyParent.com** for more ideas about how to find information about schools in your area.

Make sure you consider the various *types* of schools that may be available to your child:

➤ Public schools
  ✔ Your assigned public school
  ✔ Other schools that your child is eligible to attend (if your district has a "choice plan" that gives you options)
  ✔ Other public schools that look highly promising, even if your child is not assigned there (you may be able to petition for a transfer)
  ✔ Magnet schools
  ✔ Charter schools

➤ Private schools
  ✔ Independent schools in your local area, both large and small
  ✔ Religious schools in your local area
  ✔ Boarding schools outside of your local area (typically for older children only)

➤ Special programs housed within larger schools, public or private

➤ Home schooling

You do not need to put every school on your Target list, of course. Simply keep your sources and lists of available schools (clipped articles, etc.) handy for the next steps.

Get the Real Scoop on Schools: Read, Look, Listen

When you are ready, here are the steps you'll take to get the real scoop on schools. At first, you will ask your high priority "litmus test" questions, using those highlighted in our tables and perhaps some of your own. After you have whittled your Target School list to a manageable number (we suggest five at most), you will find out more about how each school stacks up on quality and fit. Focus on quality and your fit Must Haves, but if information about your Nice to Haves pops up, keep it for later. Follow these steps, which are summarized in *Snap To It*:

➤ *Write down questions you want to ask at* **all** *schools* on master copies of your *Great School Quality* and *Personalized Great Fit Checklists*. If writing out longer questions will help you feel more prepared, use the *Interview Forms* starting on page 273. Use the three *What to Look for in a School* tables (starting on page 380) to help. Highlight questions that are a top priority for screening schools. You may already have completed this step as you read about quality and fit in earlier chapters. Take a peek at the three *Ways to Get What You Don't Get at School* tables (starting on page 416) if you want to whittle your list of quality and fit needs down to those you cannot make up for outside of school.

➤ *Make one copy of the* **Great School Quality** *and* **Personalized Great Fit Checklists** *for each school* you consider (even if you have not yet narrowed your Target School list down to a small number). If you are using *Interview Forms*, make a copy for each individual you expect to interview.

➤ *Start a file for each school you consider.* You can use this to hold your checklists, information and notes on the school, and ultimately registration and admissions paperwork.

➤ *Record questions unique to particular schools* on each school's checklists or *Interview Forms*. You may want to complete this step only for your top five Target Schools.

➤ *Begin to investigate* schools, using the screening questions. Start by reviewing written materials and websites for basic information; use "live" questioning to delve deeper.

➤ *Record what you learn* about each school, as you learn it, in the "Notes" columns on the two checklists or on your *Interview Forms*.

➤ *Quickly eliminate schools* that clearly are a bad fit or provide inferior quality.

➤ *Add schools* you discover that may be a Great Fit or provide superior quality.

➤ *Narrow your list to the top five* schools as quickly as possible so that you may focus your time on these.

➤ *Dig to get all the information you need about your top schools.*

➤ *Grade your top Target Schools* on each Great School Quality Factor and Fit Factor using the checklists when you have enough information about each (see examples starting on page 266).

➤ *Reconsider schools you may have eliminated* earlier in the process if your Target School list gets too short.

How Do I Ask That?

Before you start calling or visiting schools, think about what questions will get you the information you need. In the early stages while you are still honing your list of Target Schools, you may want to ask *pointed* questions so that you can quickly eliminate poor fit and quality schools. For example, "My child is extremely active ("kinesthetic") and learns best when he can move around and do

Smart à la Carte

Rezoning Blues

If your child's assigned public school is on your Target School list and you live in a place where public school rezoning occurs frequently, you may want to consider the potential impact on your child and family. Rezoning is more likely in high-growth cities and "swing" neighborhoods between schools often used to balance enrollment.

While in general we advocate going for the best quality, best fit school available for each precious year of your child's life, avoiding disruption and change mid-stream can be a factor for some children and families. Rezoning is not the only cause of instability, though. Brand new schools, those under weak, new or about-to-change leadership, and those lacking a clear mission also are highly susceptible to ups and downs. If many of the items on the following list apply, make sure you have some stable options on your Target School list. You might give the nudge to more stable schools when it comes to decision time. Potentially more stable options include public ones less sensitive to rezoning (magnet schools, charter schools, special programs within larger schools), private schools and home school-ing. In all of these cases, the type of school is less important than the strength and consistency of the individual school's leadership and mission.

Factors that may make a stable school more important:

➤ Your child has great difficulty with changes. Many children will "grow out of it," but some remain sensitive to the hyper-stimulation of new situations.

➤ Your child is challenged in any way: academically, socially, emotionally or behaviorally.

➤ Your family life is full of twists and turns. You are a single parent and work out-side of school hours, both parents work and have unpredictable schedules, par-ents are divorced and sharing custody (so child is going back and forth), or there have been other major disruptions in family life.

If your child is rezoned, it is not the end of the world. Many families petition suc-cessfully for their children to remain in the former school after zoning changes. This is easier if you have clear fit needs and can explain how they are well met by the school (which you can do in a snap using your *Personalized Great Fit Checklist* as a guide). Keep in mind that most adults must endure change, and you can help your child become competent at the change game by learning to make new friends and adapt to new school cultures, policies and daily routines. Many families suc-cessfully shepherd their children through changes by helping them prepare for their new school environments (see Chapter 18).

hands-on projects: what does your school offer for a child like this?" Or "Does your school monitor children's progress during the year? How and how often?" Use the highlighted questions in our fit and quality *What to Look for in a School* tables to help weed out (and in) schools quickly.

As you investigate high-potential schools more thoroughly, you may want to start conversations with more open-ended questions that do not reveal the answer you want to hear. For example: "Does your school address children's different learning styles? How?" Or "How do your teachers know if children are making progress?" Some people will give you more accurate answers this way. You can get more and more specific until you have all the information you need and feel comfortable that you are getting an accurate picture of the school.

If you feel embarrassed about pressing for answers to your specific questions (most people do), work harder upfront to collect as much information as you can from printed materials, school websites and your friends who are already in-the-know about the school. Then you can focus your "live" time on the questions you still have rather than on learning basic facts about the school.

Where Do I Look for Information about Schools?

You can get additional information about your Target Schools from a variety of sources, including those listed below. See our Resources for Parents section starting on page 354 or visit **PickyParent.com** for more help.

➤ *Your state department of education.* All states issue "report cards" on public schools or at least have lists and contact information available. To date, much of this information has gone unused by most parents. But it can be a good way to compare past performance in the basic subjects. You can compare individual schools, as well as towns and cities if you are considering a move. Try your state's website first to get information quickly. Use our Chapter 11 guidance for comparing test scores.

➤ *Your local public school district's central office* (look in the phone book). Your district should have information about school assignments, magnet schools, choices available among other public schools and the educational approach taken by various schools from which you may choose. Look for a website, which may have useful school performance numbers (using our Chapter 11 guidance to interpret scores). Charter schools may not be included in information you get from your school district.

➤ *Individual schools*
   ✔ *Staff:* The principal, teachers and other staff should be available by appointment to help you. Receptionists may be able to answer practical

questions about school hours, transportation, costs, child care, etc., but reserve questions about the classroom for other staff.

✔ *Written materials:* Ask for anything that explains the school's mission, curriculum, teaching method, student population and other features of interest to you.

✔ *Tours and open houses:* Use these as opportunities to find out all you can about the school. Ask questions. Make sure you ask about quality and fit Must Haves, so you can eliminate schools that are a clear "no." Write down what you hear and see. Many schools will throw heaps of irrelevant information your way, often highlighting offerings having little to do with quality and addressing fit only for a few. Warm cookies, flashy performances and scripted student recitations have wooed many a well-meaning parent to the wrong school. Filter out the flash, unless it truly addresses your child's or family's needs. Focus on *real* quality and your own child and family fit concerns. (But do enjoy the cookies.)

✔ *Observation:* Reserve this for schools on your final list, as meaningful observations are time-consuming. Consider observing the grade your child would attend next year, as well as an older grade. Ideally, you would observe more than one teacher in each grade. When you observe, look for children who act like you expect yours would in the classroom. For example, if your child is very shy and quiet, observe whether teachers encourage the quiet ones to participate and give them time to respond. If your child will be the one with a hundred questions and comments, observe whether teachers act appreciative of enthusiastic children while also teaching them to focus their comments on main ideas.

✔ *Web site:* search for a school's site on the internet or simply ask if the school has one. These often contain practical information as well as philosophy and educational approach. Pay attention to what they do not say, as well as what they do say.

➤ *Parents.* One of your most valuable sources will be parents who have either child or family needs very similar to yours. In general, talking with parents of children *like yours* is as accurate a read on the experience your child would have as – and much more time efficient than – limited classroom observations. As you talk with parents, make sure that you follow up with a quick question about their child and family needs. This will help you put their opinions into perspective. Asking parents of highly gifted children about their experience may not tell you whether a school would drive home the basics in reading, writing and math for your more typical child. Asking parents of a highly visual child who loves to sit, look and listen in her traditional school will not tell you how your bustling, kinesthetic child would fare. In short: understand the perspectives of your sources before taking opinion as fact.

Screen Potential Schools

You can use a few quick short cuts to screen schools on your initial list and to add other high-potential schools. You will screen for fit and quality.

Screen for Fit: To screen for fit, consider the overall design of each school as well as the specific offerings that affect fit with your Must Have needs. First, add to your Target list any schools with *designs* that are a high-probability fit for your child's or family's Must Haves. Remove from your Target list any schools using designs that are very unlikely to fit your child's or family's Must Haves. If you are not sure, and your list is not too long, feel free to keep a school on your Target list until you gather more information. Use our *School Designs Defined* table on page 172 to help you pick and choose among designs. Use your *Personalized Great Fit Checklist* to gather information and record what you learn about each school.

Second, add schools that appear, at a glance, to be potential Great Fits because their *specific offerings* fit your needs. Remember that some schools do not use a well-known design, and that's O.K. As you scan your community to find out what schools are available to your child, ask about schools that might fit your specific Must Have needs. Remove schools if it becomes apparent that they do not offer what you need in a school to meet child and family Must Have needs. Use the limited number of top-priority, highlighted questions in our *Child and Family: What to Look for in a School* tables to screen schools without spending too much time.

In short, make these changes to your Target School list:

➤ Add schools with
  ✔ High-potential, Great Fit designs
  ✔ Offerings that fit your child and family Must Haves

➤ Remove schools with
  ✔ Low-potential, poor fit designs (but feel free to keep them for a while longer if you're not sure)
  ✔ Offerings that fail to fit your child and family Must Haves

Screen for Quality: you'll want to add to your Target list any schools that appear – at a glance – to provide stellar quality, and likewise eliminate those at the bottom of the barrel. To screen for quality, consider readily available testing results (interpreting carefully with help of our Chapter 11), each school's reputation for educating children like yours, and the highlighted questions in our *Quality: What to Look for in a School* table (page 409). Use your *Great School Quality Checklist* (page 200) to gather information and record what you learn about each school.

At a distance, quality is hard to judge accurately. However, you do not need to make fine distinctions among schools yet. If there are schools in your community that you suspect may be truly superior in real quality, add them to the list. If there are schools on your list now that you quickly discover to be of disappointing quality – especially for children or families similar to your own – drop them. You will be too busy investigating high-potential schools to spend time on mediocre prospects. If you are not sure, and your Target list is not too long, feel free to keep questionable schools on your list until you learn more. Later you can add more questions from the *Quality: What to Look for in a School* to better assess each school.

Beware of imposters. Lacking a way to identify *real* quality, parents have been unfortunately susceptible to common imposters such as lovely landscaping, a bountiful breadth of subjects, and a popular reputation. A school's reputation is remarkably unreliable. School reputations often are built on three things unrelated to quality: the capabilities of the students, the school's competence marketing itself, and potentially misleading test scores.

Many schools boast excellence when it is the pre-existing capabilities of the students, not the schools themselves, that are of high caliber. Schools populated only with bright, motivated children may have impressive overall test scores – but not necessarily when you compare to similar students elsewhere. Unfortunately, it can be oh so tempting for these schools to coast along without providing real quality. At some point, you will need to find out how well such a school follows the seven Great School Quality Factors for a child like yours.

Likewise, while a school's competence in marketing itself is an important characteristic from a school management perspective, it tells you nothing about the education quality your child will experience. And a brief reminder warning about test scores: they can help you choose, but they can just as easily mislead you. Schools with great *overall* test scores may be a disaster for children like yours. You must look at how well a school does with children similar to yours to make even a snap judgment. (Refer back to the discussion of test scores in Chapter 11 and the *Child Needs: What to Look for in a School* table on page 380 to help you here.)

Smart à la Carte

Panicky Parent Pressure Valve

Don't panic! If you find yourself strapped for time or confidence, remember:

1. Meeting even one of your child's critical learning needs better, through school or home life, can significantly improve your child's life and school performance. If you're in a time pinch, focus on your child's top Must Have only.

2. A school strong in Great School Quality Factors #2 and 3 will meet the learning needs of most children over the long haul. Make these two your top search priorities in a pinch.

In short:

➤ Eliminate from your Target School list
  ✔ Schools that clearly are not getting results, especially with children like your child
  ✔ Schools that clearly are not following the seven Great School Quality Factors, especially with children like your child

➤ Add to your Target School List
  ✔ Schools that clearly are getting impressive results, especially with children like your child
  ✔ Schools that clearly are following the seven Great School Quality Factors, especially with children like your child
  ✔ Schools with a strong reputation for educating children like yours

If you find that you still have too many schools on your Target School list, fear not. You can easily eliminate schools as you gather a bit more information. If you find later that none of your preferred schools truly satisfies your Must Have needs or is of acceptable quality, you may want to loop back and gather more information about some that you eliminate now. Try to whittle your Target list down to five or fewer schools before you dig in too far on each.

Will you need to make snap judgments sometimes to decide whether a school is a high-potential hit or a low-potential laggard? Yes. Can you do this with confidence? Yes. When you're not sure about a school, simply keep it on your list to gather more information later. Keep your reference sources of other available schools handy just in case your Target list gets too short.

Continue to Banish the Bad, Gather the Good

Once you have narrowed your search to your top five or fewer schools, you will need to gather more detailed information from several sources until you feel confident that you have a lock on each school's strengths and weaknesses. Use additional questions from the *Quality, Child and Family: What to Look for in a School* tables. You may continue to add and delete schools from your list, as needed, dropping those that just won't work and adding new high-fliers you discover. Most importantly, you will find out what you need to know about the schools you most want your child to attend.

Banish the Bad. You know quality and your fit Must Haves. Focus on these first and foremost. Based on these alone, you most likely will be able to eliminate many schools from your list in a snap. Filter out schools that clearly are a bad fit – that come nowhere near meeting your child and family "Must Haves." Eliminate schools that are clearly of bad quality – that are clearly *either* very weak in one Great School Quality Factor *or* weak across the board on quality.

This step may take nerves of steel for some of you. You may feel pressure from family, friends, neighbors or colleagues to send your child to a particular school. But if it is quite clear that the anointed school does not meet your child's or family's *Must Haves*, or if you – savvier about school quality now than most parents – detect serious problems in the school, you should eliminate it now. You need to spend your limited time investigating and choosing from among the schools that meet your needs. Certainly, though, if you have unlimited time or few other schools from which to choose, it may be worth a closer look, if only to have confidence telling curious friends why that school is *not* the right place for your child or family!

Gather the Good. Even in the middle of your school hunt, you can broaden your list with newly discovered high-potential schools. Your research into your initial Target Schools will lead some of you to discover other high-potential schools. When you meet parents who have similar child or family needs, ask what other schools they considered (and wish they had considered). In response to your probing questions, school staff who have your best interests in mind will sometimes tip you off to other potential Great Fit (or quality) schools.

Indeed, your increased understanding of your child's and family's needs and school quality may lead you down paths you hadn't considered at all. Granted, a deeper look into things may reveal that a school's fit or quality is not what you expected, but do consider schools that might not have been on your initial list. You might find "just the thing" where you least expect.

When you meet parents who have similar child or family needs, ask what other schools they considered – and wish they had considered.

Dig Deeper, Dig Wider

In some cases, you will find that information is difficult to obtain, different sources give you different answers, or you just need to know more to choose between similar schools. Stick with it! You can get what you need to know – even if the answer is "it varies from teacher to teacher." You will learn from seeking the information you really need. And if you are considering a move to gain access to your preferred public school, you *certainly* will want to look under every stone before uprooting your family.

What if a School Will Not Give You Information?

You may find that you cannot get the information you need from a school. The most likely reason is that the school simply has not addressed the issues about which you are asking. If you have asked the principal, parents and teachers what the school does to help children like yours learn, and they just do not answer the question, chances are that the answer is "not much." If you've asked many people what the mission of the school is, and none of them knows, chances are that the school is flying by the seat-of-the-pants (which means the school is less likely to be consistent and stable).

Another possibility is that you are asking about a known weakness of the school, and school staff members are embarrassed about it. If they are embarrassed, it likely indicates that problems are not addressed head-on by school leadership and there is no plan for improving the school (a bad sign if you are hoping for change!).

Making Sense of Inconsistent Information

As you take all of this in and record what you have learned, look for inconsistencies. Are teachers giving you a very different picture of the school from the one painted by the principal? Are parents of children similar to yours giving you very different perspectives depending on the teachers their children have had or grades they have attended? Does the school brochure's description of the teaching method not match what you saw in observations? Does the new school plan list lofty goals, but fail to back them up with clear and specific actions *that will achieve the goals* in the classroom?

The more consistency you see in a school, the more likely it is that the school has a stable culture on which you can depend. Less consistency often indicates one or more quality problems – an ill-defined mission, a poorly selected or managed teaching staff, or inconsistent focus of time, money and effort within the school. Sometimes, resistance by staff to change can keep real quality out of reach of a well-intentioned school. Even when a school seems to *fit* your needs quite well, you should know that less consistent *quality* will mean your child experiences more ups and downs in school. This still may be preferable to a *somewhat* higher-quality school that does not address your fit Must Haves at all.

Inconsistency is different from an openness to change. Great Schools constantly review their activities and make thoughtful improvements to better meet their mission. In Great Schools, you'll see leaders and teachers alike striving to make changes in the classroom, as well as in a written plan. Staff who can't or won't change are asked to leave. In a school with weak instructional leadership, a change in mission or school goals won't consistently change what happens for your child in the classroom.

Nice to Haves Can Matter

If you are lucky, your Nice to Haves will become important. If you find that you have two or more schools similar in overall quality and fit, gather more information about how these schools will meet your Nice to Haves. Use the same process to determine what schools should offer as you used for your Must Haves. In the end, a good fit on many Nice to Haves can push one school ahead on your most wanted list, even if the school is *slightly* less appealing in quality and fit *Must* Haves.

SNAP TO IT

What To Do

➤ *Use our School List Tool* on page 272 to keep track of schools you are seriously considering.

➤ *Find out what schools are available* to your child.
  ✔ *Start your list with schools that you know you want to consider,* including your Default Destination and others such as your assigned public school, favorite private school or a favorite among neighbors and friends.

  ✔ *Find out what other schools are available to your child* in your community, considering all school types and schools you have heard about previously.

  Estimated Time: 10 minutes – 2 hours

➤ *Get the real scoop on schools:*
  ✔ *If you have not done so already, complete preparation of your Personalized Great Fit Checklist* (page 59) *and Great School Quality Checklist* (page 200).
    • *Use the* **What to Look for in a School** *tables* starting on page 380 to identify top priority questions and additional helpful questions.
    • *Use the* **Ways to Get What You Don't Get at School** *tables* starting on page 416 to focus your hunt on needs you cannot address outside of school.
    • *Use our* **Interview Forms** on page 273 if you want to write out more questions.
    • *Make a copy of an* **Interview Form** *for each interview*.
    Estimated Time: 5 minutes – 1 hour, depending on previous preparation.

  ✔ *Start a file for each school* you consider to keep all paperwork in one place. Estimated Time: 1 minute

  ✔ *Screen for quality and fit* to shrink your Target School list to a manageable size, ideally five schools at most:
    • *Ask top priority "litmus test" questions* pointedly.
    Estimated Time: 30 minutes – 3 hours

  ✔ *Dig deeper and wider into your top Target Schools.* Focus on quality and your fit Must Haves. Ask additional questions you have for each school. Use all available sources of information to get a complete and accurate view of each school. Estimated Time: 1 hour – 5 hours or more

  ✔ *Add high potential schools* you discover. Estimated Time: as needed

  ✔ *Delete lower quality, poorer fit schools.* Estimated Time: as needed

  ✔ *Record information about Nice to Haves* as it arises.

➤ *Complete a Great School Quality Checklist and Personalized Great Fit Checklist for each school you consider,* jotting down notes and then grading each of your final Target Schools on both quality and fit. Estimated Time: 20 minutes – 1 hour per school

Need more? Want more? Got more to share? Visit PickyParent.com.

A CONFIDENT CHOICE Tool

School Name: Elm Street Elementary

Personalized Great Fit Checklist

➤ In the first blank column, list in pencil the precise names of your top child & family needs based on your *Child and Family Needs Summaries* (pages 38 and 110) and on your reading of Chapters 2–9 and related tables. For example, write "Basic Learning Capability, Typical." See a complete example on page 176.

➤ Check whether each of your needs is a Must Have or Nice to Have.

➤ In next big column, make note of the characteristics a school must have to meet your need based on your reading of Chapter 10 and related tables.

➤ Include specific questions to ask school principal, teachers, parents, and others (or use our *Interview Forms* on page 273).

➤ Make an extra copy and fill in notes for each school you consider.

➤ After you gather the information you need, grade each school on how well it fits each Must Have and Nice to Have item:

A perfect fit   **B** very good fit   **C** halfway fit   **D** poor fit   **F** very poor or no fit

FIT FACTOR	CHILD & FAMILY NEEDS: Must Haves & top Nice to Haves	MUST HAVE	NICE TO HAVE	WHAT TO LOOK FOR and QUESTIONS TO ASK	NOTES ABOUT THIS SCHOOL	GRADE
What Your Child Learns	*Child:* Basic Learning Capability – Bright/Gifted	X		• Indiv. learning goals ahead of grade level or high overall goals • Frequent monitoring • Focus on critical thinking	• Every student has "Learning Contract" at/above gr. level • Bi-weekly reports to parents • Not sure – critical thinking	A-
How Your Child Learns	*Child:* Motivation – Weak *Family:* Values about how – Classroom Behavior – controlling/strict	X	X	• Variety of teaching methods • Frequent feedback for parents • Individual work with teacher • Clear behavior expectations • Clear punishments & rewards	• Teachers trained each year in using varied methods • Bi-weekly rpts to parents • Daily indiv. work w/teacher • Several rowdy kids a handful for teacher	A C(?)
Social Issues	*Family:* Student Community – critical mass of gifted children	X		• High % of children designated "gifted" or scoring at high levels on tests (not just % at grade level)	• 17% of students in grades 3-5 are in gifted program • 23% of students scored at "advanced" on state tests	B
Practical Matters	*Family:* • Child-care – need afterschool • Transportation – bus to & from • Money – afford up to $6,000 plus $1000 for afterschool; prefer less	X		• Afterschool available • Bus to and from school available (for afterschool, too) • Tuition & fees minus aid is no more than $6,000, or total with afterschool no more than $7000	• Afterschool to 6 pm • Bus to school, but not from afterschool • Public school – no tuition (afterschool = $2,400)	B- A

Personalized Great Fit Checklist

A CONFIDENT CHOICE Tool

School Name: __Ridgefield Academy__

► In the first blank column, list in pencil the precise names of your top child & family needs based on your *Child and Family Needs Summaries* (pages 38 and 110) and on your reading of Chapters 2–9 and related tables. For example, write: "Basic Learning Capability, Typical." See a complete example on page 176.

► Check whether each of your needs is a Must Have or Nice to Have.

► In next big column, make note of the characteristics a school must have to meet your need based on your reading of Chapter 10 and related tables.

► Include specific questions to ask school principal, teachers, parents, and others (or use our *Interview Forms* on page 273).

► Make an extra copy and fill in notes for each school you consider.

► After you gather the information you need, grade each school on how well it fits each Must Have and Nice to Have item:

A perfect fit   **C** halfway fit
B very good fit   **D** poor fit   **F** very poor or no fit

FIT FACTOR	CHILD & FAMILY NEEDS: Must Haves & top Nice to Haves	MUST HAVE	NICE TO HAVE	WHAT TO LOOK FOR and QUESTIONS TO ASK	NOTES ABOUT THIS SCHOOL	GRADE
What Your Child Learns	Child: Basic Learning Capability – Bright/Gifted	X		• Indiv. learning goals ahead of grade level or high overall goals • Frequent monitoring • Focus on critical thinking	• No indiv goals; overall goals seem just a little above avg • Four report cards/year • Each child produces "major project" every year.	C+
How Your Child Learns	Child: Motivation – Weak Family: Values about how – Classroom Behavior – controlling/strict	X	X	• Variety of teaching methods • Frequent feedback for parents • Individual work with teacher • Clear behavior expectations • Clear punishments & rewards	• Most instruction teacher-directed, but frequest field trips look stimulating • Four report cards/year • Some small grp; no one-on-one • Very orderly classrooms	B- A
Social Issues	Family: Student Community – critical mass of gifted children	X		• High % of children designated "gifted" or scoring at high levels on tests (not just% at grade level)	• No scores available • Staff say majority of kids "gifted"	B(?)
Practical Matters	Family: • Child-care – need afterschool • Transportation – bus to & from • Money – afford up to $6,000 plus $1000 for afterschool; prefer less	X		• Afterschool available • Bus to and from school available (for afterschool, too) • Tuition & fees minus aid is no more than $6,000, or total with afterschool no more than $7000	• Afterschool to 6:30 pm • Bus to and from school • Full cost after $3000 aid about $7000 including afterschool. (Donations?)	A B

© 2004 by Armchair Press, LLC. All rights reserved.

Great School Quality Checklist   PAGE 1

School Name: ___Elm Street Elementary___

▲ Complete a separate *Great School Quality Checklist* for each school you consider.
▲ In Notes column, make notes about each school. Which factor elements are strengths? Weaknesses?
▲ After gathering available information, grade each school on each overall Great School Quality Factor:

✔ **A** school has all of the elements
✔ **B** school has most of the elements
✔ **C** school has about half of the elements
✔ **D** most of the elements are missing
✔ **F** school has none or almost none of the elements

GREAT SCHOOL QUALITY FACTORS	NOTES ABOUT THIS SCHOOL	GRADE
1. Clear Mission Guiding School Activities ● Written mission communicating focus and priorities ● Staff, parents & written materials state same mission ● School-wide goals support mission ● Student goals, curriculum & teaching support mission	• Principal, teachers, and parents we talked to all echo "one child at a time" motto • Literature repeats indiv. focus	A
2. High Expectations for All Students: *High Minimum Expectations for All* ● Challenging but achievable student learning goals (standards) for each grade level ● School-wide plan and actions ensure that all students achieve at least grade level in basics, no excuses ● All or near all children achieve grade level ● Progress scores high for all, including lowest scorers *Higher Expectations for Students Who are Ready* ● Learning goals raised for ready students ● Clear, written progression of goals beyond grade level ● Plan and actions ensure students meet higher goals ● At least gifted students achieve very high test scores ● Progress scores are high for top students	• School uses state standards • For children who are ahead, teachers use next-grade-up standards (and higher? Not sure) • Each child signs "Learning Contract" every six weeks setting indiv. goals	A-

Continues....

A CONFIDENT CHOICE Tool

Great School Quality Checklist   PAGE 2

School Name: ___Elm Street Elementary___

Category	Notes	Rating
3. Monitoring of Progress and Adjusting Teaching • School assesses individual student progress (weekly is ideal) to ensure that every child achieves his or her learning goals • Teachers change teaching approach	• Students have one-on-one time with teacher or aide each day • Assignments vary for diff. students	A
4. Focus on Effective Learning Tasks • Instruction approach proven to work • Class time allocated according to subjects' importance • Materials & facilities allocated in line with importance • Principal and teachers limit class interruptions	• Reading and math blocks seem shorter in this school than others • Materials, facilities out of date (?) • Classes interrupted: visitors, announc.	C
5. Home-School Connection • School tells parents what children will be learning • School tells parents how to help own children learn • School updates parents on own child performance • School works with parents to resolve problems	• Bi-weekly reports to parents on children's progress • Lots of "parent workshops" but they focus on kids who are behind	B
6. Safe and Orderly Environment • Students know how they are expected to behave • Students focus on work in the classroom • Consequences for behavior are clear and consistent • School keeps students safe from harm	• Discipline seems like an issue for some kids; most kids focused on work; teachers spending time on this • School expels worst offenders	C?
7. Strong Instructional Leadership • Clear performance expectations for teachers • Principal recruits, keeps great teachers • Teachers work together within & across grades • Principal monitors individual teacher performance • Staff regularly identifies problems, improves school • Professional development focused on school goals • Principal acts on high and low teacher performance	• Principal seems to expect a lot of teachers; one struggling K teacher was dismissed last year mid year • Teachers have a lot of workshops on individualizing teaching; principal and other teachers rate each other four times yearly	B?

A CONFIDENT CHOICE Tool

Great School Quality Checklist PAGE 1

School Name: ___Ridgefield Academy___

- Complete a separate *Great School Quality Checklist* for each school you consider.
- In Notes column, make notes about each school. Which factor elements are strengths? Weaknesses?
- After gathering available information, grade each school on each overall Great School Quality Factor:
  - ✔ **A** school has all of the elements
  - ✔ **B** school has most of the elements
  - ✔ **C** school has about half of the elements
  - ✔ **D** most of the elements are missing
  - ✔ **F** school has none or almost none of the elements

GREAT SCHOOL QUALITY FACTORS	NOTES ABOUT THIS SCHOOL	GRADE
1. Clear Mission Guiding School Activities • Written mission communicating focus and priorities • Staff, parents & written materials state same mission • School-wide goals support mission • Student goals, curriculum & teaching support mission	• Motto is "Scholarship, leadership, character" but no mission beyond that. Nobody talks about it. Resting on reputation?	C
2. High Expectations for All Students: *High Minimum Expectations for All* • Challenging but achievable student learning goals (standards) for each grade level • School-wide plan and actions ensure that all students achieve at least grade level in basics, no excuses • All or near all children achieve grade level • Progress scores high for all, including lowest scorers *Higher Expectations for Students Who are Ready* • Learning goals raised for ready students • Clear, written progression of goals beyond grade level • Plan and actions ensure students meet higher goals • At least gifted students achieve very high test scores • Progress scores are high for top students	• Generally school seems to expect all students to be a little above average • No sense that school sets specific goals for individual children if they are ahead. If they're ahead, "they're fine" we heard. Not sure what that means. (B or C overall? Not sure. B-?)	A D B- (?)

Continues...

Great School Quality Checklist   PAGE 2

School Name: Ridgefield Academy

Checklist Item	Notes	Grade
3. Monitoring of Progress and Adjusting Teaching ● School assesses individual student progress (weekly is ideal) ● Teachers change teaching approach to ensure that every child achieves his or her learning goals	• Mostly whole class instruction, same assignments across board • 4 report cards per year	C−
4. Focus on Effective Learning Tasks ● Instruction approach proven to work ● Class time allocated according to subjects' importance ● Materials & facilities allocated in line with importance ● Principal and teachers limit class interruptions	• Open Court/Saxon Math; much time! • Top of line academic equipment – library, science ctr., writing lab • No interruptions; two way mirrors	A
5. Home-School Connection ● School tells parents what children will be learning ● School tells parents how to help own children learn ● School updates parents on own child performance ● School works with parents to resolve problems	• Lots of communication to parents about school (A+ newsletter) • Less communication about my child	C
6. Safe and Orderly Environment ● Students know how they are expected to behave ● Students focus on work in the classroom ● Consequences for behavior are clear and consistent ● School keeps students safe from harm	• VERY orderly school • Students with discipline problems not admitted; or given the boot	A
7. Strong Instructional Leadership ● Clear performance expectations for teachers ● Principal recruits, keeps great teachers ● Teachers work together within & across grades ● Principal monitors individual teacher performance ● Staff regularly identifies problems, improves school ● Professional development focused on school goals ● Principal acts on high and low teacher performance	• Principal is very charismatic with us • Seems good at teacher recruiting; not sure performance and expectations? • Teachers told us "she doesn't get involved in our classrooms" • Teachers use staff training money for own interest areas	C

School List Tool

Date: _____

➤ Make your "gut" list of schools you'd like to consider
➤ Find out what other schools are available to your child in your community
➤ Add a school to your list if you think it may fit at least one of these categories:
    1. Fits your child's and family's Must Haves, or
    2. Provides better quality than other schools available to your child
➤ Consider different types of schools (public, private, religious, home)
➤ Include schools using designs likely to fit your child or family well
➤ Add each school's essential contact information (name, telephone number, website) for quick reference
➤ Eliminate schools as needed, based on quality or fit

SCHOOL TYPES	SCHOOLS WE MAY CONSIDER
Public: **Assigned**	
Magnets	
Charters	
Other	
Private Schools	
Religious Schools	
Home School	

Principal Interview

➤ List your questions in left column. Use the *Child, Family* and
  Quality: What to Look for in a School tables starting on page
  380 to help decide what questions to ask

➤ Make a copy for each interview.
  Add school-specific questions on each school's copy

➤ Complete right column for each school

Date: _____

School Name: _____

Principal's Name: _____

MY QUESTIONS	ANSWER NOTES

Teacher Interview

➤ List your questions in left column. Use the *Child, Family* and *Quality: What to Look for in a School* tables starting on page 380 to help decide what questions to ask

➤ Make a copy for each interview.
Add school-specific questions on each copy

➤ Complete right column for each teacher

Date: _____

School Name: _____

Teacher's Name: _____

MY QUESTIONS	ANSWER NOTES

Parent Interview

➤ List your questions in left column. Use the *Child, Family* and *Quality: What to Look for in a School* tables starting on page 380 to help decide what questions to ask

➤ Make a copy for each interview.
   Add school-specific questions on each copy

➤ Complete right column for each parent

Date: _____

School Name: _____

Parent's Name: _____

MY QUESTIONS	ANSWER NOTES

Make Your Choice, Make It Happen

■ ■ ■ ■ ■ ■ ■

LIGHT'NING LIST

What To Know from Chapter 16

➤ **Picky is as picky does: here's your chance to make a huge difference** in how your child spends thousands of childhood hours at school.

➤ **Comparing and ranking schools helps you not only choose a school, but prepare to parent your child** outside of school, no matter what school your child ultimately attends.

➤ **Keep an open mind** and remember that many parents choose schools they did not expect, because of better quality and fit.

➤ **Perfect quality and fit are rare,** but you can play an active role to fill the gaps for your own child and support positive changes in your chosen school.

➤ **Consider involving your older or mature child in the final decision,** especially if you have two or more similarly appealing options.

➤ **Quality and your fit Must Haves should weigh more heavily** in your school decision than Nice to Haves. You may need to rank your Must Haves if you have more than one top school option. Ask yourself this: which needs are most important for your child's school to address?

➤ **Knowing which school weaknesses you can best accommodate** outside of school is important for choosing the right school for your child and family.

➤ **If you have two or more great options, you can make a judgment with confidence,** since you will understand each school's major strengths and weaknesses.

➤ **Remember your Great School Quality Factor #2 and 3 safety valve should your decision become overwhelming:** a school strong in these two factors will meet the quality and fit needs of many children over the long haul. Focusing on these, plus one top need of your child, can improve your child's life greatly.

Decisions, Decisions: Choose the Right School

Chapter 16

It's Time to Decide

You've gotten the scoop on your Target Schools. You've talked the talk, thought the thoughts. But unless you choose your child's school – and plan your out-of-school parenting – based on your work, you lose much of the value.

This chapter will see you through finding the clear view you need to make your school choice with confidence. Now is the time to lay it all out and compare across schools. If you've been holding your breath – trying hard not to draw a conclusion about the schools you've considered – it's time to decompress and look at the facts you've gathered. If you've been ranking your Target Schools in your mind as you learned more about each, it's time to test your conclusions. Even if your choices are limited, you'll need to review the key information you have gathered about each Target School.

Knowing that you have focused on the most important aspects of quality and fit for your child and family will give you great confidence in your choice. Understanding the strengths and weaknesses of the school you choose will allow you to improve your interactions with the school and your child-rearing decisions outside of school.

Be confident if you choose an unexpected school. Every year, many parents set aside biases to choose schools for quality and fit. Their children, families and schools are all the better for it.

Open Your Mind

When you are highly informed about your child's and family's needs, as well as the real indicators of school quality, you may find that the most appealing schools are not at all what you expected. Where you began your hunt is not necessarily the same place you will end it. And parents who've been down the road of following their own needs first – only to see their children's school interest and performance wither – know that quality and crucial child needs trump parent needs, hands down.

Many parents travel an unexpected course all the way from considering only traditional, one-size-fits-all schools to considering only schools that break children into very small groups for more personalized learning. Other parents go in unpredicted directions, as well: from public to private, private to public, school-house to home school, assigned school to charter school, magnet to assigned school, and so on. Stay confident even when your destination is not what you expected. You are not alone. Every year, parents throughout the United States alter their commitment from one school, school type or design to school quality and overall fit. Their children, families and schools are all the better for it.

Smart à la Carte

"Feeder Schools": A Leg Up?

In some cities, a few elementary schools are regarded as "feeders" for particular selective middle or high schools. If your child attends the feeder school, he is presumed to have an advantage when it comes to getting into the upper-level school. If you have your eye on such a secondary school for your child's future, you might be tempted to select the feeder school now to up the admissions odds later. But should you do so?

Let's take the easy case first. If the feeder school meets your fit needs and passes quality muster, the fact that it feeds the desirable high school could well put it over the top in your decision-making, perhaps breaking a tie with a similar school. But now the tougher case – what if the feeder falls short in fit or quality? What then?

Keep this in mind: attending the feeder school will probably not guarantee your child's admission to the selective secondary school. The two schools' perennial relationship may give you an edge, but your child will still need to meet the upper-level school's exacting standards. If the feeder school is a poor fit for your child or weak in quality, what will happen? You may find that after a lackluster elementary career, he doesn't make the cut after all.

So think twice before opting for a perceived feeder school over a school that's a better fit and higher quality. Your child's elementary years are a critical period for development, not just a holding pen for a future school. (If the school you are considering is the elementary section of one larger umbrella school, similar rules of thumb apply. See the box *Up Your Odds: Understand The Admissions Game* in Chapter 17.)

Peer and Family Pressure Nipping at Your Heels

As you zero in on your final choice, peer or family pressure will undoubtedly rear its demanding head for many of you. The mere thought of telling curious neighbors at the park – let alone good friends and family members – that you may take a road less traveled can cause tremors in all but the most irreverent mavericks among us. If you have followed the steps laid out in Chapters 1 – 15, you'll find sure footing faster when asked about your choice. You know your

Smart à la Carte

Peer and Family Pressure: Let Confidence be Your Reward for Hard Work

If you live, work, or socialize among people who attend a certain school – or type of school – you may feel embarrassed that your child's or family's needs would lead you down a different path. If you've always been a gung-ho supporter of your alma mater, or public schools, or private schools, how can you explain why you've chosen to send your child elsewhere without seeming to put down the very people you've rallied with over the years?

We dare say that most of you have made many *other* parenting decisions running counter to what friends, family, neighbors and colleagues would do. School is different only because it is such a *public* parenting decision – everybody knows what you've decided in the end, and you may be faced with many folks asking "why?" – especially if you go against the grain.

Arm yourself. The clearer your decision-making, the wiser and more confident you will feel. The wiser and more confident you feel, the better you can explain your decision. You need not put down others' decisions when your decision is based on fit. This is much harder, of course, when your decision hinges on quality. But remember that different families can make up for differing school weaknesses at home – so even choosy parents may make different decisions in seemingly similar situations. The better you can explain your decision in personal terms, the less affronted others will feel, and the less rebellious you will feel.

But sharing information with others – about fit *and* quality – will help you *all* support and improve your children's schools. No school is perfect, and parents sharing ideas can only help. Indeed, any school populated by more engaged parents will likely improve. Pick and choose the right times and places to state your quality case to other parents. In turn, listen to others and learn, but stand your ground, too. Meanwhile, be proud to be thought of as a parent who goes the extra mile for your child when it really counts!

child's and family's needs, and you know about quality. You've found out what you reasonably could about schools available to your child. You've both followed your "gut" (putting these values and concerns into words) and you've been logical and smart. Stand strong. Stay confident about your choice, even while listening to others' differing views.

Perfect Quality and Perfect Fit are Rare

Some of you, particularly in cities with many school options *and* many parents making a proactive choice, will find yourselves torn between two or more promising schools. Others of you may find that one school rises to the top, plainly addressing your quality and fit needs the best. But all too many of you will find that you have little real choice in your area, or that none of your options pass muster.

We hope that pressure from better-informed parents will push more schools to do better with more children more of the time. But the reality today is that many parents must choose between the "lesser of evils," and the "best" choice is a mediocre school and an imperfect fit. You can take several paths if you come to this crossroads.

For starters, parents can accommodate many school imperfections once aware of them. *The Child, Family and Quality: Ways to Get What You Don't Get at School* tables (starting on page 416) are a great place to start. For example:

➤ School perfect academically but does not include children from your neighborhood? Sign your child up for activities or summer camps that draw children from your area, and set aside one afternoon a week just for play with neighborhood friends.

➤ School offers high quality, individually-paced education in the basics but covers few other subjects? Include science camp, language classes, drama and other "special" subjects on your child's after school and summer activity list (don't overload; spread throughout the year!).

➤ Your child needs a small school environment with lots of one-on-one teacher contact to feel motivated about academics, but only private schools in your area offer this, and you can't afford the tuition? Hire a tutor to come to your home one afternoon each week to check your child's progress and motivate your child. The cost of this should be *significantly* less than a private school. Take the lead in asking your child's teachers for regular progress updates – just asking will focus teachers' attention on your child.

➤ Really need to send your two children to different schools to accommodate their very different needs, but find the differing vacation schedules a challenge? Plan ahead to focus your family time on the vacations your children have in

Smart à la Carte

Home Sweet Home: Should You School There?

More families than ever in our country, well over a million in 2002, are providing their children's educations at home. Parents choose this route for many reasons, all of which boil down to concerns about the fit or quality of more traditional school settings. You might consider home schooling if:

➤ Available schools are low quality or a poor fit for your child or family.

➤ Your child did not get into your chosen school, and your second choice school is not of acceptable fit or quality.

➤ Your child has unusual needs that cannot be met at school or in non-school hours.

➤ Your family has strong and uncommon values – religious or other – that you want to reinforce through schooling, and no available school fits the bill.

➤ You want to provide your child with a highly tailored academic experience unavailable in many schools today.

➤ You feel confident that you can best provide the academic, social, emotional and physical developmental support your child needs by home schooling, rather than by partnering with your child's school.

Home schooling is the best choice only for the right parents and children. You must be as tough on yourself as you are on more traditional schools. Use the *Confident Choice Tools* to compare home schooling with schools in your area, grading yourself just as you have done with other schools you considered. Not all parents possess the broad range of skills and capabilities needed to support their children's development through home schooling. The older your child, the more true this becomes: the more technical and challenging your child's level of work, the broader and deeper your own academic skills must be. Not to mention that motivating your child and conveying knowledge are different skills altogether from possessing the knowledge yourself. The mental work of establishing learning goals, figuring out how you will teach each subject, and finding and choosing materials takes oodles of mental and leg work. In a traditional school, these tasks may be shared by a number of people possessing various skills and talents. When you home school, you must wear these many hats all at once. You may be able to collaborate with other home schoolers in your area, but only if you take the initiative to do so. If you feel up to the challenge, go for it. If not, remember that you are always your child's teacher in non-school hours. You can play an important role in your child's education, even if not home schooling. Check out the Resources for Parents section starting on page 354 and **PickyParent.com** for links to web sites for families considering home schooling.

common. If you can, use your child's solo time off as an opportunity for valuable one-on-one time with each child.

➤ Your academically gifted child's needs are not being met by schools in your rural area? Check out the growing array of Internet-based, self-paced educational tools. Seek out public or private schools outside your immediate local area. Some states have public schools that serve gifted students statewide; check with your state department of education. Many private boarding schools offer significant scholarships for gifted students from rural areas, but these are primarily for middle and high school years.

➤ School inconsistent in fitting your child's needs? Meet with and write a letter to the principal to ensure your child gets the best-fit teachers as often as possible. Clearly communicate your child's needs to teachers at the beginning and during each school year. Use interaction time with teachers (e.g., conferences, open houses) to steer them towards understanding and meeting your child's needs. Fill the gaps with tutoring or extracurricular activities.

If choosing between your child's needs and your own, we encourage you to bend your needs creatively to meet your child's. You'll have fewer regrets and headaches if a school fits your child well.

You can also push for change in your chosen school. Many a school, both public and private, has been spurred to change by a resolute group of parents. A willing principal and eager teachers are necessary for real and lasting change, but parents can be the catalyst that gets things moving. Just as a teacher's high expectations can change how a child performs, your expectations can redirect the energy of school staff towards quality or a common fit need. Discussions with your school's PTA chairperson and the principal are two good places to start if you are bent on change. (See more about pushing for change in Chapter 18.)

Third, this is the point in time when some parents consider home schooling. Only you can make the decision about whether this is the best course for your children and family. You'll need to consider how well you can provide the seven Great School Quality Factors and meet your child's and family's fit needs. Undoubtedly, home schooling is the best option for some children and families. But just as certainly, it is the wrong choice for many. Among other things, you'll need to consider your own personal strengths and weaknesses and how much energy you'll have to address your family's many needs when your home schooling "school day" is done (see Home Sweet Home: Should You School There? on page 283).

Conflict on the Road to Making a Choice

As you wade knee-deep into your final decision, you may start thinking: *us or them?* You may feel trapped, particularly if *either* parent or child has compelling and unchangeable needs. Rest assured, you can resolve conflicts with confidence that you've made the best overall decision for your *child and family*. In many families, parent values and needs will be the overwhelming determinant of where children go to school. In some cases, with some children, you can make this decision without an ounce of guilt and without much accommodation outside of school. When your child falls in-the-box developmentally and has a learning style compatible with your family's best-fit school, and when that school passes the quality test, your family school preference can reign supreme.

In other cases, both your child and family may have compelling needs, and they may not always seem compatible. Then, you must prioritize your own Must Haves and your child's together, deciding which needs you can most easily address outside of school. Eventually, you may even find that your

Smart à la

A Story: Parents Defer to Their Child's Needs

Sharon and Chris struggled with the private versus public question. These parents had moved to a city where many members of Chris's family had lived and developed a pleasant tradition of attending a well-regarded private day school. But these parents were not follow-the-crowd types. They thought long and hard about where to send their two children. They felt a more kindred spirit with friends and neighbors who sent their children to public school and wanted their own children to benefit from exposure to a diverse group of children.

And that is the decision they made with their first child. Unfortunately, their child, who was bright in his Basic Learning Capability, suffered from Attention Deficit Hyperactivity Disorder. Because he was bright, he was able to make grade level despite his problems focusing on work. However, he was working far below the level of which he would have been capable if not for the disability. But because he made grade level, his teachers were satisfied. His parents, however, were not. They were frustrated, and saw their son as a classic case of falling through the cracks. Eventually, they had their son formally tested by a psychologist.

Upon realizing what a tremendous gap there was between his performance and capability, they made the painful decision to switch him to a private school. They looked carefully to find one where the values of the parents and other students were aligned with their own. Ironically, they settled on the one that the husband's family had attended. This school, it turned out, had developed a strong school-wide expertise in dealing with a few specific, common disabilities, including ADHD.

Their child's learning soared under the watching eyes of teachers who would not settle for performance below the child's capability. He graduated near the top of his high school class and went on to perform well at a prestigious college. Just as important, he developed self-confidence, high expectations for himself, and the self-control to use his intellectual gifts.

child's Must Haves open windows to new ideas about which schools will meet your own needs.

Families are different from each other, and parents within a family can be, too. If you're part of a two-parent family, you may find that you have differing values, and perhaps needs, from your parenting partner. Many of these conflicts may have been resolved when you assessed your family fit needs. But sometimes, the big conflict comes when you've looked at schools available to your child, and you realize that you must choose between one parent's needs or values and those of the other. Don't let choosing a school become a war of the wills. Sit down

Smart à la Carte

A Story: A Child's Needs Open New Windows in a Family's World

Cindy and Carl assumed that they could get what they and their young child needed only in a private day school. They were a personally conservative, socially well-connected couple living in a prestigious neighborhood where most children attended old-line private day schools. The well-established local private schools seemed a natural focus for their attention. Their child was highly imaginative and conceptual, creating and solving problems he found interesting, noodling through ideas in original ways. But he was also highly sensitive to the emotional traumas of typical preschool peer interactions. To some, their son might have seemed "spacey" and overly sensitive. To his parents, though, he was highly perceptive, insightful and focused – on what interested him.

Hunting for the right elementary school, Carl and Cindy visited the private school they'd targeted (Dad's alma mater) and found the teaching method to be quite traditional. Looking through the lens of their imaginative child, they could feel the straightjacket he would feel here. Most of the day would be spent in teacher-directed activities working on very concrete tasks. At best, their child would not have the chance to develop one of his greatest strengths – his imagination – at school. At worst, he might end up feeling "different" from his peers and agitated by the structure, particularly in a school where parents and teachers value conformity. Furthermore, they'd pay a fat tuition bill for the privilege!

Their search continued, and they ultimately found two public schools that would meet the parents' and child's essential needs: in academic content, teaching method, social environment and practical concerns. These were schools where, it turned out, several families whom Cindy and Carl knew from church, preschool and other places were sending their children. They were guaranteed admission into at least one of them. How different their destination was from what they had expected. A child's needs can, indeed, open new windows in a family's world.

Smart à la Carte

Holding Back and Grading Up: Should You?

At some point, many parents consider holding a child back for a year or moving a child up a grade. How can you make this sometimes wrenching decision with confidence?

In truth, there is no simple answer. Many child development experts believe the normal variation in mental, social and emotional maturity to be very wide up until age 8 or 9. It is reasonable for you as a parent to expect a school to accept these normal variations in the early elementary years. Great Schools do. But you may have less than Great available, or your child may be an extreme case. If your child's birthday is within roughly two months of a school's birthday cutoff, the issue is less problematic – do what seems best for social and academic fit. But even then, know that there are always tradeoffs. Consider the implications not just for this year and next, but for puberty and teenage years. (e.g., How might maturing physically and getting a driver's license well before or after peers affect your child?)

Holding Back: Perhaps you're concerned about your child's academic or social readiness for school. Or perhaps you are not concerned at all, but your child's school is. Here's the score: research shows no long-term *academic* achievement benefit to delaying the start of kindergarten or holding children back a grade. This isn't surprising given the strong evidence that the more a school expects of a child, the more that child learns. Far too many complacent, one-size-fits-all schools claim to have higher grade level standards, but adopt an early birthday cutoff for entry into a grade and a frequent practice of holding children back. These schools may claim that holding back is evidence of their high standards, but in fact the opposite is true. The social costs and benefits of holding a child back are less clear. You will need to weigh the potential social benefit of your child's additional physical and social maturity compared to classmates – now through high school – against the likely long-term academic cost.

Moving Up: For ideal emotional and social development, a child should spend a large part of the day with several children close in age. While very bright children often seem to skip academic steps, they rarely skip social and emotional ones. Getting along with same-age peers will be an invaluable life-long skill quite difficult to develop at older ages. A Great School will not need to move a child up a grade for academic challenge except in the most extreme circumstances. Instead, children across the grade who have similar current academic capabilities will be taught together. But if your best school option doesn't do this well, or if your child is extraordinarily advanced, moving up may be the best move. Even then, attending academic sessions with older children but staying with same-age peers the rest of the day will enhance your child's social development for the long run. And you'll need to take extra care to help your child form and nurture friendships with same-age children outside of school. (For more help with your highly gifted child, see the Resources for Parents section starting on page 354 and visit **PickyParent.com**.)

together to assess how well schools meet *all* of your quality and fit needs. Prioritize together. In some families, parents' disagreements over educational values have led to focusing on the child's needs as a tie-breaker – not a bad outcome!

If you are a divorced parent and are making decisions with your former spouse, this can be a trying time – one where previous differences come to the fore. We say this: do your very best work and use your best self-control to focus on the needs of your child first. We know you want to. We also know that it is hard when you feel angry or hurt, or both. If you are sharing custody, your child may well spend more waking hours in the custody of school than in the custody of either parent. Think about it. It's possibly one of the most stabilizing and high-impact decisions you can make for your child at this time. Just as we recommend to other families, consider focusing on your child's needs as a tie-breaker when ranking schools if you can't agree on parent priorities.

If you can't decide, focus on Great School Quality Factors #2 and 3 and your child's top fit need that you can't meet outside of school.

Involve Your Child

If you haven't already, now is a great time to involve your child. If your child is older or mature, you likely will have involved him or her directly in identifying child needs. Discussing both child needs and family needs is a great way to reinforce your values, increase your child's self-understanding, and help your child feel committed to the school you choose. You need not give your child a primer on school quality, but it is good to point out the quality strengths of the schools at the top of your list.

Once you have narrowed your choice down to two or three equally appealing schools, you might want to consider allowing your child to make the final choice. If your child is older, a rising fourth or fifth grader for instance, he may have strong opinions and be downright insulted if not consulted in the final decision. Remember that your child is an individual, and his interests – academic, social, emotional and physical/athletic – can be child Must Haves. Hopefully, you considered this while thinking about fit. If not, now's your chance. Tell your child:

➤ Why you are proactively choosing a school for your child, instead of just doing what your neighbors and others do

➤ The big steps you've taken (reading about what makes a school really good, thinking about what your child and family need in a school, and learning more about schools in your town), and

➤ The top schools you are now considering and what you like about each one. (And, perhaps, the downsides of each. Of course, keep in mind that anything you say to your child may well be repeated around the neighborhood!)

If you really don't want to involve your child in the choice, but just want to inform him about your decision, stop there. If you do want your child to make the final choice, then ask if your child, after hearing what you like about your top pick schools, has an opinion about what sounds best to him. If admission is uncertain into your chosen school, you'll want to be clear about that with your child and be sure to emphasize the strengths of your lower ranked schools.

Smart à la Carte

When is Switching Schools Worth the Effort?

If your child is already in elementary school or is in a preschool that continues into the elementary grades, you may be wondering when switching schools is worth it. Your child will spend roughly 1,000 hours in school each year (more if you use school child care). Every year of your child's life is valuable, every year of school time precious. The temporary stress of a change is often preferable when the new school is better in quality and fit.

But a stable school situation may be important in some situations: if your child has great difficulty with changes, if your child is challenged in any way (academically, socially, emotionally, or behaviorally), or if your family life is already full of disruptions and changes.

So, how do you decide? Here's what we suggest: complete your school search just as you would if your child were being forced to make a change. Include your child's current school in that search unless you are decidedly displeased with the school's quality or fit. See how your child's school stacks up against alternative schools. In your final decision, consider the stress of change and how well your child will likely deal with that stress, but also consider the great quantity of time your child will be in school after the transition stress is over. If your best alternative is selective or has limited slots (public or private), consider whether your child will be less likely to be admitted if you wait another year.

➤ In the end, if your child's current school is a close second, you may opt to stay put to avoid the stress and inconvenience of a change. Consider how well you can make up for quality and fit differences between the current school and the best alternative.

➤ If you stay put, you'll better understand the school your child attends and feel more committed to the school.

➤ If you decide it's worth the effort to switch schools, then you'll surely be glad you spent the time to investigate alternatives! See Chapter 18 for help preparing for the new school.

The Final March to Choosing a School

When you are ready, here are the steps you'll take to make a *final choice*:

1. Compare your Target Schools directly, using the *School Comparison Worksheet* (page 292).
2. Compare Great School Quality Factors and fit Must Haves first.
3. Know which school weaknesses you can accommodate, and which you cannot.
4. If you must, rank your Must Haves.
5. If you need to, compare Nice to Haves.
6. Make a judgment and rank your Target Schools.

Whatever school you choose, and whatever its imperfections, you can make the most of the situation by carefully crafting your child's non-school experiences and your interactions with your child's school. Chapter 18 will help you take the first steps towards becoming a great partner in your child's education. But first you'll need to take the sometimes dizzying step of getting your child in to your chosen school.

SNAP TO IT

What To Do

➤ *Compare your Target Schools directly.* Use our *School Comparison Worksheet* on page 292. Here you will transfer the grades you have given each school from your *Great School Quality* and *Personalized Great Fit Checklists.* See an example on page 294. Estimated Time: 15 minutes – 1 hour

➤ *Compare Great School Quality Factors and fit Must Haves first.* Identify (highlight or circle) the schools with the highest and lowest grades on each Great School Quality Factor and Must Have Fit Factor. Are one or more schools stronger than the others *overall*? If not, notice the *particular* strengths and weaknesses of each school on your list compared to the others. Look at just *how different* the schools are on each important factor. To help you make a quick visual comparison, you may want to use green to highlight the school(s) strongest on each factor and red to highlight the school(s) weakest on each factor. If you couldn't bring yourself to narrow your Target School list to five or fewer before now, this may be a good time. Estimated Time: 15 minutes – 1 hour

➤ *Know which school weaknesses you can accommodate, and which you cannot.* What are the weaknesses of each Target School – in quality and fit? Note the schools that *fail* to meet a need you really cannot make up for at home. Now look at the opposite: highlight schools that *best address* needs you cannot accommodate at home, in non-school activities or family life. Use the *Child, Family and Quality: Ways to Get What You Don't Get at School* tables starting on page 416 to help. Estimated Time: 15 minutes – 1 hour

➤ *If you must, rank your Must Haves.* If you like to get technical, you may want to assign a numerical weighting to each Must Have. See our decision worksheet at **PickyParent.com** for more help. Or you may just want to highlight the one or two Must Haves that are *most* essential. If you are choosing between your children's needs and your own, we encourage you to bend your needs to meet theirs when possible. Estimated Time: as needed

➤ *If you need to, compare Nice to Haves.* If you are choosing between two schools very similar in quality and Must Have fit, compare how well each addresses your Nice to Have fit needs. Consider using yellow to highlight the top schools on these factors. Estimated Time: as needed

➤ *Make a judgment and rank your Target Schools.* Based on all of these factors, rank your Target Schools. Estimated Time: as needed

Need more? Want more? Got more to share? Visit PickyParent.com.

School Comparison Worksheet *PAGE 1*

▲ Use the information you have gathered about schools to do a side-by-side comparison of both fit and quality. If you are comparing more than five schools, you will need to use two of these worksheets.

▲ List school names at the top of the school columns to right (use school initials or abbreviations to fit).

▲ Page 1: Transfer informaton to the first three blank columns from your *Personalized Great Fit Checklist.* Place your grades for each school on each Fit Factor below school name. Compare how well schools fit your child and family needs.

FIT FACTOR	CHILD & FAMILY NEEDS: Must Haves & top Nice to Haves	MUST HAVE	NICE TO HAVE	SCHOOL #1	SCHOOL #2	SCHOOL #3	SCHOOL #4	SCHOOL #5
What Your Child Learns								
How Your Child Learns								
Social Issues								
Practical Matters								

Continues…

A CONFIDENT CHOICE Tool

School Comparison Worksheet — PAGE 2

▶ Page 2: Transfer quality grades from your *Great School Quality Checklist* below each school name. Compare the quality of your school options.

▶ Review pages 1 and 2 and compare the schools. Highlight particular strengths and weaknesses of each school. Remember, not all items listed here are equal in importance for you and your child.

✔ Must Haves and quality should weigh more heavily in your decision than Nice to Haves.

✔ Use the *Child, Family and Quality: Ways to Get What You Don't Get at School* tables to help you decide which Must Haves and quality weaknesses you can best accommodate outside of school, if needed.

GREAT SCHOOL QUALITY FACTORS	SCHOOL #1	SCHOOL #2	SCHOOL #3	SCHOOL #4	SCHOOL #5
1. Clear Mission Guiding School Activities					
2. High Expectations for All Students					
3. Monitoring of Progress and Adjusting Teaching					
4. Focus on Effective Learning Tasks					
5. Home-School Connection					
6. Safe and Orderly Environment					
7. Strong Instructional Leadership					

School Comparison Worksheet   *PAGE 1*

► Use the information you have gathered about schools to do a side-by-side comparison of both fit and quality. If you are comparing more than five schools, you will need to use two of these worksheets.

► List school names at the top of the school columns to right (use school initials or abbreviations to fit).

► Page 1: Transfer informaton to the first three blank columns from your *Personalized Great Fit Checklist.* Place your grades for each school on each Fit Factor below school name. Compare how well schools fit your child and family needs.

FIT FACTOR	CHILD & FAMILY NEEDS: Must Haves & top Nice to Haves	MUST HAVE	NICE TO HAVE	SCHOOL #1 Elm	SCHOOL #2 Ridge	SCHOOL #3	SCHOOL #4	SCHOOL #5
What Your Child Learns	Child: Basic Learning Capabilty - Bright/Gifted	x		A-	C+			
How Your Child Learns	Child: Motivation - Weak	x		A	B-			
	Family: Values about how - Classroom Behavior - controlling/strict		x	C?	A			
Social Issues	Family: Student Community - critical mass of gifted children	x		B	B?			
Practical Matters	Family: · Child-care - need afterschool · Transportation – bus to & from	x		B-	A			
	· Money – afford up to $6,000 plus $1000 for afterschool; prefer less	x		A	B			

Continues…

295

School Comparison Worksheet — *PAGE 2*

▶ Page 2: Transfer quality grades from your *Great School Quality Checklist* below each school name. Compare the quality of your school options.

▶ Review pages 1 and 2 and compare the schools. Highlight particular strengths and weaknesses of each school. Remember, not all items listed here are equal in importance for you and your child.

✔ Must Haves and quality should weigh more heavily in your decision than Nice to Haves.

✔ Use the *Child, Family and Quality: Ways to Get What You Don't Get at School* tables to help you decide which Must Haves and quality weaknesses you can best accommodate outside of school, if needed.

GREAT SCHOOL QUALITY FACTORS	SCHOOL #1 Elm	SCHOOL #2 Ridge	SCHOOL #3	SCHOOL #4	SCHOOL #5
1. Clear Mission Guiding School Activities	A	C			
2. High Expectations for All Students	A-	B- ?			
3. Monitoring of Progress and Adjusting Teaching	A	C-			
4. Focus on Effective Learning Tasks	C	A			
5. Home-School Connection	B	C			
6. Safe and Orderly Environment	C?	A			
7. Strong Instructional Leadership	B?	C			

LIGHT'NING LIST

What To Know from Chapter 17

➤ **Get organized and stay organized** to make sure you take all the *right steps* at the *right times* to apply or register for your child at your top five Target Schools.

➤ **Timing:** The typical school hunt process falls between August and April of the year before your child would start the next grade.

➤ **Admissions Testing:** Your child may need testing, a group observation and/or interview for admission into some schools:
  ✔ *Consolidate testing* by hiring a private tester to do one round of tests, if possible
  ✔ *Schedule smart:* plan only one admissions/testing event per week for your child and never two days in a row
  ✔ *Manage your child's stress, fatigue and health* during test and interview weeks, and
  ✔ *Consider optional test preparation* for older children only, but not the same week as actual testing.

➤ **Relationships Count.** To build a long-term relationship with the school you ultimately pick and to sell yourself and child to selective schools, stick to these four principles:
  ✔ *Be Polite* – say please and thank you; speak with respect
  ✔ *Be Genuine* – be yourself and encourage your child to do the same
  ✔ *Be Firm* – ask the questions you need to ask; get the information you need
  ✔ *Listen Well* – give schools a chance to say what they need to say

➤ **Each school type has typical steps** for admissions and registration; review these along with helpful tips in the chapter text.

➤ **Each individual school has its own calendar.** You'll need to follow the specified steps of each school you consider.

➤ **All is not lost if your child does not get a slot in your top pick school:**
  ✔ Hang on – many children are admitted off of waiting lists to both public and private schools. Let selective schools know *you* want *them* and *why*.
  ✔ Prepare to make the most of the school your child will attend.

Chapter 17

Getting In Is More Than Spin: Secure a Slot for Your Child

The Waiting Game

Once you've decided which school best matches your quality and fit needs, you will wish you could just pluck it off the shelf and ring it up at the cash register. Those of you who've chosen the assigned public school for your child can strut about while the rest of us live in a nervous twit. Alas, the real life agony of applying and waiting remains for many of you, for public and private school-of-choice hopefuls alike. If your top pick school is selective or has limited spaces, you may be left tapping your toes for a few weeks to several months or more.

Don't panic if it seems like every family you know is trying to send its children to the same school. We hope you know by now that high demand does not always equal high quality, and there are hidden gems in many towns and cities.

But the word to the wise is this: do not assume you will get your first choice or even your second, unless your child is guaranteed admission and you've completed the required registration. Make sure your child knows that your top pick school is not a sure bet (unless it is, of course).

Meanwhile, take time to point out the positive aspects of your lower-ranked school options. This will help take the pressure off any testing your child must undergo and lessen the blow if your top pick doesn't materialize. This pressure release may be particularly important for older and more mature children who are sensitive to test stress.

Getting in really is more than spin. Please, please always, always follow your particular Target Schools' admissions and registration requirements precisely.

You may feel a wee bit of stress yourself. Indeed, choosing a school is emotionally all-consuming for many parents and families during the major school choice months, from August through April. Remember that a wide range of strong feelings about this matter is normal, and even more likely if you care greatly about the quality and fit of your child's school.

Focus your energy on the practical world of applying and registering. Different types of schools – regular public, magnet, charter, private, and so forth – have different sets of steps for admitting children, and the specific steps may differ by individual school, as well. We'll cover the typical differences among school types in the second half of this chapter, but please, please *always, always* check into your particular Target Schools' admissions and registration requirements. First, though, let's focus on the similar issues most of you will encounter. As you progress from choosing a school to getting the school to choose your child, the two biggest concerns will be logistics and relationships.

Logistics: Get Organized, Stay Organized

Even if your child is a top candidate or a seeming shoo-in, you must do what is required at the right times to ensure your child's spot in your school of choice.

It's your job to stay organized during your child's school hunt, and especially so during the application and registration process. You might wish someone else would keep up with the deadlines, appointments and paperwork, but they won't, and so you must. Schools are simply too busy to keep up with you, so you must keep up with them. Public schools may send you a registration notice of some kind, particularly if you and your child live in a city with significant choice among public schools, but you won't want to count on this. Private schools have many prospective students and their parents flowing through during the typical peak admissions season from October through March. If you plan to home school, your state may have deadlines for informing the powers that be of your intent. Few schools at the elementary level will actively recruit individual students, and even then they are unlikely to cut you slack if you miss a key registration or application deadline. So, even if your child is a top candidate or a seeming shoo-in, you must do what is required at the right times to ensure your child's spot in the school of your choice. Our *Getting In Is More Than Spin!* worksheet on page 316 will help you keep tabs on your efforts school by school.

Timing

As in most areas of life, timing is not really *everything* in a school hunt – unless, that is, you miss a deadline. So, do all you can to be sure that you don't. What kind of timeline are you likely to see? This certainly will vary, and you should check the dates for each school you consider. But here is a typical set, just to familiarize you with the usual order of things:

Model School Choice Calendar

This is a model. Always follow the steps and deadlines of each individual school you consider.

August/September:
➤ You read or review this Picky Parent Guide to gain an understanding of school quality and determine your child's and family's needs (with professional help if needed)
➤ You find out what schools are available and begin to screen for quality and fit

September/October:
➤ Open houses and tours begin – you sign up to screen promising schools
➤ Written applications, registration forms and school brochures available
➤ Test score information from previous school year available
➤ You schedule and begin interviews, by appointment, with principals and teachers of most promising schools
➤ You gather documents needed for application and registration at many schools (child's birth certificate, social security number, and proof of residence)

November:
➤ Applications for some private and religious schools due
➤ Some public school initial registrations due
➤ Some private, religious, and selective public school interviews, testing begin
➤ Open houses and tours continue
➤ Your school research – gathering information, conducting interviews – continues, and you begin to narrow your list of Target Schools to five top choices

December/January:
➤ Private and religious school applications due, including reference letters from child's current teachers
➤ Public school applications and written registration due, especially for magnet schools, schools in cities with choice programs, charter schools and special programs within schools
➤ Private, religious, and selective public school interviews and testing continue
➤ Your school research continues, and you rank your Target Schools

February:
➤ Interviews and testing continue, as scheduled
➤ Your school research continues to get more details, if needed

March:
➤ You wait while schools make admissions decisions, run magnet and charter school lotteries and complete registration input
➤ Some schools notify families about admission and registration outcomes

April:
➤ Rest of schools notify families about admission and registration outcomes
➤ Public schools continue registration (but typically little choice among schools at this time)
➤ You take appropriate action if your child is waitlisted at your top pick school

Paperwork

You'll have some, though we think if you keep it organized you need not spend too much time on low-value paper shuffling. Shuffle less, learn more in the precious time you devote to choosing your child's school. Try this:

➤ *Keep a calendar.* If you are already a calendar-in-hand type, then you will sail through this step. If not, start now. As soon as a school hits your top five on the Target School list – even though you may change your mind later – record, in pencil, the application or registration deadline as well as get-ready reminders for any pre-work needed at least two weeks ahead (e.g., filling in application, getting a teacher's recommendation, finding your child's birth certificate).

➤ *File it.* Make a file for each Target School, and put the admissions or registration materials that you must return to the school in the front of the folder. Hopefully, this will be easy, since you already have a file for investigating each promising school (right?). Write in big letters on the front of each file the final date for application or registration for that school. Sure, you already have these dates recorded on your calendar, but this will just serve as another reminder.

Testing, Group Observations and the Like

Some schools will require formal assessments of your child, perhaps including learning styles, I.Q., social skills and other measures of academic readiness and fit. Testing may be done by a private third party (a child psychologist or school placement expert) or by an employee of the school. Private schools are most likely to have testing requirements, but some public schools and public charter schools may, as well. Testing also may be required for admission into a special program within a larger school, whether public or private.

The types of tests and assessments you might see include these:
➤ A written or oral test of current academic capabilities and/or intelligence
➤ Assessment of emotional, social and physical (large and fine motor) development
➤ Observation of your child in a school-like group setting
➤ Social interview
➤ Assessment of your child's previous work (that you submit to school)

If a public school requires an assessment, it almost certainly will provide it for free, usually administered by school or district staff. Private schools typically include the cost of testing in the application fee. But many schools, both public and private, will accept test results from an approved private tester (e.g., a child psychologist or education counselor). You can save yourself and your child some trouble by limiting the total number of tests and assessments. The easiest way to do this is asking if schools will accept test results from a common third party. If you can swing it financially and your child is going through lots of testing, it may be worth the money. Each assessment session is a new situation and likely to cause some stress, even if it is fun for your child (as it often will be). Some schools may want to conduct an informal social interview and group observation in addition to testing, and this certainly will de done by school staff rather than an outsider.

Testing may be done with groups of children or one-on-one with a tester. If your child is shy or sensitive to new environments, aim for a one-on-one assessment when possible. Some schools will offer a group test for free but allow you to pay for an individual assessment if that's what you'd prefer. Remember, a child won't over test, but your child may not fully show his capabilities or act like himself if tired or stressed.

Some schools want to see how your child operates in a group, since so much of the school day is spent this way. Private and selective public schools may ask you to bring your child at a specified time for a mock day at school, where children will be grouped in a class with other student candidates and a real teacher from the school. In rare circumstances, a school may offer to observe your child in his current school or group day care.

Regardless of where and how your child is tested, be a thoughtful planner for your child:

➤ *Spread out your child's school admissions events.* We might say "use your common sense," but truly you may need to be more sensible than is common. *One special event per week is enough for most children. Really.* Your child will both absorb your stress and feel his own from the new situations you are introducing. Never, ever schedule two admissions events – tests, group observations, or interviews – on the same day or two days in a row, unless you absolutely have no choice in the matter.

Start asking your friends and acquaintances, and you'll likely hear several sad stories of stressed children and frustrated parents as a result of over-scheduled school assessments. While most adults can gear up for several focused "performances" for a few days, young children typically need longer to recuperate. The stress and fatigue your child feels will lead to a lack of self-control and an inability to think clearly. This has been the downfall of many a school applicant, much to the parents' dismay. Even if your child is a gung-ho groupie, group observations can be stressful. Every group has different rules and norms, and your child will be stretched to pick up on the new norms fast. That's hard work. You might allow more than one event per week for a child in fourth grade or older. Consider your child's age, how well your child handles other new situations *and* how tired new events leave her.

If you need to reschedule an event, call as far in advance as possible and explain why you would like to make the change. Many schools will notice and appreciate your sensible parenting. If you realize after the fact that your child just wasn't "himself" on the day of observation or testing, be sure to let the school admissions/testing staff know and offer an explanation (for example: sick, tired from another event of some kind).

➤ *Avoid other stressful or tiring events.* In the day or two before your child attends a test, interview or group observation, stick to your usual routine, or if your child's life is hectic, cut back a bit. Hard as this may be for the avid parent, save play dates with new (or feisty) friends, the circus, new extra-curricular activities, and the like for weeks when your child is *not* going through the school admissions wringer.

➤ *Keep your child healthy.* Focus your child's life on the healthy basics for a few days in advance (at least) – healthy meals and snacks, plenty of outdoor exercise, an earlier-than-usual bedtime, frequent hand washing and plenty of water to drink. Whatever your child knows and can do, a healthy body will let her show her stuff at test time.

Relationships

At one school you consider (which one?) you are starting a long-term relationship, not just selling your child. That school will care for your child for 30 plus hours each week.

While you are flitting about finding facts about schools, the schools are getting to see you the parent, and sometimes your child, in action. You'll want to use this chance not just to collect the information you need and meet formal admission or registration criteria, but also to get your relationships with potential schools off to a strong start. Remember, after all, that one of these schools you are grilling is the one you'll marry – ahem – choose for your child, and you'll want those early interactions to have been warm and fuzzy even as you put schools (and perhaps they you) through the wringer.

Your relationship with a school starts the first time you call to sign up for an open house or obtain admissions materials. You are learning about how the school operates, and they are learning about your child's family. In short, you are forming a bond that may last for years, or be broken within months. Until you've chosen a school for your child, and your child has secured a spot, the dance you do is a tentative one.

From the "getting in" perspective, your job is twofold: first, to sell your child and family to a school (even as they sell themselves to you) and second, to

Smart à la Carte

To Prep or not to Prep?

You may be wondering whether you should prepare your child for tests, group observations and interviews. The best way to "prepare" your child is to play an active role in your child's overall development from day one (or before, prenatal experts would argue). Your child is far more likely to display knowledge, social skills, self control and physical prowess in a testing situation if they are part and parcel of his everyday world. Encouraging your child to use "good manners" in an interview is practically futile if your child has no ideas what "good manners" are or is not routinely asked to use them. Wishing your child could quickly learn to spell his name by Friday falls far short of asking him to recall a name he's seen written, heard spelled and touched on letter blocks for years.

Yes, for your older child, you might consider a private test preparation course in advance (*at least* several weeks ahead). But really, if you are feeling the need to do this, perhaps you should consider finding a tutor for your child during the rest of the year, not just for test preparation. The best show of what your child knows and can do will come from deeply imbedded habits, skills and knowledge.

By the time you get to choosing a school for your child age four or older, the appropriate question is, "how can I make choosing a school a positive and meaningful experience for my child?" Help your child form an attitude that will allow him to perform his best without fear of disappointing you. Let your child know that – for better or worse – life is full of tests, interviews and social judgment-making of one kind or another. Each of us will shine on some occasions and flounder on others. At some times we'll be able to show all that we know. But sometimes, our capabilities will stay locked away inside our weary or self-conscious brains and bodies. As much as you can, help your child know that we all have good days – and bad.

Manage the stress by telling him ahead of time what to expect logistically (e.g., how long each interview or test will take, generally what kinds of questions he might be asked) and by limiting the pressure to perform beyond your child's current capabilities. Well before each test, interview or group observation, tell your child what kind of reasonable behavior you expect (e.g., to try his best, to listen well, to be considerate of others). If you wait until the last minute, your child will feel your stress, and it will make him feel stressed. On the big day, do no more than this: let your child know you love him, hug him, and take care of your child's healthy routine (exercise, early bedtime, healthy breakfast, snack and so on). Afterward, congratulate your child's effort and ask if he had fun. If the event took place at the school, ask your child what he thought of the teachers, other staff and activities. Let him talk if he wishes, but don't press it.

begin building a long term relationship that will help your child in the school she ultimately attends. So while you are investigating and applying or registering with schools, you can get your relationship off to a start that will improve your child's odds of entry or, at the least, set the right tone for your relationship later.

Guiding Principles

You need to do no less than a fine balancing act to build your relationships with prospective schools. Keep these guiding principles in mind:

➤ Be polite

➤ Be genuine

➤ Be firm

➤ Listen well

Be Polite. Even as you ask tough questions to probe for a school's strengths and weaknesses, say "please" and "thank you," and speak with respect in your voice. Nobody particularly wants to deal with a crabby person, and schools are no exception (even if your child is the eighth wonder of the world). Write a brief thank you note to school staff members who are especially helpful to you in your school hunt, whether or not you think their school will be #1 on your list. Do this even for public schools and others where admissions are by lottery rather than selection (because you may be starting a long term relationship, not just selling your child). Especially praise people who are courageously candid with you about their own school's weaknesses or who help you think about other appropriate (great quality or fit) schools beyond their own.

Be Genuine. Pretending that you or your child is something different from what you are won't help anyone in the long run. Be as honest about your child's strengths and challenges as you want schools to be with you. Remember, schools know that a parent who understands her child's strengths and challenges is a better partner for a school and its teachers than a parent who wants her child to be something the child is not. Plus, a school cannot fully communicate what it can do for your child if it doesn't have an accurate picture of your child's needs and family situation. Resist the dramatic urge you feel to impersonate the wealthy socialite you may secretly wish you were to get your child into an "elite" school. It may be as important from the school's perspective that child and family will add positively to the school community – not just through donations and social connections, but also through parent volunteer work, diversity and your child's contributions both in the classroom and out.

Be Firm. Let neither politeness nor humility prevent you from getting picky about important matters. You must obtain the information you need about a school to make a good choice and work with the school later. Great Schools, and even many mediocre ones, will appreciate that you care enough to ask good questions about quality and fit. Remember, many people working with schools know that children of engaged parents perform better. If you've been through the (hopefully uplifting) toil of learning about school quality and fit, let your new know-how and enthusiasm shine through. Ask the questions you need to ask to get the information you need. If a school is not answering your questions with specifics, ask more specific questions until you understand what the school is and isn't going to offer your child.

Some principals and teachers will dismiss your questions as "not important here at our school," and this may embarrass you. One mother told us of her tough decision not to choose the school her twin sons wanted to attend (their best friends were going there). The principal repeatedly dismissed the mother's concern about whether her typical son would get the basic academic reinforcement he needed while his highly gifted twin got the very advanced instruction in mathematics that he needed. In the end, she realized that the school offered a one-size-fits-all approach. The principal's semi-rude responses to the mother's questions were simply a way of covering the unfortunate truth.

Many parents have suffered through feelings of dismay and insecurity after polite tongue lashings from principals and teachers who lacked good answers to important questions about quality and fit. You are not alone. Stay strong, and know that merely by asking your questions you may be improving the lots of children and families who follow. When principals hear a consistent and compelling demand from parents for real quality and a variety of fit options, more will feel obliged to improve.

Listen Well. While you'll want to spend much time asking your specific questions, it is just as important to hear what a school says for itself. You will need to be on the receiving end some of the time. Some parents are so eager to share what they know and want, that they walk away without a clear view of how a school sees itself (and why). At the beginning of interviews, offer a one-minute set of "headlines" of your child's and family's biggest fit and quality concerns. Listen to what they want to say first, *then* fire away with your questions when the time is right. In open houses and school tours, listen to the school's spiels, *then ask* your specific questions if they have not already been answered. You'll learn much about the focus and consistency of the school if answers are rolling off their tongues, and equally as much if you have to hunt and peck for scraps of information. Just as important, you will show yourself to be both a concerned parent and one who wants to be a school partner, not dictator.

Tips for Getting In: Public Schools

Your Assigned School

➤ Find out the required registration date. Even if you've selected your assigned public school, some cities guarantee your child a slot in a particular school only if your child is registered by a certain date. If your town or city allows parents to choose among public schools, you'll need to be especially vigilant.

➤ Get the required paperwork as soon as it is available so you won't have to rush

Smart à la Carte

Up Your Odds: Understand The Admissions Game

"Selective" schools come in two varieties. Some have admissions criteria – they accept only kids with a particular targeted combination of test scores, other capabilities and family attributes. Others (typically public schools) are open to everyone though some kind of lottery, but have more applicants than available slots. In either case, you can up your odds of getting in simply by understanding the dynamics of admission at the school.

Individual schools vary, so it's important to do some up-front homework.
➤ How many slots are available at your child's grade level? How many applicants are expected?
➤ What are the criteria for admission/registration, and do those criteria change in higher grades?
➤ Do siblings (and/or alumni relatives) get preference over other applicants?

The slots available even in the lowest grades may be fewer than you think. Most selective schools guarantee admission to returning students, who occupy most seats in the upper grades. So most of the new student slots will be in the school's starting grade, typically kindergarten or pre-K at an elementary school. In some schools, both public and private, many of those starting-class positions will be spoken for by *siblings* of current students, who usually have a leg up in the admissions/registration process (in some schools absorbing well over half of the available slots).

But you may find other windows of opportunity. In both public and private schools, some families will move each year, opening some number of slots. Some families may find the school to be a poorer fit than anticipated, and so will change schools. Seats may open up for other reasons as well. A K-12 private school, for example, may deliberately leave spaces open in higher grades (e.g., 6th and 9th) to allow for

Continues...

➤ Gather required documents in advance (may include birth certificate, copy of social security card, proof that your child lives at the residence you claim and immunization history)

➤ Don't be creative now – use the forms supplied by the school district

➤ Register – turn in that paperwork – by the assigned date

➤ You may be required to bring your child in person to a checkpoint – do it if required

➤ Make sure you have met the principal

➤ Let principal and teachers you meet know that you've made a proactive school choice for your child, even though the school is your assigned school

---

Up Your Odds...*continued*

new entrants, but those slots will typically be reserved for students with proven high academic achievement.

In many private schools, lower grades are populated by children of families who will send all of their children to the same school. Despite what some admissions officers may tell you, these schools will bend over backwards to admit siblings so that family loyalty is not split between schools. And family characteristics are typically more important for the lower-grade elementary slots. But to remain academically competitive when student achievement becomes more visible in middle and high school, these schools reserve some slots in higher elementary and middle school for very high-achieving applicants. Your child's achievement, rather than family characteristics, becomes more important in the higher grades. *Know that quality and fit may differ considerably among a K-12 school's elementary, middle and high schools, particularly if the programs have different leaders.*

If you understand these dynamics, you can "play the game" more effectively by doing things like:

➤ Applying for a school's Pre-K program. The Pre-K class may have more open slots than kindergarten, and once you're in, you're in. But scrutinize the quality and fit of the elementary program specifically before you take this leap. Every year counts a huge amount at this age. Think hard before you accept mediocre K – 5 years for the hope of better quality in grades 6 – 12.

➤ Leading with a younger sibling. It may be tough to get your rising second grader into an already full school. But if her little sister is admitted to Pre-K or K, then your second grader's chances are boosted by her sibling status.

➤ Waiting for a window. If your child's current grade level is full, ask about future grade levels. Perhaps waiting a year could up your odds considerably.

Public Magnet Schools

➤ Find out the required the registration date

➤ Get the required paperwork as soon as it is available so you won't have to rush

➤ Gather required documents in advance (may include birth certificate, copy of social security card, proof that your child lives at the residence you claim and immunization history)

➤ Complete any testing or other admissions requirements well in advance of the deadline (in case there is any delay getting results or a re-test is needed); test deadlines may be different from the paper application deadlines

➤ Gather needed teacher and other recommendations – make this easy for recommenders by providing detailed instructions, all the necessary forms, and sealable envelopes; pre-address and stamp any items they must mail

➤ Don't be creative now – use the forms supplied by the school district

➤ Register – turn in that paperwork and any test results – by the assigned date

➤ You may be required to bring your child in person to a checkpoint – do it if required

➤ Make sure you have met the principal

➤ Let principal and teachers you meet know that you've made a proactive school choice for your child

Other Public Schools in Your District

By Petition. If your overall best quality, best fit school is a public one to which your child is not assigned (and your city has no formal choice program), call your local district office to find out if petitioning for a transfer is possible. Get your hands on your school district's formal policy for transfers – why, how and when are they allowed? The more clearly your case fits the official rules, the easier a time you'll have.

But if your case does not fit the "rules," don't stop there. You should make your case anyway, telling why the preferred school will fit, why the assigned school does not fit, and the likely impact on your child, family and your child's classroom teacher if a transfer is not granted. State your case clearly and stick to your main Must Have fit needs. Do this in writing – addressed to the person or people responsible for such decisions – and follow up with phone calls. You, having very carefully considered your child's and family's needs, will be in a great position to articulate clearly why one school is a far better fit than another. Your child is less likely to be awarded a transfer based on quality than on fit, unless your assigned school has been deemed low performing by the state for several years. Under federal legislation in force as of this writing, districts must offer students in such schools transfers to better schools.

You may feel like a big squeaky wheel, and that may make you cranky. It is only because some schools (and districts) have fallen into the unfortunate habit of ignoring the differing needs of children and their families that you need squeak at all. You need not be nervous (though it's perfectly normal to feel this way), and do not worry about sounding slick. Be firm and persistent, but polite, too. You are doing the right thing for your child, and that's what's most important. By the way, if your child is granted a transfer, make sure to get the decision in writing to avoid confusion later. And thank the people who helped you.

By Choice Plan. If your school district has a formal choice plan that lets you pick from among not just magnet schools but "regular" public schools, as well, make the most of your flexibility. If you find that one of these is your best pick, take the steps to maximize your child's chances of getting in:

➤ Find out the required the registration date or dates. There may be a pre-registration to give the school district notice that your child may attend a public school and then another date by which you must indicate your preferred school(s)

➤ Get the required paperwork as soon as it is available so you won't have to rush

➤ Gather required documents in advance (may include birth certificate, copy of social security card, proof that your child lives at the residence you claim and immunization history)

➤ Complete any testing or other registration requirements well in advance of the deadline (in case there is any delay getting results or a re-test is needed); test deadlines may be different from the paper application deadlines

➤ Gather needed teacher and other recommendations – make this easy for recommenders by providing detailed instructions, all the necessary forms, and sealable envelopes; pre-address and stamp any items they must mail

➤ Don't be creative now – use the forms supplied by the school district

➤ Register – turn in that paperwork and any test results – by the assigned date

➤ You may be required to bring your child in person to a checkpoint – do it if required

➤ Make sure you have met the principal at your top pick school as well as your back-up school

➤ If your first choice isn't granted and the school your child must attend is a poor fit, consider petitioning for an exception using the guidelines above

➤ Let principal and teachers you meet know that you are an engaged parent and that you've made a proactive school choice for your child

Public Charter Schools

➤ Charter schools may follow their own time frames and procedures, so do not assume that the deadlines and steps are the same as for other public schools in your area

➤ Find out the required the registration deadline

➤ Get the required paperwork as soon as it is available so you won't have to rush

➤ Gather required documents in advance (may include birth certificate, copy of social security card, proof that your child lives at the residence you claim and immunization history)

➤ Complete any testing or other registration requirements well in advance of the deadline (in case there is any delay getting results or a re-test is needed); test deadlines may be different from the paper application deadlines

➤ Gather needed teacher and other recommendations – make this easy for recommenders by providing detailed instructions, all the necessary forms, and sealable envelopes; pre-address and stamp any items they must mail

➤ Don't be creative now – use the forms supplied by the charter school

➤ Register – turn in that paperwork and any test results – by the assigned date

➤ You may be required to bring your child in person to register – do it if required

➤ Make sure you have met the school principal

➤ Let principal and teachers you meet know that you are an engaged parent and that you've made a proactive school choice for your child

Tips for Getting In: Private Schools

Private schools generally are more complicated beasts than public ones at admissions time (See the box *Up Your Odds: Understand the Admissions Game* on page 306). Not only are you building a potential long-term relationship, you are selling your child and family. Some parents live for this moment, others dread it. If you are in the dread lane, slog through it *with confidence*, knowing that you are doing the right thing for your child (assuming you have focused on quality and fit in your choice).

Will a sufficient swagger for Dad and an extra swing in the waddle for Mom get you into that selective school? Maybe, maybe not. Just remember that arrogant is out, confident is in. And confident you'll be inside, so there's no need to cross over the line to arrogant nor to regress back to the parenting wallflower you once may have been. A great you is better than a second-rate, phony someone else. You may not wish to put on a show, anyway. Indeed, many parents are looking for a school where they can just be themselves. But know that wearing the latest designer duds to an egalitarian, crunchy granola school interview may not be the best strategy. Nor your favorite blue jeans with the just-right hole in the knee for a golf-club-dress-code school. For pure influence, you might try fitting in without going to extremes: plot your attire according to the usual garb of other parents with children attending the school. But if you are not in-the-know, don't fret. Just look like you care, but not like you planned the entire week around today's outfit. "Dress casual," "business attire" or anything clean, neat and in between will do just fine for private school tours and interviews. Leave your best outfit at home, but do get out the iron and scrounge around the back of your closet for shoe polish.

Sometimes the most effective "selling" is that done by someone else on your behalf. So, should you use your "connections" to get your child admitted to your school of choice? In reality, many private schools are founded and operated as much on social norms and values as on academic goals. While this may be unstated, and certainly frustrating for "outsiders," it is often true. Because of this, having one or more recommendations from parents of current students can give your child a valuable boost in the admissions process (all other things being roughly equal), even when such recommendations are not part of the formal admissions forms. The more a school seems to have a strong social culture – with a homogeneous (highly similar) set of students and many social events for parents and families, not just students – the more likely it is that recommendation letters or phone calls will help.

If you don't know a soul connected in any way to your top pick school, and it is a private one with a strong social following, do not assume that your child will be denied admission. If you have matched your child and family well to a school – considering the fit not only of academic offerings, but also of values and social characteristics – then your child may be admitted even though you've just moved to town or hail from across the railroad tracks. You might consider finding other ways to meet people who attend your Target Schools – religious organizations, preschool, children's extracurricular activities and carefully chosen community volunteer work are a few of the places you might meet more people whose children attend your school of choice. While a brief acquaintance is unlikely to lead to strong arm recommendations on your child's behalf, you might gain insight into the social culture of schools in your area if you have met many families with children attending a variety of schools.

If one or more private schools are on your Target School list, you'll need to:
➤ Determine when applications are due and whether you must give notice of your intent to apply in advance (like some public schools, there may be two different deadlines)
➤ Get the required paperwork as soon as it is available so you won't have to rush
➤ Gather required documents in advance (may include birth certificate, copy of social security card, and immunization history)
➤ Schedule and complete any testing or other registration requirements well in advance of the deadline (in case there is any delay getting results or a re-test is needed); test deadlines may be different from the paper application deadlines
➤ Gather needed teacher and other recommendations – make this easy for recommenders by providing detailed instructions, all the necessary forms, and sealable envelopes; pre-address and stamp any items they must mail

➤ Don't be creative now – use the forms supplied by each school

➤ Turn in that paperwork and any test results – by the assigned date

➤ If desired, line up friends, colleagues, and neighbors whose children attend the school to write letters in support of your child and family – *either* have them seal letters and include with your application or have them deliver letters separately

➤ Make sure you have met the principal at your top pick school as well as your back-up school

➤ Let your top pick school know that *you* want *them* and *why*. Use your *Confident Choice Tools* as a guide for communicating just what it is you like about a school. Some private schools are as impressed by the commitment of parents to their children's education as by test results

➤ Let principal and teachers you meet know that you are an engaged parent and that you've made a proactive school choice for your child

If the school is a religious one, you might also consider taking these steps:

➤ Include one or more recommendations from leaders in the religious organization you and your child attend; as with other recommenders, either have them seal letters and include with your application or have them deliver letters separately

➤ If applicable, make sure you have communicated your family's commitment to the religious values of the organization and have made clear that this is one of the reasons you want your child to attend this school

Tips for Getting In: Special Programs within Larger Schools

In general, you should follow the steps listed above for the type of school you are considering. But also consider taking these steps:

➤ Make clear the consequences for your child, family and the classroom teacher if your child is *not* admitted into the special program. You, having exceptional understanding of your child's fit needs, will be able to communicate this.

➤ If you are not satisfied with test results provided by the school or district, consider hiring a private counselor to retest. Include results with your child's application.

Tips for "Getting In": Home Schooling

➤ Determine the registration deadline for notifying the state (or public school district if needed) of your intention to educate your child at home.

➤ Get the required paperwork as soon as it is available so you won't have to rush

➤ Gather required documents in advance (may include birth certificate or copy of social security card)

➤ Determine what, if any, showing of an educational plan, materials and facilities are required (and by when)

➤ Complete and return the required paperwork by the assigned date; don't be creative now – use the forms supplied

➤ Start planning your school-at-home now, so that you can be sure you will be ready when the time comes

➤ Consider scoping out schools and registering for a backup in case you become disabled or otherwise unable to follow through with home schooling

When You Don't Get Your Top Pick School

Despite your best efforts, your child may not get into your top pick school – at least not right away. If you applied to a school where admission is by lottery (e.g., a public choice school, magnet or charter school), you may feel angry at "the process" that let you down. Popular schools – whether of good quality or not – often simply have too few slots to take all applicants. Hang on. Some parents of children who got into your top pick school may choose another school, change their minds, move or make other decisions that will open up a spot for your child. Find out if there is a waiting list and how far down that list your child is. This shuffling can happen right up to the last minute before school begins or even a short time into the school year.

If you have applied to one or more selective schools for your child (e.g., a private school or selective public school program), you may feel disappointed or even embarrassed by the rejection of your child and/or family. You, too, must hang on, as some families may choose other schools, allowing students from the waiting list to enter (make sure you know whether your child is on the list). Popular private and selective public schools, just like regular public ones, cannot take all the students who wish to attend.

But there is no need to brood. Remember, popular schools do not necessarily select students for qualities that you yourself might value. Every year, many stellar students are rejected from schools that claim to be "academically elite" in favor of mediocre students with the right social, alumni or sibling connections. Every year, schools supposedly seeking "diversity" reject fascinating families in favor of ones who fit each school's standard mold.

If you are waiting to see whether your child will be admitted off a waiting list, public or private, consider these steps:

➤ Let admissions staff at your top pick school know why their school was your top choice, using your knowledge of quality and fit to help communicate. Knowing how much *you* want *them*, a school may nudge your child ahead on the waiting list in some cases.

➤ Try not to let your feelings of disappointment overwhelm you. Start thinking of yourself as a partner with the school your child will attend. Know that you will have the chance soon to encourage change in that school (Chapter 18 will get you started).

➤ If the school your child will attend (barring a waiting list breakthrough) is private, you may need to pay a deposit while you wait to see if a spot in your top pick school opens up. Aside from the sting in your wallet, there's no need to feel bad about spending this money. If your child does get into the top pick later, you can think of the lost deposit as a thank you gift for the school that offered you a good alternative.

Most importantly, make lemonade from lemons. In the next and final chapter, we help you prepare to convert your disappointment into actions that:

➤ Improve the school your child will attend and

➤ Make up for its weaknesses outside of school.

SNAP TO IT

What To Do

➤ *Get organized, stay organized:* use our *Getting In Is More Than Spin! Worksheet* on page 316 to help keep tabs on your effort school by school. Estimated Time: a few minutes per school, when needed

➤ *Mark your calendar and prepare* for interviews, testing, observations and application (or registration) deadlines.
  ✔ *Keep a calendar:* record individual schools' deadlines and steps needed in advance to meet them.
  ✔ *File it:* make a file for each Target School to keep application and registration materials organized and handy.
  Estimated Time: 15 minutes per school to mark calendar with dates and set up file

➤ *Build relationships* with potential school picks:
  ✔ *To "sell"* your child and family to selective schools.
  ✔ *To begin a long-lasting relationship* with the school your child finally attends.
  Estimated Time: 15 minutes per school to plot strategy

➤ *Keep your* **Confident Choice Tools** *close at hand* to help you communicate your needs and expectations to schools. Estimated Time: saves you time

➤ *Skim our model calendar* on page 299. Estimated Time: 3 minutes

➤ *Follow the specified steps of schools you consider.* Estimated Time: as needed

Need more? Want more? Got more to share? Visit PickyParent.com.

Getting In Is More Than Spin!

A When-It's-Time-to-Get-Practical Checklist

➤ Note the names of schools you are considering in top row.

➤ Check off each step as you complete it for each school. Some items will not apply to all schools; for example, several items apply only to selective schools.

➤ Items #16 – 19 are intentionally blank. Add other steps for individual schools you consider.

GETTING IN STEPS	SCHOOL #1	SCHOOL #2	SCHOOL #3	SCHOOL #4	SCHOOL #5
1. Get application or registration materials, brochures, other materials					
2. Sign up for open house and tour					
3. Get school's previous test scores					
4. Schedule phone or live interview with principal (best after tour or open house)					
5. Schedule classroom observations (ideally with chance to ask teachers questions – or do this at open houses)					
6. Interview parents with similar family needs and children like yours					
7. Gather child's documents (birth certificate, social security number)					
8. Teacher recommendation packages delivered to recommenders					
9. Check with recommenders to ensure letters & forms complete, delivered					
10. Application/registration complete, delivered (make sure school receives)					
11. Schedule interviews and observations (where they interview you and child)					
12. Schedule child testing at schools (or private testing if allowed)					
13. Plan "spin" to get child in (friends, etc.)					
14. All Great School quality information gathered					
15. All Great Fit information gathered					
16.					
17.					
18.					
19.					

"Many of life's failures are
people who did not realize
how close they were to
success when they gave up."

–THOMAS A. EDISON

Make the Most of It

■ ■ ■ ■ ■ ■ ■

LIGHT'NING LIST

What To Know from Chapter 18

➤ *All parents contribute to their children's development* outside of school, whether by plan or default. *Choose how your child spends precious non-school time.*

➤ *You can compensate for many school weaknesses,* once you know what they are.

➤ *Your Great School Quality Checklist and Personalized Great Fit Checklist* completed for the school your child attends will help you understand the school's strengths and weaknesses.

➤ *If you take action before and during each school year*, you can
  ✔ *Prepare your child* for school and
  ✔ *Prepare the school* for your child.

➤ *Useful actions you can take during the school year* include these:
  ✔ Work with your child's school
  ✔ Work with your child
  ✔ Invest time and money in your child's school
  ✔ Make up for school shortcomings at home

➤ *Take responsibility for keeping communication flowing* with your child's teacher.

➤ *Help your child learn* to organize school work and make her best effort.

➤ *When major changes occur* in your family, your child or your child's school, you should re-evaluate school quality and fit.

➤ *Life's too short: mend fences with friends and family* if choosing an unexpected school has left relationships fragile.

Chapter 18

Get the Best Results (*Whatever* School Your Child Attends)

Make the Most of What You've Got

Whether or not you got your top pick, and whether or not you found a Great School that's a Great Fit, you surely will feel the relief of certainty about where your child will be going. A perfect school and perfect fit are rare, and nearly all parents must do at least a bit of gap-filling on the side. Whatever your circumstance, you will want to do what needs to be done to round out your child's development. Knowing your chosen school's strengths and weaknesses – in quality and fit – will allow you to do just that. Your pickiness will be rewarded not only in how your child spends time at school, but in how well you are able to parent your child the rest of the time.

Look back at your assessment of the school your child attends. Notice the school's quality and fit strengths, and take delight in them. But also plan ahead to make up for weaknesses, this year and in the future, with your child's home and non-school experiences. Specifically, you can:

➤ *Prepare* to begin the next year of school,

➤ *Partner* with your child's school during the school year, and

➤ *Watch for changes* that might require a school switch later.

For decades, parents have done wonders for their children attending schools that fall short in quality and fit. You, too, can find other ways to educate and develop your child when needed.

Prepare to Begin the Next Year of School

The first stops are your *Great School Quality Checklist* and *Personalized Great Fit Checklist* – completed for the school your child will attend. Use these to refresh your own memory about what you need and expect and to help you communicate clearly and concisely with your child's school.

Prepare the School for Your Child

Regardless of how responsive you expect your child's school to be, you can carry your child's principal and teachers far down the road towards understanding your child and family by communicating your needs in advance. Even the best of schools and teachers will benefit from a heads up in this regard.

Try the following steps during the spring and summer before your child begins or switches schools. Even if your child is staying put at the same school, you can strengthen your school relationship, information flow and the school's work with your child by taking some of these steps:

➤ Help the *principal* get to know your child and family
- ✔ Schedule a brief meeting
- ✔ Write a brief letter
- ✔ Attend an open house
- ✔ Share your child's testing results
- ✔ Share your child's previous years' report cards

➤ Help your child's *teacher*(s) get to know your child and family
- ✔ Write a brief letter
- ✔ Schedule a brief meeting
- ✔ Share your child's previous years' report cards

Help the principal. Introduce your child and family to the school's leader ahead of time, ideally starting in April or May before your child starts (assuming an August/September school start date):

➤ *Schedule a brief meeting* alone with the principal if you didn't already do so. In this meeting communicate your child's and family's Must Haves, and ask how you can work with the school to ensure that your needs are met. Let the principal know you made a proactive choice among schools, and that you've noticed the school's strengths and challenges. If the school was not your top choice, you will feel better starting your child's career there if you've expressed your concerns. Your input might even help the school initiate changes. If you already had this meeting during the school hunt (and we hope you did), go ahead to the next step: a reminder letter. If you do not already have a relationship with the principal, take this step even if your child is staying in the same school (especially if your child's needs have been poorly met there in the past).

➤ *Write a brief letter* (two pages at *most*) describing your child's and family's Must Haves. The more your principal knows, the more likely it is that your child will be assigned the most appropriate teacher and offered other appropriate assistance. Make clear that you expect your child to be assigned a lead teacher who can deal with his needs effectively. Be sure to include a description of the kinds of teaching approaches that have been effective and ineffective with your child in the past. Reiterate both what you like about the school and any concerns you have about quality or fit. You may write this letter in advance of your meeting with the principal to set the agenda or after your meeting to clarify what you discussed – whichever makes you feel more comfortable expressing your needs. You do not need to be a star author. Any good principal will appreciate your effort regardless of your penmanship and prose (they know that children of choosy parents perform better!). Take this step even if your child is staying at the same school, if you are concerned about teacher assignment or if your child's needs have not been well met in the past.

➤ *Attend an open house* or other school social event, and introduce yourself and your child to the principal, assistant principal and teachers (especially those from the grade your child will attend next year). If you have already met the principal or others, be sure to reintroduce yourself and say a quick hello. This is *not* the time for a prolonged discussion of your child's needs, as the principal will have many other parents to meet and greet, as well. If you haven't formed even the barest of relationships with your child's current principal, and your child is staying at the same school, it is never too late: make an effort to meet your child's principal now.

➤ *Share your child's testing results,* if any, from private assessments and even assessments conducted by other schools for admissions. Do this particularly if these tests cover an area not covered by your chosen school's own pre-admission testing. Attach copies of these to your letter or bring to your meeting with the principal. Do this even if your child is staying at the same school, if the information might shed light on previous challenges with your child.

➤ *Share your child's previous years' report cards* or progress reports from school or child care, if any. If your child has had behavioral or academic problems, you might be worried about biasing your child's principal. But your child's principal cannot help your child's teacher prepare or respond to a challenge they don't know exists. You should speak clearly and directly to your child's principal about past problems and future solutions. On the other hand, if your child's report card indicates that she's been a bright academic and behavioral star, you'll want to share this as well. At the very least, it will imply that you expect similar results from your child's new school. If you disagree with previous teachers' assessments – for example if your child's needs have been grossly unmet, leading to poor school behavior and performance – you should discuss your thoughts and feelings with your child's new principal. You need not take this step if your child is staying at the same school, unless you think highlighting some aspects of the report might aid your discussions with the principal.

Help your child's teacher(s). As soon as you know which teacher has been assigned to your child, and certainly by the end of the first week of school, take time to introduce your child and family:

➤ *Write a brief letter* (two pages at most) describing your child's and family's Must Haves. Use the letter you sent to the principal as a guide (indeed the principal may have shared this letter with your child's teacher already), but omit items referring to teacher selection. Summarize your child's school hunt testing results, if any. Let the teacher know you made a proactive choice among schools (unless of course this was your last-choice school). Include any descriptions of teaching tactics that have been effective and ineffective with your child in the past. Say that you look forward to working with your child's teacher (music to a teacher's ears). Write and send this letter as soon as you know who your child's lead teacher will be. As with the principal, the letter need not be perfect. Nearly all teachers will appreciate the information you provide.

➤ *Schedule a brief meeting* alone with the lead teacher soon before or after school starts. Many schools provide this time for all parents. It is a helpful way to begin building the parent-teacher relationship, and it is very helpful for those parents who are uncomfortable writing about their children's needs. If such a meeting is not routine, you may feel uncomfortable asking your child's busy teacher for special time. Consider setting up a phone call instead, if this is more convenient for all. In this meeting – by phone or in person – communicate your child's and family's Must Haves, and ask how you can work with the teacher to ensure that your child's needs are met. Ask how your child's teacher prefers for you to keep in touch informally during the year – by sending notes in your child's backpack, phone calls, e-mail, chats at carpool pickup, etc.

➤ *Share your child's previous years' report cards* or progress reports from school or child care, if any (make a copy and keep the original). If your child has had behavioral or academic problems, you might be worried about biasing your child's teachers. But your child's teachers cannot prepare for or respond to a challenge they don't know exists. You should speak clearly and directly to your child's lead teacher about past problems *and* future solutions. On the other hand, if your child's report card indicates that she's been a bright academic and behavioral star, you'll want to share this as well. If you disagree with previous teachers' assessments – for example if your child's needs have been grossly unmet, leading to poor school behavior and performance – you should discuss your thoughts and feelings with your child's teacher. You need not take this step if your child is staying at the same school, unless you think highlighting some aspects of the report might aid your discussions with your child's new teacher.

Choosing Not Just a School, But a Teacher

If you have followed the steps above with your child's principal, you'll be well on the way to an appropriate teacher match. It is in the school's interest to get this right, as your child's success on measures important to most schools – student achievement, teacher and parent satisfaction – may depend upon it. If you have found a spot for your child in a truly Great School with a Great Fit, you will have less work to do, as fitting teacher and child will undoubtedly be part of the principal's strategy for ensuring that individual students' needs are met. Alas, until schools catch up with parents' growing expectations for great quality and fit, you may have a bit of cajoling to do.

Some principals will say, "All of our teachers are good." But you, wise parent that you are from reading this book, know that both quality and fit are important. This is true for school and teacher. All teachers – just like all professionals of any kind – are going to have strengths and weaknesses. It is the principal's job to ensure that teachers are assigned to students with whom the *teachers* can be successful. It is also the principal's job to ensure that as many students as possible are assigned to the teacher with whom each *child* can be successful. It is a fine balancing act for the principal. Push to ensure your child's need are met, but know that principals sometimes must include other factors in their assignment decisions, such as balancing the number of girls and boys, and so on. Your child might not be matched with the very best fit teacher every year, but you should expect every assigned teacher to be at least a good, solid fit for your child.

Your school may have a form for you to complete to help with teacher assignment (we hope this will become standard). Be sure to shoe-horn in key Must Have information about your child and family, even if what you need to say does not fit the form precisely.

Some principals do not mind if you request a specific teacher. If you are very certain of the teachers' strengths and weaknesses and how they will meet your child's needs, that's fine. If you do not know the teachers well and have not had the chance to observe them, a general letter that will help your principal pick the best one is the better route. Most principals, especially the ones very savvy about fitting child and teacher, will appreciate the flexibility of making assignments for fit, not teacher popularity.

If your child is stuck in a school with little appreciation for the idea of "child fit," then the principal may resist any effort to match your child to the best-fit teacher. This is astonishingly, if unintentionally, cruel to those children who end up in an unfortunate mismatch. But this is the way of some principals, no doubt. You are more likely to end up in this situation if you have chosen a school with a strong one-size-fits-all approach that works for a *limited* set of children, and if that approach is not a good fit for your child (for example if you have chosen one school for all of your children, but their needs are quite different, and the school is inflexible).

If you *know* your child has been poorly matched with a teacher, make one more effort at pointing out to the principal the possible consequences to your child, the teacher, and you. Use your *Confident Choice Tools* to help you communicate clearly and specifically. Know, though, that once school has started, moving your child to a different class may have a domino effect on other children. Many principals would be hesitant to make a change at this point.

In the worst case, you might check around to see if many other parents and children are in the same situation. Consider organizing other parents to lobby the principal to change the teacher assignment policy. Failing this (and assuming you have no other schools to which you might switch), lobby the school board or board of directors to insist that the principal change the policy – or that the principal be changed for one who will better serve the interests of students. Meanwhile, you the parent may have more gaps to fill for your child this year. Get out your parental caulk and spackling. *Child Needs: Ways to Get What You Don't Get at School* (page 416) is a start.

Prepare Your Child for the School

Seize every opportunity to make a new school old hat. Prepare your child for school by making the new environment seem as familiar as possible ahead of time. The environment includes facilities and grounds, the child's future classroom, other students, parents, teachers, other school staff and school work.

Meet the Place and People. Help your child meet other same-age children and their parents, teachers and other school staff. During the spring and summer before school starts (assuming an August/September start date), take your child to at least one – more if possible – social events at the school. These are great chances to meet other newcomers as well as old timers. You need not work the room, and it is true that many of these folks won't be your best friends nor your child's. But you and your child will feel more comfortable once school begins if a few familiar faces pop up here and there.

If your chosen school does not have organized events, take the initiative. Starting the spring before your child will begin at a new school, take your child to play on the playground and just to walk the halls. Attend a spring musical performance or other organized public events at the school. Even consider organizing an event yourself, such as a picnic or afternoon playground stomp. Ask the school if it would support you in this endeavor (you will need a list of new children or children who will be in your child's grade, with phone numbers or addresses).

In the month before school starts, get together with one or more children and parents from your child's new class (or at least the same grade, if you do not know teachers' assignments yet). You might meet at the school playground for a picnic, go out for pizza, or enjoy another activity that will allow the children to interact informally. If you do not know other families who will attend the same school, call the school and ask if they can play matchmaker by giving you names and phone numbers of families who live nearby.

Meeting new schoolmates is a *big deal* to many children. Some will be nervous about even a low-key meeting of their new schoolmates, so do not be surprised if your child acts shy or clingy the first time out. Rather than shove your child away and increase his anxiety, you simply must make additional efforts to meet up with classmates just before and during the initial weeks of school. Eventually, your child will know other children and will feel at home. Of course, you may be lucky and have a child who will jump right in to play with strangers. If this is your child, encourage him to reach out to the shy ones and invite them to play along, too.

Even if you do not attend a social event, take your child to the school during the daytime to peek in on the classrooms for his future grade. You might do this at the end of a school day the spring before, and again the week before, school starts. It is comforting for many children to see the physical layout without the hubbub of other students. Your child can imagine himself pecking at that computer, working at that table or reading in that corner. With permission, your child might even spend a few minutes using the learning materials.

Get Ready for the Work. If your child's schoolwork will be significantly different from her previous school-like experiences, you may want to help her prepare. Talk about how the activities, teaching and work materials might be different. If the new school will be a great academic stretch for your child, you might consider weekly tutoring in basic subjects over the summer to prepare your child (the school may have recommended this already). Particularly in higher grades where other students will be walking a well-worn path, it is better for your child to be slightly over-prepared academically than under-prepared. Then, she may spend the first few weeks on other harrowing tasks, like making friends and learning the way to the bathroom.

Recognize Your Child's Worries. It is normal to face a new situation with a mixture of excitement and fear. Ask your child about any concerns he or she might have. Whatever they are, help your child think about how to address the reason for the worries. If your child is worried about leaving friends, commit to having old friends over to play in the afternoons or on weekends. If your child is worried about making new friends, commit to helping your child by inviting new friends over in the first few months of school. If your child is concerned that school will be too hard, commit to keeping up with your child's work and finding help if the going gets tough. If your child is worried that the school won't be challenging enough, commit to providing extra stimulation outside of school. If your child is worried about being teased, commit to helping your child develop the skills to forge new friendships and inner confidence that will insulate her from the words of rude classmates. Let your child's teacher know about your child's worries so she can help you monitor for any difficulties.

Partner with Your Child's Teachers During the School Year

Education is a partnership between child, family and school, and you can choose to form an effective partnership or not. You can coordinate with teachers, share information and work towards the same goals for your child together – or not. You and your child's teachers can plan together to use each of your strengths, or you can spend your time whining about each other's shortcomings and pointing fingers.

If you were fortunate enough to find a Great School with a Great Fit for your child, kudos. If not, what can you expect from your child's teachers? Can you expect a teacher to do it all, providing Great School quality without a Great School to back her up? In most cases, the answer is no (although some teachers perform backbreaking miracles, no doubt). But even without a Great School, you can initiate strong parent-teacher partnerships to develop your child at home and school. You simply will have more gaps to fill and more work to do than you would at a better quality and fit school.

Discuss your child's needs with teachers; let them know what you are doing at home. Share your ideas with them, and, in turn, listen to their ideas. Make the most of what you've got – in parenting skill and in your school pick. Just as a Great School can make up for many parental shortcomings, a great parent can make up for many school shortcomings.

Keep Communication Flowing

When it comes to communication between parent and teacher, too much is better than none. It is better to say too much and ask too much than to say and ask too little. The better you keep teachers informed about life at home, the better they can adapt to your child in the classroom. The better you understand what your child is experiencing at school, the better you can adapt to your child at home.

It is your job to ensure that this communication happens. Yes, it is the school's job too, but your child and family will suffer when there's a problem. So take responsibility even when, especially when, your child's teacher does not. What kinds of things should you communicate to your child's teacher between conferences and other formal meetings? Start here:

➤ Your family situation has changed in a concrete way (a move, a divorce, a very ill parent, a job change or loss for parent and so on)

➤ Your family situation has changed in a smaller, temporary way that may bother your child (living through renovations, parent traveling a lot this month and so on)

➤ You have noticed negative changes in your child (symptoms of depression, fatigue, loss of interest in school or friends, violent or angry behavior and so on)

➤ You have noticed positive changes in your child (happier, more excited about school work, making new friends and so on)

➤ You child has begun a new activity that will absorb a fair amount of time or energy

➤ Your child has made consistent positive or negative comments about school

➤ Any other noticeable change, for better or worse, in your child's academic, social, emotional or physical well-being

What questions might you ask to get communication flowing *from* your child's teacher? Start here:

➤ How are things going in your class this year?

➤ How are things going at the school in general this year? Any big changes?

➤ How is my child doing? Is (s)he _____ (the thing you fear your child is doing)? Is (s)he _____ (the thing you hope your child is doing)?

➤ Is there anything different I should be doing at home with my child?

➤ What can I do to help?

If a problem arises, try the steps outlined in the box *Resolving Parent-Teacher Conflicts* on page 330. This approach may help you address the challenge quickly. But not always. You may have to involve the school principal to get results. A principal who is a good problem-solver and facilitator will focus both on solving the problem at hand and helping you and the teacher figure out how to communicate and work together. But don't be shocked if the principal is defensive or tries to sweep your concerns under the rug (especially if you had the same experience with the same person in your school hunt). This is poor principal performance, but do not let it rattle you. As in your school hunt, stand strong (and think of the other parents who undoubtedly have had the same experience with this principal). If you cannot resolve communication issues, or the problems beneath, start looking for a new school or see the box *Changing a School.*

Smart à la Carte

Resolving Parent-Teacher Conflicts

Is your child's teacher just not working out? Is she so far down on the quality scale, and so different from what you expected, that you're in shock? Does your child bring out the worst in his teacher? Does your child's teacher seem to bring out the worst in your child? Or is something just not right – your child is showing a loss of interest in school, boredom, decreased performance or stress related to school? If the answer to any of these questions is "yes," do not wait to take action. Act now. After one month of school, the transition period should be over (give it six weeks for kindergarten and pre-K). Your goal is to get action, which starts with an understanding of the problem, continues with a plan for addressing the problem, and ends with changes – at school and home – happening according to plan.

Try these steps:

1. Schedule a face to face meeting with the teacher as soon as possible. You probably won't be the first, so do not feel like you are alone.

2. If you feel more comfortable writing than speaking, write a letter about your concern ahead of time. Either use it as the opener to schedule the meeting, deliver it a few days in advance of the meeting, or bring it to the meeting.

3. In the meeting (and letter), follow these tips for effective feedback:
   ➤ First, spend a moment or paragraph thanking the teacher for her effort. Express positive feedback about things that may be going well or qualities in the teacher that you appreciate.
   ➤ Next, on to the problem. Be very specific about the effects or symptoms you see in your child. ("My child stopped sleeping when school started. My child has lost interest in school work, and this has never happened before." Etc.)
   ➤ Be very specific about the impact this has on you and/or your family life. ("Her constant whining about school is making my younger children upset. My spouse and I are losing sleep over this now.")

Continues...

Invest in Your Child

In addition to keeping the information flowing between you and teacher (and principal when needed), consider other ways you can boost both your child's and school's performance. The biggest impact you will have on your child is the time you spend with him. You may think of other ways to help your child directly, but here's a start:

➤ Let your child know that you expect him to make his best effort in school work
➤ Teach your child to keep track of homework assignments, due dates and finished work (offer to buy your child a calendar and storage files for finished work)

Resolving Parent-Teacher Conflicts...*continued*

➤ Tell the teacher directly that you would like to do your part to make things right for your child and want the teacher's input about what to do at home.
➤ Do not make global assumptions or accusations about the teacher's shortcomings.
➤ If you have ideas about what changes might help, you may share them; but...
➤ Do not come to definitive conclusions about what changes need to occur; instead ask the teacher what ideas she has to address the situation. She may need time to think about it, get the principal's input and get back to you.

4. At the end of the meeting, ask the teacher what she sees as the next step. The goal for you: get the teacher to make a plan for specific changes and communicate the plan to you. The teacher might need a week to think about it. She or he might need to meet with the principal. Or you may need to meet with teacher and principal together. Whatever it takes to help the teacher form an action plan, be sure that that's what happens.

5. Schedule a time to talk again, in person or by phone, to decide together what actions each of you will take (one or two weeks later should allow adequate time for planning). Decide together whether and how to communicate with your child about any changes.

6. If this does not work (the teacher won't schedule a meeting; the teacher proposes no changes; the teacher proposes changes, but after two more weeks no changes have occurred), call and schedule a meeting with the principal. Let the principal decide how to proceed.

7. If your child's needs still are not met, it's time to consider looking for a new school or leading the charge to change the school.

➤ Teach your child to make sure he understands homework assignments before leaving school
➤ If your child needs help understanding homework, help him but let him do the final assignments himself
➤ Hire a tutor or seek a free school-based one if you are uncomfortable in the teaching role (ask your child's teacher about this)
➤ Check over your child's homework and school work when teachers send it home; discuss corrections with your child to make sure he understands them
➤ Let your child know that you have a willing ear for his thoughts and concerns about school (and reinforce this by asking how things are going every day)
➤ Praise your child for great effort that leads to great results, in academic and other pursuits
➤ Accept that your child might not excel in every area

Invest in Your Child's School

In addition to communicating with your child's teachers and helping your own child directly, you can help boost the school's performance by volunteering and contributing money to activities that *directly support the school's mission and goals*. In many schools, ill-focused parent volunteer efforts have little impact on educational results. Just as with school staff efforts, parent efforts should be well-planned to support the mission of the school, the goals of the school, and to fill gaps related to these. If you are disappointed by limited opportunities to make a meaningful contribution, consider getting involved in the PTA board and making changes. Even if you like what you see, consider getting involved in school parent leadership to press for continued changes and improvements.

Meanwhile, start by getting the lay of the land:
➤ Attend one or more Parent-Teacher Association meetings to learn what parents are already doing in your school
➤ Look and listen for opportunities to use your skills and knowledge to replace services the school might have to purchase otherwise (saving the school funds for other purposes)
➤ Ask your child's teacher what role you might play that would help with student learning in the classroom (e.g., tutoring a struggling child, tending – even teaching – a small group of children while the teachers focus on another small group)

Of course, some of your time may be spent just learning about the school and building a comfortable relationship with staff and other parents. And some of your time may be spent just having fun with staff, students and other parents, regardless of the impact on student learning. Indeed, if you chose a school largely for its values and family community, these activities may be the most personally rewarding for you.

Smart à la Carte

Changing a School

You may feel inspired to dig in and improve your chosen school once your child starts there. We hope that frustration will lead to action, and that parents' voices will be heard. Rather than dismissing parents as too personally motivated, we hope school leaders will hear the united voice of parents who want better quality and better fit choices among both public and private schools.

Changing a school, of course, is a tall order. Here are a few helpful tips to jump-start your thinking:

➤ Pinpoint the specific quality issues you want to address. Vague calls for "change" have little chance of success. Use our Great School Quality Factors to zero in on what matters most.

➤ Look for the source of the problem. Does the school lack a commitment to do what needs to be done? Or is there a commitment, but no plan? Or is there a plan, but no follow-through? Can the existing leadership make the needed change, or is new leadership what's needed?

➤ Build a case. Gather hard data, specific examples, and other evidence of the problems you see. Research solutions so you can back up your proposals for change with solid information.

➤ Understand how decisions are made about your issues. Do individual teachers make the call? The principal? The school leadership council or governing board? The district? You need to know where to focus your efforts.

➤ Gather a broad base of support. Include many different kinds of parents. Individual teachers can also be allies. If the problem comes from outside the school (like a bad school district policy), the principal may well agree with you and welcome your involvement. The less the issue gets framed as you vs. the school, the better.

➤ Include people who the decision-makers trust, respect, and want to please (e.g., parents who give much money or time to school; parents of high-performing students).

➤ Work through the channels first. If there's an established way to bring new ideas to the table, start there.

➤ Realize the usual channels may not work. Successful efforts to change schools sometimes require more than an amicable meeting in the principal's office. They often take considerable time and require something like a campaign to achieve results.

➤ Be honest with yourself – are you up for this? You're more likely to be if you build a team that can work together.

They may include:
➤ Attending (and helping to organize) school social functions
➤ Attending school fundraisers
➤ Attending school athletic events
➤ Volunteering for activities that make the school pleasant but that are unrelated to school quality, such as landscaping and decorating

If you have money you would like to contribute to your child's school, you may do so in several ways. Your money is best spent on items and activities that directly support the mission of the school or that directly improve the school's quality and fit for your child. Some ways to contribute money include these:
➤ Give to your school's annual fundraising campaigns
➤ Give to your school's capital campaigns (which typically fund big investments like new or better buildings and equipment)
➤ Make a gift to your child's teacher for supplies and equipment either of your choosing or hers (write the check to your child's school with the purpose designated on the check and accompanying note); deliver to your child's teacher directly
➤ Sponsor a field trip or other special event for your child's class (ask your child's teacher in advance)

Make Up for School Shortcomings at Home

Start with the sections that pertain to you in the *Quality, Child, and Family Needs: Ways to Get What You Don't Get at School* tables starting on page 416. You, lively parent that you are, will undoubtedly have much to add to this for your child. As you are thinking through your options, you can use the *Getting What You Don't Get at School Parenting Planner* on page 339 to keep you focused on what counts most. In general, consider these sources of non-school development for your *child*:
➤ Free, unstructured time at home for your child to pursue own interests (materials supplied by you the parent). A no TV policy or clear limits helps with this.
➤ Suggest that your child take homework assignments an extra step, or in a different direction of interest (after completing the required assignment, of course)
➤ Extracurricular group activities (clubs, sports, group lessons)
➤ Extracurricular individual activities
➤ Tutoring, to broaden your child's knowledge in a new area
➤ Tutoring, to challenge your child with more difficult material or to reinforce the basics
➤ Computer activities to broaden or strengthen your child's knowledge or to challenge your child with harder material
➤ Self-study at a library, museums and other public learning areas
➤ Youth and family activities at your religious organization

Make your child a partner in this process. Help her to pick and choose from among activities that will meet the needs unmet by school. Help your child learn to prioritize by considering lots of possibilities, but choosing only the most meaningful and high-impact activities. Plan for a year at a time so that you feel more at liberty to spread out structured activities over time, rather than cramming every afternoon full. If you over schedule your child, even with his consent, you will surely begin to see waning interest and symptoms of stress. Take a clue and cut back thoughtfully if this happens.

Oops! Something's Gone Wrong! When is it Time to Make a Change?

Wouldn't it be nice if things stayed the same so you could choose a school that you could count on forever, no questions asked? Yes. But in reality, changes happen that affect school quality and fit, some for the better and some for the worse.

When do changes mean you need to change schools? Sure, you'll want to make a change when your child's current school tanks in quality or fit. But you might want to consider making a change if you suspect that there's a better quality, better fit school available to your child, and a little research proves you right. Perhaps another school has made tremendous improvements, perhaps yours has slipped a bit, or perhaps your needs have changed. Keep your ear to the ground, *especially* if your chosen school was not of great quality or fit from the start.

Here are obvious signs that it might be time for a school change:

➤ *The School Has Changed*
  ✔ Your child's school leadership has changed, and your quality demands or fit needs won't be well met any longer
  ✔ The quality of your child's school has taken a nosedive
  ✔ Your child's school has made changes that do not fit your child's or family's important needs
  ✔ You were duped – your child's school does not fit as you thought it would or is not of the quality you thought

➤ *Your Family, Your Child, or What You Know About Your Child, Has Changed*
  ✔ Your family's needs have changed and the school no longer fits
  ✔ Your child's needs have changed, and the school no longer fits
  ✔ You have learned something new about your child's needs, and now understand that the school does not fit (e.g., your child has a previously undetected disability)

➤ *Something is Wrong . . . But What?*
- ✔ Your child is not happy at school for an extended period of time, and efforts to solve the problem have not worked
- ✔ Your child is not learning or performing at grade level in basic subjects
- ✔ Your child is not learning or performing above grade level, despite better previous performance or above average Basic Learning Capability
- ✔ You are not happy with your child's school – for quality or fit reasons – now that you have learned more about it

Now, you won't want to put your child through the stress of change for a minor improvement. You and your child are better off trying to improve the school or accommodate your needs outside of school. In fact, if you can successfully initiate school improvements, you'll be serving a whole community of children and families in one fell swoop. (See box on *Changing a School* on page 333.) But there is no need to suffer, and certainly no need to make your child suffer, if change is needed. And you will be oh, so much better equipped to choose a school the second time around.

Fixing Fences: When You've Flown in the Face of Friends and Family

If you have chosen a school different from the one friends, family or neighbors expected, you may be on the receiving end of cold shoulders, tongue lashings or gapes of disbelief. But you know now that you are not alone in bucking a trend or two in your child's best interest. Parents of all kinds – all kinds of viewpoints, all kinds of incomes – are getting picky when it counts, just like you. Parents who are themselves children of '60s radicals but who choose private schools. Parents who are themselves children of big givers to private schools but who opt against the family favorite for better quality and fit. Parents in neighborhoods dominated by private school attenders but who find astonishingly good quality in their assigned public schools. Parents in neighborhoods where everyone goes to the assigned public schools but who choose an alternative. Devout Catholics who rebel and go secular. You, and others like you, are all parents in search of something better and more fitting for your child and family. Your child will spend thousands of childhood hours in school. Getting picky about the school you choose should be a point of pride, not scorn.

Choosing your child's school is your first really public parenting statement, and it may be the first time that seeming wedges between you and others are revealed. You wish those wedges could be benign, but sometimes they are raw like a wound with no protective skin. We won't pretend to be family relationship experts. So let us just speak as parents, friends, neighbors, colleagues and family members. We tell our own children all the time that they can have many different kinds of friends – friends with whom they like to work, friends with whom they like to "just play," friends with whom they like to do sports, friends whom they teach, friends who teach them, friends of whom they take care, friends who take care of them, friends who really understand them, and friends with whom they are friendly but not close.

All of these relationships are important. We are all best off if we have some of each kind, whether with family, neighbors, colleagues or others. The mere fact that you have one difference – even one on which you've grown to place much importance – does not mean that you cannot continue to have a positive relationship. You need not be identical to be friends, and you need not be cut from the same mold to be family. You will be a better parent, indeed a better person, if you are a great you rather than a watered down version of your friends, neighbors, colleagues or family members. You, in turn, must accept that they may have other values, needs and wants that lead them to decisions different from yours, regarding school and other matters. (Or you can accept that they just may be mindless lemmings, dingbats or shameless self-promoters who don't give a hoot about their children's welfare. But they are *still* your friends and family. Give them a copy of this book before you give up on them.)

> *Your job as a parent is to see the big picture and make sure you provide the kind of environment, at school and elsewhere, that your child needs to become the terrific person he is meant to be.*

Parting Words

One thing is true for certain: much of what your child needs to know to become a happy, healthy, loving, achieving, contributing adult will not be learned in school. Your child's core values – about how to interact with other people and how to spend time, effort, and money – will be learned largely at home, at friends' homes and in other meaningful non-school experiences. Your job as a parent is to look at the big picture and make sure you are providing the kind of environment your child needs to become the terrific person he is meant to be. Above all, enjoy your child and the unique person he or she becomes.

What To Do

➤ *Review your chosen school's strengths and weaknesses,* in both fit and quality, using the *Great School Quality Checklist* and your *Personalized Great Fit Checklist* that you completed for the school. Estimated Time: 15 minutes

➤ *For each school weakness, think of concrete actions you can take to fill the gap* outside of school. Use our *Quality, Child, and Family: Ways to Get What You Don't Get at School* tables starting on page 416 as well as your own ideas. Use our *Getting What You Don't Get at School Parenting Planner* on page 339 to help you plan. Estimated Time: as needed (more for a poorer quality and poorer fit school, less for a Great School that's a Great Fit)

➤ *Prepare the school for your child.*
   ✔ *Help your child's principal get to know your child and family* by sharing Must Haves, previously effective teaching tactics, testing results and report cards. Share with your child's principal any information that will help assign a good-fit teacher:
   • Schedule a brief meeting (in late Spring before school begins)
   • Write a brief letter (in late Spring before school begins)
   • Attend an open house
   • Share your child's testing results, if any (with letter or at meeting)
   • Share your child's previous years' report cards (if changing schools)
   Estimated Time: as needed
   ✔ *Help your child's teacher(s) get to know your child and family* by sharing Must Haves, previously effective teaching tactics, and report cards:
   • Write a brief letter (as soon as you know teacher assignment)
   • Schedule a brief meeting (just before or during first week of school)
   • Share your child's previous years' report cards (if changing schools)
   Estimated Time: as needed

➤ *Prepare your child for school by helping him or her get familiar* with school facilities and grounds, the child's future classroom, other students, parents, teachers, other school staff, and school work in advance. Seize every opportunity to make a new school old hat. Estimated Time: as needed (1 – 2 hours plus organized events)

➤ *During the school year, consider these actions:*
   ✔ Work with your child's school
   ✔ Work with your child
   ✔ Invest time and money in your child's school
   ✔ Make up for school shortcomings at home
   Estimated Time: as needed

➤ *Re-evaluate school quality and fit when major changes occur* in your family, your child's life or your child's school. Estimated Time: as needed

➤ *Life's too short: you must mend fences with friends and family,* if choosing an unexpected school has left relationships fragile. Estimated Time: all the time you need

Need more? Want more? Got more to share? Visit PickyParent.com.

Getting What You Don't Get at School

Parenting Planner

➤ Fill in the quality and fit weaknesses of the school your child will attend.

➤ Decide and fill in what you plan to do to overcome those shortcomings. Use your own ideas and the *Ways to Get What You Don't Get at School* tables.

➤ Try not to over schedule your child in non-school hours. Use less structured, at-home materials and activities as well as more formal arrangements.

➤ Remember that trying to encourage changes in your child's school may be an option.

School's Quality or Fit *Weakness*	What will I do to make up for this weakness?	Next Steps (Research, Determine Cost, Schedule, etc.)

Glossary

Academic: Academic, as it is used in this book, means having to do with elementary school subjects required for later functioning as an independent adult in our society. These include at least reading, writing, math, science, and social studies.

Adequate Yearly Progress: A term used in the 2001 federal No Child Left Behind legislation that refers to how much schools must increase the percentage of children achieving grade level in order to meet federal requirements. This measure does not indicate how well a school helps students learn beyond grade level goals.

Advocate: The role of parent or other influential adult to understand and communicate a child's needs to teachers and principal.

Age-Appropriate: Age-appropriate means suitable for a child of a particular age. Age-appropriate capabilities are ones that most children of a certain age have mastered. Age-appropriate education uses teaching methods and subject matter that appeal to the interests, preferences, and capabilities of most children of a certain age.

Alma Mater: A school that you attended previously. In our usage, you need not have graduated from a school for it to be your alma mater. With Latin and Greek origins, the term literally means "nourishing home" or "nourishing mother," but you may or may not have such warm feelings towards every school you attended!

Analytical Thinking: Solving problems by breaking them down into logical, orderly steps. One of the two major capabilities assessed by traditional "I.Q." tests (the other is Conceptual Thinking).

Assessment: Formal test or measurement of an individual child or school using scales of commonly accepted measures generally agreed to be important. May also refer to informal monitoring of an individual child's learning.

Auditory Learner: *See* Learning Styles

Basic Learning Capability: A child's readiness for learning in core academic subjects. Includes both your child's current mental processing abilities ("I.Q.") and your child's previous learning of core academic content. Core academic content includes subjects essential to later education and adult life in our society: at least reading, writing and math in the elementary years. Often considered an unchangeable characteristic, in fact a child's Basic Learning Capability can change significantly during the elementary years.

Before and After School Care: Care for school-age children before the formal school day begins and after the formal school day ends, often during typical parent work hours.

Behavior: Behavior includes student and staff social behavior both in and out of the classroom. Aspects of behavior include manners with other children and adults, dress, discipline and honor code.

Behavioral Challenges: *See* Challenges

Breadth: Subjects, topics, and aspects of the "whole child" beyond just core academic subjects.

Capability: The state of readiness for performance or accomplishment in a particular pursuit. In the case of Basic Learning Capability, a child's readiness to learn in core academic subjects. In other areas, such as music, art, physical and hands-on activities, creativity, and English as a Second Language, includes the relevant mental, physical, and technical skills and knowledge for each pursuit.

Certification: The licensing of prospective teachers by a state. May include passing a written exam meant to assess knowledge of education principles or other requirements.

Challenges: Physical Health, Mental Health and Behavioral:

>**Physical Health:** Any physical restriction, handicap or ongoing illness that may prevent a child from participating fully in school life and learning or that requires daily treatment or special facilities.

>**Mental Health:** Any ongoing or recurring emotional upset (such as depression, anxiety, or other mental health challenges) that may prevent a child from participating fully in school learning and life or that requires regular treatment or school oversight.

>**Behavioral:** Significant, unresolved behavior or discipline problems in group settings that prevent a child or others in same class from effectively learning.

Charter School: A public school that has a "charter" or contract to educate students in exchange for receiving public education operating funds. Charter schools typically are released from many of the regulatory constraints placed on other public schools, but must achieve specified educational results to continue receiving public money.

Choice Plan: A plan within a public school district that allows parents to choose from among several schools, not just an assigned school. A choice plan may allow choice from among all schools or from among a limited number within the district.

Clear Mission Guiding School Activities: A written school plan that is used to guide all decisions about how to spend time, money and other resources in the school. The mission should clearly define why the school exists, the major guiding principles (values) of the school and whom the school will serve. All members of the school community should understand the key points and follow them in daily school activities. One of the seven Great School Quality Factors.

Conceptual Thinking: Making comparisons between things not obviously related, seeing similarities and large patterns in a collection of smaller events. One of major capabilities assessed by traditional "I.Q." tests (the other is Analytical Thinking).

Confidence: The feeling that you can do a good job, so trying hard is worth the effort. If you read this book, you will both feel and act more confident when choosing and working with your children's schools.

Content: The subjects, topics, skills and knowledge that a student learns or is taught at school.

Controlling Classroom Behavior Management: A method of managing students' behavior in which teachers maintain order through clear rules, rewards and consequences. Also called "Strict." Contrast with Developmental approach.

Core Academic Subjects: Subjects that all students must master in preparation for independent adult life and further education in our society, including at least reading, writing and math in the elementary years. Also includes science and social studies in most curriculums.

Creative Thinking: Thinking of new ideas and ways to do things, rather than imitating others or doing things the way they have been done before; may apply to varying activities.

Critical Thinking: Thinking that includes making judgments. Requires both analytical and conceptual thinking to assess logic and completeness of previous work, and in some instances creative thinking to determine alternatives not presented in previous work.

Culture: *See* School Culture.

Curriculum: The combination of learning goals (grade level and/or individualized) that define what children are supposed to learn in a school. Sometimes also refers to the materials and teaching method used to meet learning goals.

Default Destination: Our term for the school to which a parent would send a child if not making a proactive school choice.

Design: *See* School Design.

Developmental Classroom Behavior Management: A method of managing students' behavior in which teachers maintain order by coaching and developing students' self-control and using peer and parental pressure. Contrast with Controlling/Strict approach.

Differentiation: An instruction approach in which both the difficulty of material taught and the teaching methods used differ according to each individual child's current achievement level, learning styles, interests and other child characteristics. This is used as an alternative to teaching one level of skill and knowledge and using one teaching method for all children in a class. Differentiation combines Great School Quality Factor #2 (High Expectations) for children ahead of grade level and Great School Quality Factor #3 (Monitoring Progress and Adjusting Teaching) for all children. Also called "individualized instruction."

Disorders: *See* Learning Disabilities and Disorders

District School: *See* Public District School

Diversity: A school is diverse when the students or parents are different from each other in certain respects. A school may be diverse in students' academic capabilities; race; religion; gender of students; values and ethics of students and parents; family income and wealth; student and family residence; or interests of students. Different students and families may value different aspects of diversity.

Education: Education includes what a child learns and how he learns, both in school and out of school. Education includes not just academics, but also development of a child's social, emotional and physical capabilities.

Educational Goals: Individual Educational Goals are the specific skills and knowledge that a school expects an individual student to learn, either based on the child's grade level or based on the child's previous mastery. School Educational Goals are goals for average levels of achievement or progress that a school has for all students or for students in various subgroups (e.g., by race, income, or previous performance).

Elementary Schools: Schools that serve children in grades kindergarten through 5th or 6th grade.

English as Second Language: When a language other than English is spoken by a person, and a person is not already fluent in speaking, reading, writing and understanding English, and learning English is desired or required, then English is called the person's "Second Language" ("ESL"). ESL programs in schools follow varying formats. Schools vary in the amounts of time spent on English instruction, the range of subjects taught in English and the quantity of instruction in the student's first language. The long term goal of most ESL programs is for each student to understand, speak, read and write English at the level expected of same age children for whom English is the first language.

Essential Activities: The activities that a child must continue in order to address the child's compelling interests or capabilities.

Ethics and Morals: *See* Morals and Ethics

Extracurricular Activities: Activities conducted outside of the school's regular academic curriculum. May be done at school or with an unrelated group. May include traditional academic content or other areas. Examples include sports; fine arts such as drama, art, music, or dance; chess clubs; math and science clubs; book clubs; volunteer community service; and non-school religious activities. *See also* Essential Activities.

Fees: Fees are amounts of money parents pay over and above tuition to fund non-core elements of a child's education, most often at private schools. Examples include sports fees, locker fees, and field trip fees. Fees are distinct from tuition only because a school chooses to charge for them separately, often because the fee purchases an optional element of the child's experience. Inquiring about fees in advance can help you determine which ones are truly optional and which are necessary to include in your school budget.

Fit: The match between child, family and school. A Great Fit school is one that completes a particular child's education and development in ways complementing the family's values and needs. Fit, along with school quality, is one of the two major considerations for choosing the right school for a child. *See also* Fit Factors.

Fit Factors: The four areas to consider for determining how well a school fits the needs and values of a particular child and family. Each Fit Factor is comprised of specific elements for child, family and school. *See also* definitions of the individual factors: What Your Child Learns, How Your Child Learns, Social Issues, and Practical Matters.

Focus on Effective Learning Tasks: The multi-task process of ensuring that students' school learning time is focused effectively on the work of learning. Includes using well-tested teaching approaches; allocating class time, materials, and facilities in line with each subject's and topic's importance; and ensuring that class time is not interrupted. One of the seven Great School Quality Factors.

Four Fit Factors: *See* Fit Factors

Gifted: Traditionally, students who possess some combination of unusually high learning ability and unusually high performance in traditional academic areas: reading, writing, math, science, social studies, and the thinking skills that underlie each. Today, the term "gifted" may refer to children with combined unusually high learning ability and performance in other areas as well, such as music, art, athletics, social interactions and leadership.

Goals for Your Child: Goals important to a parent that the child is at risk of not meeting. Common goals influencing school choices include grade progression, academic performance at the child's full level of capability, and college opportunity.

Grade Level Standards: The specific knowledge and skills that a school expects all children to acquire and demonstrate by the end of each grade level. Grade level standards may be written as end-of-year goals only or as a series of steps spanning multiple grades and phases within each grade.

Great Fit: *See* Fit

Great Fit Triangle: Triangle picture with three puzzle-piece sections – child needs, family needs and school offerings. The Great Fit Triangle illustrates how the fit among child, family and school determines the completeness of an individual child's education and development.

Great School: A school in which students of all abilities and types learn dramatically more than similar students in other schools. Research has consistently shown that schools meeting this definition exhibit the seven Great School Quality Factors used in this book far more often than schools producing lesser academic results with their students.

Great School Quality Factors: The seven characteristics of schools shown through repeated research to distinguish Great Schools from average ones. Great Schools are ones in which students of all abilities and types learn dramatically more than similar students in other schools. *See* Chapter 11.

Hands-On: Activities, or a person who pursues activities, requiring strength, agility, speed, balance and/or flexibility of hand muscles. Includes creating ideas or objects and solving problems using small muscles of the hand. *See also* Physical. *See also* Learning Styles: Kinesthetic/Tactile.

Health, Mental and Physical: *See* Challenges

High Expectations: Combined challenging learning goals and a consistent expectation by school staff that all students can meet the goals. Includes high minimum grade level expectations for all students, with clearly defined actions taken for students at risk of not meeting. Also includes a defined process to set higher expectations for students ready to learn beyond grade level, including clear actions to help those students meet individual goals. One of the seven Great School Quality Factors.

Home School: Formal education offered primarily in a child's own home and guided by a child's own parent(s). Home schooling may include multiple families collaborating for academic instruction, music, sports, art and other activities. Instruction may be done by hired tutors. Some aspects of home schooling may take place away from home, such as art and science museums, other local educational facilities, and homes of other families.

Home-School Connection: The communication between school and parents of information important for each child's learning and development. Includes school informing parents what children will be learning, how to help at home, and how each parent's own child is faring. Also includes school working effectively with parents to resolve problems. One of the seven Great School Quality Factors.

How Your Child Learns: One of the four Fit Factors. "How Your Child Learns" includes features of a child or family that influence how a school should teach and interact with the child, both in and out of the classroom.

Implementation: This is what schools actually do day-to-day, as opposed to what they say they will do or plan to do.

Independent School: A private, non-government school that is owned, operated and funded without control by any larger body (e.g., religious or other group).

Individualized Instruction: *See* Differentiation

Instructional Leadership: Leadership of a school. The seventh Great School Quality Factor. Includes ensuring that all staff members are focused on implementing the first six Great School Quality Factors. Specifically: maintaining clear, high expectations for teachers; recruiting and keeping great teachers; organizing teachers to work together; monitoring and improving teacher performance; and acting on high and low teacher performance (recognizing and rewarding high performers, ridding school of low performers). *See* Leadership.

Kinesthetic/Tactile Learner: *See* Learning Styles

Leadership: The capability of establishing a vision and/or goals and organizing and managing a group of people to implement the vision and goals. Term applies to both children's capabilities (*see* Social Skills) and adults' capabilities (*see* Instructional Leadership).

Learning Content: *See* Content

Learning Disabilities and Disorders: Disabilities and disorders are imbalances and severe challenges that may keep a child from learning and performing at the level of which the child would be capable if not for the disability or disorder. A disability is a problem with an important, basic part of your child's physical or mental functioning that is significantly different from your child's other capabilities or that significantly hampers your child's learning. A disorder is a problem with an important, but not necessarily basic, part of your child's physical or mental functioning. Both disabilities and disorders may keep a child from fully utilizing other capabilities. Both may affect academic, social, emotional and physical learning and performance. Some disabilities and disorders can be overcome entirely if detected and addressed early enough in a child's development. The impact of most others, once diagnosed, can be lessened.

Learning Goals: The specific skills and knowledge that a school expects a child to acquire and demonstrate. Learning goals may be the grade level standards or may be determined for each individual child, particularly for children who meet or surpass grade level before the end of the school year or who are Extremely Challenged in Basic Learning Capability.

Learning Styles: Auditory, Visual and Kinesthetic/Tactile. Strengths and preferences your child has for using the senses — particularly sight, hearing/talking, and movement/touch — to absorb new information and act in a learning environment.

> **Visual:** child learns best seeing things written or in pictures; stimulated by how things look; bothered by disorder, clutter.

> **Auditory:** child learns best listening, talking, discussing; stimulated by sounds; bothered by loud, disorganized noises.

> **Kinesthetic/Tactile:** child learns best by moving body; stimulated by activity; bothered by sitting still. Tactile learning is specific type of kinesthetic learning: child learns best by working with hands, including both handwriting and other activities.

Lottery: A process through which a school randomly selects students for admission. Most often used by public schools when the number of applications for admission exceeds the number of slots. Some schools hold separate lotteries for different grade levels, genders, family incomes, and other dimensions.

Magnet School: A school in a public school district that offers a special curriculum (e.g., math and science, performing arts) or teaching method. The term "magnet" is used because these schools are intended to attract students from across a district.

Mental Challenges: *See* Challenges

Mission: The purpose of the school. The mission should define why the school exists, the major guiding principles (values) of the school and whom the school will serve. Actual "mission statements" vary in completeness. A mission is necessary to guide a school in choosing its curriculum and teaching methods, both to fit the school values and to meet the needs of students attending the school.

Monitoring of Progress and Adjusting Teaching: The twin process teachers and other school staff use to assess individual students' learning progress frequently and adjust teaching approaches to ensure that all children meet their learning goals, whether grade level or beyond. One of the seven Great School Quality Factors.

Morals and Ethics: Morals are a person's definition of what actions, thoughts and words are right and wrong; a person's definition may be guided or determined by a larger group (religion, family, community). The term "ethics" is often used interchangeably with "morals." Ethics entails a specific determination of right and wrong when the moral definition is not entirely clear; such a determination often is guided by priorities about which morals carry more weight than others in certain situations.

Motivation: Your child's internal drive to learn and perform academically. This includes setting goals, working to meet them and overcoming obstacles. While there are other motivations, this is the one used in this book to help match children with schools.

Multiple Intelligences: The areas of intelligence possessed by all people in varying degrees, not limited to traditional verbal and mathematical capability. The seven core intelligences include those two as well as musical, bodily-kinesthetic, spatial, interpersonal (social), and intrapersonal (self-knowledge). Howard Gardner, who defined the concept of multiple intelligences, urges educators to recognize that stimulation of one intelligence may increase others, as well (e.g., music to help teach math or language). Aspects of multiple intelligence theory important for choosing a school have been incorporated into the *Confident Choice Tools.*

Must Have: A Must Have need is a child or family characteristic that parents decide is both very important (to the child or family) and essential for their child's school to address.

Nice to Have: A Nice to Have need is a child or family characteristic that parents would prefer for a school to address. Nice to Have needs may be less important than ones that families "Must Have" addressed at school, or these needs may be more easily met outside of school than Must Haves.

Ownership and Control: Ownership and control determine who funds and makes decisions about the operations of a school, including mission, curriculum, teaching method, discipline and other matters. Who owns and controls a school defines the school type: public district, charter, private, religious, home, etc.

Parent Community: The relationships of parents to each other and the school and the feelings of belonging created. Feelings of belonging are influenced by individual parents' fit with other parents in a school, including where parents live, pre-existing friendships, values, social behavior and manners, and diversity of parent social groups, economic status, race and ethnicity. An element of Fit Factor #3, Social Issues, for families.

Parent Involvement: The level and type of involvement in a school by parents. Level of involvement is influenced by the types of roles available to parents in the school, the school's expectation for parent involvement, and the number of parents who actually are involved. Roles typically include decision-making boards, helping with daily school life and fundraising. An element of Fit Factor #3, Social Issues, for families.

Parochial School: A school operated by a religious group. Typically, a parochial school would include religious instruction and possibly worship as part of the school day.

Phonics: A reading instruction method in which children are taught not just letter sounds, but the sounds of common letter combinations which, all together, form words.

Physical: Having to do with the body. Displaying bodily strength, agility, speed, balance and/or flexibility; or creating ideas and solving problems using whole body. *See also* Hands-On. *See also* Learning Styles: Kinesthetic.

Physical Health Challenges: *See* Challenges

Picky Parent: A parent who makes well-informed, thoughtful choices about important matters for his or her child.

Practical Matters: Matters of logistics (scheduling, transportation, and the like) and money, rather than matters of education content or values. This is one of the four Fit Factors for matching your child and family to a school.

Principal: The primary leader of a school's instruction and operations, responsible for ensuring school quality and adherence to the school's mission. This is the instructional leader, responsible for managing teachers and other staff to ensure high quality and mission-fitting curriculum and teaching methods. This person may have ultimate responsibility for additional operations, including parent and community relations, fundraising, finance, facilities and grounds, admissions/registration and other areas. May also be called the school Director, Head of School, or other similar titles.

Private School: A school owned, operated and funded by a group other than a government. Typically, private schools are funded through tuition and fees paid by parents and through fundraising. Private schools may be independent or parochial (religious).

PTAs and PTOs: "Parent Teacher Associations" and "Parent Teacher Organizations." These are groups of parents within individual schools organized to help parents stay informed and contribute time and money to the school.

Public District School: A school owned, operated and funded by a school district. Typically, these schools are funded through a combination of local, state and federal money collected through various taxes (e.g., income tax, property tax). Public schools most often are operated by local governments, but must abide by state and federal regulations, as well.

Quality Factors: *See* Great School Quality Factors

Religious School: *See* Parochial School

Safe and Orderly Environment: A school environment in which students are kept safe from harm by other people, facilities and equipment. Also one in which students know how they are expected to behave in and out of the classroom, and they behave as expected because consequences are clear and consistent. One of the seven Great School Quality Factors.

Schedule: The school schedule includes the daily start, finish and class schedule; the yearly beginning and end dates for the school; and the periodic holiday and vacation days during the school year.

School Achievement: The overall average level of attainment by a whole school on a defined measure, regardless of progress made within a given year. Measures might include percent of children who test at grade level or average test scores. A school can have high achievement without helping students learn (e.g., if school has many academically gifted students). A school can have low achievement despite making large progress (if student achievement started low).

School Advisory Committees or Boards: Typically, an advisory group – made up of parents, staff and community members – that advises the principal on school leadership matters. In district schools, this group's role is often limited to advice and fundraising assistance. In charter and private schools, this group may play a larger role in establishing major school policies, choosing principals, fundraising and other critical functions.

School Culture: The values, policies, organizational structures, and practices of the school community that determine how the school spends time and money, how people at the school treat each other, and which values – such as honesty, kindness, individual achievement, respect for different ideas, and teamwork – are reinforced and which are not.

School Design: A cohesive plan for a school's overall mission, curriculum and teaching method. Some school designs also include particular types of school management, teacher training, facilities, discipline and other elements of a school. Not all schools follow a preexisting design. Not all schools have a cohesive design at all.

School Fit: *See* Fit

School Improvement Plan: A written plan for improving a school. Such a plan usually follows a grading or assessment of a school's strengths and weaknesses (from test scores, parent and staff surveys and the like). A good school improvement plan includes specific goals, action steps to help reach each goal, a list of people and money needed to reach the goals, and a time target for reaching each goal.

School Progress: How much a school improves on any defined measure of success. Example measures include percent of children at grade level, parent satisfaction scores, and average student progress made by individual children in the school. School progress on one measure, such as number of students at grade level, does not always indicate success on other measures, such as growth/learning by students above grade level. For example, a school with many academically gifted students may have a very high percentage of children at grade level without students making a full year's worth of individual student progress. Likewise, individual students in a school may make great learning progress while the school makes little progress in number of students at grade level if many are low achieving at the start. *See also* Student Progress.

School Quality: The level of excellence in helping students learn in core academic subjects, consistently demonstrated across an entire school. The highest quality schools are ones in which students of all abilities and types learn more than similar students in other schools. Research has consistently shown that schools meeting this definition of school quality exhibit the seven Great School Quality Factors used in this book far more often than schools producing lesser academic results with their students. Quality, along with school fit, is one of the two major considerations for choosing the right school for a child.

School Type: School type, in this book, refers to who owns and controls a school. This is not related to course content, teaching method, or quality. School types included in this book (some of which overlap): district public schools, public magnet schools, public charter schools, private independent schools, private parochial (religious) schools, and home schools.

Secondary Schools: Schools that serve children in grades 6 through 12 (some may begin in 5th or 7th grade). These include middle school (or "junior high," "intermediate school") and high school (or "upper school").

Selective School: A school that actively chooses children based on criteria other than lottery results or pre-determined zoning assignments. Criteria may include individual child and family characteristics, such as test scores, demonstrated capabilities, and values/ interests, as well as overall goals for the school's population (e.g., mix of ages, gender, race, income).

Self-Understanding: A child's demonstrated ability to understand his or her own strengths, weaknesses and interests and to use that understanding to make decisions.

Seven Great School Quality Factors: *See* Great School Quality Factors

Social Issues: Issues affecting your child's and family's feelings of belonging and connectedness to other people in a school. This is one of the four Fit Factors for matching your child and family to a school. *See also* Social Skills.

Social Skills: Understanding and interacting well with many kinds of people. Also includes social leadership of groups, including organizing and leading others.

Special Needs: In education lingo, students with "special needs" are those with extraordinary challenges in one or more areas, including traditional academic pursuits, physical abilities, emotional skills, or life skills.

Special Program: A self-contained school program for a limited number of students housed within a larger school. Typically, the curriculum and/or teaching method differs from the larger school in which the program is housed. May focus on students with particular needs differing from most other students (e.g., extremely gifted, disabled) or on a specialized course of study (e.g., foreign language immersion). Level of interaction with other students in school varies.

Standards: *See* Grade Level Standards

Structure: The level of pre-defined activity in a school. Includes pre-defined learning goals, curriculum and teaching methods required of teachers as well as pre-defined activities required of students. In a very structured school, teachers within each grade use the same learning goals, topics and materials for teaching students. In addition, teachers direct and lead students through most learning activities. A structured curriculum helps ensure that all students are exposed repeatedly to the step-by-step facts and skill practice needed to build basic knowledge, but may prevent more motivated and capable students from excelling in some areas and less capable students from getting the extra help they need. A less structured school allows more differences across classrooms, more differences in individual student instruction, and more student participation and choice in learning activities. Less structure allows highly-skilled and well-supported teachers to tailor teaching and learning to the needs of each student, but may allow less motivated students to fall behind their learning potential. A school may be structured in one way, such as pre-defined grade level standards, but less so in others, such as allowing students to choose from among self-directed learning activities.

Student Achievement: Achievement is the level of skill or knowledge attained. A school that focuses on pre-set achievement goals, usually called "grade level," will work to ensure that all students achieve specified goals by year end. Better schools set higher student achievement goals for individual students when they are ready to learn beyond grade level.

Student Community: The relationships of students to each other and the feelings of belonging those relationships create. Feelings of belonging are influenced by individual students' fit with other students in a school, including where students live, pre-existing friendships, values, social behavior and manners, and diversity of student social groups, economic status, race and ethnicity.

Student Discovery: A teaching method in which teachers allow students to choose activities for themselves, and teachers provide materials that allow students to discover new knowledge and skills for themselves. Contrast with Teacher-directed teaching method.

Student Progress: How much individual students learn in a school year, as demonstrated in end-of year assessments. Often called "growth" scores and often calculated numerically. This is distinct from School Progress, which is how much a school improves on any one of several measures, including percent of students at grade level, parent satisfaction scores, and average student progress. A school that focuses on student progress will ensure that all students, including those already ahead of grade level, increase their skills and knowledge as much as possible during the school year.

Tactile Learner: *See* Learning Styles

Target Schools: A Picky Parent term for the short list of schools available to your child (up to five) with the best chance of providing great quality and fit for your child and family. Once you've pared your list down to a manageable number, these are the schools that you will investigate in detail.

Teacher Quality: The level of excellence demonstrated in helping students learn. This includes combined mastery of the academic subject matter and an ability to influence a variety of students with different interests, capabilities, and other characteristics to learn.

Teacher-directed: A teaching method in which teachers directly transmit knowledge to students and guide student activities in detail. Contrast with Student Discovery teaching method.

Teaching Method: The process a teacher uses to help students learn at school. Method may be teacher-directed, focused on student discovery of knowledge for themselves, or a combination. Teaching method may include classroom behavior management, which may be controlling/strict, developmentally oriented, or a combination.

Tuition: The money that parents pay for the core elements of a child's education at a private school. Tuition often does not cover the entire cost of a private education. Schools make up the shortfall with fees charged to parents for non-core elements of education (sports, lockers, field trips, etc.) and fundraising.

Uniformity: A school is uniform when the students or parents are the same in certain respects. A school may be uniform in students' academic capabilities (e.g., schools for gifted or special needs children); race; religion; gender of students; values and ethics of students and parents; family income and wealth; student and family residence (e.g. neighborhood schools); or special interests of students (e.g., performing arts schools). Different students and families may value different aspects of uniformity.

Values: Values are core beliefs about what things are more important and less important in life. Values may be expressed through thoughts, words and actions and help determine how people spend time, money and other resources. Values help define and distinguish individuals, families, and schools.

Visual Learner: *See* Learning Styles

What Your Child Learns: One of the four Fit Factors. "What Your Child Learns" includes features of a child or family that influence what subjects and level of difficulty should be taught to a child.

Whole Child: A view of children's development and education that focuses not just on academic or cognitive learning, but on other aspects of a child's growth, too. Includes at least social, emotional and physical learning, as well as cognitive. May be divided into more detailed categories and may include spiritual development.

Whole Language: A reading instruction method in which children are exposed to reading materials so that they become familiar with common words, phrases and contexts of stories and are able to build off of those to read on their own.

Resources for Parents

This appendix contains a list of organizations, websites, books and other resources that can help you find out more about specific topics covered in this book. Web links change over time, and there are many more great books and sites that we could not include here. Visit *PickyParent.com* for more resources and up-to-date links.

The list is organized by major topic:

Discover Your Child's Needs
1. *Information about Diagnostic Testing*
2. *General Resources on Child & Schooling Challenges*
3. *Gifted Children*
4. *Other Capabilities / Multiple Intelligences*
5. *Learning Styles*
6. *Learning Disabilities and Disorders*
7. *Other Disabilities*

Get the Scoop on Schools
1. *Basic Information about Local Schools*
2. *Information on Your School's Standards*

Make the Most of Your Child's Schooling
1. *Building a Solid Foundation in Reading*
2. *Helping Your Child With Homework*
3. *Finding a Tutor for Your Child*
4. *Talking with Your Child's Teacher*

Learn More about School Types and Designs
1. *Financial Aid for Private Schools*
2. *Homeschooling*
3. *Charter Schools*
4. *School Designs*

When You Need to Know More...
How to Research Any Education Topic

Discover Your Child's Needs

1. Information about Diagnostic Testing

- *Special Educator's Complete Guide to 109 Diagnostic Tests* by Roger Peirangelo and George Giuliani. (The Center for Applied Research in Education, 1998).

- National Association of Child Psychologists
  http://www.nasponline.org/index2.html

2. General Resources on Child & Schooling Challenges

(see also the more specific topics following Gifted Students section)

- *Finding Help When Your Child is Struggling in School* by Lawrence J. Greene. (Golden Books, 1998).

- *501 Ways to Boost Your Child's Success in School* by Robert D. Ramsey. (Contemporary Books, 2000).

- *The Fussy Baby Book: Parenting Your High-Need Child from Birth to Age Five* by William Sears and Martha Sears. (Little Brown & Company, 1996).

- *The Difficult Child* by Stanley Turecki and Leslie Tonner. (Bantam, 2000).

- *Raising Your Spirited Child: A Guide for Parents Whose Child Is More Intense, Sensitive, Perceptive, Persistent, Energetic* by Mary Sheedy Kurcinka. (Perennial, 1998).

- *Real Boys: Rescuing Our Sons from the Myths of Boyhood* by William Pollack. (Random House, 1998).

- *Reviving Ophelia: Saving the Selves of Adolescent Girls* by Mary Pipher. (Putnam, 1994).

3. Gifted Children

- Hoagie's Gifted Education Page collect numerous gifted resources in one place.
  http://www.hoagiesgifted.org

- The Association for the Gifted was organized to help professionals and parents support gifted children.
  http://www.cectag.org

- Educational Resources Information Center (ERIC) has information on a wide variety of topics related to gifted education.
  http://ericec.org/gifted/gt-menu.html

- The National Association for Gifted Children (NAGC) is an organization of parents, educators, and other professionals interested in gifted issues.
  http://www.nagc.org

- Supporting Emotional Needs of the Gifted (SENG) provides information on identification and effective ways to live and work with the gifted.
  http://www.SENGifted.org

- The National Research Center on the Gifted and Talented provides links to gifted associations in each state.
http://www.gifted.uconn.edu/stategt.html
- *Guiding the Gifted Child: A Practical Resource for Parents and Teachers* by James T. Webb, Elizabeth A. Meckstrom, and Stephanie S. Tolan. (Great Potential Press, 1999).
- *Teaching Gifted Kids in the Regular Classroom: Strategies and Techniques Every Teacher Can Use to Meet the Academic Needs of the Gifted and Talented* by Susan Winebrenner. (Free Spirit Publishing, 1992).
- *Helping Gifted Children Soar: A Practical Guide for Parents and Teachers* by Carol Ann Strip with Gretchen Hirsch. (Great Potential Press, 2000).
- *Gifted Children: Myths and Realities* by Ellen Winner. (BasicBooks, 1996).

4. *Other Capabilities / Multiple Intelligences*

- The Family Education Network website includes checklists to determine your child's natural capabilities.
http://familyeducation.com/topic/front/0,1156,21-12410,00.html
- *Frames of Mind: The Theory of Multiple Intelligences* by Howard Gardner. (Basic Books, 10th Anniversary Edition, 1993).
- *Intelligence Reframed* by Howard Gardner. (Basic Books, 1999).
- *Gifted Children: Myths and Realities* by Ellen Winner. (BasicBooks, 1996).

5. *Learning Styles*

- Site with general information about learning styles and multiple intelligences.
http://www.ldpride.net/learning_style_work.html
- *So Each May Learn: Integrating Learning Styles and Multiple Intelligences* by Harvey Silver, Richard Strong and Matthew Perini. (Association for Supervision & Curriculum Development, 2000).
- *Learning Styles: Putting Research and Common Sense into Practice* by Anne Lewis and Elizabeth Steinberger. (American Association of School Administrators, 1991).
- *Discover Your Child's Learning Style* by Mariaemma Willis and Victoria Hodson. (Prima Publishing, 1999).
- *Marching to Different Drummers,* 2nd Edition by Pat Burke Guild and Stephen Garger. (Association for Supervision and Curriculum, 1998).

6. *Learning Disabilities ("LD") and Disorders*

- LD Online is a website designed for parents and teachers offering a range of information about LD, including links to national and state level resources.
http://www.ldonline.org

- National Center for Learning Disabilities has links to research articles, tips for living with LD for parents and students, as well as information about legislation that affects LD students:
  http://www.ncld.org/LDInfoZone/index.cfm

- Schwab Learning is a parent's guide for helping children with LD:
  http://www.schwablearning.org/index.asp

- *When Your Child Has LD: A Survival Guide for Parents* by Gary Fisher, Rhoda Cummings and Pamela Espeland. (Free Spirit Publishing, 1995).

- *Teaching Kids with Learning Difficulties in the Regular Classroom: Strategies and Techniques Every Teacher Can Use to Challenge and Motivate Struggling Students* by Susan Winebrenner and Pamela Espeland. (Free Spirit Publishing, 1996).

- All Kinds of Minds is a non-profit institute that helps families, educators, and clinicians understand why children are struggling in school and provides practical strategies to help them become more successful learners.
  http://www.allkindsofminds.org

7. Other Disabilities

- National Information Clearinghouse for Children and Youth with Disabilities (NICHCY)
  http://www.nichcy.org

- The Beach Center on Disability has many resources for families of children with disabilities.
  http://www.beachcenter.org/

- Disability Resources provides links to many resources on the web, including national and international sites, documents, databases, and other informational materials.
  http://www.disabilityresources.org

- ERIC has information on a wide variety of education topics related to children with disabilities.
  http://ericec.org/osep-sp.html

Get the Scoop on Schools

1. Basic Information about Local Schools

- GreatSchools.net is a nonprofit organization that provides information about public, private and charter schools in all 50 states and detailed school profiles for California, Arizona, Texas, Florida and Washington.
  http://www.greatschools.net

- The School Information Partnership provides public school and district performance information.
  http://www.schoolresults.org

- Achieve.org links to each state's department of education.
  http://www.achieve.org/achieve.nsf/StateResources?openform
- National Center for Education Statistics has a site providing access to basic
  public school and district information.
  http://nces.ed.gov/ccd/search.asp
- National Center for Education Statistics has another site including both public
  and private school information.
  http://nces.ed.gov/globallocator/

2. Information on Your School's Standards

- Achieve.org links to each state's standards for its public schools.
  http://www.achieve.org/achieve.nsf/StateResources?openform
- No Child Left Behind website developed by the U.S. Department of Education.
  There is a section specifically for parents.
  http://www.nclb.gov
- The American Federation of Teachers has written a report, *Making Standards
  Matter*, that evaluates state standards and details how each state measures up
  against its criteria for high-quality.
  http://www.aft.org/edissues/standards99/toc.htm
- The Fordham Foundation has been evaluating state standards for many years.
  The 2000 review is available at:
  http://www.edexcellence.net/library/soss2000/2000soss.html
- Education Week has an annual report evaluating state's efforts to improve K-12
  education by setting rigorous academic standards. The 2003 report is available
  online (free registration required).
  http://www.edweek.org/sreports/qc03

Make the Most of Your Child's Schooling

1. Building a Solid Foundation in Reading

- The National Reading Panel Report was commissioned by the U.S. Department
  of Education.
  http://www.nationalreadingpanel.org
- Reading First is a U.S. Department of Education initiative to foster strong reading
  skills in all students.
  http://www.ed.gov/offices/OESE/readingfirst
- The International Reading Association has several online resources offering
  tips for parents who want to encourage reading. Also available in Spanish.
  http://www.reading.org/publications/brochures/brochures.html

2. *Helping Your Child with Homework*

- National PTA
  http://www.pta.org
- National Parent Information Network site is sponsored by the U.S. Department of Education.
  http://www.npin.org
- The Family Education Network website, a commercial site, has information for parents about homework help, general parenting issues, and learning resources.
  http://www.familyeducation.com/home
- *Math Coach: A Parent's Guide to Helping Children Succeed in Math* by Wayne A. Wickelgren and Ingrid Wickelgren. (Berkley Books, 2001).

3. *Finding a Tutor for Your Child*

- Parents interested in getting supplementary services for their child such as tutoring and after school care can get information on state-approved providers by going to this U.S. Department of Education website:
  http://www.nclb.gov/parents/supplementalservices/index.html

4. *Talking with Your Child's Teacher*

- National PTA resources:
  http://www.pta.org/parentinvolvement/bts/a12_ptconferences.asp and
  http://www.pta.org//parentinvolvement/helpchild/oc_parentteacher.asp
- The National Parent Information Network has several articles about how to work effectively with your child's teacher.
  http://www.npin.org
- The National Education Association offers information about how to have a successful parent teacher conference.
  http://www.nea.org/parents/ptconf.html

Learn More About School Types and Designs

1. *Financial Aid for Private Schools*

- The National Association of Independent Schools website has helpful information about financing a private school education.
  http://www.nais.org/financialaid/parents
- This commercial website offers information and links to lending companies that specialize in private school loans.
  http://www.finaid.org/otheraid/privateschool.phtml
- In some cities, organizations make scholarships available for private school attendance, usually targeting lower-income families.
  http://www.childrenfirstamerica.org

2. Homeschooling

- American Homeschooling Association.
  http://americanhomeschoolassociation.org
- National Home Education Network. http://www.nhen.org
- Ann Zeise's A to Z Home's Cool Homeschooling website.
  http://www.gomilpitas.com/homeschooling

3. Charter Schools

- The U.S. Department of Education's charter school page.
  http://www.uscharterschools.org
- Center for Education Reform
  http://www.edreform.com

4. School Designs

- The Northwest Regional Education Lab (NWREL) has an online catalog of
  school reform models.
  http://www.nwrel.org/scpd/catalog/index.shtml
- Parents' Guide to Alternatives in Education by Ronald Koetzsch. (Shambhala,
  1997).

When You Need to Know More... How to Research Any Education Topic

- What Works Clearinghouse on Education Research is a resource currently
  being developed by the U.S. Department of Education to synthesize the latest
  research on a variety of important education topics.
  http://ww.w-w-c.org
- National Parent Information Network site is sponsored by the U.S. Department
  of Education. It offers research-based information about a wide range of education topics.
  http://www.npin.org
- ERIC is a national information system funded by the U.S. Department of
  Education to provide access to education literature and research. ERIC Digests are
  short, research-based papers that outline the existing research on a given topic.
  http://www.eric.ed.gov
- The Regional Educational Laboratories are educational research and development organizations supported by contracts with the U.S. Department of
  Education. These regional offices act as resources for schools and districts in
  their regions and are a source of current research on various topics.
  http://www.nwrel.org/national
- National PTA
  http://www.pta.org

Confident Choice Tools

■ ■ ■

CONFIDENT CHOICE Tools

These are the three tools you need to complete your research, compare your Target Schools and make your choice. We've repeated them here for easy access.

Other tools included in this Appendix:

For a complete list of *Confident Choice Tools*, see page ix.

A CONFIDENT CHOICE Tool

Personalized Great Fit Checklist

School Name: _____

▶ In the first blank column, list in pencil the precise names of your top child & family needs based on your *Child and Family Needs Summaries* (pages 38 and 110) and on your reading of Chapters 2–9 and related tables. For example, write:"Basic Learning Capability, Typical." See a complete example on page 176.

▶ Check whether each of your needs is a Must Have or Nice to Have.

▶ In next big column, make note of the characteristics a school must have to meet your need based on your reading of Chapter 10 and related tables.

▶ Include specific questions to ask school principal, teachers, parents, and others (or use our *Interview Forms* on page 273).

▶ Make an extra copy and fill in notes for each school you consider.

▶ After you gather the information you need, grade each school on how well it fits each Must Have and Nice to Have item:

   A perfect fit   **C** halfway fit

   B very good fit   **D** poor fit   **F** very poor or no fit

FIT FACTOR	CHILD & FAMILY NEEDS: Must Haves & top Nice to Haves	MUST HAVE	NICE TO HAVE	WHAT TO LOOK FOR *and* QUESTIONS TO ASK	NOTES ABOUT THIS SCHOOL	GRADE
What Your Child Learns						
How Your Child Learns						
Social Issues						
Practical Matters						

Great School Quality Checklist   PAGE 1

School Name: _____

▶ Complete a separate *Great School Quality Checklist* for each school you consider.
▶ In Notes column, make notes about each school. Which factor elements are strengths? Weaknesses?
▶ After gathering available information, grade each school on each overall Great School Quality Factor:

✔ **A** school has all of the elements
✔ **B** school has most of the elements
✔ **C** school has about half of the elements
✔ **D** most of the elements are missing
✔ **F** school has none or almost none of the elements

GREAT SCHOOL QUALITY FACTORS	NOTES ABOUT THIS SCHOOL	GRADE
1. Clear Mission Guiding School Activities ● Written mission communicating focus and priorities ● Staff, parents & written materials state same mission ● School-wide goals support mission ● Student goals, curriculum & teaching support mission		
2. High Expectations for All Students: *High Minimum Expectations for All* ● Challenging but achievable student learning goals (standards) for each grade level ● School-wide plan and actions ensure that all students achieve at least grade level in basics, no excuses ● All or near all children achieve grade level ● Progress scores high for all, including lowest scorers *Higher Expectations for Students Who are Ready* ● Learning goals raised for ready students ● Clear, written progression of goals beyond grade level ● Plan and actions ensure students meet higher goals ● At least gifted students achieve very high test scores ● Progress scores are high for top students		

Continues....

Great School Quality Checklist ▸ PAGE 2

School Name: _____

3. Monitoring of Progress and Adjusting Teaching
- School assesses individual student progress (weekly is ideal)
- Teachers change teaching approach to ensure that every child achieves his or her learning goals

4. Focus on Effective Learning Tasks
- Instruction approach proven to work
- Class time allocated according to subjects' importance
- Materials & facilities allocated in line with importance
- Principal and teachers limit class interruptions

5. Home-School Connection
- School tells parents what children will be learning
- School tells parents how to help own children learn
- School updates parents on own child performance
- School works with parents to resolve problems

6. Safe and Orderly Environment
- Students know how they are expected to behave
- Students focus on work in the classroom
- Consequences for behavior are clear and consistent
- School keeps students safe from harm

7. Strong Instructional Leadership
- Clear performance expectations for teachers
- Principal recruits, keeps great teachers
- Teachers work together within & across grades
- Principal monitors individual teacher performance
- Staff regularly identifies problems, improves school
- Professional development focused on school goals
- Principal acts on high and low teacher performance

School Comparison Worksheet *PAGE 1*

➤ Use the information you have gathered about schools to do a side-by-side comparison of both fit and quality. If you are comparing more than five schools, you will need to use two of these worksheets.

➤ List school names at the top of the school columns to right (use school initials or abbreviations to fit).

➤ Page 1: Transfer informaton to the first three blank columns from your *Personalized Great Fit Checklist.* Place your grades for each school on each Fit Factor below school name. Compare how well schools fit your child and family needs.

FIT FACTOR	CHILD & FAMILY NEEDS: Must Haves & top Nice to Haves	MUST HAVE	NICE TO HAVE	SCHOOL #1	SCHOOL #2	SCHOOL #3	SCHOOL #4	SCHOOL #5
What Your Child Learns								
How Your Child Learns								
Social Issues								
Practical Matters								

Continues....

School Comparison Worksheet ···· PAGE 2

▶ Page 2: Transfer quality grades from your *Great School Quality Checklist* below each school name. Compare the quality of your school options.

▶ Review pages 1 and 2 and compare the schools. Highlight particular strengths and weaknesses of each school. Remember, not all items listed here are equal in importance for you and your child.

✔ Must Haves and quality should weigh more heavily in your decision than Nice to Haves.

✔ Use the *Child, Family and Quality: Ways to Get What You Don't Get at School* tables to help you decide which Must Haves and quality weaknesses you can best accommodate outside of school, if needed.

GREAT SCHOOL QUALITY FACTORS	SCHOOL #1	SCHOOL #2	SCHOOL #3	SCHOOL #4	SCHOOL #5
1. Clear Mission Guiding School Activities					
2. High Expectations for All Students					
3. Monitoring of Progress and Adjusting Teaching					
4. Focus on Effective Learning Tasks					
5. Home-School Connection					
6. Safe and Orderly Environment					
7. Strong Instructional Leadership					

Know Your Child's Needs

How to Use This Table:
➤ Use this table to help identify and clarify your child's top needs that should be addressed at school.
➤ This table is organized by the four Fit Factors: *What* Your Child Learns, *How* Your Child Learns, Social Issues and Practical Matters.

➤ You do not need to read all items here. Instead, focus on characteristics you think *might be* Must Haves and Nice to Haves for your child at school. Use Chapters 2 – 5 and the *Child Needs Summary* on page 38 to help narrow your reading of the table.
➤ Search for Fit Factor items by name in the far left column.
➤ Based on the criteria listed, record Must Haves and Nice to Haves on your *Child Needs Summary* (page 38).

Child Characteristic	*Criteria for Determining Must Haves and Nice to Haves*
	WHAT **YOUR CHILD LEARNS**

Basic Learning Capability

➤ Extremely Challenged
➤ Challenged
➤ Typical
➤ Bright/Gifted
➤ Highly Gifted

Your child's readiness for learning in core academic subjects. A Must Have for all children. All parents should determine the best-fit categories for their children. (When identification is not possible, seeking both Great School Quality Factors #2 and 3 in a school becomes essential.)

Basic Learning Capability is a combination of your child's *mental processing* capability and the knowledge and skills developed through prior *academic exposure* in the core academic subjects. Mental processing, for this purpose, includes analytical thinking (problem solving) and conceptual thinking (comparing, contrasting, seeing similarities and differences) in both language and math. Core academic subjects include at least reading, writing and math in the elementary years.

➤ Basic Learning Capability may be measured using traditional I.Q. (intelligence quotient) testing or, even better, a combination of this and assessments of demonstrated learning in language and math compared to same-age children.
➤ If your child's I.Q. and academic learning are different, use the higher of the two to choose a school.
➤ If your child tests differently in math and language, use the higher of the two to choose a school.
➤ If your child's academic learning is far below I.Q., consider further testing for specific disabilities, disorders, motivation challenges, need for additional academic exposure, or other barriers that may keep your child from absorbing or expressing knowledge.
➤ The categories below are guidelines. If your child falls near a border, you should read about the categories on both sides to determine which best fits your child currently.
➤ Opt for the higher category if uncertain, but read advice for both levels so that you will be prepared for academic and social challenges your child may face.
➤ I.Q. and language/math testing is quite accurate, but does *not* measure a child's creativity, motivation or other competencies needed to use intelligence in work and life.

Basic Learning Capability:
Extremely Challenged

➤ Tests below 70 on standard I.Q. test, and/or
➤ Is significantly delayed in all language and mathematical areas compared to others same age
➤ Has extreme difficulty interacting independently as peer of Typical children
➤ Difficulty learning self-care and daily routines compared to most same-age children
➤ Future challenge: may have trouble living independently unless educated to meet specific needs

Basic Learning Capability:
Challenged

➤ Tests between 70 and 85 on standard I.Q. test, and/or
➤ Is consistently somewhat delayed in language and mathematical areas
➤ May have difficulties interacting as peer of Typical children
➤ If child is already in school: child consistently has been a low performer in all academic subjects
➤ Despite academic challenges, child learns self-care and daily routines adequately

Continues…

Know Your Child's Needs   ...*continued*

Child Characteristic	Criteria for Determining Must Haves and Nice to Haves
Basic Learning Capability: **Typical**	➤ Tests between 85 and 120 on standard I.Q. test, and/or ➤ Is close to expected development and achievement in most language and mathematical areas; may be somewhat ahead or behind in some areas ➤ Most children (about 7 out of every 10) are in this category
Basic Learning Capability: **Bright/Gifted**	➤ Tests between 120 and 130 on standard I.Q. test, and/or ➤ Is developmentally advanced, or learns more quickly than most peers, in most language and mathematical areas; or is advanced and learns quickly in at least one major area, and/or ➤ Scores between 90th and 97th percentile on language and/or math achievement tests. ➤ If child is already in school, may display one or more symptoms of inadequate academic challenge at school: May say schoolwork is easy. May say school is boring generally. May say basic subjects are boring (reading, math). May have trouble listening, paying attention or sitting still in whole-class learning activities in basic subjects, yet be very focused in small achievement-level groups, individual work, and subjects introducing new topics (breadth). May perform well in basic academic subjects without seeming to study very much. May learn new school material quickly once introduced.

Basic Learning Capability:
Highly Gifted
	➤ Tests above 130 on standard I.Q. test, and/or
	➤ Is developmentally advanced in most language and mathematical areas or extremely advanced in at least one major area, and/or
	➤ Scores at or above 97th percentile on language and/or math achievement tests, and/or
	➤ Displays most behaviors below, when compared to children of same age:*
	  • Very large vocabulary
	  • Able to read early, often before elementary school
	  • Longer attention span, persistence, intense concentration in areas of interest
	  • Learns basic skills quickly, with less practice
	  • Wide range of interests
	  • High curiosity level; asks limitless questions
	  • Likes to experiment, do things differently
	  • Puts ideas or objects together in new, unusual, not obvious ways
	  • Remembers a great deal of information
	  • Unusual sense of humor
	  • May express feeling of "being different" from other children in abstract ways (e.g., "other kids not interested in my ideas" or "I am different") beginning at very early ages (3 – 4 years).
	  • If child is already in school, also may display one or more symptoms of inadequate academic challenge at school: May say schoolwork is easy or boring. May say basic subjects are boring (reading, math). May have trouble listening, paying attention or sitting still in whole-class learning activities in basic subjects, yet be very focused in small achievement-level groups, individual work, and study of new topics. May perform well in academic subjects without seeming to study much. May seem to know new school material before it has been taught or learn immediately once taught. Because they tend to go unchallenged early in life and become accustomed to being "the best" always, may develop perfectionist tendencies when faced with challenges later (e.g., won't try new skills if aren't sure they'll be the best, won't finish projects unless they are certain they are "perfect," avoid competition from equally gifted students).
	➤ Future challenge: may have difficulty using intelligence in adult life unless learns to face challenges and develops strong social and emotional skills.

*Adapted from *Guiding the Gifted Child* (Great Potential Press, 1994).

Continues...

Know Your Child's Needs ...*continued*

Child Characteristic	Criteria for Determining Must Haves and Nice to Haves

WHAT YOUR CHILD LEARNS ...*continued*

Other Capabilities
➤ Musical
➤ Artistic
➤ Physical & Hands-on
➤ Social & Leadership
➤ Creativity
➤ English as Second Language

These are Must Haves only if they are extreme strengths or weaknesses of your child and you cannot help your child with continued development outside of school. Weakness in English as Second Language is a Must Have need that should be addressed at school in nearly all cases. See Chapter 3 for more detailed descriptions of strengths and weaknesses in each capability listed here.

➤ **Musical:** senses, appreciates, composes, and/or performs music, including rhythm, pitch, and tone
➤ **Artistic:** understands and appreciates others' art; creates original works of art pleasing or interesting to others
➤ **Physical & Hands-on:** displays strength, agility, speed, balance and/or flexibility; or uses all or part of the body to create ideas or objects and to solve problems
➤ **Social & Leadership:** understands & interacts well with many kinds of people; or organizes & leads other children
➤ **Creativity:** thinks of new ideas and ways to do things, rather than imitating others or using standard methods; may apply to varying activities
➤ **English as Second Language:** understands, speaks, reads, and writes English at age-appropriate level, and English is the child's second language.

Note: If there is a content area that *you as a parent* value highly, it may be a Must Have for family Fit Factor #1 regardless of your child's capability or personal interest. In addition, you are not limited to considering the capabilities listed here; you may want to include any other *strength* of your child's that *you consider valuable* and in which your child also has a strong *interest*.

➤ **Strengths:** A strength is an area (other than the core academic ones addressed in Basic Learning Capability) in which your child has shown strong or early capability beyond most peers of the same age. Consider these capabilities to be school Must Haves only if your child is also *interested* in using the strength. Otherwise, you may want to nurture the strength outside of school until (s)he develops a strong interest, as well.
➤ **Weaknesses:** Weaknesses in these areas are Must Haves if your child has shown very weak *or* late capability *and* you either do not have time or resources to help your child develop the capability or the weakness is one that may prevent your child from fully using other capabilities (Physical & Hands-on, Social & Leadership, and English as Second Language). In general, the capabilities listed are ones that can bring joy and fulfillment even to those who are not masters of the craft. For that reason, you should help your child develop (through school or family life) at least the level of capability and skill that will allow him/her to function as a happy, healthy person. English as a Second Language should be addressed at school in most cases.

Interests
➤ Subjects or topics
➤ Ways of thinking (analytical, conceptual or creative thinking)
➤ Other interests, regardless of talent or current skill (e.g., interpersonal, musical, artistic)

An interest is something that your child loves to think about or do, regardless of capability or current skill level. A Must Have if:

➤ Interest is strong: child voluntarily spends large amounts of time on interest, and
➤ Interest is long-held: one or more years for child 6 or under; two or more years for child over 6, and
➤ Interest will continue: your child wants to continue pursuing the interest, and
➤ Interest is unusual: your child's interest is not shared by many others of similar age/grade (so unlikely to be addressed in typical school curriculum), and
➤ Child's interest is one that would be difficult to satisfy without support of the school, or
➤ For child already in school: child is not motivated in school unless interest is major part of curriculum

Assume that a *very* extreme level of interest, even in a traditional academic subject, is unusual, period.

 Continues...

Know Your Child's Needs ...continued

Child Characteristic	Criteria for Determining Must Haves and Nice to Haves
HOW YOUR CHILD LEARNS	
Learning Styles ➤ Visual ➤ Auditory ➤ Kinesthetic/Tactile	A Must Have if: 1. Child is very strong in one style only (and weak in other two) or Child is very weak in one style And ... 2. Child has trouble learning, is not interested in school, or is easily upset when needs of dominant style are not met
Learning Style: **Visual**	➤ Like to see things written down or in a picture: • Remember what they see well • Want to see and show others timelines, illustrations, charts, diagrams • Learning aided by copying and organizing notes ➤ Very attuned to physical environment – desk or table arrangement, things on walls, how things look: • Bored by lack of things on walls • Excited by stimulating, but neatly organized, physical environment • Overstimulated and bothered (may become upset) if classroom materials and equipment are disorganized • Has trouble focusing without own workspace that child can organize neatly – own desk or assigned place at table • May have difficulty with changes involving new physical surroundings
Learning Style: **Auditory**	➤ Like to talk: • Remember what they say well • Want to discuss and talk through what they have heard, what they are thinking • Thrive on classroom discussion • Like to read out loud • Will repeat ideas and words aloud when they are trying to remember • Will assume you remember what they've told you (because they will) • Silence rare – they are bored by silence and will interrupt it with talk • Difficulty working quietly at desk for a long time – need to talk to selves or others ➤ Stimulated by sound: • Remember what they hear without visual or physical cues, without writing it down • Like teachers to explain things orally • Like and ask for storytelling without books • Overstimulated and bothered by extreme or poorly organized noises – crowds, loud music, very noisy classrooms
Learning Style: **Kinesthetic/Tactile**	➤ Like to move their bodies ("kinesthetic"): • Like to act out a situation or do simulations • Like to be busily moving while working • Like to do hands-on projects to represent their ideas • Express enthusiasm with large physical movements (jumping, running in circles) • May wiggle body constantly; may be labeled hyperactive • Difficulty sitting still for long periods ➤ And/or like to touch ("tactile" aspect of Kinesthetic style, also called "fine motor skills" and "small motor skills"): • Like to build, do detailed work by hand, and handle materials constantly • Understand ideas best when they can touch a physical object • Like to write, take notes or doodle to keep hands busy, even though may not look at notes later • Like to make a physical product by hand • May fidget constantly; may be labeled hyperactive • May have trouble focusing and completing tasks unless holding something in hands

Continues...

Know Your Child's Needs ...continued

Child Characteristic	Criteria for Determining Must Haves and Nice to Haves

HOW YOUR CHILD LEARNS ...continued

Motivation	Your child's self-motivation to achieve (learn and perform) academically. A Must Have if motivation is a strength or weakness. May be a Must Have if child is typical and parent cannot provide general supervision of child's work and progress at school.

Summary identification:
➤ Strength: child sets challenging goals for self, tries hard things on own, works to overcome barriers and problems
➤ Typical: child works to meet goals set by teachers, parents; or sets achievable goals for self; stops if problems arise
➤ Weakness: child not bothered when does not perform well; or is bothered but takes no action to improve

Levels of Motivation (lowest to highest):*

1. Child not bothered when does not perform as well as (s)he or others expect on tasks
2. Child is bothered when (s)he does not do as well as (s)he or others expect on tasks, but takes no steps on own to improve
3. Child works to meet goals set by parents or teachers; stops when problems or barriers arise
4. Child sets achievable goals for self; often lowers goal or stops when problems or barriers arise
5. Child sets challenging (but achievable) goals for self; or tries to do new hard things on own; and often works to overcome barriers and problems to achieve goals
6. Child thinks of entirely new, unusual, or very challenging goals for self, makes a plan, involves others as needed for help, usually works to overcome even difficult barriers to achieve the goal.

Your child's current level is the highest number that describes how your child acts with regularity (often when needed, but not necessarily always).
✔ If your child is at level 1 or 2, then motivation is a weakness.
✔ If your child is at level 3 or 4, your child's motivation is typical.
✔ If your child is at level 5 or 6, your child's motivation is a strength.

Signs that motivation is a weakness for your child who is already in school:
➤ Your child's school performance is usually below capability in most subjects (and no recent or recurring emotional upset, disability or disorder explains the low performance), or
➤ Your child is rarely bothered by below-capability performance on school work (tests, quizzes, papers, etc.), or
➤ Your child is bothered by below-capability performance, but does not take steps on own to improve performance during the year (e.g., studying more before tests, completing homework correctly more often)

*Adapted from *Competence at Work* (John Wiley & Sons, Inc., 1993). |
| **Physical or Mental Health Challenges**

...continues | A Must Have if either of the following might keep your child from participating effectively in daily school life or from developing academically, socially, emotionally or physically:
➤ *Physical Health Challenges:* Your child has a physical handicap, ongoing illness or other physical condition that could prevent your child from participating fully in school life, that requires treatment during school hours (at school or elsewhere), or that is noticeable to other children; or
➤ *Mental Health Challenges:* Your child has experienced ongoing or recurring emotional upset, such as severe depression, extreme anxiety, bi-polar disorder, or other debilitating mental health illnesses (may be related to specific events such |

Know Your Child's Needs ...continued

Child Characteristic	Criteria for Determining Must Haves and Nice to Haves
	HOW YOUR CHILD LEARNS ...continued

Physical or Mental Health Challenges

...continued

as death of parent or divorce, or may have unspecified causes). Seek professional diagnosis if you suspect mental illness. Some signs of mental illness include:

- Big changes or ongoing problems in your child's sleep – sleepy all the time, not able to sleep, or suddenly begins erratic schedule (e.g., sleepy all day, awake all night).
- Big changes or ongoing problems in your child's eating – packing it away in gorging sessions or prolonged loss of appetite. Extreme or sudden weight gain and loss are also signs of a problem.
- Loss of joy – your child always seems to be unhappy, laughs very little.
- Loss of excitement – your child loses interest in school and activities that used to get her excited.
- Loss of self-control – your child is lashing out in anger frequently, acting violent towards siblings or parents, or wildly excited for extended periods.
- Social changes – your child is suddenly not interested in former friends, without explanation. Your child suddenly stops talking with you and/or siblings.
- Changes in academic performance – your child's grades drop suddenly.

Behavior Challenges

A Must Have if:

➤ Your child has had
  - significant, unresolved behavioral or discipline problems in group settings, or
  - behavior problems that prevent your child or others in classroom from learning effectively, or
  - behavior problems that have lead to serious or multiple formal disciplinary actions against your child (or you believe might lead to formal disciplinary actions in the future) in school, preschool or child care

Learning Disabilities & Disorders

In general, a *disability* is a problem with an important, basic part of a child's physical or mental functioning that is significantly different from your child's other capabilities or that significantly hampers your child's learning. A *disorder* is a problem with an important, but not necessarily basic, part of your child's physical or mental functioning. Visit *PickyParent.com* for links to more information about disabilities and disorders.

This is a Must Have for any recognized learning disability (see *Special Needs Table* on *PickyParent.com*) and any disorder severe enough to require special services at school in order to meet your child's academic, social, emotional or physical needs.

Signs that your child may have a disability or disorder include:

➤ Your child does well in most or all *subjects*, except one.

➤ Your child does well with most *aspects* of his school work, except one that may cut across many subjects (e.g., reading, writing, speaking aloud).

➤ Your child speaks well, but *does not write well* compared to others of same age (e.g., takes a very long time, makes many errors, gets very frustrated).

➤ Your child writes well but *does not speak* so that others understand (compared to others of same age).

➤ Your child follows written instructions well, but *not spoken instructions*.

➤ Your child follows spoken instructions well, but *not written ones*.

➤ Your child *does not focus* on his school work for long enough periods of time to accomplish what is expected of children his age.

➤ Your child is unable to work and learn in a *group of children*; behavior problems or emotional outbursts regularly prevent him from doing his school work.

➤ Your child has extreme difficulty forming relationships with others his own age.

...continues

Continues...

Know Your Child's Needs

Child Characteristic	Criteria for Determining Must Haves and Nice to Haves
HOW YOUR CHILD LEARNS ...continued	
Learning Disabilities & Disorders ...*continued*	➤ Your child has trouble *moving or working his body,* so that typical, day-to-day activities are difficult. This may be a Nice to Have rather than a Must Have if your child has a learning disorder or disability that is: ➤ Resolvable with appropriate development, and ➤ You as parent have the ability yourself or means, through a counselor or tutor, to address your child's developmental needs outside of school Consider the following characteristics of your child in deciding what kinds of school to seek: ➤ The *severity of the disability* and the resulting level of *specialized* services your child requires to meet academic, social, emotional and physical needs ➤ Your child's *ability to function socially* in a group with typical children (the higher this ability, the more likely that your child will fare well in some activities of a typical classroom)
Self-Understanding	Child's demonstrated ability to understand self, including own strengths, weaknesses, interests, wants and needs and to use that understanding in making life decisions. This is a Must Have if your child is very weak in this area. Signs that this is a Must Have include your child: ➤ Focuses little time on activities she enjoys and does well, or ➤ Spends too much time on activities that are of little consequence (no enjoyment for child, no help for schoolwork or other achievements, and no help to others), or ➤ Has few interests of her own (usually lets a sibling, parent or friend choose) ➤ Chooses friends who are unkind to her or who do not bring out the best in her, or ➤ Expresses little recognition of her own strengths and weaknesses
SOCIAL ISSUES	
Friends	A Must Have if: ➤ Child has well-established friendship(s) with child(ren) attending a certain school, and ➤ Child does not have friends attending other schools you might choose, and ➤ Your child does not have social skills needed to meet and make new friends and ➤ You are unable to help your child continue current friendships outside of school or establish new friendships Here are some signs that your child may have difficulty making new friends in a new school: ➤ Your child often chooses not to play with other children ➤ Your child never approaches new children, or is rarely successful when trying to do so (at the park, at school) ➤ Your child sticks rigidly with the same friend every day, refusing to make other friends or let others join in
PRACTICAL MATTERS	
Essential Activities	➤ A Must Have if child has non-school interests or activities that: • cannot be addressed fully at school, • must continue, and • often conflict with typical school scheduling. This is a Must Have for very few children. Let your child's interest, capability and own motivation lead the way.

Know Your Family's Needs

How to Use This Table:
➤ Use this table to help identify and clarify your family's top needs that should be addressed at school.
➤ This table is organized by the four Fit Factors: *What* Your Child Learns, *How* Your Child Learns, Social Issues and Practical Matters.

➤ You do not need to read all items here. Instead, focus on characteristics you think *might be* Must Haves and Nice to Haves for your family at school. Use Chapters 6 – 9 and the *Family Needs Summary* on page 110 to help narrow your reading of the table.
➤ Search for Fit Factor items by name in the far left column.
➤ Based on the criteria listed, record Must Haves and Nice to Haves on your *Family Needs Summary* (page 110).

Family Characteristic	Criteria for Determining Must Haves and Nice to Haves
WHAT YOUR CHILD LEARNS	

Values about what *content* is important
 	
➤ Core academic subjects
➤ Other academic subjects (list)
➤ Morals, ethics, character, religion
➤ Other non-academic subjects
➤ Other topics important to you
	A Must Have if:
	➤ You very strongly value a particular subject or set of subjects *and* you need for school to cover the subject(s), including
	  • Core academic subjects (reading, writing, math)
	  • Other academic subjects (foreign language, etc. – make your own list of subjects you value)
	  • Morals, ethics, character, religion
	  • Other non-academic (for example: social, emotional and physical development)
	  • Other topics important to you
	or
	➤ If your child is already in school: you are concerned that subjects important to you are getting short shrift at your child's school

Goals for your child ➤ Grade progression ➤ Academic performance ➤ College opportunity	A Must Have only if both of these are true: ➤ This is a goal you have for your child, *and* ➤ Your child is at risk of not meeting the goal. (If goal is learning a particular subject, use *Values about Content* above.) Common examples of goals parents are concerned about include: ➤ **Grade progression:** Your child is at risk of failing a required subject or not meeting the required standards for progressing from grade to grade. Some of the risk factors include single parent, parents did not finish high school, child's family is below or near federal poverty line, language or cultural barriers, child is challenged in Basic Learning Capability (see *Know Your Child's Needs*). You or your child may have other factors that put your child at risk of not meeting this goal. ➤ **Academic performance:** Your child is capable of performing above grade level, but is at risk of not performing as well academically as (s)he is able. Some of the risk factors include single parent, parents did not finish high school, child's family is below or near federal poverty line, language or cultural barriers. You or your child may have other factors that put your child at risk of not meeting this goal. ➤ **College opportunity:** You would like your child to attend college, you believe your child is capable of getting into college, but you believe that this goal will be difficult to attain. Some of the risk factors include single parent, neither parent attended college, child's family income below or near federal poverty line, language or cultural barriers.
HOW YOUR CHILD LEARNS	
Values about school-wide expectations and rules on student conduct *…continues*	A Must Have if: You have a strong opinion about school *rules and expectations* regarding children's social behavior and general conduct (based on religious, moral, ethical, or other values), *especially if…*

    Continues…

Know Your Family's Needs ...*continued*

Family Characteristic	Criteria for Determining Must Haves and Nice to Haves
	HOW YOUR CHILD LEARNS...*continued*

Values about school-wide expectations and rules on student conduct ...*continued*
➤ Manners with other children
➤ Manners with adults
➤ Dress
➤ Discipline
➤ Honor code
➤ Other behaviors

➤ Your time with your child after school is very limited, or
➤ You have difficulty teaching the religious, moral or ethical lessons you want your child to learn, or
➤ Your child is particularly susceptible to peer influence, or
➤ If child is already in school: you are concerned about the values and behavior your child seems to be adopting from other students at current school

May be less important if:
➤ You feel comfortable reinforcing religious, moral and ethical beliefs at home, and
➤ Your child is an independent thinker who is able to withstand peer influence, or
➤ Your child is already in school: your child often describes and evaluates other students' behaviors and expresses how his/her own values and behavior are different (or asks for your help understanding and evaluating others' behavior)

Values about how children should *learn*:
➤ Teaching method
  • Teacher-directed
  • Student discovery
  • Mixed approach
➤ Classroom behavior management
  • Controlling/Strict
  • Developmental
  • Mixed approach

A Must Have if you have a strong opinion about:

➤ **Teaching method: how children should be taught** in school
  • Teacher-directed: You want teachers to play the role of "expert," transferring their knowledge to children directly, and "director," guiding all of children's activities in detail.
  • Student-discovery: You want teachers to play role of "facilitator," helping students figure out new knowledge for themselves and allowing students to make some choices about their own activities.
  • Mixed approach: You want some of both teacher-directed and student-discovery learning.

➤ **Classroom behavior management: how teachers should manage student behavior** in the classroom
  • Controlling/Strict: You want a school where teachers are expected to maintain order through clear behavior rules, punishments and rewards.
  • Developmental: You want a school where teachers are expected to maintain order by improving students' self-control, coaching students about how to improve behavior, and indirect pressure through peers, parents and principal.
  • Mixed Approach: You want a school where teachers are expected to maintain order by using a combination of controlling and developmental approaches.

➤ If your child is already in school: you are concerned about the effectiveness of either the teaching method or classroom management (as defined above) in your child's current school

Your role as advocate
for child (understanding, communicating and influencing school to address *your* child's learning needs).

The greater your ability, the less important for school to help you.

A Must Have if:

➤ You have difficulty *understanding* or *responding* to your child's academic, social, emotional, or physical needs, or
➤ You believe that you will have difficulty *communicating* with your child's teacher and principal about your child's needs, or
➤ Your child is already in school: you are having difficulty communicating with your child's teacher and principal, and your child's current school does not fit your child's Must Have needs

You may feel challenged in these areas because of lack of time (if you are a single parent, working or otherwise occupied), lack of confidence in your own abilities to understand or communicate about your child, language barriers, cultural differences or other reasons.

Continues...

Know Your Family's Needs   ...continued

Family Characteristic	*Criteria for Determining Must Haves and Nice to Haves*
	S O C I A L I S S U E S

Parent Community

I want my child's school to have parents with particular characteristics

A Must Have if:
- You have a strong opinion about the kinds of parents, and families, with whom you want to associate through your child's school or
- Your child is already in school: you are concerned about the negative impact on yourself and your child of other parents

Make a list of characteristics important to you, including:
- Friends: Parents you already know?
- Neighbors: Neighborhood parents?
- Location: Parents from a particular neighborhood other than your own?
- Values: Same values as you? Which values?
- Social behavior and manners: Ways you want, or don't want, other parents to act?
- Social and economic status: Do you have preferences about the diversity or make-up of the parent community?
- Race and ethnicity: Do you have preferences about the diversity or makeup of the parent community?
- Other parent characteristics you do or do not want?

Parent Involvement in School

- Helping
- Decision-making
- Fundraising activities

A Must Have if you have a strong preference about the type or level of parent involvement:
- Types of parent involvement include:
  - Helping with school's daily life (e.g., volunteering for classroom activities, helping in the media center, chaperoning field trips, organizing a book fair, and the like)
  - Decision-making (e.g., volunteering as a member of a school advisory or governing board and similarly empowered roles)
  - Fundraising (e.g., organizing or participating in fundraising activities, such as school carnivals, book fairs, dances, candy and wrapping paper sales, giving campaigns and so forth)
- Levels of parent involvement you might prefer include:
  - You strongly want to participate personally in school, or
  - You strongly want a school where most or all *other* parents participate in school life, or
  - You do not want to or cannot participate significantly in school life (due to work, health, preferences, or other constraints)

Student Community

I want my child's school to have students with particular characteristics

A Must Have if:
You have a strong opinion about the kinds of students with whom you want your child to associate at school, and
- Your time with your child after school is limited, or
- You have difficulty teaching the social, religious, moral or ethical lessons you want your child to learn, or
- Your child is particularly susceptible to peer influence, or
- Child is already in school: you are concerned about the values and behavior your child seems to be adopting from other students at current school

May be less important if:
- You feel comfortable reinforcing strongly held social, religious, moral and ethical values at home, or
- Your child is an independent thinker who is able to withstand peer influence, or
- Your child is already in school: your child often describes and evaluates other students' behaviors and expresses how his/her own values and behavior are different (or asks for your help understanding and evaluating others' behavior)

...continues

Continues...

Know Your Family's Needs   *...continued*

Family Characteristic	*Criteria for Determining Must Haves and Nice to Haves*
	SOCIAL ISSUES... *continued*

Student Community

I want my child's school to have students with particular characteristics

...continued

Make a list of characteristics important to you, including:
➤ Friends: Do you want to keep your child with current friends? Are you seeking new friends for your child?
➤ Neighbors: Your child's neighbors?
➤ Location: Students from a particular neighborhood other than your own?
➤ Values: Same values as you? Which values?
➤ Social behavior and manners: Ways you want, or don't want, other students to act?
➤ Student achievement: Higher, lower or same-performing students compared to your child?
➤ Social and economic status: Do you have preferences about the diversity or make-up of the student body?
➤ Race and ethnicity: Do you have preferences about the diversity or makeup of the student body?
➤ Gender diversity: Do you want an all-boys or all-girls program for your child?
➤ Other student characteristics you do or do not want?

I want my child to attend certain school, school type, or school design

A Must Have only if:
➤ You would choose this school (or school type or design) over other schools of better quality and fit.
A Nice to Have if:
➤ You would choose this school (or school type or design) over other schools only in the case of a close "tie" in overall fit and quality

| | **PRACTICAL MATTERS** |

Child Care

➤ Before school
➤ After school
➤ Holiday
➤ Summer

A Must Have if:
➤ You have no other affordable child care options of acceptable quality for the hours and days needed
A Nice to Have if:
➤ You have at least one other affordable option of acceptable quality for the hours and days needed
Determine your needs in the following areas:
➤ Hours and days of care
➤ Transportation to/from school and to/from home
➤ Snacks or meals for child
➤ Safe supervision of child
➤ Academic or developmental assistance for child
➤ Structured or unstructured time for your child
➤ Care for your multiple children
➤ How much you can pay

Schedule

➤ Daily hours
➤ Yearly (start/finish and holidays)

...continues

A Must Have if:
➤ You have unchangeable commitments, such as work or other children's schedules, that must be accommodated and
➤ You do not have access to other child care and/or transportation for child that would accommodate your scheduling needs
A Nice to Have if:
➤ You have other commitments that would make it less convenient, but not impossible, for you to deal with certain school schedules

Continues...

Know Your Family's Needs

Family Characteristic	Criteria for Determining Must Haves and Nice to Haves
PRACTICAL MATTERS..._continued_	

Schedule ➤ Daily hours ➤ Yearly (start/finish and holidays) ...*continued*	Consider: ➤ Timing of morning and afternoon transportation for child(ren), especially with regard to multiple school schedules and conflicts with parents' work ➤ Impact of schedules on children's non-school activities ➤ Desirability of having time alone with each child ➤ Desirability of your children having time together or with friends ➤ Impact of schools with differing vacation schedules on your family's vacations and time together ➤ Other schedule issues you may have
Transportation Needs ➤ To school ➤ After school ➤ After school activities	A Must Have if: ➤ You have unchangeable commitments that prevent you from providing transportation for your child, and ➤ Your child does not have access to (or is too young for) other non-school sources of transportation (e.g., carpool, city bus, subway)
Location Proximity to your home or work	A Must Have if: ➤ You have unchangeable commitments that prevent you from considering schools farther away from home, work, or other critical location, *or* ➤ Your child has unchangeable needs that prevent you from considering schools far away from home (or other critical location), *or* ➤ You plan to visit your child's school very frequently (e.g., for volunteer work, observation) And: ➤ Transportation provided by school would not change the need for having school in certain location.
Your other children	A Must Have if: ➤ You definitely want child to go to same school as siblings (for other than logistical reasons above), or ➤ You definitely do not want child to go to same school as sibling(s) Consider: ➤ Impact on child of positive or negative reputation of your other child(ren) at school ➤ Independence of this child and her ability to "be true to self" in shadow of sibling(s) at same school ➤ Personal support your other child(ren) might lend to this child at school
Money available to pay for school	A Must Have if money available for school each year is less than the most expensive school option (minus any scholarship funding your child might obtain). Use Heads or Tails Money Worksheet to calculate your financial situation. Current = Amount you *actually* spend yearly on your child's education now (tuition, fees, child care during school hours, supplies, donations): _____ Target = Amount you could spend yearly *without major changes* in work, lifestyle, or debt (may be same as Current or Maximum): _____ Maximum = Most you are willing to spend yearly, *with acceptable changes* in work, lifestyle and debt: _____ Your Target and Maximum may be the same as Current, if increasing income and decreasing non-school spending are not possible or desirable.

Child Needs: What to Look for in a School

How to Use This Table:
➤ Make sure you have identified your child's top needs for school before using this table.
➤ For each of your child's Must Haves and Nice to Haves, find the companion section of this table.
➤ Read general information about the characteristic where provided (e.g., Basic Learning Capability, Learning Styles).
➤ Then read specific information about your child's category (e.g., Basic Learning Capability: Typical, Learning Styles: Visual).

➤ **Bolded** questions and things to seek are the most important. Focusing on them will help you quickly target the best-fit schools and eliminate poor-fit schools.
➤ Note top things to seek and ask at schools on your *Personalized Great Fit Checklist* (page 59).

If This is a Must Have or Nice to Have	...Then Look For This in a School	...And Ask These Questions
	WHAT Y O U R C H I L D L E A R N S	
Basic Learning Capability ➤ Extremely Challenged ➤ Challenged ➤ Typical ➤ Bright/Gifted ➤ Highly Gifted *...continues*	Using the information below for your child's specific BLC category, look for right combination of the following for your child's Basic Learning Capability: ➤ Pace: Your child is both *challenged* to learn new things *and able* to learn what is taught, particularly in basic subjects. Look for school either: • Focused primarily on children of your child's Basic Learning Capability, or • With frequent monitoring of individual children's progress and frequent changes in teaching approach and individual child's learning goals (may be done one-on-one with teacher or in very small groups of up to 4 children grouped by *current* level, maybe more if children are very similar), or • With significant time spent on supervised independent work in basic academic areas. Schools should not put children into one level of learning group for the entire year. Instead, students should be moved to different learning groups when monitoring shows they've made extra progress or are lagging behind. ➤ Breadth: Multiple topics and subjects are taught. Look for time spent on multiple subjects – e.g., science, foreign languages, geography, art, music. Breadth may be used to: • Reinforce basic areas: provide new, interesting contexts for learning reading, writing, math (topics should be connected to or "integrated" with math, reading and writing), • Motivate students: keep students interested in school with interesting topics, especially important when basic subjects are too easy or too hard, and/or • Broaden knowledge: taught for intrinsic value of the special subjects.	See questions below for your child's Basic Learning Capability

                                    Continues...

Child Needs: What to Look for in a School ...cont.

If This is a Must Have or Nice to Have	...Then Look For This in a School	...And Ask These Questions
WHAT YOUR CHILD LEARNS...continued		

Basic Learning Capability ➤ Extremely Challenged ➤ Challenged ➤ Typical ➤ Bright/Gifted ➤ Highly Gifted ...*continued*	➤ Critical thinking: Children learn to use the basic knowledge they are acquiring to make judgments, solve problems, apply ideas across topics and subjects, and create new ideas: • Analytical Thinking: problem solving by breaking ideas and objects into orderly steps and parts • Conceptual Thinking: connecting existing ideas in new ways; comparing and sorting things or ideas for similarities and differences • Creativity: creating new ideas and objects Look for the following common ways to teach critical thinking: • Supervised research by individual students or small groups; • Projects by individuals or small groups; • Writing: not just describing an object, book or event, but also evaluating, creating steps, comparing, connecting ideas, and creating new ideas; • Teaching method in which students must formulate own questions, think of possible answers, and evaluate own and others' ideas and work; • Academic exercises and materials specifically intended to develop thinking skills. ➤ Social Environment: Your child's successes and challenges in developing positive relationships with other children, both one-on-one and in groups. Look for: • Social opportunity: time during school day when students may work or play in unstructured groups or pairs without adults setting rules (except safety, basic behavior rules) • A significant number of students of your child's Basic Learning Capability also attending same school (and *at least* two or three others in your child's classrooms), and if your child is different from norm of school ... • Social tolerance for students of differing capabilities (children discouraged from teasing others who are more or less academically capable than norm of school) ➤ Test Score Indicators: Standard results of academic testing that allow you to compare across schools, overall for whole schools, for children in your family's economic and racial group, and for	See questions below for your child's Basic Learning Capability
...*continues*		

 Continues...

Child Needs: What to Look for in a School ...cont.

If This is a Must Have or Nice to Have	...Then Look For This in a School	...And Ask These Questions
\multicolumn{3}{c}{WHAT YOUR CHILD LEARNS...continued}		

If This is a Must Have or Nice to Have	...Then Look For This in a School	...And Ask These Questions
Basic Learning Capability ➤ Extremely Challenged ➤ Challenged ➤ Typical ➤ Bright/Gifted ➤ Highly Gifted ...*continued*	children with previous performance similar to your child's. *Overall* school scores may not be a good indicator unless schools you compare have similar student populations. Types of scores include: • Percent (%) of students at grade level, which tells you how many children have met at least grade level on tests. • Growth scores, which tell you how much progress each child has made on average. Should be at least one full year's worth on average, ideally more (since some students may be catching up and others can learn faster). Sometimes called "progress" scores. (Do not confuse this with "Adequate Yearly Progress" which is a technical term in federal legislation requiring schools to increase percent of students achieving grade level.)	See questions below for your child's Basic Learning Capability
Basic Learning Capability: **Extremely Challenged** ...*continues*	In general, look for: ➤ **School sets *individualized* learning goals for students *or* school has alternative set of *challenging but achievable* learning goals for students testing into this category.** ➤ **School monitors students' individual learning frequently during year** (*at least* every 6 weeks; weekly ideal) ➤ **School adjusts teaching approach to ensure goals are met** ➤ **School provides breadth:** independent living skills taught; multi-sensory activities used to stimulate learning (art, music, dance) ➤ **Social Needs:** school includes some other students who are similarly challenged Pace, Breadth, Critical Thinking, Social and Testing Indicators: ➤ **Pace: Must Have.** School sets individualized learning goals for students. • School admits only children in this category and focuses on their special needs, or • School groups these children together for most learning, or • School has some other viable method for ensuring that extremely challenged students' needs are met in the regular classroom.	**Principal:** ➤ Pace • **How are learning goals set for each child?** Do they change during the year? • **How are children grouped for learning?** • **How do you monitor individual progress during the year? How often?** • What changes do you make for children who are struggling? ➤ Breadth • What subjects are taught? **How are life skills addressed?** • How much time is spent on each subject weekly? • What is the purpose of each "special" class? How is that purpose achieved? • How is each special subject taught? Separate class or woven into basic subjects? ➤ Social • **How many children in each classroom do you think will be at a learning level similar to my child's?** • **Do children have a chance to interact informally with each other at school?** When, and how much time per day is that? **With children from other classrooms?**

Continues...

Child Needs: What to Look for in a School ...cont.

If This is a Must Have or Nice to Have	...Then Look For This in a School	...And Ask These Questions
WHAT YOUR CHILD LEARNS...continued		

Basic Learning Capability:
Extremely Challenged

...continued

Few if any schools can make one set of learning goals appropriate for all children in this group, as their needs are very diverse.

➤ **Breadth: Must Have.** School focuses on skills for independent living as well as academic content, and school uses multiple sensory activities to stimulate learning (art, music, dance). Look for mix of hands-on, visual and listening/talking exercise to round out your child's skills.

➤ Critical Thinking Skills: Less important

➤ **Social Needs: Must Have.** School should have some similar-ability peers in your child's class.

➤ Test Score Indicators: Look for high growth/progress scores for similar students.

Note: See **PickyParent.com** to learn more about your child's eligibility for special education services in public schools.

➤ Test Scores
 • Ask about this if you have not been able to get information elsewhere
 • Ask about any problems you see with test score results – does the principal have a plan for addressing problems?

Teachers:
➤ Same as principal. Look for answers consistent with principal's and consistent across teachers within each grade level.

Parents:
➤ Same as principal. Look for answers consistent with principal's and teachers'.
➤ Speak with other parents of extremely challenged children. Ask how well their children's academic and other developmental needs have been met.

Written Materials:
➤ Look for information consistent with what you have heard from principal, teachers, and parents.

Observations:
➤ Are the learning activities described to you by principal, teachers and parents taking place?
➤ Are teachers taking advantage of small group or one-on-one work to engage every child; are teachers trying different approaches with different children?
➤ Do teachers deal with children like yours effectively?

Basic Learning Capability:
Challenged

...continues

In general, look for:
➤ School sets high minimum expectations for all students
➤ **School vigorously pursues goal of all students meeting grade level,** trying different approaches when needed
➤ **School spends significant portion of school time on basic subjects** – reading, writing, math
➤ **School monitors students' individual learning frequently during year** (*at least* every 6 weeks, weekly is ideal)
➤ **School adjusts teaching approach to ensure goals are met**
➤ School offers individual *or* small group teaching (equally effective) according to students' current capability in basic subjects to ensure all achieve grade

Principal:
➤ Pace
 • Are grade level expectations challenging? How can I tell?
 • **Do you expect *all* children to meet grade level?**
 • **What kinds of kids do not make grade level in your school, usually? Why? What are you doing to change this?**
 • **How do you monitor individual progress during the year? How often?**
 • **What changes do you make for children who are struggling or behind in a subject? How often?**
 • What changes do you make if a former struggling student begins to

Continues...

Child Needs: What to Look for in a School ...cont.

If This is a Must Have or Nice to Have	...Then Look For This in a School	...And Ask These Questions
WHAT YOUR CHILD LEARNS...continued		

If This is a Must Have or Nice to Have	...Then Look For This in a School	...And Ask These Questions
Basic Learning Capability: **Challenged** ...continued	level performance; children are not "stuck" in low-performing groups all year, but are moved to more advanced work as soon as they are ready ➤ Academically challenged children are taught by staff as skilled as more advanced groups' teachers. Avoid schools where teaching gifted children is the "prize" for star teachers. ➤ Breadth (e.g., science, languages) used primarily to reinforce basics ➤ Test scores: high percentage of students achieve grade level; high percentage of students with previous low scores now at grade level; high growth by lowest scoring students. Pace, Breadth, Critical Thinking, Social and Testing Indicators: ➤ **Pace: Must Have.** Look for frequent monitoring of progress in basics (reading, math and writing) throughout school year, teaching done with very small ability-level groups, and individual tutoring; OR significant time in large group spent on drills and repetition in basic areas, with frequent individual tutoring as needed. ➤ Breadth: Nice to Have. Must reinforce basic subjects to be useful, e.g., using science to teach math basics, using geography to teach reading. ➤ Critical Thinking: Nice to Have ➤ Social Needs: Typical school population. ➤ Test Score Indicators: See above.	make fast progress? • How are teachers chosen to work with struggling students? Advanced students? ➤ Breadth • What subjects are taught? • How much time is spent on each subject weekly? • What is the purpose of each of these "special" classes? How is that purpose achieved? • How is each special subject taught? Separate class or woven into basic subjects? Do teachers of special subjects coordinate with teachers of basic subjects each week? ➤ Social • How many children in each classroom do you think will be at a learning level similar to my child's? ➤ Test Scores • Ask about this if you have not been able to get information elsewhere • Ask about any problems you see with test score results – does the principal have a plan for addressing problems? **Teachers:** ➤ Same as principal. Look for answers consistent with principal's and consistent across teachers within each grade level. **Parents:** ➤ Same as principal. Look for answers consistent with principal's and teachers'. ➤ Speak with parents of academically challenged children. Ask if their children's academic and social needs have been met. **Written Materials:** ➤ Look for information consistent with what you have heard from principal, teachers, and parents. **Observations:** ➤ Are the learning activities described to you by principal, teachers and parents taking place? ➤ Are teachers taking advantage of small group or one-on-one work to engage every child; are teachers trying different approaches with different children? ➤ Do teachers deal with children like yours effectively?
...continues		

Continues...

Child Needs: What to Look for in a School ...cont.

If This is a Must Have or Nice to Have	...Then Look For This in a School	...And Ask These Questions
WHAT YOUR CHILD LEARNS...continued		

Basic Learning Capability: **Typical** *...continues*	In general, look for: ➤ **School sets high minimum expectations for all students; the higher, the better,** especially for child in top half of Typical range ➤ School vigorously pursues goal of all students meeting grade level ➤ School spends significant portion of school time on basic subjects – reading, writing, math ➤ **School monitors students' individual learning frequently during year** (*at least* every 6 weeks; weekly ideal) ➤ **School adjusts teaching approach to ensure goals are met** ➤ **Students moved to more advanced work as soon as they are ready** ➤ Breadth (e.g., science, languages) used to reinforce basics ➤ Breadth of topics, both academic and nonacademic, used to help students discover own interests and strengths that will distinguish them from "the pack" of other Typical students ➤ Test scores: high percentage of students overall achieve grade level; high growth by all students, especially middle scorers; more students than those classified as "gifted" score at top levels (indicating children in middle are pushed beyond grade level – *especially* important if your child is in top half of the Typical range) Pace, Breadth, Critical Thinking, Social and Testing Indicators: ➤ **Pace: Must Have.** Typical schools will pace to meet this group's needs, but *challenging grade level expectations* for all is essential. Monitoring student progress is ideal to determine if student falls behind, needs additional challenge, or needs new approach ➤ Breadth: Nice to Have. Will help Typical students find special interests that distinguish them from "the pack." ➤ Critical Thinking: Nice to Have. Look for some time spent on special projects, writing, research, and exercises specifically geared to teach thinking skills. ➤ Test Score Indicators: see above. ➤ Social Needs: Typical school population.	**Principal:** ➤ Pace • **Are grade level expectations challenging? How can I tell?** • Do you expect *all* children to meet grade level? • What kinds of kids do not make grade level in your school, usually? Why? What are you doing to change this? • **How do you monitor individual progress** during the year? How often? • **What changes do you make for children who are struggling or behind in a subject? How often?** • **What changes do you make for students who learn new material more quickly than others?** ➤ Breadth • What subjects are taught? • How much time is spent on each subject weekly? • What is the purpose of each of these "special" classes? How is that purpose achieved? • How is each special subject taught? Separate class or woven into basic subjects? Do teachers of special subjects coordinate with teachers of basic subjects each week? ➤ Critical Thinking Skills • Does your school teach critical thinking skills? • For all students or just some (e.g., gifted)? • How are these skills taught? • If answers do not include these items, ask: Do your students do independent projects, research or writing? Can you give me a few examples of what they do? ➤ Social • Are the students in this school pretty typical academically? If not, in what ways? ➤ Test Scores • Ask about this if you have not been able to get information elsewhere • Ask about any problems you see with test score results – does the principal have a plan for addressing problems? **Teachers:** ➤ Same as principal. Look for answers consistent with principal's and consistent across teachers within each grade level.

Continues...

Child Needs: What to Look for in a School)...cont.

If This is a Must Have or Nice to Have	...Then Look For This in a School	...And Ask These Questions
WHAT YOUR CHILD LEARNS...continued		

If This is a Must Have or Nice to Have	...Then Look For This in a School	...And Ask These Questions
Basic Learning Capability: **Typical** ...continued		**Parents:** ➤ Same as principal. Look for answers consistent with principal's and teachers'. ➤ Speak with parents of academically typical children. Ask if their children's academic and social needs have been met. **Written Materials:** ➤ Look for information consistent with what you have heard from principal, teachers, and parents. **Observations:** ➤ Are the learning activities described to you by principal, teachers and parents taking place? ➤ Are teachers taking advantage of small group or one-on-one work to engage every child; are teachers trying different approaches with different children? ➤ Do teachers deal with children like yours effectively?
Basic Learning Capability: **Bright/Gifted** ...continues	In general, look for: ➤ **School sets higher, individualized learning goals for students ahead of grade level;** if not, school's learning goals are set higher for all students ➤ **School monitors students' individual learning frequently during year** (*at least* every 6 weeks; weekly ideal) ➤ School adjusts teaching approach to ensure goals are met ➤ **School offers individual *or* small group teaching according to students' current capability** in basic subjects to ensure all students are challenged to next level ➤ **School focuses on critical thinking** skills, with significant time spent on research, writing, projects, and exercises specifically geared to teach thinking skills ➤ School offers advanced courses for students in higher elementary grades (at school or at other nearby schools) ➤ School places students with children in higher grades for advanced study (if very few other children in same grade are equally advanced in a subject) ➤ School's extracurricular activities include academic ones, such as Odyssey of the Mind, Chess club	**Principal:** ➤ Pace • Are grade level expectations challenging? How can I tell? • **Do you set higher goals for students who are ready to go beyond grade level? How and how often?** • **How do you monitor individual progress** during the year? How often? • How are children grouped for learning in basics? Why? • Do you make any other changes for students who progress beyond grade level? ➤ Breadth • What subjects are taught? • How much time is spent on each subject weekly? • What is the purpose of each of these "special" classes? How is that purpose achieved? • How is each special subject taught? Separate class or woven into basic subjects? Do teachers of special subjects coordinate with teachers of basic subjects each week? ➤ Critical Thinking Skills • **Does your school teach critical thinking skills?** • **How are these skills taught?** • How much time is spent each week on this?

Continues...

Child Needs: What to Look for in a School ...cont.

If This is a Must Have or Nice to Have	...Then Look For This in a School	...And Ask These Questions
WHAT YOUR CHILD LEARNS...continued		
Basic Learning Capability: **Bright/Gifted** ...continued	➤ Social Needs: school has some other children who are gifted; typical school population is usually adequate ➤ Test scores: Top 10% of students have very high scores; large % students score in top category; high average scores (not a good indicator if school also has many challenged students); high growth scores by top scoring students. Pace, Breadth, Critical Thinking, Social and Testing Indicators: ➤ **Pace: Must Have.** Your child needs a school that does not let bright students coast along at grade level when they are capable of more. Look for school that monitors student progress frequently in reading, math and writing, and groups children by current achievement; or by other methods school individualizes most class work and homework at each student's current level of capability. Alternately, look for schools that set learning goals higher than other schools for *all* students; this is an inferior approach for students in this BLC category, so if you consider such a school, ensure that goals are *actually* higher in basic subjects than other schools (often they are not, despite school claims). ➤ Breadth: Nice to Have. More important when pacing in basic subjects is inadequate to keep child challenged. Breadth may keep bright child motivated when not challenged in basics. ➤ **Critical Thinking: Must Have.** Many of these students will need advanced critical thinking in their future school and work. Extremely important if pace in basic subjects is inadequate to keep child challenged. ➤ Social Needs: Nice to Have. Typical school population. Some other bright students in your child's classroom. ➤ Test Score Indicators: see above.	• If answers do not include these items, ask: Do your students do independent projects, research or writing? Can you give me a few examples of what they do? ➤ Social • How many children in each classroom do you think will be at a learning level similar to my child's? ➤ Test Scores • Ask about this if you have not been able to get information elsewhere • Ask about any problems you see with test score results – does the principal have a plan for addressing problems? **Teachers:** ➤ Same as principal. Look for answers consistent with principal's and consistent across teachers within each grade level. **Parents:** ➤ Same as principal. Look for answers consistent with principal's and teachers'. ➤ Speak with parents of academically bright/gifted children. Ask if their children's academic and social needs have been met. **Written Materials:** ➤ Look for information consistent with what you have heard from principal, teachers, and parents. **Observations:** ➤ Are the learning activities described to you by principal, teachers and parents taking place? ➤ Are teachers taking advantage of small group or one-on-one work to engage every child; are teachers trying different approaches with different children? ➤ Do teachers deal with children like yours effectively?
Basic Learning Capability: **Highly Gifted** ...continues	In general, look for: ➤ **School sets higher, individualized learning goals for students ahead of grade level** ➤ **School monitors students' individual learning frequently during year** (*at least* every 6 weeks; weekly ideal)	**Principal:** ➤ Pace • Do you set higher goals for students who are ready to go beyond grade level? How and how often? • How do you monitor individual **progress** during the year? How often?

Continues...

Child Needs: What to Look for in a School *...cont.*

If This is a Must Have or Nice to Have	...Then Look For This in a School	...And Ask These Questions
— **WHAT YOUR CHILD LEARNS...**continued		

If This is a Must Have or Nice to Have	...Then Look For This in a School	...And Ask These Questions

Basic Learning Capability:
Highly Gifted
 	
...continued
	➤ School adjusts teaching approach to ensure goals are met
	➤ **School offers individual or small group teaching according to students' current capability** in basic subjects to ensure all students are challenged to next level
	➤ **School focuses on critical thinking** skills, with significant time spent on research, writing, projects, and exercises specifically geared to teach thinking skills.
	➤ School offers advanced courses (at school or at other nearby schools)
	➤ School places students with children in higher grades for advanced study (if very few other children in same grade are equally advanced in a subject)
	➤ School's extracurricular activities include academic ones, such as Odyssey of the Mind, Chess club
	➤ **Social Needs: school has a substantial percentage of children who are gifted or highly gifted**
	➤ Test scores: Top 3 – 5% of students have very high scores; large % students score in top category; high average scores (not a good indicator if school also has many challenged students); high growth scores by top scoring students
	
	Pace, Breadth, Critical Thinking, Social and Testing Indicators:
	➤ **Pace: Must Have.** Unless a child has a disability or similar barrier, students in this group will rapidly learn and exceed grade level in any school not focused on the highly gifted. Few if any schools can make one set of learning goals appropriate for children in this group, as their needs are very diverse. Look for a school admitting *only* children in this ability range; and/or a school that monitors student progress frequently in reading, math and writing, and groups children by current achievement; or that individualizes most class work and homework at each student's current level of capability by other methods.
	➤ Breadth: Nice to Have. More important when pacing in basic subjects and teaching of critical thinking are inadequate to keep child challenged. Breadth unlikely to keep highly gifted child satisfied and motivated when not challenged in basics.
		• How are children grouped for learning in basics? Why?
		• Do you make any other changes for students who progress beyond grade level?
		➤ Breadth
		  • What subjects are taught?
		  • How much time is spent on each subject weekly?
		  • What is the purpose of each of these "special" classes? How is that purpose achieved?
		  • How is each special subject taught? Separate class or woven into basic subjects? Do teachers of special subjects coordinate with teachers of basic subjects each week?
		➤ Critical Thinking Skills
		  • **Does your school teach critical thinking skills?**
		  • **How are these skills taught?**
		  • How much time is spent each week on this?
		  • If answers do not include these items, ask: Do your students do independent projects, research or writing? Can you give me a few examples of what they do?
		➤ Social
		  • **How many children in each classroom do you think will be at a learning level similar to my child's?**
		➤ Test Scores
		  • Ask about this if you have not been able to get information elsewhere
		  • Ask about any problems you see with test score results – does the principal have a plan for addressing problems?
		
		Teachers:
		➤ Same as principal. Look for answers consistent with principal's and consistent across teachers within each grade level.
		
		Parents:
		➤ Same as principal. Look for answers consistent with principal's and teachers'.
		➤ Speak with parents of academically highly gifted children. Ask if their children's academic and social needs have been met.
		
		Written Materials:
		➤ Look for information consistent with what you have heard from principal, teachers, and parents.

...continues		

Continues...

Child Needs: What to Look for in a School ...*cont.*

If This is a Must Have or Nice to Have	...*Then Look For This in a School*	...*And Ask These Questions*
WHAT YOUR CHILD LEARNS...*continued*		

Basic Learning Capability: **Highly Gifted** ...*continued*	➤ **Critical Thinking: Must Have.** Essential component to both challenge and satisfy these children. Critical thinking will be essential for future school and work at this level of capability. ➤ **Social Needs: Must Have.** School must have some similar-capability peers in your child's *class* to prevent isolation. ➤ Test Score Indicators: See previous	**Observations:** ➤ Are the learning activities described to you by principal, teachers and parents taking place? ➤ Are teachers taking advantage of small group or one-on-one work to engage every child; are teachers trying different approaches with different children? ➤ Do teachers deal with children like yours effectively? ➤ Isolation: no child should be doing work all by him or herself all day. Even if a student is very far ahead academically, some of day should be spent with other children and some working with an adult.
Other Capabilities ➤ Musical ➤ Artistic ➤ Physical & Hands-on ➤ Social & Leadership ➤ Creativity ➤ English as Second Language ...*continues*	**Strengths,** look for: ➤ **School clearly describes its mission and curriculum** so that you know what content will be covered and can count on continuity of content And: ➤ Curriculum *focuses* on your child's strength (e.g., school of fine arts), or ➤ Some required or optional courses in child's area of strength, or ➤ Allows for significant independent study, research, or projects of student's choosing so that child may pursue area of strength on own, or ➤ Daily school schedule includes time for your child to pursue area of strength informally at school, or ➤ Established *extracurricular* activities at school in child's area of strength, or ➤ Will accommodate child's scheduling needs to pursue area of strength outside of school ➤ And school attracts similar students **Weaknesses,** look for: ➤ **Does not focus curriculum or teaching method primarily on your child's area of weakness (except ESL: see below)** ➤ Curriculum includes some exposure to your child's weakness. Uses teaching methods that address varying "learning styles," "multiple intelligences," or "whole-child" development or that	**Strengths,** ask: **Principal:** ➤ **What opportunities are there for my child to further strengthen his/her capability at school?** In regular curriculum? In individual work? In clubs or after-school activities at school? Required or optional? ➤ How much time is committed to this subject or type of activity each week? ➤ What training do teachers have in this subject or activity? ➤ How many students do you have with similar strength? ➤ Other questions that help you understand specifics of how well and how often your child's strength will be addressed **Teachers:** ➤ Same as principal. Ask about teachers' individual classes. Look for consistency at different grade levels and throughout school. **Parents:** Speak with parents of children with similar strength: ➤ How has this school helped to develop your child's strength? ➤ Have you and your child been satisfied? How? ➤ Have there been any problems or challenges? **Written Materials:** ➤ Look for mention of how your child's area of strength is incorporated into the school's curriculum, extracurricular

Continues...

Child Needs: What to Look for in a School ...cont.

If This is a Must Have or Nice to Have	...Then Look For This in a School	...And Ask These Questions

WHAT YOUR CHILD LEARNS...continued

Other Capabilities

➤ Musical
➤ Artistic
➤ Physical & Hands-on
➤ Social & Leadership
➤ Creativity
➤ English as Second Language

...continued

employ other techniques for ensuring your child's well-rounded development. This will allow your child to develop weaknesses while also using strengths.

➤ English as Second Language (ESL): school includes intensive language skill training for ESL students during regular school day, covering speech, reading, writing and listening comprehension

Examples of How To Develop Specific Capabilities at School

➤ Musical:
• School curriculum focuses on learning about music (rhythm, pitch and tone), or
• School uses music as one method to teach other subjects (e.g., math, reading), or
• Some music included in curriculum, or
• Extracurricular music offered

➤ Physical or Hands-on:
• School enhances body awareness and skills through subjects such as Physical Education, or
• School uses physical movement and the sense of touch as one method to teach about other subjects, including drama to teach language, construction of physical models and products to represent ideas (see Kinesthetic/Tactile Learning Style), or
• Extracurricular sports offered

➤ Social or Leadership:
• School explicitly teaches children interpersonal skills (recognizing and identifying emotions and needs of others, acting and communicating appropriately in response), or
• Requires children to do significant daily work or projects in pairs or small groups, or
• Includes significant time in day during which children interact informally (e.g., allowed to talk and interact at lunch time and/or recess), or
• Offers extracurricular activities requiring small group or paired interactions where children must work out their own rules (not structured by an adult),
• And has students living close enough to your family for informal play time outside of school

...continues

activities and other elements of school life. Is what you read consistent with what you have heard from principal, teachers and parents?

Observations:
➤ Observe classrooms teaching or using your child's area of strength. How would your child fit in? Is what you see consistent with written materials and what you have heard from principal, teachers and parents?

Weaknesses, ask:

Principal:
➤ **How is my child's weakness addressed in the curriculum?**
➤ What effort does your school make to ensure that children are well-rounded, not just academically, but socially, artistically, physically and in other ways?
➤ English as Second Language: exactly what services are offered to improve my child's English? During regular school day? Covering speech, reading, writing and listening comprehension?

Teachers:
➤ Same questions as principal. Look for consistency.

Parents: Speak with parents of children with similar challenges:
➤ Ask same questions as principal.
➤ Has this school helped develop your child's weakness?
➤ Has your child ever been socially excluded or felt uncomfortable because of his/her weakness? If so, what did the school do in response?

Continues...

Child Needs: What to Look for in a School ...cont.

If This is a Must Have or Nice to Have	...Then Look For This in a School	...And Ask These Questions
WHAT YOUR CHILD LEARNS...continued		

Other Capabilities

➤ Musical
➤ Artistic
➤ Physical & Hands-on
➤ Social & Leadership
➤ Creativity
➤ English as Second Language

...continued

➤ Creativity:
- School spends a significant portion of school week on projects in which children are able to make work products of their own choosing, or
- Allows children some choice about what activities to pursue and what their "work product" will look like, or
- Includes creative writing in curriculum for all grades, or
- Allows some choice by students about what kinds of books they read, or
- Significant time spent on creative arts – art, music, dance, drama

Interests

➤ Subjects or topics
➤ Ways of thinking (analytical, conceptual or creative thinking)
➤ Other interests, regardless of talent or current skill (e.g., interpersonal, musical, artistic)

➤ **School clearly describes its mission and curriculum** so you know what content will be covered.

And:

➤ Curriculum *focuses* on your child's interest (e.g., school of math or fine arts, foreign language immersion), or

➤ Some required or optional *courses* in child's interest area, or

➤ Allows for significant independent study, research, or projects of student's choosing so that child may pursue interest on own, or

➤ Daily school schedule includes time for your child to pursue area of interest informally at school, or

➤ Established *extracurricular* activities in child's interest area, or

➤ Will accommodate child's scheduling needs to pursue interest outside of school

➤ Social development: School attracts students with similar interests

Principal:

➤ **What opportunities are there for my child to pursue his/her special interest at school?** In regular curriculum? In individual work? In clubs or after-school activities at school? Required or optional?

➤ How much time each week is devoted to the interest area?

➤ Do you think that this school's coverage of this interest area will change in the next several years? How?

➤ Does the school have other students with the same interest? How many?

➤ If the interest is not addressed, ask questions specific to accommodating your child's schedule outside of school to pursue the interest.

Teachers: Look for answers that are consistent with the principal's and that show teachers value the interest area.

➤ How do you include this interest area in your weekly classroom teaching?

➤ Are there any other ways that you address the interest during the year (special projects, etc.)?

➤ Do you think it is a good idea to keep addressing this interest area in the future?

Parents: Look for answers that are consistent with the principal's and teachers' comments.

➤ How is this interest area covered in school?

➤ Is this an interest of your child's, too?

➤ Have you and your child been pleased with the coverage? Is there anything you hope they'll change?

...continues

Continues...

Child Needs: What to Look for in a School ...cont.

If This is a Must Have or Nice to Have	...Then Look For This in a School	...And Ask These Questions
WHAT YOUR CHILD LEARNS...continued		
Interests ➤ Subjects or topics ➤ Ways of thinking (analytical, conceptual or creative thinking) ➤ Other interests, regardless of talent or current skill (e.g., interpersonal, musical, artistic) ...continued		**Written Materials:** ➤ Consistent mention of the topic, subject, way of thinking or activity of interest, or ➤ Consistent mention of opportunities for children to pursue individual interests **Observations:** ➤ Look for bulletin boards, wall displays, facilities, materials and other visible signs that your child's interest area is valued at the school.
HOW YOUR CHILD LEARNS		
Learning Styles ➤ Visual ➤ Auditory ➤ Kinesthetic/Tactile	In general, for either extreme strengths or weaknesses, seek a school that: ➤ **Has mission and teaching methods geared to all three major learning styles,** or *both* of the following: ➤ **Includes your child's learning style strength(s) as** *major* **part of teaching method,** and ➤ Includes at least some, but not too much, of your child's weaker style(s) so that child may become more adaptable	**Principal:** ➤ **What does your school do to engage children with different learning styles?** ➤ **Do children with certain learning style strengths do better in your school? Why?** **Teachers:** ➤ Same as principal, but ask about teachers' own classrooms. **Parents:** ➤ Ask to speak with parents of children who have strengths and weaknesses similar to your child's. ➤ Ask how their children have fared academically and socially. ➤ What challenges have they faced in the classroom that may be related to learning style? How has the school responded? **Written Materials:** ➤ Look for mention of school's efforts to meet the needs of children with differing learning styles or your child's strengths in particular. **Observations:** ➤ How would your child respond to this environment – the look of furniture, walls and materials (visual); the noises, talking and discussion (auditory); the movement, activity, and hands-on work of the classroom (kinesthetic/tactile)? ➤ How do teachers respond to children who act like yours in the classroom?
Learning Style: **Visual** ...continues	The visual learner will enjoy and succeed in a school that: ➤ **Adjusts the teaching approach to ensure that students meet learning goals**	See general learning style questions above.

Continues...

Child Needs: What to Look for in a School ...cont.

If This is a Must Have or Nice to Have	...Then Look For This in a School	...And Ask These Questions
HOW YOUR CHILD LEARNS...continued		
Learning Style: **Visual** ...continued	➤ **Has visually stimulating and interesting walls, classroom equipment, materials** ➤ Has neatly organized classrooms ➤ Values neatness and requires frequent clean up of materials; uses teaching method unlikely to lead to messy or disorganized looking classrooms ➤ **Uses visual reinforcement in teaching: overheads, bulletin boards, diagrams, charts, etc.** ➤ Allows children to take notes while listening ➤ Provides children with their own assigned workspace that they may keep neat ➤ Limits movement of children from room to room	See general learning style questions above.
Learning Style: **Auditory**	The auditory learner will enjoy and succeed in a school that: ➤ **Adjusts the teaching approach to ensure students meet learning goals** ➤ **Uses group discussion, storytelling and other oral teaching methods** ➤ **Encourages students to work in pairs or small groups (and allows talking) more than large group or alone** ➤ Encourages students to present work orally (presenting projects to class, reciting poems, etc.) ➤ Allows students to talk quietly to selves while working ➤ Includes some one-on-one work time between teacher and child, or very small work groups with teacher ➤ Is not overcrowded in each classroom ➤ Trains teachers to manage overall noise level in classroom – encourages quiet talk and discussion, does not allow loud talk, yelling ➤ Trains teachers and staff to manage noise level in lunch room and other crowded places, allowing talk but not too loud	See general learning style questions above.
Learning Style: **Kinesthetic/ Tactile** ...continues	The Kinesthetic learner will enjoy and succeed in a school that: ➤ **Adjusts the teaching approach to ensure students meet learning goals**	See general learning style questions above.

Continues...

Child Needs: What to Look for in a School ...cont.

If This is a Must Have or Nice to Have	...Then Look For This in a School	...And Ask These Questions
HOW YOUR CHILD LEARNS... *continued*		

Learning Style: **Kinesthetic/ Tactile** ...*continued*	➤ **Has significant amount of "choice time" for children to move among work stations of their own interest** ➤ **Has much open physical space within the classroom for children to move** ➤ **Allows children to work in multiple appropriate positions – on floor, at table, sitting, standing, lying down** ➤ Uses physical movement to teach about other subjects ➤ Includes multiple daily breaks for activity: stretching, walking, recess ➤ Uses teaching method including dramatizations and simulations ➤ Has a major emphasis on PE, dance, after school sports, etc. ➤ Encourages completion of tasks (in combination with allowing movement) The Tactile learner will enjoy a school that: ➤ **Uses "hands-on" activities, such as models, crafts, puzzles, blocks, felt or magnetic storyboards, gardening, etc. for significant part of each school day** ➤ Includes a significant number of projects that encourage children to create models and physical products ➤ Uses the sense of touch to teach about other subjects ➤ Allows students to "fidget" and "doodle" without reprimand, but teaches them how to do so without disrupting others	See general learning style questions above.
Motivation ...*continues*	If motivation is a **weakness** (level 1 or 2), seek a school that: For child of *any Basic Learning Capability*: ➤ Is a small school, has a small program within the school, or has small classes (18 or fewer students), and ➤ **Individual students' academic capability (BLC) is assessed, and students are required to set and meet individualized goals appropriate to capability, and** ➤ **Individual academic progress is monitored frequently** (every six weeks is absolute minimum, weekly is ideal), and ➤ **School uses a wide variety of teaching methods to engage students** by appealing to different learning styles, interests, ways of thinking, etc. (ask how school engages child with *your* child's strengths and interests), and	If motivation is a **weakness** (or typical, with limited parent supervision): **Principal:** ➤ **Who sets goals for individual student' learning? How and when?** ➤ **Who monitors student progress toward goals and how often?** ➤ Is student work supervised? How? ➤ **What actions are taken to ensure that students meet goals?** ➤ **Do teachers work one-on-one or in very small groups (how small?) with students in core academic subjects? How often?** ➤ How often are parents informed about their children's progress? **Teachers:** ➤ Same as principal for teachers' own classes.

Continues...

Child Needs: What to Look for in a School ...*cont.*

If This is a Must Have or Nice to Have	...*Then Look For This in a School*	...*And Ask These Questions*
HOW YOUR CHILD LEARNS...*continued*		

Motivation

...*continued*

➤ **Teachers have one-on-one or very small group contact with each student** in core academic subjects most days, and

➤ School frequently informs parents about child's progress; weekly is best

OR for child of *Challenged or Typical Basic Learning Capability only*

➤ School sets **very clear, standard goals for students; requires students to achieve these goals** (does not allow excuses from child or parent; provides mandatory extra practice work if needed), and

➤ **Monitors your child's academic progress frequently** (every six weeks is absolute minimum, weekly is ideal), and

➤ **Teachers have one-on-one or very small group contact with each student** in core academic subjects most days, and

➤ School frequently informs parents about child's progress; weekly is best

If motivation is **typical** (level 3 or 4), and parental supervision of school work is limited:

➤ School sets high minimum expectations for all students

➤ School monitors children's individual learning frequently (*at least* every 6 weeks, weekly is best) during year to ensure that unexpected barriers to child's achievement have not arisen; school addresses problem if child's achievement falls below expected

➤ If child is gifted or highly gifted, school raises learning goals for individual children

If motivation is a **strength** (level 5 or 6), seek school that:

➤ Allows students to set some of own learning goals (within spectrum of school's overall curriculum)

➤ Gives students some freedom to determine *how* they will accomplish learning goals

➤ Allows students to work beyond pre-established learning goals, and recognizes accomplishments beyond standard curriculum

➤ Allows students to establish or improve school's extracurricular activities.

Parents:

➤ Ask to speak with parents of children who may have similar motivation challenges.

➤ Ask how their children have fared academically.

➤ What challenges have they faced in the classroom that may be related to motivation? How has the school responded?

➤ Has school communicated clearly and often about student progress toward goals?

Written Materials:

➤ Do written materials make clear how goals for individual students are set?

➤ How progress is monitored?

➤ How progress toward goals is communicated to individual students and parents?

Observations:

➤ Are all students in classrooms engaged in learning?

➤ Do teachers quickly redirect and engage students who seem not to be paying attention?

➤ Do you see any one-on-one or very small group contact between teachers and students?

If motivation is a **strength**:

Principal and Teachers:

➤ **What opportunities will my child have to set some of own work goals?**

➤ **What opportunities will my child have to decide how to accomplish own work** (e.g., timing, exact nature of work product)?

➤ Does the school allow children to do more than is asked? Will teachers recognize and give feedback on this extra work, too? How?

   Continues...

Child Needs: What to Look for in a School ...cont.

If This is a Must Have or Nice to Have	...Then Look For This in a School	...And Ask These Questions
	HOW YOUR CHILD LEARNS...continued	

If This is a Must Have or Nice to Have	...Then Look For This in a School	...And Ask These Questions
Physical or Mental Health Challenges	**Physical Health Challenges** ➤ School accommodates child's condition with facilities and equipment that allow child to participate as fully as possible in school *academic* life (make your own list of activities that may be affected and facilities and equipment needed), and ➤ School accommodates child's condition with facilities and equipment that allow child to participate in social and athletic activities (make your own list of activities that may be affected and facilities and equipment needed), and ➤ On-site health care professional qualified to provide required treatment, medication and to deal with potential emergencies, and ➤ School schedule is flexible enough to accommodate child's treatment outside of school, and ➤ Social environment is supportive of children who are different (especially if your child's condition is noticeable); teasing and taunting are not allowed **Mental Health Challenges** ➤ Small school, or small program within school, in which **staff know students and are attentive to students' social and emotional needs (as well as academic needs),** and/or ➤ School with personal counseling services for students (that you feel comfortable using) *or* ➤ School schedule is flexible enough to accommodate child's counseling or treatment outside of school ➤ And school maintains very frequent communication with parents Note: See **PickyParent.com** to learn more about your child's eligibility for special education services in public schools.	**Physical or Mental Health Challenges** **Principal:** ➤ Has your school had other children with my child's physical or mental health challenge? ➤ What have you done to help children like mine overcome obstacles to participating fully in school life? ➤ Does your school provide health services needed for my child (be specific)? ➤ Does your school have the facilities my child needs to participate fully in school (be specific)? ➤ Will your school allow my child time off for counseling or treatments? Do you have a policy or usual procedure for coordinating missed work with teachers? ➤ What have you done to help children like mine overcome any social obstacles? How does your school handle teasing by other students (ask only if child's condition is noticeable)? **Teachers:** ➤ Talk, if possible, to teachers who have had a child like yours in their class at this school. ➤ Ask same questions as principal about children that teacher has had in own class. **Parents:** ➤ Ask to speak with parents of children who may have same or similar condition as your child. ➤ Ask how their children have fared academically, socially and physically. ➤ What challenges have they faced in the classroom or socially that may be related to the mental or physical condition? How has the school responded? **Written Materials:** ➤ In its written materials, does the school openly support children with physical and mental health challenges (good), or is it a hidden secret (not good)? **Observation:** ➤ How would your child respond to this environment and learning activities? ➤ How do teachers respond to children like yours in the classroom?

Continues...

Child Needs: What to Look for in a School ...cont.

If This is a Must Have or Nice to Have	...Then Look For This in a School	...And Ask These Questions
HOW YOUR CHILD LEARNS...continued		
Behavior Challenges	➤ School's approach to discipline should be planful and clear to you. ➤ In general, look for: • Clear behavior expectations, • Consistent consequences (both rewards and punishments), • Frequent praise and discussions about good behavior, and • Firm but fair punishments when needed ➤ School discipline also should be: • Consistent with your parenting values (see Family tables), and • Effective with your child at home and elsewhere (think about what environments have worked best in past) ➤ And school should have a formal policy for working with students and parents to develop behavioral discipline and ➤ Maintain very frequent communication with parents about child (daily is best) ➤ For extreme behavior challenges or ones that have not been resolved with methods above, consider a school focused *exclusively* on children requiring significant development of behavioral discipline ➤ Note that changes in discipline method used at home (and child care) may be necessary to help your child develop age-appropriate self-control	**Principal:** ➤ **What is your school's approach to discipline in the classroom? Outside of the classroom?** ➤ **What happens when a child has repeated behavioral discipline problems?** ➤ How, and how often, does the school communicate with parents about their children's behavior at school? **Teachers:** ➤ Ask same questions as principal about children that teacher has had in own class. **Parents:** ➤ Ask to speak with parents of children who have had behavior challenges. ➤ Ask how their children have fared academically, socially, and emotionally/behaviorally. ➤ How has the school responded to problems? **Written Materials:** ➤ In its written materials, does the school openly acknowledge that some children have behavioral challenges and clearly express the school's approach to developing behavioral discipline? **Observation:** ➤ How would your child respond to this environment and the discipline approach used? Would your child's behavior likely improve? ➤ How do teachers respond to children like yours?
Learning Disabilities & Disorders *...continues*	Seek least restrictive school environment addressing children like yours: ➤ Fully meets child's needs in the regular classroom, or ➤ Pulls child out of regular classroom for part of day, or ➤ Focuses only on children with varying disabilities, or ➤ Focuses exclusively on children with disabilities like your child's. ➤ And school monitors children's individual learning frequently during year (at least every 6 weeks; weekly ideal), and ➤ School adjusts teaching approach to ensure goals are met	**Principal:** ➤ **Has your school had other children with my child's disability or disorder?** ➤ **What have you done to help children like mine overcome learning obstacles?** How successful have these strategies been? Have test scores of children with learning disabilities improved? ➤ What have you done to help children like mine overcome any social obstacles? ➤ Do you set individual goals for children with my child's disability? How? ➤ **Do you monitor child's progress and make changes during the year to child's goals and/or teaching method used? How?**

Continues...

Child Needs: What to Look for in a School ...cont.

If This is a Must Have or Nice to Have	...Then Look For This in a School	...And Ask These Questions
HOW YOUR CHILD LEARNS...continued		
Learning Disabilities & Disorders ...continued	➤ Test scores: scores for students with learning disabilities are relatively high and/or show high rates of growth ➤ Social: school has some other students like your child Note: See **PickyParent.com** to learn more about your child's eligibility for special education services in public schools.	**Teachers:** ➤ Talk, if possible, to teachers who have had a child like yours in their class at this school. ➤ Ask same questions as principal about children that teacher has had in own class. **Parents:** ➤ Ask to speak with parents of children who may have same (or similar) disability as your child. ➤ Ask how their children have fared academically and socially. ➤ What challenges have they faced in the classroom that may be related to the disability? How has the school responded? **Written Materials:** ➤ In its written materials, does the school openly support children with disabilities and disorders (good), or is it a hidden secret (not good)? **Observation:** ➤ How would your child respond to this environment and the learning activities used? ➤ How do teachers respond to children like yours in the classroom?
Self-Understanding	**Weakness**, seek: ➤ School closely fits child's other needs, or ➤ School explicitly teaches children to identify their own strengths, challenges, feelings and needs and to make decisions based on this knowledge ➤ And school communicates with parents frequently about child's academic, social, emotional and physical development	**Principal:** ➤ Does your school do anything to help children develop better self-awareness, such as understanding of their own feelings, strengths and challenges? If so, what? How often? ➤ Are children asked to make choices about their school work? If so, is guidance provided? ➤ How does your school communicate with parents about their children's progress? Academically? About social, emotional and physical development? How often? **Teachers and Parents:** ➤ Same questions as principal. Look for consistency. **Written Materials:** ➤ Look for specific description of efforts school makes to develop students' understanding of their own strengths and challenges, needs and wants (may be called "emotional intelligence," "intrapersonal intelligence," or "self-understanding").

Continues...

Child Needs: What to Look for in a School

If This is a Must Have or Nice to Have	...Then Look For This in a School	...And Ask These Questions
SOCIAL ISSUES		
Friends	➤ Seek school where child will know particular friends with whom your child wants to attend school; or ➤ Seek a school where your child will know at least some children, even if not your child's best friends; or ➤ Encourage parents of your child's friends to choose same school with you ➤ If considering very small school or special program with small number of children, ensure that other children of your child's gender will be in class	**Principal:** ➤ **Where do children who attend this school live?** ➤ Are there events that allow parents to get to know each other so we can get children together? ➤ Does your school provide a directory with students' family phone numbers? ➤ If very small school or special program: Are both boys and girls in every class? How do you achieve this balancing? **Parents:** ➤ Do your children play with other children from school? How often? **Other:** ➤ **Find out where your child's friends plan to attend school,** and include those schools on your Target School list.
PRACTICAL MATTERS		
Essential Activities	➤ Seek school that will actively collaborate with students and families for off-campus learning, or ➤ Seek school with established schedule that is compatible with extracurricular activity, or ➤ Seek school that will allow child time off from school to engage in activity, or ➤ Seek school that has some related activities or independent study time and will accommodate child's remaining needs using one of the methods above, or ➤ Consider home schooling, by yourself, in collaboration with other parents, or using a tutor	**Principal:** ➤ **Explain need for child to pursue extracurricular activity.** Touch on your child's own interest, capability and motivation to pursue the activity. ➤ **Then ask:** Could we work out a plan for my child to pursue this outside interest while also attending this school? Have other children ever done that at this school? ➤ Follow-up questions as needed: • What is daily and yearly school schedule? Is this likely to change from year to year? • Are children ever allowed time off or independent study credit for outside activities? • Is this activity addressed in the school's curriculum or extracurricular activities?

Family Needs: What to Look for in a School

How to Use This Table:
➤ Make sure you have identified your family's top needs for school before using this table.
➤ For each of your family's Must Haves and Nice to Haves, find the companion section of this table.
➤ Read general information about the family need or value where provided.

➤ Then read specific information about your family's Must Haves and Nice to Haves.
➤ **Bolded** questions and things to seek are the most important. Focusing on them will help you quickly target the best-fit schools and eliminate poor-fit schools.
➤ Note top things to seek and ask at schools on your *Personalized Great Fit Checklist* (page 59).

If This is a Must Have or Nice to Have	...Then Look For This in a School	...And Ask These Questions
WHAT **YOUR CHILD LEARNS**		

Values about what *content* is important ➤ Core academic subjects ➤ Other academic subjects (make your own list) ➤ Morals, ethics, character, religion ➤ Other non-academic: e.g., social, emotional and physical development ➤ Other topics important to you	➤ **School clearly states its mission, goals, and curriculum so you know what content will be covered,** And: ➤ Includes your valued subject(s) as a stated part of curriculum, including class time devoted exclusively to the subject, or ➤ Includes your valued subject(s) as a stated part of curriculum, and regularly weaves teaching of the subject into other subjects (e.g., science taught as part of math curriculum), or ➤ Includes optional classes or established extracurricular activities in subject, and you are confident child will be able to pursue these opportunities, or ➤ Includes special events, mini-courses, or other non-routine, limited-time exposure to subject	**Principal:** ➤ **Ask specifically about the subjects or topics of interest to you** ➤ **What subjects are covered in the curriculum** (for grades your child will attend at this school)? ➤ Are these taught in separate classes or woven into basic subjects? ➤ **How much time is spent on these subjects** (that are of interest to parent)? ➤ Are there other opportunities – elective courses, mini-courses, extracurricular clubs, etc. – to cover other topics that are not part of regular curriculum? ➤ Are the subjects covered likely to stay the same in the future (especially ones of interest to you)? ➤ What kind of training do teachers have in subjects (most important if math or science is your valued area)? **Teachers:** ➤ What subjects do you cover in your class? ➤ Separately or as part of basics? ➤ How much time do you spend on each subject in a week (ask about subject of concern to you)? ➤ Do you help with any of the other topics covered in mini-courses, clubs, etc? (If so, describe.) **Parents:** ➤ Confirm principal's and teachers' comments ➤ How have your children liked these subjects (of interest to you)? ➤ Is there anything that you think the school should do better in covering these subjects? **Written Materials:** ➤ Look for mention of subject important to you (this indicates that it is a valued and stable part of curriculum) **Observation:** ➤ May want to observe coverage of critical topics in the classroom to ensure that your expectations for what is included are met

Continues...

Family Needs: What to Look for in a School ...cont.

If This is a Must Have or Nice to Have	...Then Look For This in a School	...And Ask These Questions
WHAT YOUR CHILD LEARNS...continued		
Goals for your child: **Grade Progression**	➤ **School clearly states that all students are expected to meet grade level requirements** ➤ **School focuses large portion of school day on basic subjects** (reading, writing, math) and any other subjects required for grade progression ➤ **School has high percentage of children** *like yours* **meeting grade level** (e.g., percent at grade level for your child's race, family income, previous performance) ➤ School provides individual or small group tutoring for children not meeting grade level requirements ➤ School changes teaching approach if child's progress falls below expected	**Principal:** ➤ Are all children expected to meet grade level, or do you expect that some will fail each year? Why? ➤ What does your school do to help children who are struggling to meet grade level? ➤ How much time in each day is spent on reading, math and writing? Other subjects required for students to pass from grade to grade? ➤ My child is _____ (describe why you think your child may be at risk of not making grade level). What does your school do to help make sure children like that achieve at grade level? **Teachers and Parents:** ➤ Same as principal for each teacher's class **Parents:** ➤ Ask to talk with parents of similar children ➤ Ask how the school has helped their children succeed ➤ Ask what problems they see **Written Materials:** ➤ Look for emphasis on grade level achievement for all **Observation:** ➤ Are teachers engaging all of the children in class: • Making sure that *all* children get a chance to participate and • Making sure that all children are paying attention and • Insisting that all children learn the material?
Goals for your child: **Academic Performance** *...continues*	➤ **School clearly states that it expects children to achieve** *beyond* **grade level** requirements when they are ready ➤ **School assesses individual student readiness and sets individual goals,** with grade level as a bare minimum; goals are continually raised as child progresses beyond grade level ➤ **School monitors children's individual learning frequently** (*at least* every 6 weeks, weekly ideal) during year to ensure that unexpected barriers to child's achievement have not arisen ➤ School changes teaching approach if child's progress falls below expected	See Basic Learning Capability section of table *Child Needs: What to Look for in a School.* Ask questions for children of your child's current capability.

Continues...

Family Needs: What to Look for in a School ...cont.

If This is a Must Have or Nice to Have	...Then Look For This in a School	...And Ask These Questions
WHAT YOUR CHILD LEARNS...continued		
Goals for your child: **Academic Performance** ...continued	➤ School does what it should to meet requirements of child with your child's Basic Learning Capability (see *Child Needs: What to Look for in a School*)	See Basic Learning Capability section of table *Child Needs: What to Look for in a School*. Ask questions for children of your child's current capability.
Goals for your child: **College Opportunity**	➤ If child is Challenged or Typical in Basic Learning Capability, choose school for Grade Progression, above ➤ If child is Gifted or Highly Gifted in Basic Learning Capability, choose school for Academic Performance above ➤ For all students: curriculum in elementary should allow entry into middle and high school courses *required* by colleges and universities and *optional* advanced placement level classes in subjects where your child excels	➤ If child is at risk of not passing grade level, see questions above for Grade Progression. ➤ If child may be able to perform beyond grade level, see Basic Learning Capability section of *Child Needs: What to Look for in a School*. Ask questions for children of your child's current capability. **Also ask Principal and Teachers:** ➤ What exactly does your school do to ensure that students in higher elementary grades will be ready to take honors or advanced classes in middle and high school?
HOW YOUR CHILD LEARNS		
Values about school-wide expectations and rules on student conduct: ➤ Manners with other children ➤ Manners with adults ➤ Dress ➤ Discipline ➤ Honor code ➤ Other behaviors ...continues	➤ School clearly states its overall values, and ➤ **School clearly states its expectations for student conduct both in and out of the classroom,** including consequences for not meeting expectations, and ➤ **School's rules and expectations for students are consistent with your family's values,** including your opinions about these: • Manners with other children • Manners with adults • Dress code • Honor code • General discipline policy (what acts are punished and how punishment is administered) And ➤ School actually adheres to its own values, rules and expectations in daily school life.	**Principal:** ➤ **What social values are most important in your school?** ➤ **Does your school expect certain behaviors and conduct from students** in and out of the classroom? ➤ How is that communicated to students and parents? ➤ What are the consequences for not meeting the student conduct expectations? ➤ **May want to ask about specific rules and expectations regarding items of particular importance to you:** manners expected (e.g., on playground, at lunch), dress code, general discipline policy, honor code. **Teachers:** ➤ Do you find that you are able to enforce your school's conduct rules (be specific: honor code, discipline policy, character code, etc.)? What's the biggest challenge? ➤ What social values do you think are most important in your school? ➤ What kinds of problems do you see with student behavior outside of the classroom, in the lunch room, playground and so forth? ➤ How do students treat other students who are different from the norm?

Continues...

Family Needs: What to Look for in a School ...cont.

If This is a Must Have or Nice to Have	...Then Look For This in a School	...And Ask These Questions
HOW YOUR CHILD LEARNS...continued		

Values about school-wide expectations and rules on student conduct: ➤ Manners with other children ➤ Manners with adults ➤ Dress ➤ Discipline ➤ Honor code ➤ Other behaviors ...*continued*		**Parents:** ➤ How have you found the social behavior of the other students in your child's school? ➤ Do you like the social values that the school reinforces? Which values? How are they reinforced? ➤ Have you noticed any problems with student social behavior? What? How does school deal with that? **Written Materials:** ➤ Look for clear statement of school's social values. ➤ Look for clear statement of student conduct rules and expectations (especially ones important to you). ➤ Look for clear statement of how school expects students to behave in and out of classroom. **Observation:** ➤ During your observation time, notice whether teachers insist that children adhere to expected behaviors. ➤ Do teachers treat infractions as mere chances to inflict punishment, or do they use them as a chance to reiterate the underlying values and teach children better ways to behave? ➤ How are students who appear different from others treated? ➤ How do teachers who hear students treating others unkindly respond?
Values about how children should *learn*: **Teaching method** ➤ Teacher directed ➤ Student discovery ➤ Mixed approach ...*continues*	**Look for clear school statement of teaching methods used** throughout the school, and look for method that fits your values. ➤ Teacher directed, look for: • Teachers set goals for whole class and define activity steps • Teachers, not students, do most of the talking, or teachers direct and control class discussions • More whole-class, big-group learning, less small group and individual learning ➤ Student discovery, look for: • Students set some individual and group goals within pre-defined topic areas • Teachers encourage students to think of questions and discuss or research answers before teachers "tell answer"	**Principal:** ➤ **Is there a certain teaching method teachers are expected to use here?** Please describe. ➤ Do the teachers decide what activities children will engage in all day or do students have some choice? Is the answer the same for all subjects, or does it vary? Can you give me examples? ➤ Do teachers do most of the talking and directing of discussions? Or are students asked to come up with some of own questions and do some activities on their own? Examples? Vary across subjects? ➤ How much time is spent in whole class, small group and individual activities each day? Does this vary in different classrooms or grades?

Continues...

Family Needs: What to Look for in a School ...cont.

If This is a Must Have or Nice to Have	...Then Look For This in a School	...And Ask These Questions
HOW **YOUR CHILD LEARNS**...*continued*		

Values about how children should *learn*: **Teaching method** ➤ Teacher directed ➤ Student discovery ➤ Mixed approach *...continued*	• More small group and individual learning, less whole-class, big-group learning	**Teachers:** ➤ Same as principal for each teacher's own class. **Parents:** ➤ Same as principal and teachers – confirm consistency of school's approach. **Written Materials:** ➤ Look for written statement about teaching method expected in school. **Observation:** ➤ Are teachers instructing students in the way described by principal, teachers, parents and written materials?
Values about how children should *learn*: **Classroom behavior management** ➤ Controlling/Strict ➤ Developmental ➤ Mixed approach	Look for clear school statement of behavior management used throughout the school's *classrooms*, and look for method that fits your values. ➤ Controlling/Strict, look for: • Clear, written rules of classroom behavior expectations • Clear punishments for breaking rules, rewards for adhering to rules • Little tolerance for not fitting into behavior guidelines ➤ Developmental, look for: • Frequent, small rewards or recognition for positive behaviors • Before exacting punishments, teachers coach students to understand their own emotions (students') and to improve self-control in response to emotions • Teachers modify teaching method to ensure all students are engaged • Teachers use peer group pressure, parents and principal to reinforce expected behaviors	**Principal:** ➤ **Do you expect teachers to take a certain approach to managing children's behavior in the classroom? What approach is expected or commonly used?** ➤ If you do expect a certain approach, do teachers receive any training in this approach? ➤ What does a teacher do if he or she is having trouble managing children's behavior? (Look for principal who acts as coach to teachers, helps them resolve problems and improve behavior management.) **Teachers:** ➤ How do you keep children's behavior in the classroom focused on school work? ➤ What do you do if a child is having behavior problems? **Parents:** ➤ How have you felt about the teachers' handling of classroom behavior? ➤ Have you known about any serious behavior problems among children in the classroom? What do the teachers and principal do about that? **Written Materials:** ➤ Look for mention of how teachers manage classroom behavior. **Observation:** ➤ Does teacher behavior match what you expect based on principal and teacher comments?

Continues...

Family Needs: What to Look for in a School ...cont.

If This is a Must Have or Nice to Have	...Then Look For This in a School	...And Ask These Questions
HOW YOUR CHILD LEARNS...continued		

Your role as advocate for child (understanding, communicating and influencing school to address your child's learning needs). The greater your ability, the less important for school to help you.	➤ School that fits all of your *child's* needs very closely, *or* ➤ School uses individualized approach to student education, including *frequent assessment* of child's academic, social, emotional and physical development. School *changes* child's learning goals and the teaching approach accordingly *And* ➤ **School communicates very frequently with parents about individual children's progress and behavior** (at least weekly is ideal), and ➤ School has very strong and consistent leadership and teacher quality (see Great School Quality Factor #7: Instructional Leadership)	All questions related to your child's specific fit needs, *or:* **Principal:** ➤ How closely are you able to track the individual development (academic, social, emotional and physical) of children at this school? Who is responsible for this? How do they do it? Is it consistently done in all grades? ➤ What changes are made to a child's learning goals and the teaching approach to respond to children's individual needs? ➤ How do teachers communicate with parents about their individual children's progress and behavior? How often? **Teachers:** ➤ Same as principal for teachers' own classes. **Parents:** ➤ Same as principal for parents' own children. ➤ How closely has school monitored your child's development? ➤ How often has school communicated with you about your child's development? ➤ How well has school met your individual child's needs? **Written Materials:** ➤ Look for mention of monitoring children's progress and development not just academically, but also socially, emotionally and physically. ➤ Look for specifics about changing learning goals and teaching approach for individual students. ➤ Look for mention of how teachers are expected to communicate about children with parents.
SOCIAL ISSUES		
Parent Community I want my child's school to have parents with particular characteristics *...continues*	**Look for school with parent population that matches the list you have created.**	**Principal:** ➤ Ask questions about parent population, according to the profile you have created **Teachers:** ➤ Ask questions about parents each teacher has encountered, according to the ideal list you have created

Continues...

Family Needs: What to Look for in a School ...cont.

If This is a Must Have or Nice to Have	...Then Look For This in a School	...And Ask These Questions
SOCIAL ISSUES...continued		

Parent Community

I want my child's school to have parents with particular characteristics

...continued

Parents:
➤ Ask questions about parent population, according to the ideal list you have created
➤ Ask questions of individual parents you meet to see if values and other characteristics are consistent with what you want

Written Materials:
➤ Look for information about parents that informs you about the characteristics important to you

Observation:
➤ How do parents speak and act – with their own children, other students, teachers, principal and each other? Does this match what you want?
➤ Do you feel comfortable with other parents from this school? How will your comfort level affect your ability to participate in the school community and help your child build social relationships?

Parent Involvement in School

➤ Helping
➤ Decision-making
➤ Fundraising activities

Look for parent *policy* and *actual* parent involvement that match types and level of involvement you want, including:

➤ Parent Involvement Policy: formal opportunities or requirements for parents to participate in school in ways and at level you want, without obligation to participate in ways or at level undesirable or unfeasible for you

➤ Actual Parent Involvement Level: percentage of parents and time committed actually volunteering at school match what you want

➤ Actual Parent Roles: parents actually participate in school life in ways you want

Principal:
➤ **Do you have a parent involvement policy? What is it?**
➤ What opportunities are there for parents to participate in the school? Can you give me examples? (Ask about any specific roles you might want to play.)
➤ Is participation required or optional?
➤ What percentage of parents actually volunteer at the school each year?
➤ How much volunteer time per parent is typical?
➤ Where is most of parent time spent?

Teachers:
➤ How do parent volunteers help you? Do you find that helpful? Are there other things you wish parents would do to help?

Parents:
➤ Have you volunteered in the school? What have you done? Was it satisfying? How did it help the school?
➤ What expectations do parents have for each others' involvement?

Written Materials:
➤ Read parent involvement policy.
➤ In other materials (newsletters, etc.), look for mention of current parent involvement and requests for help from parents – does this match what you want?

Continues...

Family Needs: What to Look for in a School ...cont.

If This is a Must Have or Nice to Have	...Then Look For This in a School	...And Ask These Questions
SOCIAL ISSUES...continued		
Student Community I want my child's school to have students with particular characteristics	Look for school with student population that matches the list you have created.	**Principal:** ➤ Ask questions about student population, according to the profile you have created **Teachers:** ➤ Ask questions about student population each teacher has encountered, according to the profile you have created **Parents:** ➤ Ask questions about student population, according to the profile you have created ➤ Ask questions of individual students you meet to see if behavior and other characteristics are consistent with what you want **Written Materials:** ➤ Look for statistics about student population ➤ Look for mention of student actions and behaviors – do they match what you want in student population? **Observation:** ➤ How do students speak and act – with each other, parents, teachers and principal? Does this match what you want?
I want my child to attend a certain school, school type, or school design	The school, type or design you prefer	➤ If your bias is toward a particular school, confirm that the school has the offerings and characteristics you expected. ➤ If your bias is toward a type of school, confirm that the school has the offerings and characteristics you expect in a school of that type. ➤ If design, confirm that school is in fact using the design as you expect.
PRACTICAL MATTERS		
Child Care ➤ Before school ➤ After school ➤ Holidays ➤ Summer	School meeting your needs in the following areas: ➤ Hours and days that care is provided ➤ Transportation to/from school and to/from home ➤ Snacks or meals provided ➤ Safe supervision of child ➤ Academic or developmental assistance ➤ Structured or unstructured time for your child ➤ Care for your multiple children ➤ Cost Stop by your community's child care resource and referral agency for more information about non-school care options.	➤ From any source available to you, find out facts about this school's child care offerings ➤ Ask parents who have used care services about their satisfaction with each aspect important to you (see list to left).

Continues...

Family Needs: What to Look for in a School

If This is a Must Have or Nice to Have	...Then Look For This in a School	...And Ask These Questions
PRACTICAL MATTERS...continued		
Schedule ➤ Daily hours ➤ Yearly (start/finish and holidays)	**Look for school accommodating your daily and annual scheduling needs.** ➤ If available, be sure to look at the coming years, not just the current one, for any changes. ➤ Ask if the schedule is likely to change significantly from year to year	➤ From any source available to you, find out facts about this school's schedule ➤ School web sites and written sources often have the basics of current daily schedule and yearly calendar
Transportation Needs ➤ To school ➤ After school ➤ After school activities	School ➤ Provides transportation or ➤ Is within walking or bicycling distance for you and child (or child alone) to and from home, child care, and extracurricular activities. ➤ Find out what, if any, cost is involved in school-provided transportation	➤ From any source available to you, find out facts about this school's transportation offerings ➤ School web sites and written sources often have the basics of current transportation offerings and cost Parents who have used school transportation: ➤ Have you found school transportation to be reliable (on time, shows up every day)? ➤ Safe (good drivers, good behavior on bus)? If there have been serious behavior problems on the bus, how has the school responded? ➤ Reasonable in cost (if any)? How much?
Location proximity to your home or work	**Look for school in location desired,** near home, work or other critical location	➤ Just note whether location meets your need. May want to rank your school options according to how well they meet your need, e.g., #1= best location, #2 = next best.
Your Other Children	**Same School: Look for school that may be suitable for all of your children** (e.g., that accommodates varying ages and learning needs) **Different Schools: Look for schools with compatible schedules, locations, and transportation** to accommodate your different children without disrupting family life	From whatever source available: ➤ Same School: Determine how well school meets your children's differing individual needs (See Child Needs tables) ➤ Different Schools: Determine schools' schedules, locations, transportation and fit with other family needs to determine compatibility
Money available to pay for school	➤ **Schools with combined total cost (tuition, fees, supplies, dress, lunch, and expected donation, etc.) within your Target (or Maximum)** ➤ Subtract potential scholarship and voucher funds from total cost to determine schools that you could afford	From whatever source available (web sites and written materials are good places to start): ➤ What are tuition and fees for the year? ➤ What other costs should we expect? (Be sure to ask about these: books, supplies, dress/uniforms, lunches, snacks, special fees for trips or other activities, expected donations, class gifts for teachers.) ➤ What scholarships might be available to a child like mine? How do we apply? What are our chances (or how many children get a scholarship like that each year)? ➤ Are government vouchers available that can be used to pay some of tuition here?

Quality: What to Look for in a School

How to Use This Table:

➤ Use the *Great School Quality Checklist* on page 200 as a starting point.

➤ If you want more help understanding a Great School Quality Factor, find the companion section in this table.

➤ Make a note of specific questions you want to ask or quality details you'd like to seek in a school.

➤ Also use this table to make finer distinctions between two or more schools very similar in quality.

➤ Focusing on **bolded** questions and things to seek will help you quickly identify important quality strengths and weaknesses in each school you consider.

Great School Quality Factors: What to Look for in a School	*Questions to Ask*

GREAT SCHOOL QUALITY FACTOR #1

Clear Mission Guiding School Activities

Look for:

➤ **School has written mission that *accurately* communicates school's focus and priorities**

➤ School has memorable motto that communicates one or two most important points of mission – and everyone knows this by heart

➤ **School consistently communicates its mission through principal, teachers, parents, and written materials**

➤ School has goals for overall student achievement, overall student improvement and other important indicators of whether school is meeting its mission. These are adjusted yearly, but may include longer-term goals, too (e.g., progress towards higher student achievement over 5 years).

➤ School has clear set of skill and knowledge goals for all students in each grade and subject ("standards"). These should clearly show what students should know ("knowledge") and be able to do ("skills") by the end of each year. School should also have a method for raising goals for students who are ready. Do both of these support mission?

➤ **School's curriculum (class materials and activities), teaching method and other activities (e.g., parent volunteer work) support school mission.**

Principal:

➤ **What is the mission of your school?**

➤ What is your school motto?

➤ Does your school have certain goals it is trying to meet overall for this year? What are they? How will meeting these goals support your mission?

➤ Does your school have a written set of skills and knowledge students are expected to gain ("standards")? Are goals ever changed for some students? How do all of these learning goals for students support the mission?

➤ **How does the curriculum (class materials and activities) support the mission?**

➤ How do teaching methods support the mission?

➤ How do parent activities support the mission?

Teachers:

➤ Same as principal – look for consistency.

Parents:

➤ Same as principal – look for consistency.

➤ Has your child had a *stable and consistent* experience:
  • **Has the school turned out the way you expected for your child?**
  • **Have the teachers been similar in quality and approach?**
  • Has what your child learned each year built on the past year?

Written Materials:

➤ **Look for clear, consistent expression of school's mission, including repetition of motto summarizing mission.**

➤ Look for communication of school-wide achievement and improvement goals. May include student achievement, parent satisfaction, student turnover, teacher turnover and other factors that support mission.

➤ Are the grade level student goals clear and consistent with mission?

➤ **Look for explanations about how the student goals, curriculum, teaching method and parent activities support the mission.** Is this consistent with what you've heard from principal, teachers, and parents?

Observations:

➤ Do you see activities in classrooms consistent with what you have read and heard about curriculum and teaching method?

➤ Do you see the school motto and/or key mission points posted and used throughout the school?

Continues...

Quality: What to Look for in a School ...continued

Great School Quality Factors: What to Look for in a School	Questions to Ask
GREAT SCHOOL QUALITY FACTOR #2	

High Expectations for All Students:
High Minimum Expectations for All

Look for:

➤ **The school's minimum expected skill and knowledge goals for each grade and subject ("standards") are challenging for most students,** but attainable by all *

➤ **Principal & teachers have school-wide plan to ensure that** *all* **students** a*chie*ve at least grade level goals in basics (reading, math, writing)
  • Principal, teachers express expectation that all children will meet grade level
  • Principal, teachers take planned steps to ensure grade level achievement by all
  • Principal, teachers do not make excuses for failing students; maintain consistent expectation for grade level achievement

➤ Test scores show that a very high percentage of students actually achieves at least grade level in basics by year end, regardless of starting achievement level, race, and family income

➤ Progress or growth scores show that a very high percentage of students makes significant progress, at least one grade's worth, from beginning to end of school year

Principal:

➤ **What is the source of minimum grade level standards – state, national or school's own?** (May be helpful for comparison if source of standards is pre-existing one that has been rated. See the Resources for Parents section starting on page 354 for links to information about standards.)

➤ **Do most students in your school find the grade level goals challenging** to meet?

➤ *If your child tests Extremely Challenged in Basic Learning Capability only: Is there a clear set of challenging but achievable learning goals for students like my child? What is the source of these standards? Or, is there a defined process for the school and parents to agree on individualized learning goals for each student?

➤ **What specific actions does your school take for children who are at risk of not meeting the grade level standards?**

Teachers:

➤ Same as principal. Look for consistency

Parents:

➤ Same as principal. Look for consistency

➤ Ask parents of students who have struggled: What has school done to help your child meet grade level?

Written Materials:

➤ Written grade level goals or standards: how challenging are they? (Compare to state or national standards or to other schools you are considering.)

➤ Look for explanation of steps taken to ensure that all children achieve at least grade level expectations

---

High Expectations for All Students:
Higher Expectations for Students Who are Ready

Look for:

➤ **Skill and knowledge goals are adjusted upward throughout year,** to stay challenging but achievable, for all students who are ready to proceed beyond grade level

➤ Principal & teachers have and use a school-wide plan to ensure that individual students with higher learning goals achieve them

...*continues*

Principal and Teachers:

➤ **What does your school do for children who are ready to go beyond grade level?**

➤ What about students who are already beyond grade level in a subject?

➤ **Do all teachers in your school approach this in a similar way, or does it vary?**

➤ Do you have anything written that shows the levels of skill and knowledge through which students advance in basic subjects? Does this extend beyond grade level?

Parents:

➤ Same as principal and teachers. Look for consistency

➤ Ask parents of students who are advanced academically: What has school done to challenge your child? (Look for advanced goals and work in core academic areas for significant portion of each school day.)

Continues...

Quality: What to Look for in a School   *...continued*

Great School Quality Factors: What to Look for in a School	Questions to Ask

GREAT SCHOOL QUALITY FACTOR #2 ...continued

➤ Test scores are *not* clustered only at grade level; some students – *at least* number classified as "gifted" — have very high test scores ➤ Progress or growth scores show that top students make significant progress from beginning to end of school year	**Written Materials:** ➤ Look for mention of how school addresses academic needs of students who are advanced, ahead of grade level, or "gifted." Is this consistent with what you have heard? ➤ Look for written set of progressively more challenging skills and knowledge students are expected to master, at least in basic subjects. This should extend well beyond grade level.

GREAT SCHOOL QUALITY FACTOR #3

Monitoring of Progress and Adjusting Teaching

Look for:

➤ **School frequently monitors/assesses students' individual progress** towards their learning goals, at least in basic subjects (continual informal assessment by teachers, plus formal assessment every 6 weeks *minimum*)
  • Monitoring may be done in very small groups or one-on-one
  • Monitoring may be done by lead teacher or other skilled staff (or using computer technology)

➤ **Teachers change teaching approach, when needed, to ensure that every child** achieves his or her learning goals (whether grade level or higher)
  • Teachers have freedom and flexibility to make changes in classroom teaching that help students meet goals
  • Teachers regularly consider and address as needed a broad range of potential barriers to – and opportunities to enhance – learning, including: sound social, emotional and physical health; children's interests, nonacademic strengths, and learning styles; and learning disorders and disabilities
  • Changes are used to help students meet learning goals, not to lower goals or overall academic expectations

➤ Students are grouped for instruction in core academic subjects so that:
  • Groups are small enough that teachers can engage and monitor each child
  • Children are assigned to groups based on their current readiness / understanding   *...continues*

Principal:
➤ **How do you monitor individual student progress during the year? How often?**
➤ What systems do teachers have to obtain and keep track of data about how their students are learning?
➤ **What changes do you make for children who are having trouble** meeting grade level goals? How often?
➤ What changes do you make if a child is ahead of grade level, but not making further progress? How often?
➤ How are children grouped for learning, especially in basics (reading, math, writing)? How large are the groups? How often do these groupings change? (Schools that place each student in a fixed "ability" group for the entire year are not meeting this Great School Quality Factor. This is "tracking," and it indicates that the school does not use monitoring to change student learning goals. If you hear something that sounds like tracking, ask whether groupings change during the year.)

Teachers:
➤ Same as principal. Look for answers consistent with principal's and consistent across teachers within each grade level

Parents:
➤ Same as principal. Look for answers consistent with principal's and teachers'
➤ Ask parents of children similar to yours if their children's work has been monitored and if teachers have consistently made changes to ensure their children's progress

Written Materials:
➤ Look for consistent references to:
  • Monitoring or assessment of children's progress during school year
  • Clear, continuous efforts to ensure all children make progress, even ones already ahead of grade level
  • Clear, continuous changes made to ensure that struggling students reach grade level
  • Reference to one or more of the models used to understand and address individual children's capabilities and needs (multiple intelligences, learning styles, All Kinds of Minds, whole child, etc.), but not as a substitute for high expectations in core academic subjects

Observations:
➤ Are the learning activities described to you by principal, teachers and parents taking place?

Continues...

Quality: What to Look for in a School   ...continued

Great School Quality Factors: What to Look for in a School	Questions to Ask

GREAT SCHOOL QUALITY FACTOR #3 ...continued

• Children can move between groups as they learn (no "tracking" or fixed "ability" groups) • No child works by him or herself all day	➤ Are teachers taking advantage of small group or one-on-one work to engage every child? ➤ Are teachers trying different approaches with different children? ➤ Are there any negative consequences of how the class has been arranged to monitor progress? Look for: • Noise: class should not be too noisy for multiple groups to work in room • Order: children should know what they are supposed to be doing at all times – are they *engaged* in their small group and individual work? • Isolation: no child in elementary grades should be doing work all by him or herself all day. Even if a student is very far ahead or behind academically, part of day should be spent with other children and some working with an adult.

GREAT SCHOOL QUALITY FACTOR #4

Focus on Effective Learning Tasks

Look for:

➤ Teaching, learning approaches, and materials used are effective for most of the school's students

- **School staff have a regular process for assessing which methods and materials work** with the students in the school
- **School staff have an established process for keeping up with academic research about what works best** in each subject and with different children (by age, background and other differences)
- Methods, materials that work best with most students in a school are used most often
- Methods, materials that are not working for actual students attending a school are replaced

➤ **Class time is allocated according to importance of subjects** (consistent with school's mission and learning goals)

- Significant time spent on core academic subjects
- Time spent on each additional subject reflects school mission

➤ Materials and facilities are allocated according to importance of subjects (consistent with mission and learning goals)

➤ Principal and teachers limit class interruptions (e.g., announcements, students leaving room, visitors)

Principal:

➤ **What does your school do to stay current with best education techniques?** Have you made any recent changes? (Listen for continuous, regular changes in school curriculum, teaching methods and materials, based on current research)

➤ **Do you think your school is using the most effective teaching techniques now? What are areas you might be changing soon?**

➤ **What part of your facility and materials do you think is closest to "state of the art"?** (Should include academic items – library, classrooms well-stocked with core materials, science center or science materials in classrooms, computers used for core academics.)

➤ Do you think there are any shortages or problems with materials and facilities at your school? How does this affect what students learn in core academic subjects?

➤ **How does your school prevent class time from being interrupted** in the middle of learning activities? (Look for clear policies.) Does that work?

Teachers:

➤ Same as principal, for each teacher's own class.

➤ **What is the daily and weekly schedule?** (Look at a sample of the grades your child will be attending. Look at how time is allocated among subjects. Do reading, writing, and math receive significant time? Is coverage of other items consistent with school's mission and learning goals?)

Parents:

➤ Does your child complain about class interruptions?

➤ Do you think there are any shortages or problems with materials and facilities at your school? How has this affected your child?

➤ Has your child experienced any problems with what is taught or how it's taught at your school?

➤ Have you seen any changes in what your school is teaching or how? Has that worked for your child?

Written Materials:

➤ Describe use of learning programs, especially in reading, that have been shown by research to work (see the Resources for Parents section starting on page 354 for information about research on reading and other topics)

Continues...

Quality: What to Look for in a School ...*continued*

Great School Quality Factors: What to Look for in a School	Questions to Ask

GREAT SCHOOL QUALITY FACTOR #5

Home-School Connection

Look for:

➤ **School tells parents in advance what children will be learning** at school
  • At beginning of each year
  • Frequently during year as new topics and more challenging work are introduced

➤ **School tells parents how they should help** with children's learning (homework, attendance, etc.)
  • In general
  • On specific assignments

➤ **School updates parents frequently on each child's achievement and progress,** in academics, class behavior, and other measures important to the school's mission
  • Frequently on a pre-set schedule and
  • As needed when problems arise

➤ **School works with parents to resolve problems** through changes at school and home
  • By setting expectation that education is a family-school partnership
  • By including parents in problem identification and problem solving

➤ School identifies common challenges among parents and families of children attending the school and works proactively to strengthen families and important parenting skills
  • School partners with social services organization when needed to serve school's parents and families
  • School offers programs to increase parent skills in needed areas (general parenting skills, language, academic know-how, etc.)

Principal:

➤ **Do you tell parents in advance what their children should be learning?** How often? How is this communicated?

➤ **Do you have certain expectations about how parents will help their children with learning at home?** How do you communicate that?

➤ **How often do teachers update parents on their children's progress and behavior? How?**

➤ What happens if a student is having an academic or behavior problem?

Teachers:

➤ Same as principal.

Parents:

➤ Has your child's school told you what your child will be learning at the beginning of each year? How?

➤ Do you know how you are expected to help your child with school work?

➤ How often do teachers keep you updated on your child's progress? How? Does that work for you?

➤ Do you know what the school does if a child is having problems? Does that work for you?

Written Materials:

➤ Look for clear, parent-friendly communication in newsletters, websites, and other materials about the school's standards and learning programs

➤ Look for mention of how school communicates with parents, when, and expected role of parents with regard to their own children's educations

➤ Examine materials used by the school to communicate with parents *about their own children* (e.g., report cards, folders sent home weekly, daily behavior reports). How frequently do parents receive these? Do they contain useful information?

GREAT SCHOOL QUALITY FACTOR #6

Safe and Orderly Environment

Look for:

➤ Students know where they are supposed to be and how they are supposed to behave, both in and out of the classroom

➤ **Students focus on school work in the classroom**
  ...*continues*

Principal:

➤ **Do you have certain behaviors expected of students in the classroom and other activities?** How is this communicated?

➤ **Do you have problems with students not complying** with expected behaviors?

➤ When problems with student behavior happen, what do teachers do? What is your role in discipline?

➤ Do you have a policy about how students are supposed to act towards each other? What happens if a student violates this?

➤ **What are your biggest safety concerns here?** What do you do about that?

Continues...

Quality: What to Look for in a School ...*continued*

Great School Quality Factors: What to Look for in a School	Questions to Ask

GREAT SCHOOL QUALITY FACTOR #6 ...*continued*

➤ Consequences for behavior problems – from the mildest to most challenging – are clear and consistently applied

➤ **School communicates and enforces policies that keep students and staff safe** from harm by outsiders, other students or staff. Policies are appropriate for the location and population. For example:
- Criminal background checks for all staff
- Other job-appropriate checks, e.g., driver record for bus drivers
- Clear, enforced procedures for visitor sign in and tracking
- Clear, enforced procedures for pick-up of students by adults during and after school
- Clear policies for staff to follow regarding one-on-one interactions between students and staff (e.g., open doors, two-way mirrors on doors)

➤ School communicates and enforces policies that keep students and staff safe from harm by equipment and facility:
- Policies to cover extraordinary situations (e.g., fire, threats to school)
- Policies regarding routine cleaning and repair of equipment and facilities

---

➤ What is your policy on visitors?
➤ Do you have rules about how staff and students interact in one-on-one situations to keep students safe?
➤ How do you screen staff for basic safety issues?

Teachers:
➤ Same as principal, except last two bullets.

Parents:
➤ **Have your child's classrooms (or other school activities, including bus) experienced any problems with disruptive student behavior?** Was the problem resolved?
➤ Has your child or any child you know experienced problems with bad behavior by other students (e.g., too much teasing, threats)? What did the school do about this?
➤ **Do you feel that your child is safe at school? Why or why not?**

Written Materials:
➤ Look for clear, written policies on the following (at least):
- Student behavior expected – in the classroom and out
- Behavior that is not tolerated
- Bus behavior
- Consequences for violations
- Visitor sign in and tracking
- Pick-up of students during and after school
- Staff background checks
- Staff-student interactions
- Extraordinary situations (e.g., fire, threats to school)
- Routine cleaning and repair of equipment and facilities

Observations:
➤ Are classrooms, halls, lunchroom and other places in school orderly? (Note: "orderly" does not necessarily mean "silent" or "still." In a school that expects students to participate in conversation and hands-on activities, there will be a constant buzz and movement. As long as this represents engagement rather than chaos, you shouldn't regard it as a sign of "disorder.")
➤ Are students engaged in appropriate activity, not too loud and not bothering other students and staff?
➤ Is behavior observed consistent with behavior guidelines and teaching methods of school?
➤ Do equipment and facility appear clean and in good repair?

GREAT SCHOOL QUALITY FACTOR #7

Strong Instructional Leadership

Look for:
➤ **Principal sets clear, challenging expectations for teacher performance**
➤ Principal actively recruits and keeps teachers who meet or exceed performance expectations
            ...*continues*

Principal
(see Chapter 14 for more information about what to ask principals):
➤ How do you recruit good quality teachers?
➤ **Have you been able to keep good teachers? How?**
➤ **What do you expect of teachers once they are here?**
➤ Do teachers work together? How?
➤ How do you keep up with individual teachers' performance?
➤ How do you help teachers who need to improve in an area?
➤ If the school needs to improve in an area, how is that determined?

Continues...

Quality: What to Look for in a School

Great School Quality Factors: What to Look for in a School	Questions to Ask
GREAT SCHOOL QUALITY FACTOR #7 ...continued	

Great School Quality Factors: What to Look for in a School

➤ Principal actively ensures that teachers work together, within and across grades, to meet school learning goals

➤ Principal monitors individual teacher performance

➤ Principal and teachers regularly identify school-wide problems and make improvements

➤ Principal ensures that teachers engage in professional development that helps staff achieve school mission and learning goals by:
- Addressing common gaps in student achievement
- Addressing problems keeping individual teachers from helping students meet learning goals
- Not: teachers choose whatever they want, regardless of school needs

➤ **Principal holds staff accountable**
- Rewards and recognizes high performance
- Rids school of low performers

Questions to Ask

➤ What kinds of improvements have you been able to make?
➤ How are professional development activities for teachers chosen?
➤ **Have you ever had to fire a teacher who was not getting students to learn?**

Teachers:
➤ Do you have freedom to make changes in how you teach day-to-day to make sure every student is learning? Examples?
➤ Do you feel pushed by the principal to perform? Examples?
➤ Do you think the principal recognizes good teacher performance?
➤ Does the principal help you if you are having trouble teaching a student in your class? How?
➤ Do you like your job? (Listen for: "Yes. It's hard work, but we achieve a lot." Or "Yes. It's hard work, but we have a huge impact on children here.")

Parents:
➤ Has your child had *consistently* good teachers?
➤ If not, what did principal do about the ineffective teacher(s)? Is that teacher still at the school?

Written Materials:
➤ Look for kudos given to high-performing teachers who help school meet its goals
➤ Beware if principal or written material gives only blanket praise to all teachers, regardless of performance (blanket "thank you" is fine, but also look for recognition for highest performers)
➤ Do test scores show weakness in a single grade or class that goes unaddressed by principal?

Observations:
➤ Do you see consistent teacher quality across school? If not, does principal have a plan for improving the situation quickly?

Child Needs:
Ways to Get What You Don't Get at School

How to Use This Table:
➤ Read sections matching your child's Must Haves and Nice to Haves.
➤ Identify which child needs you can most easily meet outside of school.
➤ Once you have chosen a school, use to help plan non-school experiences for your child.
➤ Some of the suggested actions, such as hiring a tutor, seeing a counselor, and enrolling your child in activities, can be expensive. Local community organizations, public libraries, and other agencies, however, may offer some of these services and activities free or at reduced prices.
➤ Add your own ideas! (And, if you like, share them with other parents at **PickyParent.com**)

Child Characteristic	Ways to Get What You Don't Get at School
WHAT YOUR CHILD LEARNS	

Basic Learning Capability

Your child's readiness for learning in core academic subjects

If school is not a good fit for your child's Basic Learning Capability, keep track of the following items, especially ones that are Must Haves for your child (see BLC categories below)

➤ **Pace:** What your child knows and can do, particularly in reading, math and writing. Look at your child's work after it is completed and graded. Ideally, compare your child's current level of mastery to the school's standards for current and surrounding grades (or state or national standards).

➤ **Breadth:** Topics covered, and not covered, in your child's curriculum. Assess how the non-basic subjects covered *reinforce* basic subjects, *motivate* and interest your child, and cover broadening topics that *you value*.

➤ **Critical Thinking:** How much your child's program includes analytical problem solving (non-fiction writing, projects, research, other chances to figure out problems and organize steps to reach a goal), conceptual thinking (projects, research, all writing except purely descriptive) and creative thinking (creative writing of stories, poetry, drama; creative art; thinking of own topics or research questions for study; other chances to think of new ideas)

➤ **Social Needs:** Keep track of your child's successes and challenges in developing positive relationships with other children, both one-on-one and in groups.

In general, consider the following non-school sources for educational and developmental assistance with your child:
➤ Extracurricular activities with other children in groups outside of school
➤ Individual private lessons or tutoring
➤ Individual counseling with a psychologist or other trained counselor
➤ Set aside work time, and help your child pursue activities independently (e.g., provide needed transportation, materials, equipment and space for work at home)
➤ Take your child to public facilities, such as museums and libraries, that have information and exhibits
➤ Help your child find biographies of people who have traits in common with your child
➤ Help your child find websites to educate and develop
➤ Purchase computer software to develop your child's skill and knowledge
➤ Form an out-of-school club with similar children
➤ Help your child find friends with similar characteristics
➤ Seek out community organizations that support children and families like yours

Basic Learning Capability:
Extremely Challenged

...continues

➤ **Pace:** Must Have.
  • Arrange private at-home or small group tutoring tailored to your child's current level of capability
➤ **Breadth:** Must Have.
  • Arrange private at home or small group activities to teach life skills (taking care of self, organizing the steps of a healthy and safe day)
  • Select activities to stimulate multiple senses and brain regions. For example: playing

    Continues...

Child Needs:
Ways to Get What You Don't Get at School ...continued

Child Characteristic	Ways to Get What You Don't Get at School
WHAT YOUR CHILD LEARNS...continued	

Basic Learning Capability: **Extremely Challenged** ...*continued*	and moving to music; painting, clay work and other "touch" activities; physical activity with whole body (e.g., swimming, dancing) and small muscles (e.g., ball play, painting, drawing); viewing a stimulating visual environment (e.g. pictures on walls of animals and nature, posters of basic life skill activities) • Enroll your child in enjoyable non-school activities, with similarly able children or more typical ones. Discuss your child's abilities and needs with instructors in advance ➤ **Critical Thinking:** Less Important. • Help your child learn basic life skill problem solving (taking care of self, organizing the steps of a healthy and safe day) ➤ **Social Needs:** Must Have. • Join or organize community groups or small "play group" so your child may enjoy social and/or learning activities with similar children • Arrange one-on-one play time with similar children
Basic Learning Capability: **Challenged**	➤ **Pace:** Must Have. • Review your child's completed and graded school work and home work • If child is having difficulty, immediately discuss with teacher tactics for helping with school work at home • Do drills (repetitive studying) and try other ways of helping your child study current school topics at home. Or, hire tutor (or see if school can provide) for additional study of basic school topics • If child is "acing" every assignment in some subjects, but struggling in others, have your child tested immediately to see if a learning disability is leading to uneven performance. School may provide testing or you may seek through a private counselor ➤ **Breadth:** Nice to Have. • Help your child choose a *limited* number of extracurricular activities to pursue (in groups, with private tutors, etc.) • Ensure that, *over time,* your child is exposed to mix of physical, creative, analytical, artistic, language and mathematical/scientific topics and sensory experiences. Non-school activities are more likely to broaden knowledge than to motivate or reinforce school academic learning, since activities will not be coordinated with current school work ➤ **Critical Thinking:** Nice to Have. • Encourage creativity and problem solving in your child's home life. Get child's input into creative activities (e.g., decorating, landscaping). Allow or pay child to take on multi-step home projects; help child plan work steps before doing the work, and encourage self-critiquing of own work at end • Provide materials at home that encourage creativity (art, music, story tapes, fiction books) and problem solving (crosswords, puzzles, step-by-step models, brain teasers, non-fiction books) • Help your child find extracurricular activities of interest that develop creative and conceptual thinking (e.g., art, drama, science) and problem solving (e.g., chess club, carpentry) ➤ **Social Needs:** • Encourage child to develop friendships with many types of children from many sources (school, neighborhood, religious organizations, extracurricular activities)
Basic Learning Capability: **Typical** ...*continues*	➤ **Pace:** Must Have. • Review child's completed and graded school work • If child is having more difficulty than previously, discuss with teacher tactics for reinforcing school work at home

Continues...

Child Needs:
Ways to Get What You Don't Get at School ...continued

Child Characteristic	Ways to Get What You Don't Get at School
WHAT YOUR CHILD LEARNS...continued	

| Basic Learning Capability:
Typical

...continued | • Do drills (repetitive studying) and try other ways of helping your child study current school topics at home. Or, hire tutor (or see if school can provide) for additional study of basic school topics
• If child is "acing" every assignment, add pacing activities:
  • Teach your child to face new mental challenges in core academic areas (reading, math, writing) by introducing more advanced skills and concepts than school offers
  • Do "school at home" in non-school hours, either yourself or by hiring a tutor in core areas (math, reading, writing). Use school's own standards, learning goals or curriculum outline to determine next challenging steps, if possible
• If child is "acing" assignments in some subjects or types of work, but struggling in others, have your child tested immediately to see if a learning disability is leading to uneven performance. School may provide testing or you may seek through a private counselor

➤ **Breadth:** Nice to Have.
• Help your child choose a *limited* number of extracurricular activities to pursue (in groups, with private tutors, etc.)
• Ensure that, *over time,* your child is exposed to mix of physical, creative, analytical, artistic, language and mathematical/scientific topics and sensory experiences. Non-school activities are more likely to broaden knowledge than to motivate or reinforce school academic learning, since activities will not be coordinated with current school work

➤ **Critical Thinking:** Nice to Have.
• Encourage creativity and problem solving in your child's home life. Get child's input into creative activities (e.g., decorating, landscaping). Allow or pay child to take on multi-step home projects; help child plan work steps before doing the work, and encourage self-critiquing of own work at end
• Provide materials at home that encourage creativity (art, music, story tapes, fiction books) and problem solving (crosswords, puzzles, step-by-step models, brain teasers, nonfiction books)
• Help your child find extracurricular activities of interest that develop creative and conceptual thinking (e.g., art, drama, science) and problem solving (e.g., chess club, carpentry)

➤ **Social Needs:**
• Encourage child to develop friendships with many types of children from many sources (school, neighborhood, religious organizations, extracurriculars) |
| Basic Learning Capability:
Bright/Gifted

...continues | ➤ **Pace:** Must Have.
• Teach your child to face new mental challenges in core academic areas (reading, math, writing) by introducing more advanced skills and concepts than school offers
• Do "school at home" in non-school hours, either yourself or by hiring a tutor in core areas (math, reading, writing). Use school's own standards for current and higher grades to determine next challenging steps, if possible

➤ **Breadth:** Nice to Have.
• Help your child choose a *limited* number of extracurricular activities to pursue (in groups, with private tutors, etc.)
• Ensure that, **over time,** your child is exposed to mix of physical, creative, analytical, artistic, language and mathematical/scientific topics and sensory experiences. Non-school activities are more likely to broaden knowledge than to motivate or reinforce school academic learning, since activities will not be coordinated with current school work |

Continues...

Child Needs:
Ways to Get What You Don't Get at School *...continued*

Child Characteristic	Ways to Get What You Don't Get at School
	WHAT YOUR CHILD LEARNS...continued
Basic Learning Capability: **Bright/Gifted** *...continued*	➤ **Critical Thinking:** Must Have. • Encourage creativity and problem solving in your child's home life. Get child's input into creative activities (e.g., decorating, landscaping). Allow or pay child to take on multi-step home projects; help child plan work steps before doing the work, and encourage self-critiquing of own work at end • Provide materials at home that encourage creativity (art, music, story tapes, fiction books) and problem solving (crosswords, puzzles, models, brain teasers, nonfiction books) • Help your child find extracurricular activities of interest that develop creative and conceptual thinking (e.g., art, drama, science) and problem solving (e.g., chess club, science club) ➤ **Social Needs:** • Encourage child to develop friendships with many types of children from many sources (school, neighborhood, religious organizations, extracurriculars) • If child attends school with few bright/gifted children, then play match-maker to help your child meet and develop relationships with similar-capability peers
Basic Learning Capability: **Highly Gifted**	➤ **Pace:** Must Have. • Teach your child to face new mental challenges in core academic areas (reading, math, writing) by introducing more advanced skills and concepts than school offers • Do "school at home" in non-school hours, either yourself or by hiring a tutor in core areas (math, reading, writing). Use school's own standards for higher grades to determine next challenging steps, if possible ➤ **Breadth:** Nice to Have. • Help your child choose a *limited* number of extracurricular activities to pursue (in groups, with private tutors, etc.) • Ensure that, *over time,* your child is exposed to mix of physical, creative, analytical, artistic, language and mathematical/scientific topics and sensory experiences. Non-school activities are more likely to broaden knowledge than to motivate or reinforce school academic learning, since activities will not be coordinated with current school work • Consider choosing activities likely to draw other highly gifted children for combined breadth and social development (discuss with program directors, if possible) ➤ **Critical Thinking:** Must Have. Critical component to challenge and satisfy these children. • Encourage creativity and problem solving in your child's home life. Get child's input into creative activities (e.g., decorating, landscaping). Allow or pay child to take on multi-step home projects; help child plan work steps before doing the work, and encourage self-critiquing of own work at end • Provide materials at home that encourage creativity (art, music, story tapes, fiction books) and problem solving (crosswords, puzzles, models, brain teasers, nonfiction books) • Help your child find extracurricular activities of interest that use creative and conceptual thinking (e.g., art, drama, science) and problem solving (e.g., chess club, science club) ➤ **Social Needs:** Must Have. • Play match-maker to help your child meet and develop relationships with similar-capability peers • Coach (or hire psychologist skilled in this area to coach) child in social skills needed to develop friendships with others, even when child "feels different" • Seek "matches" from many sources (school, neighborhood, religious organizations, extracurriculars)

Continues...

Child Needs:
Ways to Get What You Don't Get at School ...continued

Child Characteristic	Ways to Get What You Don't Get at School

WHAT YOUR CHILD LEARNS...continued

Other Capabilities

➤ Musical
➤ Artistic
➤ Physical & Hands-on
➤ Social & Leadership
➤ Creativity
➤ English as Second Language

If your child's school does not nurture your child's strengths or develop weaknesses adequately, consider these alternatives:

➤ Extracurricular activities with other children in groups outside of school; this allows your child to develop the capability while meeting others who value the same capability

➤ Individual private lessons or tutoring in area of capability; this allows child to maximize individual achievement in capability

➤ Set aside independent work time, and help your child pursue the capability (e.g., provide needed transportation, materials, equipment and space for activity at home)

➤ Take your child to public facilities – such as museums, libraries, and parks – that have information, exhibits and equipment where your child can pursue or learn about child's area of capability

➤ Help your child find biographies of people who have excelled in this area of capability

➤ Help your child find websites about the area of capability

➤ Purchase computer software to improve your child's skill and knowledge

➤ Help child form out-of-school club with friends and others who share the capability

➤ Help your child find friends who share the capability for informal play and work

To develop or nurture **Social & Leadership Capability**:

➤ Enroll your child in group extracurricular activities in which children are able to work together as a group or in pairs. Structured, adult-directed activities alone are not enough. Some of this time needs to be unstructured, with children allowed to make some decisions and work as a group and in pairs

➤ Arrange one-on-one play time and small group activities for your child. Some of these interactions should be with school classmates and can be at your home or the friend's or in extracurricular activities. Some of this time needs to be unstructured, with no grownup dictating activities, for child to develop these skills fully

➤ Take on the role of coach to develop your child's interpersonal skills. Help child recognize and identify emotions and needs of others, and act and communicate appropriately in response. Coach before and after social interactions, not during, so as not to embarrass your child

➤ Hire counselor if your child needs significant interpersonal development or is emotionally fragile as a result of *under*developed social skills

To develop or nurture **Creativity**:

➤ Read your child stories about imaginary people, places and things, including stories about other children who use their imaginations

➤ Tell your child stories about imaginary places and people; encourage your child to tell you similar stories; take turns with your child telling one line each from a story and see how the story progresses as you create together

➤ Once your child is reading, obtain books about imaginary people, places and things, including stories about other children who use their imaginations

➤ Provide toys and materials that require imagination, and make sure your child has big blocks of time each week time with no TV, computer or other "spoon fed" activities. Example indoor materials – plain wooden blocks and other building materials; cloth scraps, yarn, string; a large stack of plain paper, colored pencils, crayons, markers, a glue stick, scissors and tape; plain paper bags, cups and plates; modeling clay or dough. Example outdoor materials – a pile of sticks, mulch, and/or rocks; a small wooden bridge, shovels and buckets, a bird house, a sand box; a simple playhouse

...continues

Continues...

Child Needs:
Ways to Get What You Don't Get at School ...continued

Child Characteristic	Ways to Get What You Don't Get at School

WHAT YOUR CHILD LEARNS...continued

Other Capabilities
➤ Musical
➤ Artistic
➤ Physical & Hands-on
➤ Social & Leadership
➤ Creativity
➤ English as Second
  Language

...continued

(*without* "real" cookware, furniture, etc.)

➤ Model creativity yourself. Think out loud with your child about different ways to do things, from decorating the dinner table to new ways to solve problems you face in your adult life (at work, in volunteer activities, in planning home life). Ask yourself out loud in front of child, "what if ...?"

➤ Prompt your child to think of new ideas and different ways to do things. Include concrete tasks like decorating the child's bedroom or deciding what flowers to plant in the window box. Include less tangible tasks like writing about new ideas and imaginary situations in school assignments. Ask your child "what if ...?"

To develop **English as a Second Language** skills:

➤ Search your community for an international support organization, either focusing on people from your country of origin (or your child's if adopted) or on immigrants in general. Find out what services are available for children

➤ Enroll your child in English classes for children in your community

➤ Invite native English-speaking children over to your house to play. This will ensure that your child has one-on-one conversations to teach "social" English speaking and listening

➤ Check out books and books-on-tape in English at your local library. Books on tape paired with accompanying paper books allow your child to *hear and see* the words at the same time. Ask your librarian for help or get an English-speaking friend to go with you to help communicate with the librarian the first time. Get to know one librarian who can help you and your child on later visits. Your child's school librarian may be able to help you find materials in your child's school library

➤ Check out or purchase computer software specifically designed to teach English reading, listening, speaking and writing to children

➤ Check out or purchase software designed to teach *English-speaking* children letters, reading and writing. Start with preschool software, and encourage your child to advance as quickly as possible until reaching the grade your child currently attends

➤ Hire a private tutor to provide individual or small group English lessons to your child

➤ Strive to learn English yourself, and force yourself to speak it at designated times (e.g., at the dinner table or when you are in public with your child)

Interests

If your child's school does not cover your child's interest adequately, consider these alternatives:

➤ Extracurricular activities with other children in groups outside of school; this allows child to develop the interest while meeting others who share interest

➤ Individual private lessons or tutoring in area of interest; this allows child to maximize individual achievement in interest area

➤ Set aside independent work time, and help your child pursue the interest (e.g., provide needed transportation, materials, equipment and space for work at home)

➤ Take your child to public facilities, such as museums and libraries, that have information and exhibits about child's area of interest

➤ Help your child find biographies of people who have excelled in your child's area of interest

➤ Help your child find websites about the area of interest

➤ If appropriate to interest, purchase computer software to improve your child's skill and knowledge

➤ Help child form out-of-school club with friends and others who share the interest

➤ Help your child find friends who share the interest for informal play and work

Continues...

Child Needs:
Ways to Get What You Don't Get at School ...continued

Child Characteristic	Ways to Get What You Don't Get at School
HOW YOUR CHILD LEARNS	

Learning Styles
➤ Visual
➤ Auditory
➤ Kinesthetic/Tactile

In general, if school does not emphasize child's strengths or develop child's weaknesses:
➤ Help your child become aware of his/her favored and less-favored learning styles
➤ Help your child feel proud of and use learning style strengths at home and in non-school activities
➤ For child with extreme strength that is making school difficult or unpleasant (for self or others), discuss with child possible ways to minimize the negative impact on the child and others
➤ Help child develop weaker learning styles through consistent exposure to materials and activities that develop those senses, at home and through other non-school activities
➤ Plan and discuss your efforts with teacher, when possible

Learning Style:
Visual

To develop or nurture **Visual Learning** when school does not, try these:
➤ Create home environment with visually stimulating and interesting walls and decorations (e.g., let child help decorate own room or space in room)
➤ Ensure child has at least one neatly organized place to spend time at home; help child set up routines to keep personal space neat; provide containers, shelves that help child with organization
➤ Provide materials (paper, colored pencils) and show child how to make a visual reinforcement for things learned at school: diagrams, tables, lists, etc.
➤ Encourage child to take notes and draw diagrams while listening to teacher

For **extreme visual learners:**
➤ Remind child about room changes in advance of each day's school activities (e.g., "remember, you have art and science lab today at school"). Ask teacher to do the same when possible
➤ Teach child relaxation techniques to use when school becomes too visually stimulating (deep breathing, closing eyes for 5 seconds, etc.)
➤ Teach child focusing techniques when school is not visually stimulating enough (e.g., taking notes, drawing pictures or diagrams related to learning task)

Learning Style:
Auditory

To develop or nurture **Auditory Learning** when school does not, try these:
➤ Encourage child to talk about school. Ask child very specific questions about what happened at school (e.g., what they learned today, favorite activities, the children with whom they played or ate)
➤ Ask child to tell you what (s)he learned in each academic area that day at school.
➤ Ensure that some non-school activities are done in small groups (or one-on-one with tutor) where talking is allowed or encouraged
➤ Encourage family discussions at dinner time and other meals. Make sure everyone takes a turn. Teach your child that it is important to participate by talking and by listening.
➤ Encourage child to read homework assignments aloud
➤ Obtain a tape recorder the child can operate and urge child to use to record thoughts and answers to homework assignments prior to writing them down

For **extreme auditory** learners:
➤ Help child organize social events (one-on-one or small groups) with other children who like to talk
➤ Provide a place in your home where your child may "talk to self" while she unwinds after school
➤ Teach child relaxation techniques (e.g., deep breathing, count one-two-three) to use when school is too loud
➤ Teach child focusing techniques when school does not allow enough talking (e.g., quietly verbalizing material, asking teacher relevant questions)

Continues...

Child Needs:
Ways to Get What You Don't Get at School ...continued

Child Characteristic	Ways to Get What You Don't Get at School
HOW YOUR CHILD LEARNS...continued	

Learning Style: **Kinesthetic/ Tactile**	To develop or nurture **Kinesthetic Learning** (whole body) when school does not, try these: ➤ Preserve a significant amount of time after school and on weekends for child to engage in physical activities of choice (at home, in group extracurriculars, at local park, etc.) ➤ Create open space in home where child can move body (less furniture, more wide spaces); change house setup and rules to allow child to dance, do somersaults, dramatize, etc. ➤ Set aside time every day for your child to do outdoor exercise ➤ Allow child to do homework in multiple appropriate positions: on floor, at table, sitting, standing, lying down ➤ Encourage child to dramatize or build models at home to help learn school material; show teacher when practical ➤ Allow some breaks for physical activity (stretching, short walk around block, jump rope) while child does homework ➤ If child is an **extreme kinesthetic learner**: Encourage your child to set and stick to time goals for completion of tasks (allowing for movement while doing) To develop or nurture **Tactile Learning** ("fine motor" work with hands) when school does not, try these: ➤ At home, provide "hands-on" materials that support your child's school learning, including models, crafts, puzzles, blocks, felt or magnetic storyboards, art paper and drawing materials, a wide variety of pencils and pens, scissors, glue sticks, beads and string, cloth to cut, and small gardening tools. Let child do own work with these ➤ Encourage child to create models and physical products related to school work; allow child to show products to teacher ➤ If Child is an **extreme tactile learner**: Teach your child how to "fidget" and "doodle" without disrupting others (hands under desk, small movements); teach your child note-taking to keep hands busy during class
Motivation *...continues*	If motivation is a **weakness** and school is not tracking your child's progress and achievement compared to capabilities, try these activities: ➤ Let each of your child's teachers know that you are concerned about your child not making his best effort on work and that you want to be informed right away if they see problems arise ➤ With your child's participation, set very clear academic goals for child. Goals should be challenging but achievable "next steps" starting from child's current capabilities. Make a plan that includes steps to attain each goal (including what child and parent will do, how you will involve teacher, amount of time needed each day or week, and when you think each goal should be met) ➤ Ensure that your child has uninterrupted time to complete homework each day ➤ Check your child's completed homework and school work. Praise good effort often. If you see mistakes, ask child to check his own work and correct problems (on his own before you help) ➤ Consider hiring a tutor once each week to work with your child one-on-one, especially if your child responds well to personal attention. Tutor may perform some of parent tasks listed above, as well ➤ Communicate frequently (at least weekly) with teacher; write a little note or call teacher (ask which method she prefers) about progress or problems you see at home in child's development and learning If motivation is **typical** and school is not keeping track of progress compared to child's capability, regularly remind your *child* to take these steps on own: ➤ Set small next-step goals ➤ Set aside homework time each day

Continues...

Child Needs:
Ways to Get What You Don't Get at School ...continued

Child Characteristic	Ways to Get What You Don't Get at School
HOW YOUR CHILD LEARNS...continued	

Motivation

...continued

➤ Check own work and make corrections
➤ Tell teacher and parents if struggling with schoolwork, not feeling motivated

If motivation is a **strength** but child does not have the chance to set own goals and work beyond grade level at school:

➤ Provide child plenty of free time and materials of interest to pursue own goals after school
➤ Support child's decisions to pursue learning or extracurricular goals, even when they seem to be "beyond" what parent would expect from child of this age
➤ Do not hover over child regarding homework; let child structure and plan own work time after school (but do help child when asked)
➤ If child becomes too tired or overburdened by taking on too much, coach child to choose highest priority interests. Help child learn to plan day to accomplish his/her priority goals

Physical or Mental Health Challenges

Physical Health Challenges
➤ Before school begins:
  • Determine with principal and child's teachers which activities will be affected for your child due to your child's physical condition and lack of proper facilities
  • Determine with principal and teachers how any required treatment, medication and likely emergencies will be handled
  • Communicate your expectations for how child should be treated by teachers in classroom and other school activities
  • Express your desire for teachers to monitor teasing, taunting and other inappropriate behavior by other students; discuss how you can help your child respond to minimize bad treatment by others
  • Ask principal for names of other parents with similar children in the school; make an effort to get to know these parents and share ideas
➤ During school year:
  • Monitor child's academic, physical, social and emotional development. Discuss any concerns immediately with teachers and/or principal
  • Coach, or hire counselor to coach, your child in how to build friendships (and deal with rude peers)

Mental Health Challenges
➤ Before school begins:
  • Determine with principal and teachers how any required treatment, medication and potential emergencies will be handled
  • Provide your child's teacher with a short written list of the symptoms of your child's mental illness, and ask teacher to let you know if symptoms appear to be worsening at school
➤ During school year:
  • Ask your child about school work and school social interactions *every day*. Listen
  • Monitor child's academic, physical, social and emotional development. Discuss any concerns immediately with teachers and/or principal
  • Ensure that your child is receiving appropriate counseling and medication outside of school

Behavior Challenges

...continues

➤ Before school begins:
  • Be sure that you have considered having or have had your child tested by a psychologist for underlying causes of poor behavior; address those underlying causes as well as the behavior that results

Continues...

Child Needs:
Ways to Get What You Don't Get at School ...continued

Child Characteristic	Ways to Get What You Don't Get at School
	HOW YOUR CHILD LEARNS...continued

Behavior Challenges
...continued

- Consider formulating a behavioral discipline plan with your child's psychologist; include actions that parent(s) should take at home and teachers should take at school. Share with school and discuss with child's teacher and principal
- Provide your child's teachers and principal with a short written list of *specific behaviors your child has displayed* previously that are disruptive to his own and other student's learning
- Provide your child's teachers and principal with a short written list of *parent and teacher actions that have been effective* in helping your child learn and display self control and focus on school work
- Ask your child's teacher to inform you *immediately* when your child's behavior hampers his own or other students' learning
- Discuss and determine with your child's principal and teachers how each of you will respond to child's behavior at school and at home

➤ During school year:
- Monitor child's academic, physical, social and emotional development. Discuss any concerns immediately with teachers and/or principal
- Increase the frequency of contact and informal communication with your child's teacher: escort your child to class or pick child up from class several times each week
- Hire a counselor for your child to help him learn to understand his feelings and control behavior in response
- Consider obtaining counseling for yourself and other adults who take care of your child outside of school to improve your own effectiveness and consistency dealing with your child's behavior

Learning Disabilities & Disorders

If school does not address your child's educational, social or other developmental needs, try the following:

➤ **All needs:**
- Communicate regularly – before and during school year – with both principal and teacher about child's progress in school and any steps you are taking outside of school to help child
- Join or form group of parents who have children with similar disabilities for support and information exchange

➤ If your child's **educational needs** are not met at school: Hire private tutor or enroll your child in after school tutoring service. Tutors should be trained to educate children with your child's specific disability. You should establish with the tutor
- a regular schedule for appointments and
- clear goals for your child's educational progress

➤ If your child's **social needs** are not met at school:
- Join group or sign child up for activities with children who share the same or similar disability. You need not isolate your child from more typical peers, but most children will benefit from having some relationships with others who are coping with similar challenges
- Help your child find individual friends who share same or similar disabilities. Coach your child to improve social skills. The more "different" your child feels, the stronger his social skills need to be to build social bridges between himself and others
- Acknowledge that many children, particularly ones with an obvious disability, will feel socially awkward around more typical children. Help your child cope with these feelings while learning to reach out to other children despite setbacks

➤ If your child's **developmental** needs are not met at school: Hire counselor or therapist to help your child overcome the disability/disorder to the extent possible, learn to

...continues

Continues...

Child Needs:
Ways to Get What You Don't Get at School ...continued

Child Characteristic	Ways to Get What You Don't Get at School
HOW YOUR CHILD LEARNS...continued	

Learning Disabilities & Disorders

...continued

accommodate the disability using child's stronger capabilities, and cope with feelings of frustration about the disability. Counselors and therapists should be trained to help children with your child's specific disability. This person may be the same as the educational tutor, but note that your child may need developmental and emotional support that a tutor focusing on educational achievement cannot provide. You should establish with the counselor or therapist

• a regular schedule for appointments and
• clear goals for your child's developmental progress

Self-Understanding

If school does not fit your child's other needs well or does not actively teach children self-understanding:

➤ Work extra hard to accommodate your child's other needs outside of school (see sections regarding your child's specific Must Have needs)
➤ Hire a counselor (psychologist, social worker, or education counselor) trained to coach children your child's age to develop self-awareness (also called "intrapersonal intelligence," "emotional intelligence")
➤ Ask your child daily after school to tell you about best and worst parts of day, how he/she felt, what he/she plans to do to address any problems or take advantage of good things that may have arisen. Give advice only after child has had chance to express and think through issues on own
➤ Allow your child to make simple choices often (among options amenable to you), starting as young as possible. Regularly ask why she made choices, what she's giving up, how someone else she knows might have made a different decision, whether the choice was hard, and how she feels about it after the fact
➤ Help your child make thoughtful decisions about activities, friends, and school work
➤ Encourage your child to consider own strengths, weaknesses, likes and dislikes in decisions
➤ When your child makes a decision about activities, friends or school work, affirm the decision and also ask him why he's made that particular decision ("That sound's great – you may go over to Jane's house tomorrow. Tell me what you like about Jane?" or "Sure, you may switch from soccer to Karate lessons this year. What got you interested in that?")
➤ In general, encourage your child to value his own time and to make thoughtful decisions about how he uses it
➤ Ask your child often about what he likes and doesn't like, what his own strengths are, what his challenges are, and how he feels
➤ Tell your child's teachers about improvements or changes you see in your child's academic, social, emotional and physical development

SOCIAL ISSUES

Friends

If school does not include your child's current friends:

➤ Before school starts, invite children (and parents) who are going to new school to meet at your house, nearby park, school playground, skating rink or other social setting and
➤ Help your child build new friendships by having other children from new school over to your house after school starts (ask your child who to have and/or get teacher's advice)
➤ Help your child continue old friendships for some time after starting new school with activities outside of school (e.g., play dates, non-school extracurricular activities)
➤ Help your child strengthen neighborhood and other non-school friendships by inviting friends over on a regular basis

...continues

Continues...

Child Needs:
Ways to Get What You Don't Get at School

Child Characteristic	Ways to Get What You Don't Get at School
SOCIAL ISSUES...*continued*	
Friends ...*continued*	➤ Take steps yourself, or through a counselor, to coach and develop your child's inter-personal skills with peers (for one-on-one and group interactions) If school class will not have enough other children of your child's gender: ➤ Discuss with school leadership possibility of recruiting additional children of your child's gender to school and classroom ➤ Plan one play date each week with a friend of your child's same gender from outside of school ➤ Consider scheduling afternoon or weekend activities with child's non-school, same-gender friends
PRACTICAL MATTERS	
Essential Activities	If school schedule does not allow your child to pursue high-priority non-school activities: ➤ First, decide if the extracurricular activity or need is truly important enough to inter-rupt your child's school schedule. If it is, and your chosen school's schedule cannot accommodate the activity, then ... ➤ Make special arrangements with school for missed time and schoolwork: • Hire tutor (or parent may tutor) in subjects where work is missed, and • Coordinate both daily schedule and missed work with teachers and principal ➤ Ensure that your child's academic performance does not suffer. A school is far more likely to be accommodating if your child's academic performance is high ➤ Consider home schooling – alone, with a tutor, or in conjunction with parents of similar children

Family Needs:
Ways to Get What You Don't Get at School

How to Use This Table:
➤ Read sections matching your family's Must Haves and Nice to Haves.
➤ Identify which family needs you can most easily meet outside of school.
➤ Once you have chosen a school, use to help plan non-school actions and experiences for your child and family.
➤ Add your own ideas! (And, if you like, share them with other parents at **PickyParent.com**)

Family Characteristic	Ways to Get What You Don't Get at School
WHAT YOUR CHILD LEARNS	
Values about what *content* is important	If your child's school does not cover valued subject or topics, try these actions: ➤ Afternoon, evening or weekend family activities that cover subject area ➤ Extracurricular activities in subject with group of other children outside of school ➤ Individual private lessons or tutoring for child in subject ➤ Set aside independent work time for child, and help child pursue the subject (e.g., by providing needed transportation, materials, equipment and space for work at home) ➤ Parent tutors or coaches child ➤ Summer camps or classes
Goals for your child: ➤ Grade progression ➤ Academic performance ➤ College opportunity	If your child's school may not be well-suited to ensure that your child reaches your goals, see the row below that corresponds to that goal
Goals for your child: **Grade Progression**	➤ Tell teachers that you want them to expect a lot from your child, and ask how you can support them at home ➤ Tell your child that you expect him/her to try hard at school ➤ Check your child's home and school work frequently ➤ Praise your child's good efforts, and help your child recognize and solve problems with school work ➤ Set aside time each day for your child to do homework and other basic skill practice ➤ Seek tutoring assistance in required subjects through school – discuss with teacher and principal ➤ Hire private tutor for child or seek assistance of private tutoring service
Goals for your child: **Academic Performance**	➤ Check your child's school and home work frequently ➤ If child is consistently having difficulty, try steps for grade progression above ➤ If child consistently performing at very top, seek teacher and principal's advice for ways to challenge child outside of school ➤ See Basic Learning Capability section of Child Needs tables for ways to ensure that your child performs *at least* at level of current academic readiness
Goals for your child: **College Opportunity**	➤ See Basic Learning Capability in Child Needs tables for ways to develop your child's academic performance outside of school. Consider schools outside of your immediate location (across county or state lines; family move)
HOW YOUR CHILD LEARNS	
Values about school-wide expectations and rules on student conduct ...*continues*	If your child's school does not have rules or other reinforcement of the social behaviors you value: ➤ Keep a written list of values you want to encourage, and have clear conversations with your child about your expectations ➤ Discuss with your child how to get along with others who are different in values, beliefs and behaviors

Continues...

Family Needs:
Ways to Get What You Don't Get at School *...continued*

Family Characteristic	Ways to Get What You Don't Get at School
HOW YOUR CHILD LEARNS...*continued*	

<table>
<tr>
<td>

Values about school-wide expectations and rules on student conduct

➤ Manners with other children and adults
➤ Dress
➤ Discipline
➤ Honor code
➤ Other behaviors

...continued

</td>
<td>

➤ Discuss with child values of others, why others have different values, and why you have yours
➤ Discuss ways of dealing with peers who behave in undesirable ways and who pressure your child to do the same
➤ Consistently reinforce your valued manners, dress, ethics and other behaviors with your children at home
➤ Model, with your own words and actions, expected values and behaviors
➤ Buy or borrow books and audio stories (fiction and nonfiction) for your child that reinforce your family's values; make sure materials are appropriate for your child's age
➤ Help your child find friends outside of school who reflect your family's values; encourage these friendships by inviting friends to your house to play and by getting to know parents
➤ Use discipline methods at home that are consistent with your values

</td>
</tr>
<tr>
<td>

Values about how children should *learn*:

Teaching method

➤ Teacher directed
➤ Student discovery
➤ Mixed approach

</td>
<td>

➤ **Teacher directed.** *If you can't get this at school:*
• Discuss with teacher at beginning of year any concerns you have about less-directive teaching style with your child
• Regularly (at least weekly) discuss current school learning goals and activities with your child to ensure that they are clear
• Encourage child to speak in class
• Encourage child to ask teacher questions when uncertain about what to do
• Encourage child to take initiative in choosing and completing own work
• Arrange or provide tutoring for your child if you become concerned about mastery of basic subjects
➤ **Student discovery.** *If you can't get this at school:*
• Discuss with teacher at beginning of year any concerns you have about more-directive style with your child
• Encourage your child to take school assignments beyond prescribed bounds at home, when child is interested in doing so
• Leave significant unstructured time for your child to pursue own interests and ideas at home
• Encourage child to be respectful of teacher's directive style, not to interrupt, to raise hand and wait patiently for questions

</td>
</tr>
<tr>
<td>

Values about how children should *learn*:

Classroom behavior management

➤ Controlling/Strict
➤ Developmental
➤ Mixed approach

</td>
<td>

➤ **Controlling/Strict.** *If you can't get this at school:*
• Ask teacher or principal to clarify expectations for child's behavior so that you can reinforce at home
• Set your own expectations, and consequences, for child's positive and negative behavior at school
• Communicate with your child's teacher frequently to get feedback on your child's behavior
➤ **Developmental.** *If you can't get this at school:*
• Give your child lots of positive attention at home – hug your child, listen to your child, spend time with your child
• Provide frequent, small rewards or recognition for positive behaviors at home
• Coach your child to improve self-control at home: help child identify sources of own emotions and control behavior in response
• If child gets into trouble at school, coach child about how to act differently next time
• Adapt after-school time to your child's unmet needs, if any, that may be leading to behavior problems (see *Child Needs: Ways to Get What You Don't Get at School*)
• Be sure you understand what behaviors are expected of your child at school, and reinforce at home, to help child adapt to school; inform teacher of your efforts

</td>
</tr>
</table>

Continues...

Family Needs:
Ways to Get What You Don't Get at School ...*continued*

Family Characteristic	Ways to Get What You Don't Get at School
HOW YOUR CHILD LEARNS...*continued*	

Your role as advocate for child (understanding, communicating and influencing school to address your child's learning needs). The greater *your* ability, the less important for school to help you.

If your child's school does not provide the help you need understanding and communicating about your child:
- ➤ Improve your *understanding* of your child's needs, through paid child/family counseling, reading about relevant topics, or joining appropriate community support groups
- ➤ Hire a tutor or counselor to help your child with unmet academic, social, emotional or physical needs
- ➤ Improve your *assertiveness and communication* skills through counseling or by joining a community support group
- ➤ Increase your *confidence communicating* with teachers and principal by volunteering at your child's school on a regular basis
- ➤ Communicate frequently with teacher about your child and your parenting efforts at home that affect school; use methods that are comfortable and manageable for you (e.g., short notes, phone messages, e-mail, dropping child off at classroom in person)
- ➤ If language or cultural differences are a barrier, ask a friend or family member who is more comfortable to help by joining you for parent conferences and other meetings with teacher; if this is a problem common in your child's school, consider meeting with principal to suggest that a school staff person help parents similar to yourself communicate well with teachers

SOCIAL ISSUES

Parent Community

I want my child's school to have parents with particular characteristics

If your child's school does not have the parents you prefer:
- ➤ Engage your child in extracurricular activities with children who have parents better matching your desired profile
- ➤ Engage your family in religious or other community organizations with families that better match your desired profile
- ➤ Encourage parents meeting your desired profile to send children to same school as your child
- ➤ If your child is exposed to parent behaviors you find objectionable, freely discuss with your child your opposing views, how you would act differently in a situation, and why other parents might have different values and behaviors
- ➤ Limit your interaction with other parents from child's school to essential activities

Parent Involvement in School
- ➤ Helping
- ➤ Decision-making
- ➤ Fundraising activities

If parents' role in school is not as extensive or of the type you would like:
- ➤ Be useful: discuss with principal, PTA chair or other school leader possible roles you might play that both utilize your talents and contribute to the school's quality, mission and goals
- ➤ Change the school: take on a leadership role in PTA and make increased or changed parent involvement your mission. Most principals are glad to have the help when parent involvement supports the school's quality, mission and goals
- ➤ Create new roles: if parent roles have been limited to helping with school's daily life, and you would rather play a decision-making or fundraising role (and have matching skills to contribute), discuss with principal, PTA chair or other leader how you might use your talents to help school

If parent role required is too much:
- ➤ Discuss with principal, PTA chair or other appropriate leader alternative ways you might help that fit your time and other constraints
- ➤ Ask for an exception, even if temporary
- ➤ Have a grandparent, other family member, family friend, or other adult make a time contribution as your substitute

Student Community ...*continues*

If your child's school does not have the students you prefer:
- ➤ Reserve time after school for play with children not attending your child's school
- ➤ Engage your child in extracurricular activities with children who better match desired profile

Continues...

Family Needs:
Ways to Get What You Don't Get at School ...continued

Family Characteristic	Ways to Get What You Don't Get at School
SOCIAL ISSUES...*continued*	
Student Community I want my child's school to have students with particular characteristics *...continued*	➤ Engage your family in religious or other community organizations with families that better match your desired profile ➤ Encourage parents with children meeting your desired profile to send their children to same school as your child ➤ If your child is exposed to other students' behaviors you find objectionable, freely discuss with your child your opposing views, how they could act differently in a situation, and why other students might have different values and behaviors ➤ Speak to the school's principal about any other concerns, particularly if you think your child's academic, social, emotional or physical development is being negatively affected by school peers
I want my child to attend a certain school, school type, or school design	If your child cannot attend your preferred school, school type, or school design: ➤ Using the *Great School Quality* and *Personalized Great Fit Checklists*, make a note of the offerings and characteristics you wanted or needed in your preferred school, school type, or school design, and ➤ Attempt to find an alternate school that most closely mimics the offerings you desired in preferred school, and ➤ For those characteristics you cannot find in a school elsewhere, use this table and the *Child Needs: Ways to Get What You Don't Get at School* table to get what you and your child need outside of school ➤ Consider re-applying or re-registering in following year(s)
PRACTICAL MATTERS	
Child Care ➤ Before school ➤ After school ➤ Holidays ➤ Summer	If you are unable to find a school with appropriate care, try these steps: ➤ Consider whether you can change your work hours (or other commitment times) to match your child's school schedule ➤ Consider alternative sources of child care you may not have considered before (e.g., neighbors, child's friends' parents, relatives, smaller child care settings such as family day care, swapping afternoon care for weekend evening care with a friend); check with your local child care resource and referral center about other options ➤ Consider extracurricular activities that might keep your child occupied during non-school hours, holidays, and vacations (e.g., camps, after school care at local children's centers)
Schedule ➤ Daily hours ➤ Yearly (start/finish and holidays)	If your children's schools have unchangeable schedule conflicts with each other or with your work: ➤ Consider whether you can change your work hours (or other commitment times) to match your child's school schedule ➤ Carpool, with you driving the segments that fit your schedule ➤ Take advantage of before or after school care offered by one of your children's schools so that you can stagger start/finish times for a manageable schedule; make sure you can use and pay for just the limited amount of care time you need ➤ For essential extracurricular activities, try to change extracurricular activity times or seek alternative instruction if there is conflict with school schedule ➤ For vacation conflicts, check school policies on children missing school; if you ensure that your child makes up missed work, you may be able to take one child out of school to match other child's vacation schedule
Transportation Needs *...continues*	If you cannot transport your child and no busing (or other school-provided transportation) is offered: ➤ Reconsider alternative means of transportation, according to child's age and maturity (e.g., city bus, subway)

Continues...

Family Needs:
Ways to Get What You Don't Get at School

Family Characteristic	Ways to Get What You Don't Get at School
PRACTICAL MATTERS...continued	

Family Characteristic	Ways to Get What You Don't Get at School
Transportation Needs ➤ To school ➤ After school ➤ After school activities ...*continued*	➤ Form carpool, and you drive segments that fit your schedule ➤ Pay neighbor (adult with nearby work or student at same or nearby school) to drive your child to school ➤ Organize vanpooling (a van with paid driver to take several children to and from school) at your child's school for your neighborhood ➤ If timing or child care is the issue, see Child Care and Schedule suggestions above
Location proximity to your home or work	➤ See suggestions in Child Care, Schedule, and Transportation sections above ➤ If need is related to child's health, explore alternative ways of meeting need; discuss with your doctor, local community agencies serving children like yours, principal and school nurse ➤ Consider home schooling your child, alone or in collaboration with other parents
Your other children	**Same School.** If all your children cannot attend same school even though you would like them to: ➤ See Child Care, Scheduling and Transportation sections above ➤ Reapply next year to family school if child was not admitted (if selective school, discuss reasons for not admitting with school admissions office, and work to develop child's school readiness) ➤ Seek multiple schools with compatible schedules ➤ Make time for siblings to interact after school and on weekends **Different Schools.** If your best option this year means sending children to same school even though you would prefer not to: ➤ Consider reapplying to suitable alternative school(s) in future years ➤ Help children distinguish themselves and develop confidence in their unique talents through extracurricular activities ➤ Discuss any concerns you may have with your children's principal and teachers to minimize any negative effects (e.g., assign different teachers to your children to reduce "shadow" of older siblings)
Money available to pay for school	If your best school option is too expensive: ➤ Discuss your conflict with principal or admissions office to see if any additional financial support is available ➤ Consider whether child's grandparents or other relatives might contribute financially to child's education ➤ Contact local agencies that may have private school assistance programs ➤ Review your overall family budget one more time to see if there are any areas where you can feasibly – and actually – cut spending ➤ Review your overall income options one more time to see if you have any ways of earning additional money If you are surprised that your best school option costs less than you anticipated: ➤ Donate money to your child's school ➤ Use some money for extracurricular activities, educational toys and educational travel ➤ Offer to reimburse your child's teachers up to a specified dollar amount for supplies they purchase for the class; or make an outright gift to school designated for your child's teacher to spend ➤ Offer to fund an extra class field trip related to child's class studies ➤ Offer to purchase school supplies and school clothes for a needy child attending the same school ➤ Spend less time making money and more volunteering at your child's school (or with your children after school)

Quality:
Ways to Get What You Don't Get at School

How to Use This Table:
➤ Read sections matching each Great School Quality Factor.
➤ Identify which Great School Quality Factor weaknesses you can most easily make up for outside of school.
➤ Once you have chosen a school, use to help plan non-school actions and experiences for your child and family.
➤ Add your own ideas! (And, if you like, share them with other parents at **PickyParent.com**)

Great School Quality Factor	*Ways to Get What You Don't Get at School*
GREAT SCHOOL QUALITY FACTOR #1	
Clear Mission Guiding School Activities	➤ If school has unclear or no written mission: Ask principal, teachers and parents about other Great School Quality and Fit Factors most important to your child and family. Are answers consistent, even though school does not have clear written mission?
	➤ If a Great School Quality or Fit Factor important to you is *inconsistently* addressed in school (because of unclear mission, goals, curriculum or teaching method): ask principal if you can influence which teachers your child is assigned to ensure quality and fit
	➤ Ask if principal would support formation of group to write new mission statement; be sure to show how mission is supported by school-wide achievement and improvement goals, student learning standards, curriculum and teaching method
	➤ If one or more aspects of school – school-wide goals, student learning standards, curriculum or teaching method – do not support mission: let principal know your concerns, discuss with other parents, and join or form committee to address specific areas that are out of alignment with mission
GREAT SCHOOL QUALITY FACTOR #2	
High Expectations for All Students ➤ High Minimum Expectations for All ➤ Higher Expectations for Students Who are Ready	➤ Set high expectations for both achievement and progress for your own child; do not rely on school to do this
	➤ Discuss with each of your child's teachers your expectations for your own child's achievement and progress; let teachers know that you want them to expect a lot of your child and that you will support them at home
	➤ Check your child's completed school and home work; praise your child's good efforts, help your child recognize and solve problems with work
	➤ If your child is at risk of not meeting grade level, ask teacher or principal about tutoring opportunities at school, hire a private tutor, or tutor child yourself. See *Child Needs: Ways to Get What You Don't Get at School* section for students Challenged in Basic Learning Capability for more ideas
	➤ If child is ready to advance beyond grade level but is not making further progress at school: obtain learning goals for higher grades, and hire tutor or provide your own "school at home" after school to help your child advance at faster pace. See *Child Needs: Ways to Get What You Don't Get at School* sections for children Gifted and Highly Gifted in Basic Learning Capability for more ideas
	➤ Inform child's teacher about your activities; the teacher may have ideas to help you
	➤ Consider organizing other parents and students to start academic clubs that foster a culture of thinking and academic pursuit, such as Odyssey of the Mind, chess, and the like. Get teacher support. Make the clubs visible on campus with posters, announcements, and contests that encourage many children to participate
GREAT SCHOOL QUALITY FACTOR #3	
Monitoring of Progress and Adjusting Teaching *...continues*	➤ Discuss with teacher your expectations for your own child's achievement and progress
	➤ Check your child's completed school and home work
	➤ If you do not see progress, and if your child is at risk of not meeting grade level: ask teacher or principal about tutoring opportunities at school, hire private tutor, or tutor child yourself. You may want to ask if school can provide (or you pay for private) assessment of child's interests, capabilities (academic, social, emotional and physical),

Continues...

Quality:
Ways to Get What You Don't Get at School *...continued*

Great School Quality Factor	*Ways to Get What You Don't Get at School*

GREAT SCHOOL QUALITY FACTOR #3...*continued*

Monitoring of Progress and Adjusting Teaching
...continued

learning styles, potential disabilities and other factors that might affect child's learning. Consider non-academic sources of stress (social, emotional, physical) that may be affecting child's learning. Inform teacher of results and discuss how school might alter teaching approach with your child. See *Child Needs: Ways to Get What You Don't Get at School* section for students Challenged in Basic Learning Capability for additional ideas

➤ If child has higher-than-grade-level learning goals but is not making progress, discuss with teacher. Reevaluate the child's mastery of more basic material. Consider non-academic sources of stress (social, emotional, physical) that may be affecting child's learning. If goals are appropriate, hire tutor or provide your own "school at home" after school to help your child

➤ If child is not being challenged (no higher goals and no monitoring of progress), you will need to hire tutor or provide your own "school at home" after school to challenge your child. See *Child Needs: Ways to Get What You Don't Get at School* sections for Gifted and Highly Gifted children for more ideas

➤ In all cases, inform child's teacher about your activities; the teacher may have ideas to help you

GREAT SCHOOL QUALITY FACTOR #4

Focus on Effective Learning Tasks

➤ Using a tutor, your own efforts or extracurricular group activities, supplement your child's education in subjects where your child's school is not using instructional approaches that work for your child (or not enough time spent on subject at school)

➤ Read parenting magazine articles about school instruction research findings. Ask your principal how you might help the school stay abreast of the latest research about effective curriculum and teaching methods. Ask about specific ideas you have seen. The more you stay informed and concerned, the more reinforcement your child's school will have to keep current

➤ Express your specific concerns about class time, interruptions, materials, facilities or instructional approaches to your child's teacher *and* principal. Be clear about how you think the situation may be keeping your child from learning as well as your child could. Sometimes, a simple change will improve the situation dramatically (e.g., bathroom breaks between classes, children leave for appointments or tutoring between subjects not in middle, limited use of loudspeaker for school announcements, putting most valued subjects at time of day when children are most focused, changing how facilities are used)

➤ In coordination with principal and teachers, organize fundraising effort to ensure that appropriate materials are available to all children. Fundraising sources include parents, neighbors living near school, community groups, foundations that support education, and special government grants

GREAT SCHOOL QUALITY FACTOR #5

Home-School Connection

➤ In spring before school starts, write your principal a letter telling as much as you know about your child's academic, social, emotional and physical development (use your *Child Needs Summary* and *Personalized Great Fit Checklist* as guides). Also describe the kinds of teachers who have been effective (and ineffective) with your child. Mail or meet with principal to deliver

➤ During or just prior to the first week of school, write your child's teacher a note similar to the one you wrote the principal, focusing on your child. Most teachers will appreciate the help understanding your child and knowing what challenges and opportunities they'll have working with your child

➤ Periodically, drop off or pick up child at classroom so that teachers know who you are. If time, ask how things are going with your child. If lengthy discussion is needed, make an appointment to meet or call teacher after school hours

...continues

Continues...

Quality:
Ways to Get What You Don't Get at School   *...continued*

Great School Quality Factor	*Ways to Get What You Don't Get at School*

GREET SCHOOL QUALITY FACTOR #5...*continued*

GREAT SCHOOL QUALITY FACTOR #5...*continued*

Home-School Connection

...continued

➤ Offer to volunteer in class (read a story, tutor a child, decorate for party, whatever you can do well) to gain teacher access and trust

➤ Generally, take the initiative to ask teacher how things are going for her and for your child this year. The more you understand your child's teacher's strengths and challenges (everybody has both!), the better you can shape your child's life outside of school

➤ Get a copy of the learning standards for your child's grade (and beyond if child is advanced), so you will know generally what your child should be learning during year. This may be available on school website, or you may call your child's school office and ask for a copy. If your child attends public school, these standards may also be available from the district office or state education agency. If you meet resistance, be firm but polite, saying that you want to help make sure your child is keeping up in school

➤ Check your child's completed school and home work, and check off skills/knowledge on the learning standards once you believe your child has mastered them

➤ If you have questions or concerns about your child's report card, call teacher right away to discuss. Ask what you can do at home to support your child's success. Then ask what the teacher plans to do

➤ If conflict with a teacher arises, call principal. Helping parents and teachers figure out how to work together is part of the principal's job. See the box *Resolving Parent-Teacher Conflicts* in Chapter 18 for more

GREAT SCHOOL QUALITY FACTOR #6

Safe and Orderly Environment

➤ Be clear with your child about how you expect him or her to behave at school, in class and elsewhere

➤ Ask your child how (s)he and other children behaved each day at school. Ask how other children's good and bad behavior affected your child. Discuss how your child's good and bad behavior affected other students and teacher. Ask how your child feels about things at school, and listen for social and emotional challenges. Encourage and help your child to address underlying conflicts or problems that affect behavior. Encourage child to keep improving own behavior

➤ If you are concerned about behavior of other children on your own child, discuss your concern with teacher (and principal if needed). Be specific about the effect on your child's social, emotional, academic and physical well-being

➤ Bring any *general safety* concerns to the immediate attention of principal. If the concern is only about your child's classroom, discuss with teacher first. Chances are good that other parents have similar concerns

➤ If you are concerned about *specific, immediate threats* of harm to your child (e.g., another child is threatening harm), inform teacher immediately. If teacher does not act right away, inform principal immediately. If risk is extreme, inform teacher and principal immediately upon realizing the risk of harm. Do not wait. If you are not satisfied with actions taken, take your concern to the next level (call school board member or district office)

GREAT SCHOOL QUALITY FACTOR #7

Strong Instructional Leadership

...continues

➤ When teacher quality is uneven, all the more important to ensure the best fit with your child. In spring before school starts, write your principal a letter telling as much as you know about your child's academic, social, emotional and physical development (use your *Child Needs Summary* and *Personalized Great Fit Checklist* as guides). Also describe the kinds of teachers who have been effective with your child in the past. Mail or meet with principal to deliver

Continues...

Quality:
Ways to Get What You Don't Get at School

Great School Quality Factor	Ways to Get What You Don't Get at School
GREAT SCHOOL QUALITY FACTOR #7...continued	
Strong Instructional Leadership ...continued	➤ At the beginning of the year, share with your child's teacher any techniques for teaching that have been especially effective with your child in previous school years, at home, or in extracurricular activities. Teachers may or may not be able to follow this advice, but you improve the odds if they are informed ➤ When a teacher is effective in helping your child learn, tell her, thank her, and tell principal ➤ Identify your child's teacher's strengths and weaknesses early (by observing your child's progress or by talking with parents of similar children who have had teacher). Make up for weaknesses outside of school with extracurricular activities or tutoring ➤ If your child is not responding well to school – academically, socially or emotionally – be assertive: ask your teacher and principal how you can work together to ensure that your child's needs are met ➤ If you are concerned about the quality of your child's teacher, express your concern confidentially to principal (call or make an appointment). At the end of the meeting, be sure you understand what will happen next to resolve the problem

Sources

We studied reams of research in assembling this book. In this summary, we highlight the major sources of information we used by chapter.

Chapter One

We drew our information about the number of children attending schools other than their assigned public schools from a survey conducted by the National Center for Education Statistics, *The Condition of Education: 2000.* The statistic about how many families say that schools influenced their decisions about where to live is from Jeffrey Henig's 1999 article, "School Choice Outcomes" in *School Choice and Social Controversy: Politics, Policy, and Law*, edited by Stephen Sugarman and Frank Kemerer. The information about how many states allow some choice across or within school districts is from a 2003 state-by-state profile on the Heritage Foundation website, "Snapshots of Choice in the States." Data on the growth of magnet schools are from Rolf Blank, Roger Levine and Lauri Steel's 1996 article "After 15 Years, Magnet Schools in Urban Education" in *Who Chooses? Who Loses?* edited by Richard Elmore and Bruce Fuller. The 2003 statistics about how many charter schools there are in the United States is from The Center for Education Reform website at http://edreform.com. Information about the number of home schooled children comes from a report by the National Center for Education Statistics, *Home Schooling in the United States: 1999.*

In the box entitled, "Get Smart About School Types," we refer to the research literature on the comparative advantage of attending different types of schools (e.g. public vs. private). This research has returned a hodge-podge of mixed results, with no clear advantage emerging for one type of school over another once parental education and income levels are factored out. From the hodge-podge of results, studies showing benefits of attending private schools show the strongest benefit for African-American students. See the 2001 RAND study *Rhetoric Versus Reality,* by Brian P. Gill and others, for an overview of this research.

There is considerable research that parents who actively choose their children's schools are more satisfied overall with their schools' performance and that they are more involved in various aspects of the school than parents of children in assigned schools. For more information on this subject, see the survey data reported in the *Condition of Education 2000*, published by the U.S. Department of Education, and the RAND *Rhetoric Versus Reality* study. The research on how well active choosers perform is more mixed. Choosers do seem to perform better, but it is often difficult to tell whether these outcomes result from choosing or from the fact that choosers tend to come from more education-oriented and motivated families. Again, the RAND *Rhetoric Versus Reality* study provides a recent, balanced treatment of this question.

The finding that I.Q. can increase dramatically during childhood comes from James Webb, Elizabeth Meckstroth, and Stephanie Tolan's 1994 book *Guiding the Gifted Child: A Practical Source for Parents and Teachers.* There are many examples of Great Schools that dramatically increase students' performance. For one compilation, see The Education Trust's *Dispelling the Myth,* available at http://www.edtrust.org.

Our discussion of school quality rests on decades of research examining effective schools to determine the characteristics they have in common. On the Web, The Association for Effective Schools, Inc at http://www.mes.org/ is one source for more information about this research, and we drew heavily on the information there to craft how we explained school quality. If you would like to read some of the more recent studies, see M.C. Wang and colleagues' 1993 article "Toward a Knowledge Base for School Learning" in the *Review of Educational Research;* and Charles Teddlie and Samuel Stringfield's 1993 book *Schools Make a Difference: Lessons Learned From a 10-Year Study of School Effects.* These resources contain references to the many other studies that explore this topic.

Chapter Two

In Chapter Two, we refer to various theories regarding how children differ from one another in their capabilities, interests, intelligence, development, and learning styles. For Howard Gardner's theory of multiple intelligences, see his 1983 book *Frames of Mind: The Theory of Multiple Intelligences* and his more recent work *Intelligence Reframed* (1999). Mel Levine's work is featured in his 2002 book *A Mind at a Time* and the *All Kinds of Minds* website at http://www.allkindsofminds.org/. Authors who focus on "whole child" thinking when it comes to children's development include Joanne Hendrick in the 2000 book *The Whole Child: Developmental Education for the Early Years.* More a reference for educators than parents, this textbook provides an overview of the "whole child" concept. The "high-need child" is described by William Sears and Martha Sears in *The Fussy Baby Book: Parenting Your High-Need Child From Birth to Age Five* (1996). The "difficult child" is the subject of Stanley Turecki and Leslie Tonner's *The Difficult Child* (2000). The concept of a "spirited child" derives from Mary Sheedy Kurcinka's *Raising Your Spirited Child: A Guide for Parents Whose Child Is More Intense, Sensitive, Perceptive, Persistent, Energetic* (1998).

Chapter Three

In Chapter 3, we explore the concept of determining your child's Basic Learning Capability. See Webb, Meckstroth, and Tolan's *Guiding the Gifted Child*, first cited in Chapter One. This work is also the source of the finding that children's I.Q. can increase with proper stimulation and challenge. On gifted education, we also drew on Ellen Winner's 1996 book *Gifted Children: Myths and Realities.*

The Viewpoint box on Howard Gardner's theory of multiple intelligences draws on his 1983 book *Frames of Mind: The Theory of Multiple Intelligences* and his more recent book *Intelligence Reframed* (1999).

Chapter Four

There are several books and articles that explore learning style theory, including Harvey Silver, Richard Strong and Matthew Perini's 2000 book *So Each May Learn: Integrating Learning Styles and Multiple Intelligences;* Anne Lewis and Elizabeth Steinberger's 1991 book *Learning Styles: Putting Research and Common Sense into Practice;* Mariaemma Willis and Victoria Hodson's 1999 book *Discover Your Child's Learning Style* and the Association for Supervision and Curriculum Development's 1998 volume *Marching to Different Drummers,* 2nd Edition.

There is considerable academic debate regarding whether modifying instruction to match an individual's learning style enhances student achievement, particularly for low achieving students. For a discussion of how learning style matching improves student achievement, see Rita Dunn and Shirley Griggs' book, *Learning Styles: Quiet Revolution in American Secondary Schools* (National Association of Secondary School Principals, 1988). For a thorough and critical discussion of the research surrounding learning styles, see Lynn Curry's article "Critique of the Research on Learning Styles" (Oct. 1990, *Educational Leadership*).

Our discussion of motivation was informed by the work of psychologist David McClelland. See Lyle M. Spencer, Jr. and Singe M. Spencer's 1993 book *Competence at Work: Models for Superior Performance.*

The controversy, both legal and academic, surrounding inclusion, the practice of placing students with disabilities in the least restrictive environment, is well documented in numerous publications. One good resource is the Office of Special Education and Rehabilitative Services within the U.S. Department of Education: http://www.ed.gov/offices/OSERS/.

The Viewpoint box on Mel Levine draws on his books *All Kinds of Minds* (1992) and *A Mind at a Time* (2002).

Chapter Seven

In this chapter, we refer to the research supporting exposure to a foreign language. In addition to the direct benefits of speaking another language, language study seems to have a positive effect on children's ability to understand and use their native languages as well. See the Center for Applied Linguistics' website for links to such research (http://www.cal.org). Similarly, there seem to be additional benefits to learning music. One example of a study connecting musical exposure with mathematical performance is Amy Graziano, Matthew Peterson and Gordon Shaw's 1999 article in the journal *Neurological Research*.

Chapter Nine

In Chapter Nine, we discuss the large body of research surrounding parent involvement in school and at home. For a summary of this research, see Amy Baker and Laura Soden's 1998 review, "The Challenges of Parent Involvement Research," available online at http://www.ed.gov/databases/ERIC_Digests/ed419030.html.

We also refer to the literature on how peers influence academic achievement. For more information, see Roslyn Mickelson's 2001 article, "Subverting Swann: First and Second-Generation Segregation in the Charlotte-Mecklenburg Schools," in the *American Educational Research Journal;* Michal Kurlaender and John Yun's 2000 article "Is Diversity a Compelling Educational Interest? Evidence from Metropolitan Louisville," a report issued by the Civil Rights Project at Harvard University; Caroline Hoxby's 2000 paper, "Peer Effects in the Classroom: Learning from Gender and Race Variation," available from the National Bureau of Economic Research at http://papers.nber.org/papers/w7867; and Eric Hanushek, John Kain, Jacob Markman, and Steven Rivkin's 2001 paper, "Does the Ability of Peers Affect Student Achievement?" available at http://www.utdallas.edu/research/greenctr/Papers/pdfpapers/paper24.pdf.

See the section above on Chapter One for information about research on the performance of different school "types" (e.g. public and private.) For information about the research related to a wide range of school "designs" see the Northwest Regional Educational Laboratory's *Catalog of School Reform Models* at http://www.nwrel.org/scpd/catalog/.

Finally, we cite research showing that how much a school spends has little correlation with its quality. Academic debate rages over this topic, on display in such collections as *Developments in School Finance, 1997- Does Money Matter?* (available from the National Center for Educational Statistics, http://nces.ed.gov) and *Does Money Matter? The Effect of School Resources on Student Achievement and Adult Success* (1996). Few scholars, however, argue that one should judge a school's quality by how much it costs or spends. *How* it spends the money is also critical, and this, as we have noted, continues to pose a challenge for many wealthy schools.

Chapter Ten

This chapter mentions research showing that schools are more effective when they "differentiate," or tailor instruction to meet the needs of individual students. For a review of this extensive literature and its nuances, see Tom Loveless's 1998 report, "The Tracking and Ability Grouping Debate," available from the Thomas B. Fordham Foundation at http://www.edexcellence.net/. Findings in this area have heavily influenced the recommendations for instructional practice outlined by such organizations as the National Research Council (http://books.nap.edu/html/nses/) and the National Reading Panel (http://www.nationalreadingpanel.org/). The benefits of differentiation have been shown especially high for gifted students. See the website of the National Research Center on the Gifted and Talented (http://www.gifted.uconn.edu/nrcgt.html) for a number of research articles exploring this topic.

In this chapter, we again cite research about the lack of connection between how much a school costs or spends and how well it performs. See the discussion under Chapter Nine, above.

Chapter Eleven

The effective schools research that is the basis for the seven Great School Quality Factors is referenced in the section above on Chapter One. The research on differentiating instruction to meet varied students' needs is cited in the section on Chapter Ten. The research on approaches to teaching reading is discussed under Chapter Twelve, below.

Research on class size is filled with claims and counterclaims. There is certainly no consensus that smaller classes are necessarily better, and little evidence that small reductions (e.g., from 35 to 30) make any difference. Some of the best studies, in which students were randomly assigned to *very* small classes, have shown positive effects. One often cited example is Tennessee's STAR program, which compared K-3 students in classes of 22-26 with those in classes of 13-17 and found lasting benefits for students in the smaller classes. See Frederick Mosteller's 1995 summary, "The Tennessee Study of Class Size in the Early School Grades" in the journal *The Future of Children.*

Studies on the value of smaller *schools* are summarized in Mary Ann Raywid's 1999 review "Current Literature on Small Schools," available at: http://www.ericfacility.net/databases/ERIC_Digests/ed425049.html.

For a concise summary of the research on what characteristics of teachers influence students' success, see Dan Goldhaber's Spring 2002 article "The Mystery of Good Teaching" in the journal *Education Next.*

Chapter Twelve

For more information on the research supporting language immersion programs, see the website of the Center for Applied Linguistics (http://www.cal.org). The most conclusive evidence to date about reading instruction can be found by looking at a review conducted by the National Reading Panel. Their report is available at (http://www.nationalreadingpanel.org/).

Chapter Sixteen

For a summary of the research on delaying the start of kindergarten, see "When to Start Kindergarten? Suggestions for Parents from the National Association of School Psychologists," available online at http://www.teachersandfamilies.com/open/parent/kg1.cfm. The National Research Council's 1999 study *High Stakes: Testing for Tracking, Promotion, and Graduation* also discusses the research on delayed kindergarten and reviews studies on the consequences of having students repeat a grade of school.

Index

ARMCHAIR PRESS

Share the wisdom of *Picky Parent Guide* with family, friends and colleagues.

Easy Order Form

FAX: Fax this form to 913-362-7401

POSTAL: Mail this form to Armchair Press,
P.O. Box 411037, Kansas City, MO 64141-1037

INTERNET: Go to www.PickyParent.com

E-MAIL: orders@PickyParent.com

TELEPHONE: Call 1-888-PICKY88 (742-5988) toll free   Source code: PPG1

❑ Please send _____ copies of *Picky Parent Guide: Choose Your Child's School with Confidence, The Elementary Years (K–6)* at $19.95 each. I understand that I may return any of them for any reason for a full refund.

❑ *Please add me to your mailing list for announcements about new books and seminars.*

Name: _____

Address: _____

City: _____ **State:** _____ **Zip:** _____

Telephone: _____

E-mail address: _____

Sales tax: Please add 7.5% for products shipped to California addresses

Shipping: U.S.: $4.95 for first book and $1.95 for each additional book
International: $9.95 for first book; $4.95 for each additional book (estimate)

Payment: ❑ Check   ❑ Visa   ❑ MasterCard   ❑ American Express   ❑ Discover

Card Number: _____

Name on Card: _____ **Exp. Date:** _____

Signature: _____

Thank you for your order!

Share the wisdom of *Picky Parent Guide* with family, friends and colleagues.

Easy Order Form

FAX: Fax this form to 913-362-7401

POSTAL: Mail this form to Armchair Press,
P.O. Box 411037, Kansas City, MO 64141-1037

INTERNET: Go to www.PickyParent.com

E-MAIL: orders@PickyParent.com

TELEPHONE: Call 1-888-PICKY88 (742-5988) toll free   Source code: PPG1

❑ Please send _____ copies of *Picky Parent Guide: Choose Your Child's School with Confidence, The Elementary Years (K–6)* at $19.95 each. I understand that I may return any of them for any reason for a full refund.

❑ *Please add me to your mailing list for announcements about new books and seminars.*

Name: _____

Address: _____

City: _____ **State:** _____ **Zip:** _____

Telephone: _____

E-mail address: _____

Sales tax: Please add 7.5% for products shipped to California addresses

Shipping: U.S.: $4.95 for first book and $1.95 for each additional book
International: $9.95 for first book; $4.95 for each additional book (estimate)

Payment: ❑ Check ❑ Visa ❑ MasterCard ❑ American Express ❑ Discover

Card Number: _____

Name on Card: _____ **Exp. Date:** _____

Signature: _____

Thank you for your order!